COMPUTERS AND ASTROLOGY:

A Universal User's Guide and Reference

by

Patricia L. Foreman

HERE IS WHAT PEOPLE ARE SAYING ABOUT

COMPUTERS AND ASTROLOGY!

"It's exciting! I wish I had this book eight years ago when I first bought my computer and astrology program. I would have saved a lot of money that I spent on reference books and programs that ultimately never gave me what I needed. Now here, in one book *Computers and Astrology* provides me with everything I need for casting charts. I keep it by my computer constantly".

Rosalind McKnight
Creative Living Institute
Evington, Virginia, USA

"I wish I had this book before I spent hours alternatively fuming at the computer and feeling stupid because I couldn't understand the astrological terms used in program documentation."

"This is a clear description of both computer and astrological terms so that everyone, from novice to master can assemble a computer system to fit their personal needs. While you can practice the art of astrology without a computer, serious students and professionals now find that instant computations expand their horizons. A complete chart analysis can be done in the time previously required to erect a chart. When we can calculate transits, progressions, directions, returns, midpoints, and more with a few keystrokes, we can fine tune both psychological and predictive analysis. This book provides both students and professionals a means to analyze their needs. Buy it!"

Nancy Hastings
NCGR National Board and Executive Committee
AFA Gold Card Astrologer
Concord, Massachusetts, USA

"We have long needed an introduction to astrological computing presented without any particular ax to grind. I especially appreciate the book pointing out that choosing software is not a trivial matter to leave to a snap judgement, first appearance or someone else's opinion...you need to do some work to get a program that will work well for you. This book brings together a lot of information useful to someone getting into astrological computing."

Mark Pottenger
Los Angeles, California

"...A much needed book for todays modern astrologer. It's complete, concise, easy to follow, well planned and accurate...take an 'A' for a job well done!"

Alphee Lavoie
A.I.R. Software
West Hartford, Connecticut

"...an excellent manual which holds a space on my dwindling shelving near my computer...it is masterful!"

Margaret M. Meister
NCGR Advisory Board
Malibar, Florida, USA

"...particularly appealing are the clear graphics, charts and tables, which delineate many of the processes and principles of astrology. *Computers and Astrology* is fun to read, and is an excellent reference to have on hand."

Nancy McMoneagle
The Monroe Institute
Faber, Virginia, USA

"The content is magnificent! I've been studying astrology for over a decade yet this book contains information that I haven't found anywhere else. It explained a good many things that are only casually referred to in other texts. It is fascinating to know that there is so much variety within astrology."

Rick Goode,
Whole Health Group,
Boston, Massachusetts

Cover Type Design by **Koeller Graphics**
Burlington, Vermont

Cover Artist **John Churchman,**
Burlington, Vermont

Line Art and Diagrams by Patricia L. Foreman

Library of Congress Cataloging-in-Publication Data
Foreman, Patricia L., 1950-
Computers and astrology : a universal user's guide and reference / by Patricia L. Foreman. --
p. 300 cm.
Includes bibliographical references and index
ISBN 0-9624648-1-3

1. Astrology. 2. Computers. 3. Astrology--Data processing.
4. Horoscopes--Data processing. 5. Horoscopes. I. Title.

BF1708.1 133.5
92-82652

Published by:

Good Earth Publications
Box 4352
Burlington, Vermont 05406-4352

Printed in the United States of America

DEDICATION

In general, prejudice seems to be the only factor standing in the way of a serious scientific consideration and evaluation of astrology.

Perhaps through the use of computers, astrological research can prove the validity of the unseen planetary forces and influences upon living systems, including human kind.

In this spirit, this book is dedicated to all seekers of wisdom, who, by studying the cosmos, gain an understanding of the workings of the self and essence of the soul as reflected by the universe.

ACKNOWLEDGEMENTS

As with all efforts, this book owes its existence to many people. Thanks to all the many representatives of software companies for the descriptions and demo diskettes of their computer programs. A deep appreciation and respect goes to Robert Hand and the staff of Astrolabe for so generously sharing their time, expertise, documentation, notes, and enthusiasm. Thank you Gary Christen, Patricia White, William Sweeney, Arthur Blackwell, Linda Sherrill and Nancy Lavoie. Also thanks to Alphee Lavoie of A.I.R. Software, Dennis Haskell of Time Cycles Research and Tom Bridges of Matrix Software.

Deep gratitude to Mark Pottenger, CCRS creator, for reviewing the final manuscript and finding innumerable errors that escaped the rest of us. Your perfection and eye for detail is appreciated Mark.

Much appreciation goes to Peter Ashe, for his long-term friendship and expert technical input on this book.

Also thanks to: Monica Dimino, professional astrologer, for so candidly sharing comments and providing direction at the early stages of the book.

Special thanks to my colleagues who reviewed and edited draft manuscripts:

Judy Curley, owner of *What an Interesting Bookstore!*

Rhiannon Hanfman, astrologer and former editor of *One Earth*, the Findhorn Foundation Magazine.

Nancy Hastings, AFA gold card astrologer, NCGR Executive Committee member, author and international teacher.

Margaret Meister, astrologer and member NCGR Advisory Board.

Nancy McMoneagle, for her gift of a detailed review of the book while there was so much happening around her - Thank you Scooter!

Janet and Jessie Mills, special friends for their almost daily support, enthusiasm, and suggestions.

Gorden Stubbs, my wizard, whose friendship and computer assistance has literally changed my life.

A tribute to Marie and Dick Foreman, who survived my childhood, and who, in spite of my wandering off several beaten paths, are still proud parents.

A special thanks for the love, support and encouragement from Andy Lee, who has joined me in discovering astrology as a means of understanding the nature of our selfs, and thereby helping to manifest the many great potentials that lie within.

Table of Contents

LIST OF FIGURES AND GRAPHICS

LIST OF TABLES

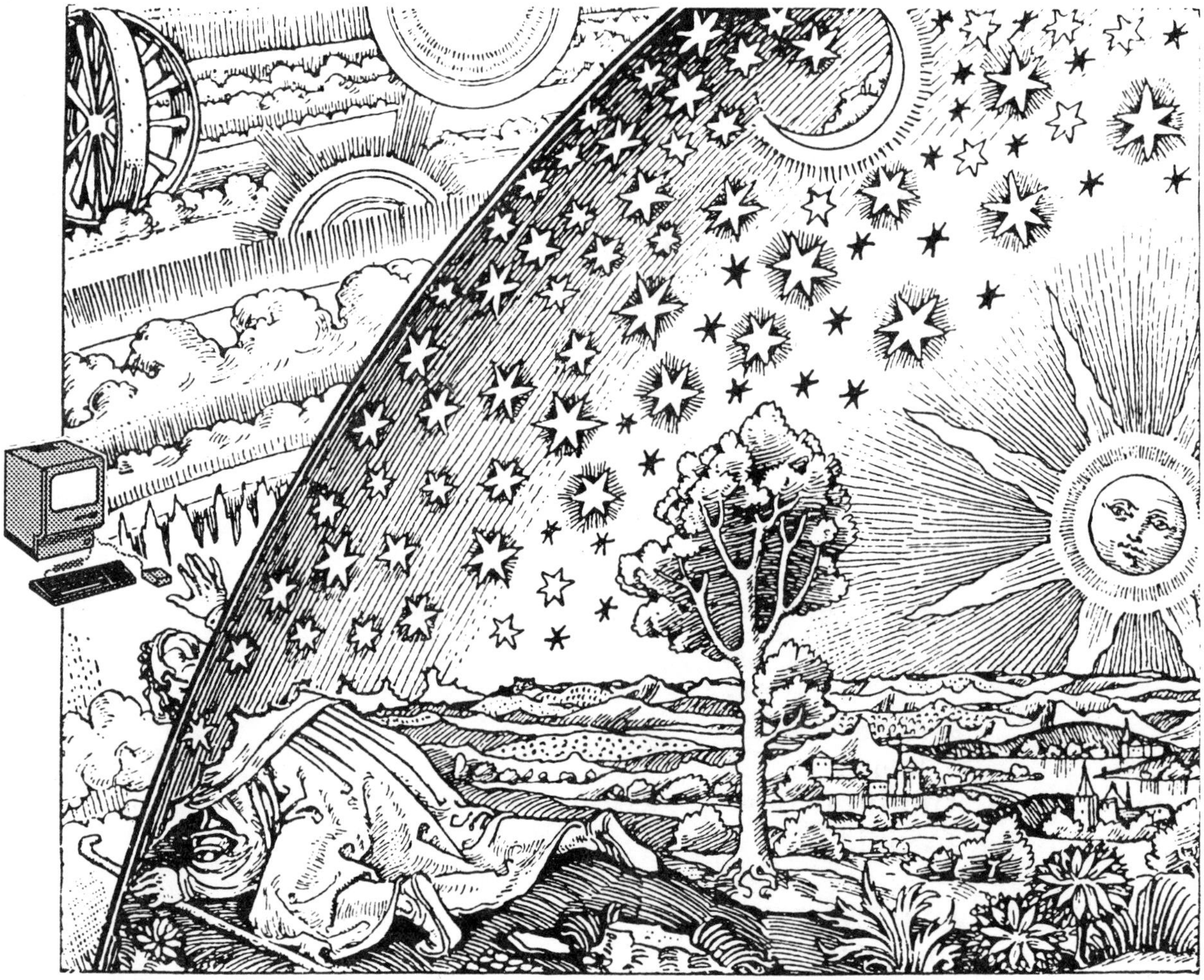

An astrologer/scholar/seeker reaches out of the known world to gain knowledge of other worlds. Modified Swiss woodcut circa 1500.

INTRODUCTION

The computer is an all purpose tool that is changing the way people work, including astrologers. The ease of electronically casting charts allows astrologers at all levels to test theories and experiment with many different methods.

Those who dislike math no longer must do the complex calculations to construct a birth chart. With a few keystrokes, they are free to use their intuition and talents on chart interpretation.

Those who are scientifically inclined, will find that computers offer a research and analytical tool with accuracy and power not here-to-fore available. The use of computers is rapidly becoming a life skill of our culture, regardless of profession.

How can any astrologer's life be made easier by computers? There are many ways. There are things a computer can do that the average person simply cannot, or would not do. These are:

- **Calculations.** A computer can do many complex calculations quickly and accurately.

- **Graphics.** The computer can print many types and styles of charts and tables quickly and clearly.

- **Databases.** Through its electronic memory, a computer can store, retrieve and manipulate vast amounts of information. Data bases can include ephemerides, charts, geographic locations, and other astrological data.

Astrology is literally embarking upon a new age, the age of modern computers that can perhaps finally prove the validity of this ancient science.

What is this book all about? Currently, there are very few references available on the use of computers in the astrological arts. This book has been written for the general public to complement the documentation that accompanies astrology software. It is intended to serve as a *universal reference guide* and has four objectives:

> **User's Guide (Part 1).** To provide a reference on the terminology and features that can be available in different astrological software packages. This book does not cover such items as specific keyboard commands or the operating procedures necessary to use a certain model of computer. It does describe the many choices and options that an astrologer must make when casting charts.
>
> **Software Comparison Methodology (Part 2).** To present a method for astrological software comparison that systematically includes all the features a casting program might offer.
>
> **Astrological Dictionary (Part 3).** To provide, in alphabetical order, information that might be useful, interesting, or needed in the study of astrology. There is extensive use of the index and cross references throughout the book.
>
> **Useful Casting Information (Part 4)** To provide a collection of information and data that can be valuable when casting or interpreting charts. Included are major world-city coordinates, time zones, major life transits, and astronomical data.

Who can use this book?
This book is written for readers ranging from professional astrologers to those who are mildly curious about astrology. Specifically:

1. *Professional Astrologers* who would like to know what astrology software packages offer, and have a systematic methodology to compare software packages.

2. *Casual Astrologers* who do not have the time or interest in tediously casting charts by hand, but would like to have the advantages of casting charts electronically.

3. *Astrologers with no interest in computers*, but who are looking for a technical reference. This book provides sometimes hard to find information on house systems, coordinates, chart types, and other facets of astrology.

4. *Computer Owners* who are looking for new uses for their computers, such as casting charts.

How and Why Was This Guide Written?

Research for this book began in 1987, when the author was looking for astrology programs for a Macintosh and a traveling lap top (MS-DOS). Then, no book or reference was available that identified programs, or explained the terms found in promotional brochures. Two obstacles became immediately apparent. These were:

> *Too much unexplained terminology* that included obscure terms and concepts not readily available in references from local libraries or bookstores.
>
> *Scanty documentation* that accompanied most programs tended to be "Swiss cheese" that is, it contained too many holes or assumed astrological knowledge.

Information received from software distributors was usually in the form of catalogues or brochures. Hours were spent pondering, scanning and dissecting the many documents. From these promotional materials, we developed a check list to compare features offered by different software packages. This check list became the table of contents for *Computers and Astrology.*

As a final note, the author plans to revise and update *Computers and Astrology* and would appreciate hearing from readers regarding the usefulness of the information and format. She is open to suggestions for additions to the next edition. Send all correspondence care of the publisher If you request a reply, please include a self addressed, stamped envelope.

Computers and Astrology was created using desktop publishing using both MS-DOS and Macintosh computers and programs.

Sphæræ Materialis Formula.

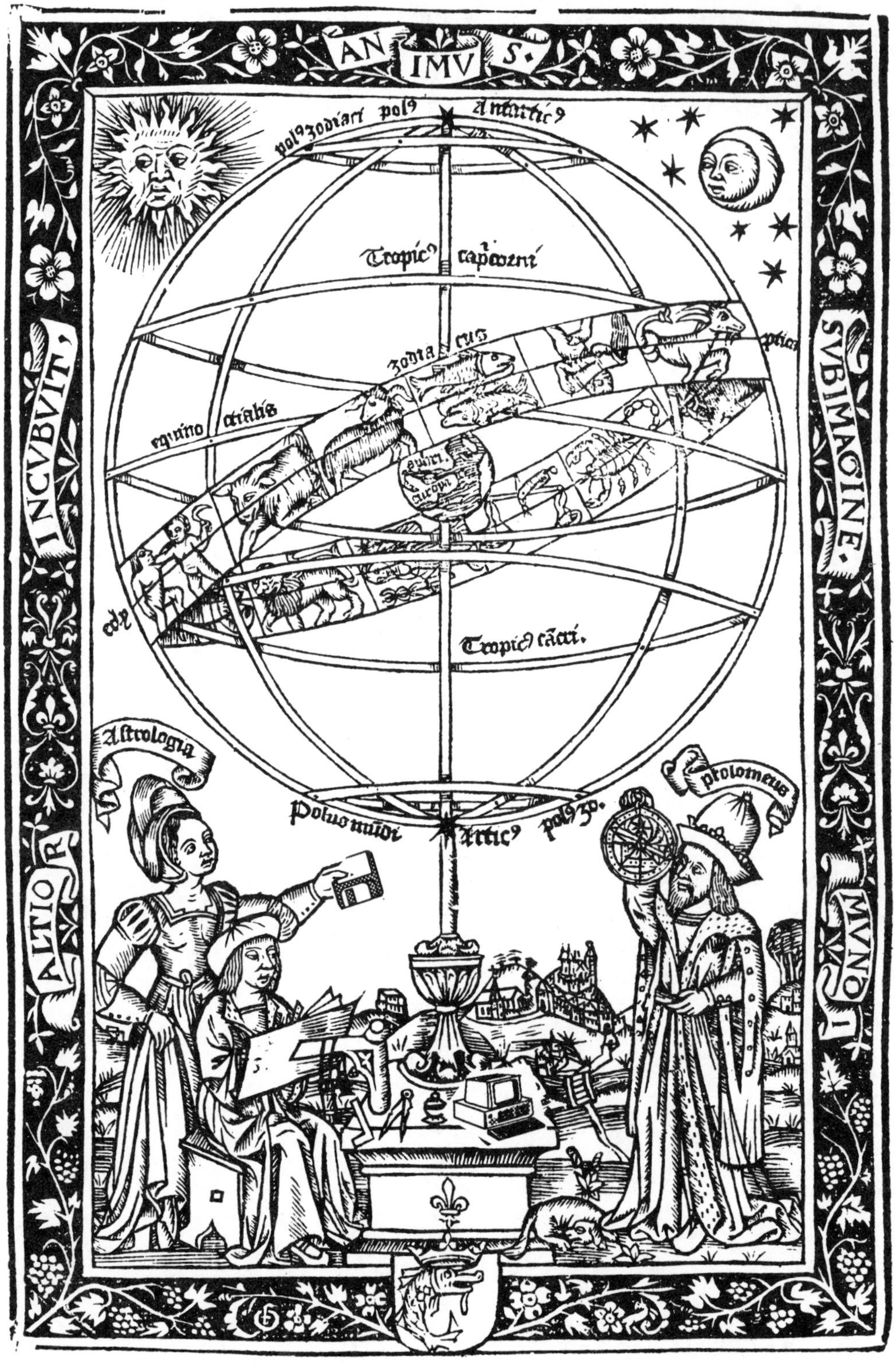

VRANIA PTOLEMAEVS

The Celestial Sphere. At the right Ptolemy is taking a sighting while Astronomy is handing him a newly formatted disk. Woodcut (slightly modifed) by Erhard Schon made at Nuremburg in 1515 as the title plate to Leonard Reymann's Birth Chart.

PART ONE

USER'S GUIDE

CHOICES IN CASTING

This section explains the terms, concepts and choices an astrologer must consider when casting a chart. It sequentially builds upon terminology you need to understand the astronomical and mathematical basis of astrology. For example, you need a basic understanding of the coordinate systems before the differences in house systems can be discussed. The order of this section is:

A. Choices You Must Make When Casting a Chart

   1. Zodiac Types
   2. Coordinate Systems
   3. House Systems
   4. Charts and Tables
   5. Graphics and Chart Styles

B. Other Program Features

   A description of the many features and options that can be included in astrological programs.

1. ZODIAC TYPES

The term "zodiac" is from *zoe*, the Greek word for life or animal, and *diakos*, which means wheel. A literal translation could be either "Wheel of Life" or "Animal Circle". "Zodiac" refers to the 16° to 18° wide band of sky through which the Sun and Moon appear to move. Except for Pluto, the planets also appear always to be within this band. This imaginary band is divided into twelve signs of 30° each, with signs bearing the name of a star group (constellation). Today, because of the Precession of the Equinoxes, the signs and constellations no longer align.

There is only one band in the sky that is the "zodiac" belt, but there are several ways to look at it. Thus you might encounter the plural "zodiacs". As astrologer Patricia White points out: *"The plural 'zodiacs' is used because there are several zodiac systems, depending upon where you put the starting point. The zodiac also depends upon whether you use equal 30° divisions or unequal divisions reflecting the actual extent of each constellation".*

Still, keep in mind that the term "zodiacs" (plural) is a misnomer, because there is only one band in the sky that is the zodiac. Whether you call this band the tropical or sidereal zodiac depends on the beginning point.

Ptolemy in the second century AD. defined a third zodiac system, the astronomical zodiac. This system divides the zodiacal belt into twelve unequal constellations. Ptolemy defined a total of 48 constellations, encompassing 1,022 stars.

By far the two most common zodiac systems used today are the tropical and the sidereal. Robert Powell wrote an excellent description of the various zodiac systems in *The Zodiac: A Historical Survey.*

Tropical Zodiac

The tropical zodiac has been in wide use for over 2,000 years. Hipparchus, a Greek astronomer, discovered the Precession of the Equinoxes in 130BC. Since then there has been differentiation between the sidereal and tropical zodiacs. The tropical zodiac is based on the ancient Greek approach that divides the sky into 12 equal parts according to the seasons on Earth. This zodiac uses the positions of the Sun at the beginning of each of the four seasons. The first day of spring (the Vernal Equinox) is the starting point.

Figure 1. Seasons, Solstices and Equinoxes

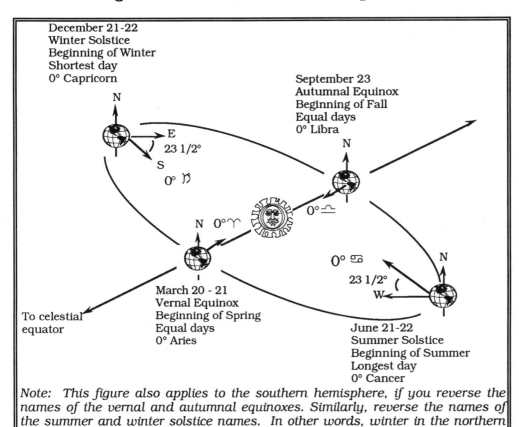

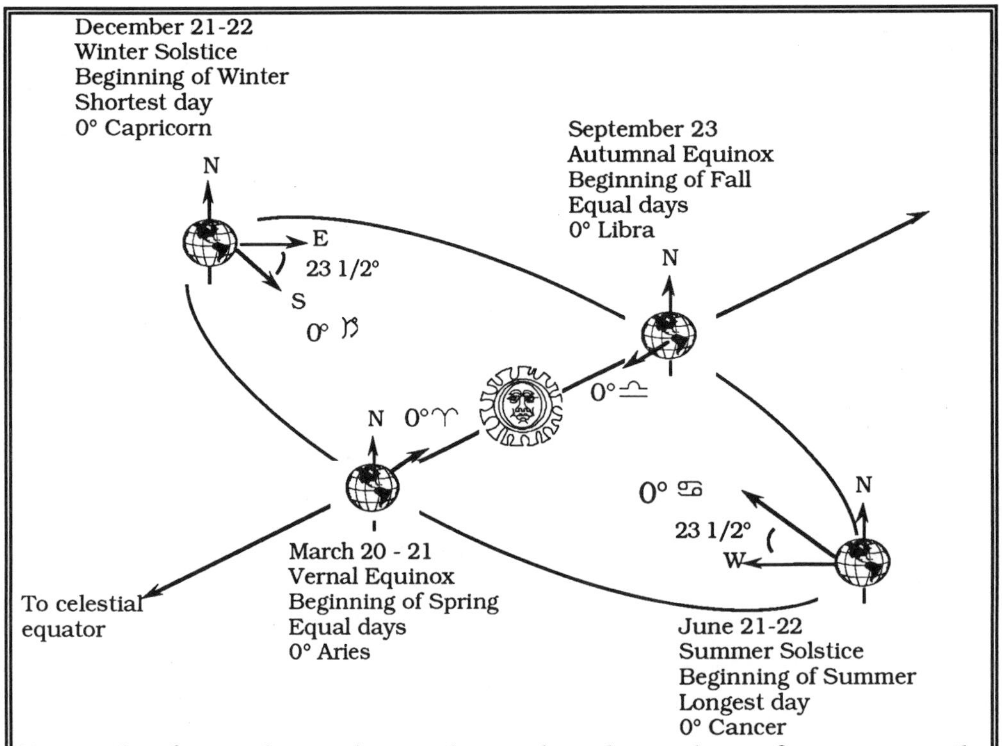

Note: This figure also applies to the southern hemisphere, if you reverse the names of the vernal and autumnal equinoxes. Similarly, reverse the names of the summer and winter solstice names. In other words, winter in the northern hemisphere is summer in the southern hemisphere.

The first day of spring is around March 20th to 21st, when night and day are equal in length. This is the vernal equinox point and is the intersection of the ecliptic and the celestial equator. The ecliptic is the apparent path of the Sun through the sky in the middle of the zodiacal belt.

The celestial equator is the extension of the Earth's equator into space. The exact time and place when the Sun's apparent path crosses the equator is the beginning of the zodiac for that year. In the tropical zodiac this point is zero degree Aries (0°♈).

In a similar fashion, the summer solstice is the longest day of the year. It occurs around June 21st, when the Sun at zero degree Cancer (0° ♋). At this time, the Sun is at its highest elevation at local noon.

The beginning of fall is the fall equinox, at zero degree Libra (0° ♎). This occurs around September 22nd or 23rd when, the Sun's apparent path crosses the equator and night and day are equal in length.

Finally, the shortest day of the year is the winter solstice with the Sun at zero degree Capricorn (0° ♑). This occurs around December 21st, when the Earth is closest to the Sun at local noon.

Figure 2. Tropical Zodiac Chart

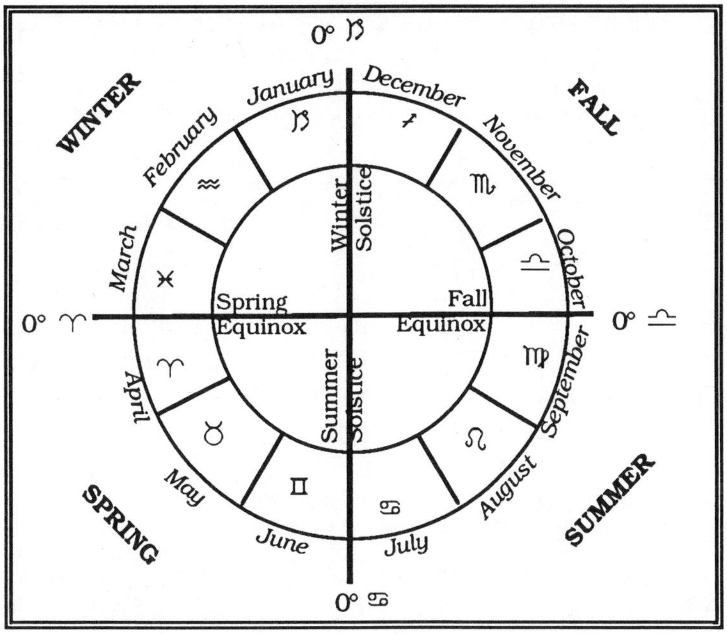

Keep in perspective that the pole of the Earth's rotation tilts (about 23.5°) to the pole of its orbit. The angle between these two poles is the obliquity of the ecliptic. If it were not for this tilt, the Earth would be vertically perpendicular to its orbit and there would no change of seasons. The seasons are due to the varying altitude of the Sun, and are a purely terrestrial effect caused by the Earth's motion around the pole of the ecliptic.

In summary, the tropical zodiac system uses the point in time when the Sun crossed the equator into the northern hemisphere. This point, zero degrees Aries (0°♈), is the starting point for a new annual cycle. The tropical zodiac system, point for a new annual cycle. The tropical zodiac system, more than any other zodiac system, reflects the seasons of the year.

Sidereal Zodiac

There are some astrologers that view the zodiac of constellations, or the sidereal zodiac, as the true zodiac. The sidereal zodiac relates a planet's position to the background of "fixed" stars. About 2,000 years ago, the tropical and sidereal zodiacs coincided. Because of the Precession of the Equinoxes, the two zodiacs no longer are in line with each other. This is shown in Figure 3. After one complete Precession cycle of 26,000 years, the tropical and sidereal zodiacs will again coincide.

In astrological practice, sidereal astrologers subtract a certain number of degrees from the positions of the planets given in the reference tables for the tropical zodiac. Ephemerides and tables of houses for the sidereal zodiac are somewhat difficult to find.

Currently, the tropical zodiac is about 24° to 26° ahead of the sidereal zodiac. Be aware that there is dissent among sidereal astrologers where the sidereal zodiac begins. This is even more complicated because "fixed stars" are not actually fixed or stationary. They move extremely slowly from our human life-span perspective on Earth. This means that the constellations and the sidereal zodiac itself have changed during the past 2,500 years. Therefore, merely subtracting the number of degrees to compensate for the Precession is still not entirely accurate, but accurate enough for practical purposes.

The sidereal zodiac uses the constellations (the fixed stars) in the same 16 to 18 degree wide band of sky (8 to 9 degrees to either side of the ecliptic).

Hindu astrologers and the school of Cyril Fagan and Garth Allen advocate the sidereal zodiac. Some promotional materials for astrology programs call this the "Fagan-Allen Zodiac", or Fagan-Allen System. The Rudolf Steiner writings also refer to the sidereal zodiac.

Figure 3. Difference Between the Sidereal and Tropical Zodiacs

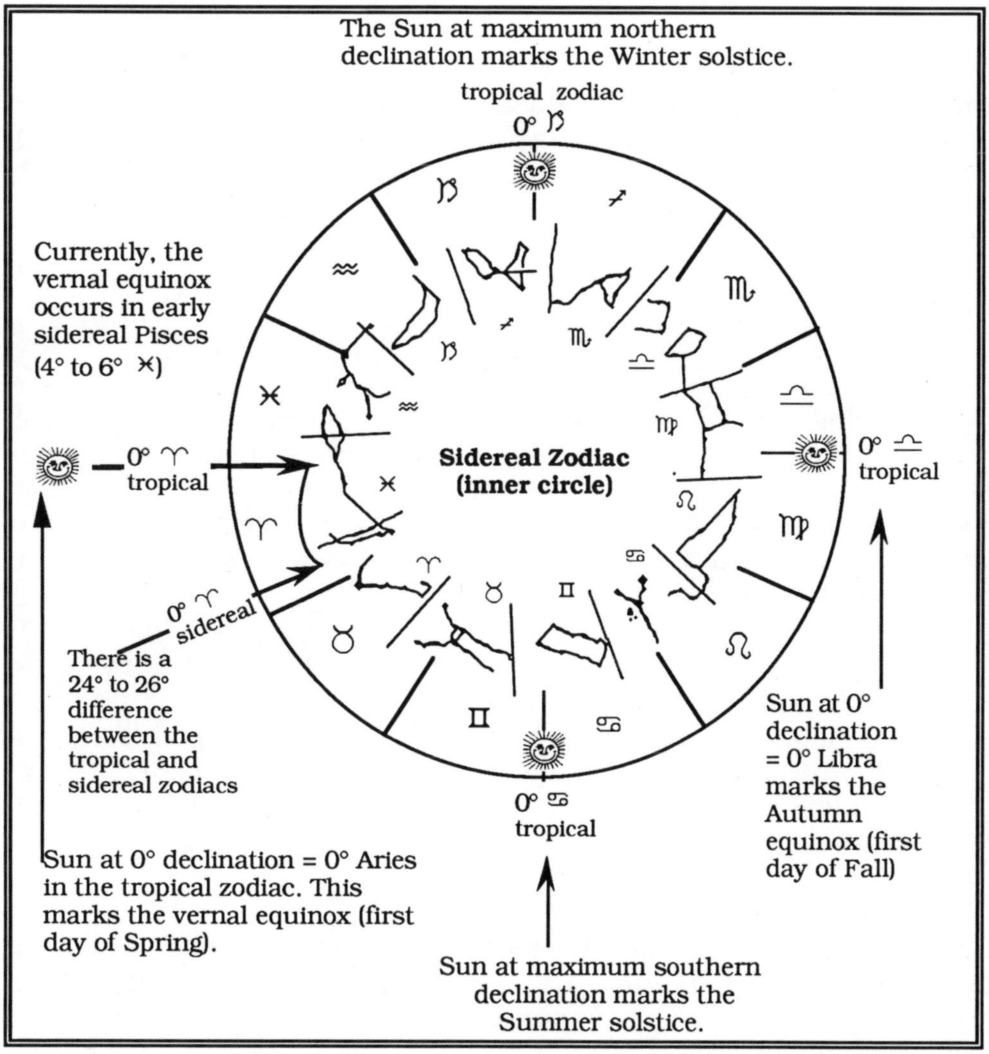
The Sun at maximum northern declination marks the Winter solstice.
tropical zodiac
0° ♑
Currently, the vernal equinox occurs in early sidereal Pisces (4° to 6° ♓)
0° ♈ tropical
Sidereal Zodiac (inner circle)
0° ♎ tropical
0° ♈ sidereal
There is a 24° to 26° difference between the tropical and sidereal zodiacs
0° ♋ tropical
Sun at 0° declination = 0° Libra marks the Autumn equinox (first day of Fall)
Sun at 0° declination = 0° Aries in the tropical zodiac. This marks the vernal equinox (first day of Spring).
Sun at maximum southern declination marks the Summer solstice.

Several sidereal zodiacs are used in the Far East and Asia (especially India). Each zodiac system can have a slightly different ayanamsa, or beginning point. An ayanamsa is an ancient Sanskrit term that means "yearly degree". In modern astrology, it describes the difference between the beginning points of the tropical and sidereal zodiacs.

In Summary, sidereal astrology takes into account the Precession of the Equinoxes. The difference between the tropical and sidereal zodiacs is the starting point. Sidereal astrologers must subtract about 24 to 26 degrees from the positions given in a tropical zodiac ephemeris. For example, in the sidereal zodiac, the Sun is at about four to six degrees Pisces (4° to 6° ♓) on the first day of spring (March 20 - 21 of each year). In the tropical zodiac, the first day of spring is always at zero degrees Aries (0° ♈).

Both the tropical and sidereal zodiacs use the same names for planets and signs. There has been considerable debate and controversy regarding which of the two zodiac types is better.

2. COORDINATE SYSTEMS

An astrologer needs to understand the concepts and technical terms behind the various coordinate systems. This is important so that advantages and disadvantages of the different house systems can be understood and applied appropriately. The next section describes house systems. But first, let's think about coordinates.

A coordinate system refers to the frame of reference astrologers and astronomers use to plot the positions of the stars and planets. The coordinate system measures the positions of objects. Mundane or local positions use Earth coordinates. Astronomical or space positions are measured on the celestial sphere using one of three coordinate systems: horizon, equator or ecliptic.

In addition, there is the observer's center-of-reference, which is from one of two points: the Earth (geocentric) or the Sun (heliocentric). This is the point of reference from which you view the zodiac, either from the Sun, or Earth. Each coordinate system and center-of-reference creates a different emphasis and viewpoint of the same event.

Centers of Reference

Geocentric

Geocentric literally means: *geo* (Earth) *centric* (center). This coordinate system uses the Earth as the reference point. The positions of the signs, planets and stars are plotted as seen from the center of the Earth.

Heliocentric
Heliocentric means *helio* (Sun), *centric* (center). Heliocentric coordinates use the positions of the stars, planets and signs as they would appear if viewed from the center of the Sun.

Earth Coordinates

Geographic Longitude and Latitude
To locate a place on Earth, geographic coordinates use imaginary circles named *Meridians of Longitude* and *Parallels of Latitude.* The figure below shows the Earth coordinates.

Figure 4. Earth Coordinates: Latitude and Longitude

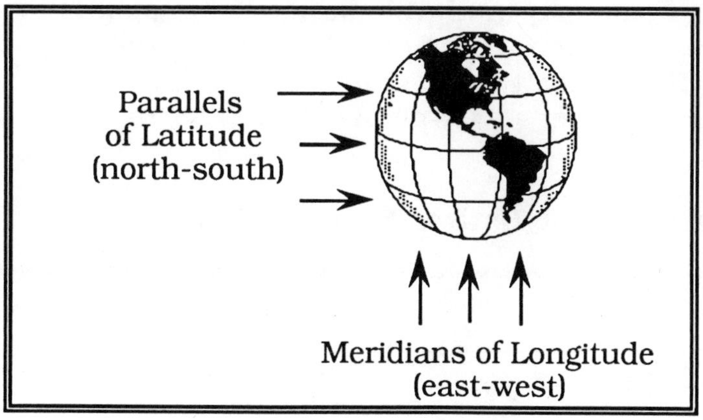

Longitude is the distance measured along the Earth's equator. The zero point of geographic longitude is the Prime Meridian, which passes through Greenwich, England. We measure Longitude east to west from Greenwich. Terrestrial longitude of 15° is equal to one hour of time.

Note that celestial longitude is different from geographic longitude. You measure celestial longitude along the ecliptic beginning at 0° Aries. Geographic longitude begins at the prime meridian that passes through Greenwich, England. Also note that if you extend the geographic latitude and longitude into space these are the equatorial coordinates: declination and Right ascension. *Latitude,* also measured in degrees, is distance north or south of the equator.

Astrologers also use the equatorial coordinate system. In this coordinate system, the plane of reference is the celestial equator, which is the Earth's equator projected out into space.

Closely related to the Earth's coordinates is the idea of a celestial sphere that surrounds the Earth, extending out into space. The technical definition of the celestial sphere is an imaginary sphere that exists at an infinite distance from the Earth. The celestial equator, also termed the *equinoctial*, is a projection of the Earth's equator onto the celestial sphere. The celestial north and south poles are directly overhead at the terrestrial poles. Figure 5, The Horizon System - Observer at North Pole, illustrates the basic idea of the celestial sphere.

The Horizon Coordinate System

Normally, when we refer to the horizon, we mean the *visible* joining of the sky and the land. This is different from the *rational* or *celestial* horizon that is a circle on the celestial sphere. Below are two diagrams that show the horizon system from an observer's viewpoint at the north pole, and at the equator.

Figure 5. The Horizon System - Observer at North Pole

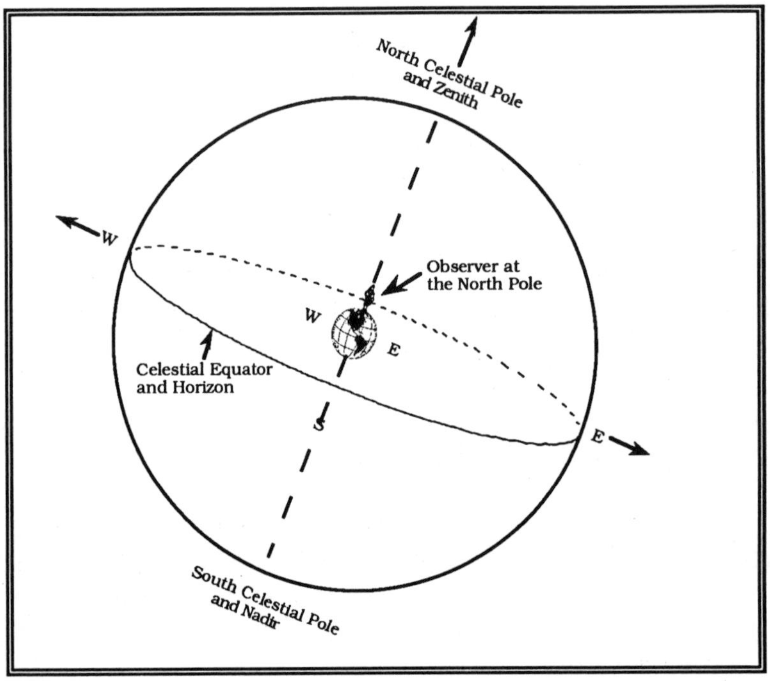

Figure 6. The Horizon System - Observer at Equator

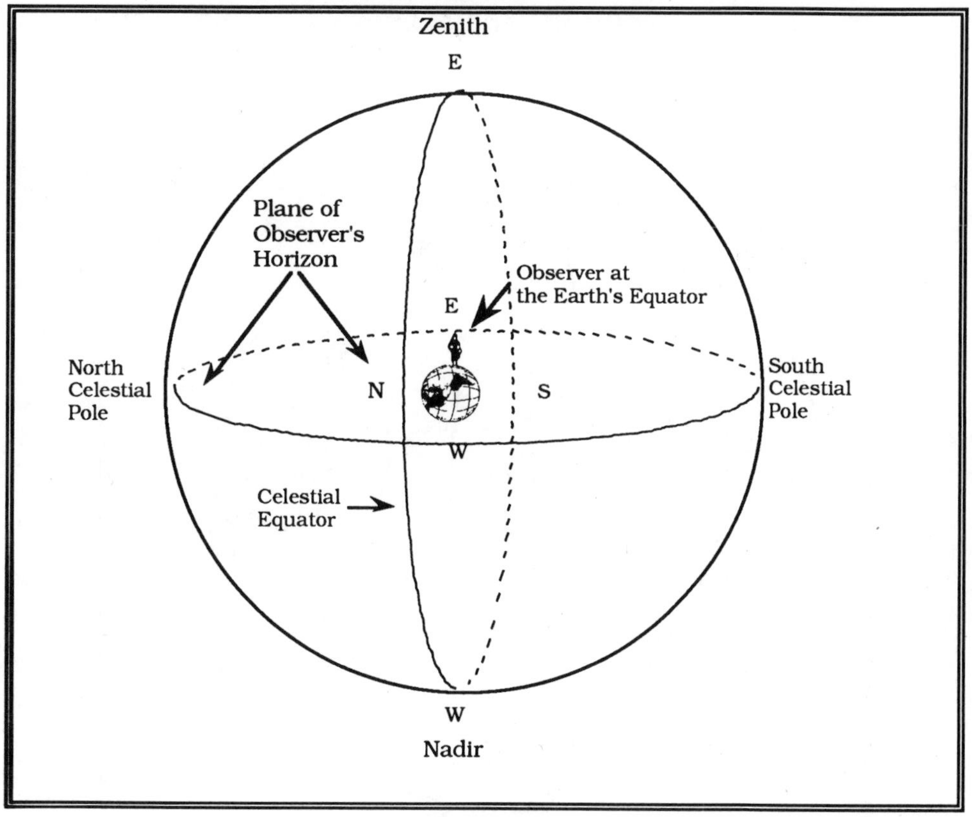

As shown in the two diagrams above, the horizon system uses the observer as the primary point of reference. The horizon coordinate system uses the coordinates of *altitude* and *azimuth.*

The altitude is the angular distance of an object above the horizon. Azimuth is the angle around the horizon from a reference point (usually north) to a great circle passing through the zenith and the object.

Figure 7. Horizon System Coordinates Altitude and Azimuth

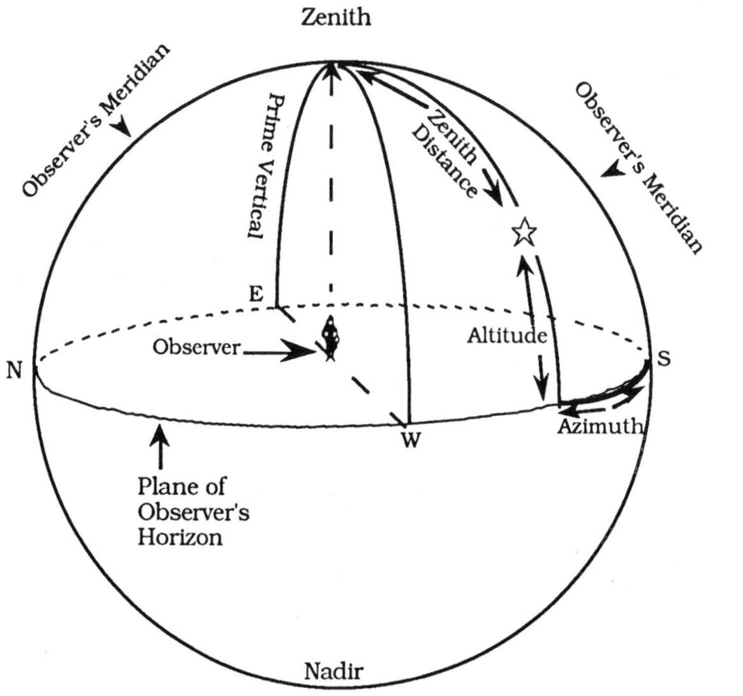

The Horizon System Uses the Coordinates of Altitude and Azimuth

Local Space Coordinates

Local space is the same as the horizon coordinate system. It uses the astronomical horizon as the frame of reference. In a strict sense, geomancy implies the use of the horizon system.

"Local space charts" are astrological maps of the sky that use the horizon system to describe planets' positions. Local space uses the person and local environment as the center. The individual chart (location) is the center, with the zenith directly overhead, and the nadir directly below. The azimuth or east/west is 360° around the center, and this is +0° to +90° of altitude to the zenith overhead, and -0° to -90° of altitude to the nadir below. See Figure 7, *Horizon System Coordinates: Altitude and Azimuth.*

The standard local space charts are opposite the standard natal, or ecliptic horoscopes. You draw the ecliptic chart from the view of facing the equator from the northern hemisphere. This places the midheaven on top (south and up), and the ascendant (east) on the left.

The local space chart has north at the top, with the cardinal directions positioned as you usually see on topographical maps. West is on the left of the chart; east is on the right. In a similar way, this also reverses the houses from the ecliptic horoscope as the figure below shows. Astrologers sometimes refer to a local space chart as an *azimuth chart*.

Figure 8. Local Space Chart

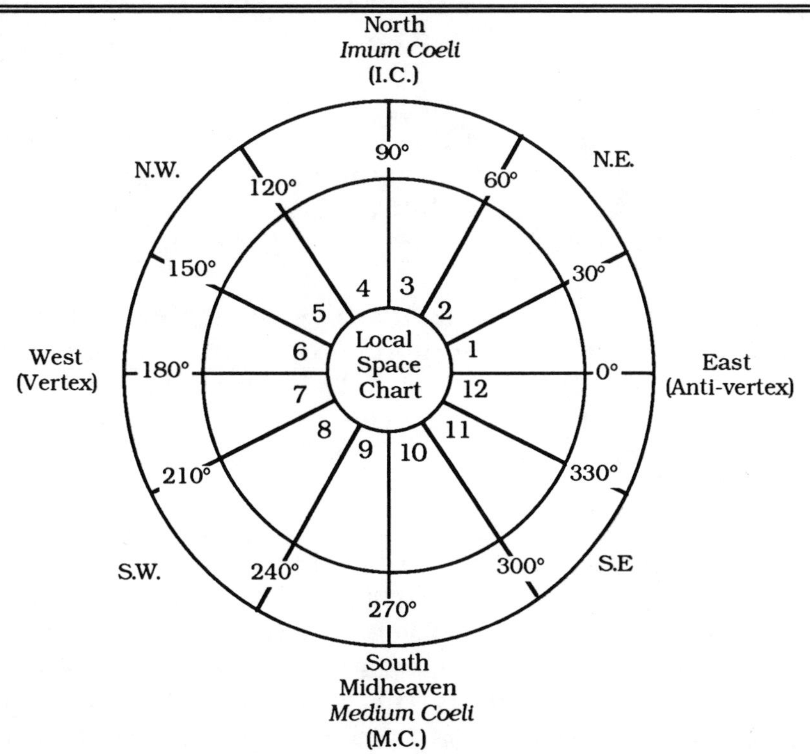

A local space chart reverses the houses and places the planets on the horizon as we would see them from our personal viewpoint.

Two good references on the local space system are Steve Cozzi's book: *Planets in Locality*, and Zipporah Dobyns booklet: *Working with Local Space.*

The Equatorial Coordinate System

Two geographical coordinates of latitude and longitude pinpoint any place on Earth. Similarly, you can find any object in the heavens if you know its coordinates on the celestial sphere. The celestial coordinates are *declination (Dec)*, and *right ascension (RA)*. The equator coordinate system, just as its name implies, uses the great circle of the Earth's equator as its primary reference.

In summary:

north/south = latitude on Earth, and declination on the Celestial Sphere.

east/west = longitude on Earth and Right Ascension on the Celestial Sphere.

Right Ascension (RA)
Right Ascension is the measurement of the stars' and planets' distances along the celestial equator, measured eastward starting at 0° Aries (the vernal equinox). Zero degrees Aries (♈) is like a "celestial Greenwich", and is one of two points of intersection of the celestial equator and the ecliptic.

The measurement of RA is sometimes in degrees (0° to 360°) around the equator, but is more often expressed in sidereal time. One hour of sidereal time (ST) is equal to 15 degrees of distance along the equator. See Figure 8, The Equator Coordinate System.

The right ascension is also the angle between the *hour circle*, and the first point of Aries (0° ♈). The hour circle is an imaginary circle that passes through a celestial body and the celestial poles. The angle between the hour circle through the object and the observer's meridian is sometimes used as an alternative coordinate. This is the *hour angle*. See *Hour Circle*, and Figure 44. *Hour Circle and Hour Angle*, in the Astrological Dictionary.

In the hour angle coordinate system you plot the planets' locations in relation to the celestial equator, starting from the intersection of the celestial equator and the meridian arc. Hour angle is the east-west measurement and the declination is north-south.

Declination

Declination is the complement of right ascension and terrestrial longitude, and refers to a body's distance north or south of the celestial equator, measured from 0° to 90°. That is, you measure how far the planet, star, or point is above or below the celestial equator. A heavenly body position north of the celestial equator is often noted by a + (positive), and a position south of the celestial equator by a - (negative) degree.

Figure 9. The Equator Coordinate System

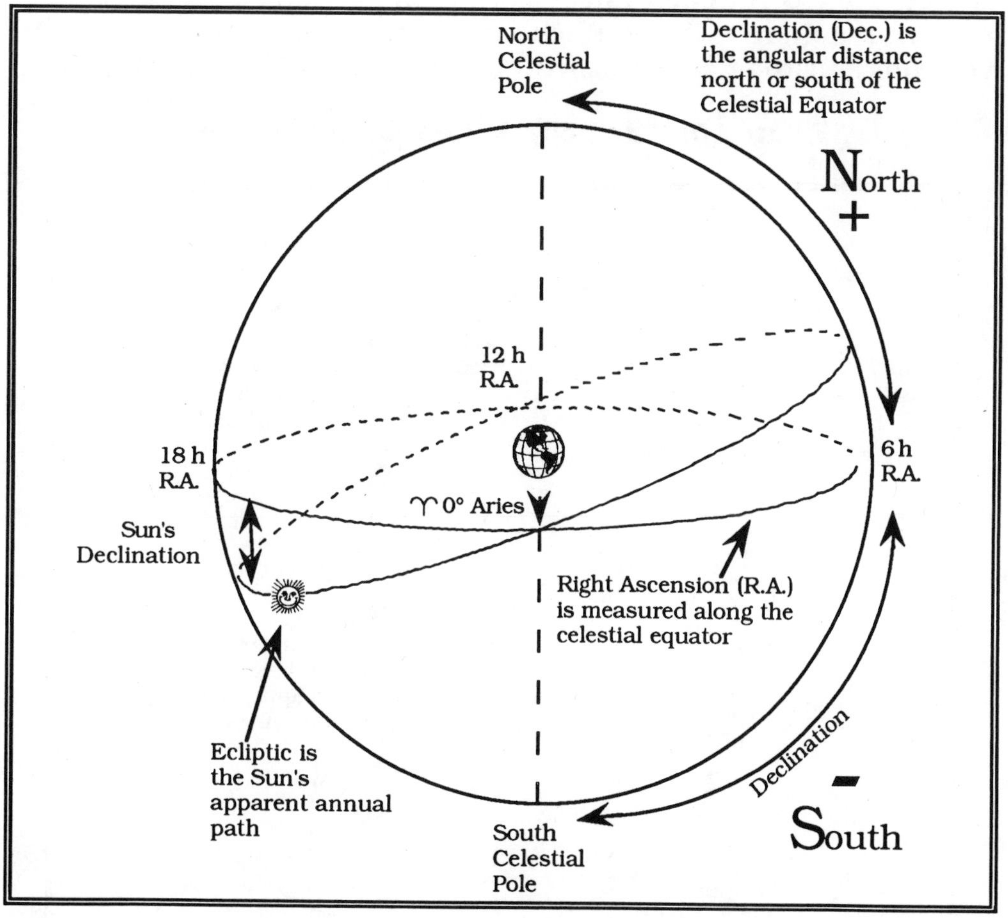

Astrologers usually use right ascension for some methods of progressions and directions, or for finding the culmination and anticulminating times of planets.

Ecliptic Coordinate System

The ecliptic is the yearly path of the Sun's center on the celestial sphere as seen from Earth. Another way to look at the ecliptic is the yearly path of the Earth, as seen from the Sun. Where the circle of the ecliptic intersects the celestial equator marks the zero point, which is the first degree of Aries (0° ♈).

Just as the Earth coordinate system uses latitude and longitude, the ecliptic coordinate system uses a similar grid of lines on the celestial sphere. These lines are the celestial latitude and celestial longitude as described, and shown in the figure below.

Figure 10. The Ecliptic Coordinate System

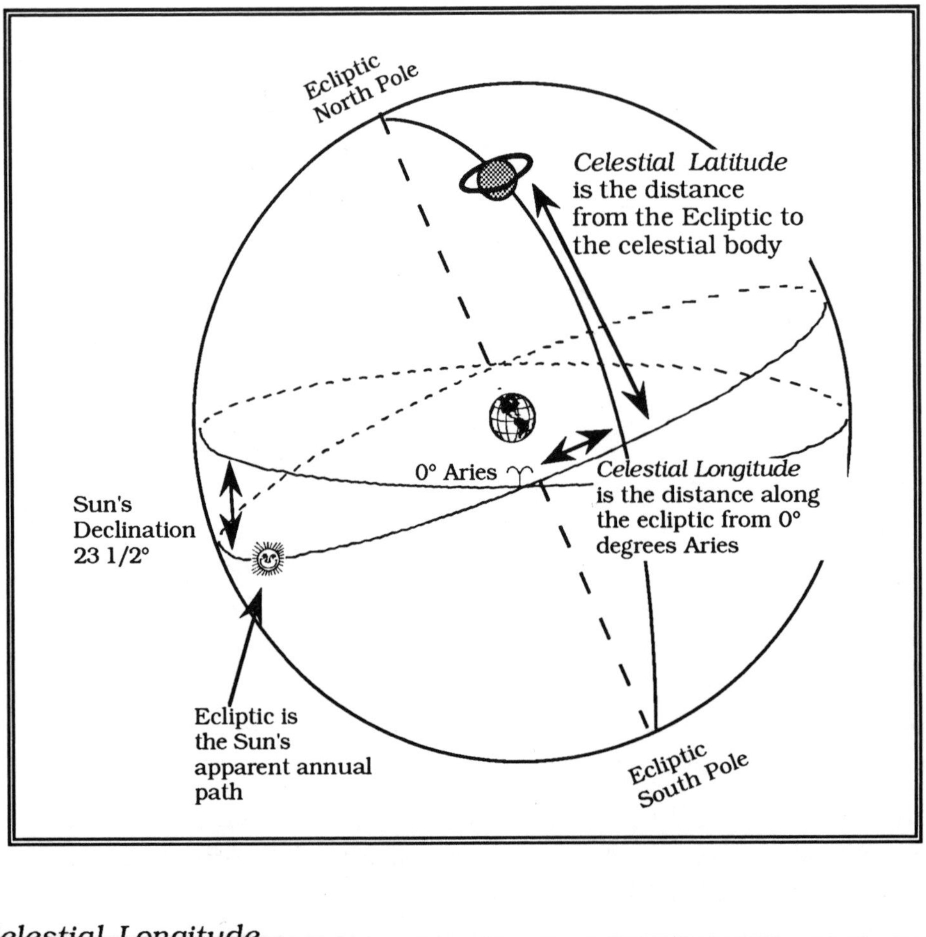

Celestial Longitude
Celestial Longitude is the angular distance along the ecliptic between a plane perpendicular to the ecliptic that passes through an object, and the first point of Aries (0°♈). You

measure this distance in degrees and minutes of arc eastward from 0° ♈ Aries. For example, if the Sun is 55° eastward from the 0° ♈, then you would conclude that its longitude is 25° ♉ (Taurus). You obtained this from adding 30° Aries + 25° Taurus = 55° celestial longitude.

Celestial Latitude
Celestial Latitude is the other coordinate of the ecliptic system. This is the perpendicular (north or south) angular distance of an object from the Ecliptic, measured in degrees and minutes. A planet is exactly on the ecliptic when its latitude is zero degrees. You would use celestial latitude to calculate the rising and setting times of planets in certain types of progressions and directions.

Astrologers usually express the positions of the planets in a combination of ecliptic coordinates (celestial longitude), and equatorial coordination (declination).

Mundoscope Coordinates

Sometimes called Campanus Mundoscope Coordinates, this system measures positions along the prime vertical moving westward starting at the zenith, or the point directly overhead.

The prime vertical is the plane that extends due east-west from the observer and straight up through the zenith, directly above the observer. The prime vertical plots the location of planets along its circle starting from the east down toward the nadir, then up to the west, and finally back to the zenith. Prime vertical longitude is the east-west measurement. Prime vertical latitude is the measurement perpendicular to the prime vertical. Amplitude is north south measurement along the horizon. See Figure 7: *Horizon System Coordinates Altitude and Azimuth.*

The mundoscope coordinates relate the position of planets, stars, and other points to their true position in a given house system. Normally you relate the positions of the planets to the zodiac without taking certain positionally distorting factors into account.

For example, Pluto can be as much as 17 degrees north or south of the ecliptic. Fixed stars can be as much as 90 degrees from the ecliptic and are even more prone to distortion. If you incorporate these positions into a house system without correcting the distorting factors, you will get an incorrect impression of the position. This can lead to a misinterpretation of its significance in the chart.

The high latitude of the birthplace is another situation that can cause the distortion of many intercepted signs in a horoscope.

Coordinate Systems Summary

Each coordinate system has a slightly different function in both astronomy and astrology. The table below summarizes the coordinate systems and the respective coordinate terms.

Table 1. Coordinate Systems

Coordinate System	North-South Up-Down	East-West Across	Reference Points	Great Circles
Earth	Latitude	Longitude	Greenwich	Prime Vertical
Horizon	Altitude	Azimuth	•Zenith •South Point	•Vertical circles Meridians
Equatorial	Declination	Right Ascension	•North Celestial Pole •0° ♈	•Hour Circles •Circles of declination
Ecliptic	Celestial Latitude	Celestial Longitude	•North ecliptic pole •0° ♈	•Ecliptic circle
Local Space	Altitude	Azimuth	•Cardinal directions	•Horizon
Mundoscope	Amplitude Latitude	Longitude	•Zenith •Nadir	•Prime Vertical

3. HOUSE SYSTEMS

House systems are essentially an artificial division of the space around the Earth. The first house is always in the same area, no matter what time of day it is. Each house symbolically relates to a different area of life, such as finances, home, career, communications, etc. In other words, you use house systems as a way of relating the zodiac to a place and time on Earth. Houses bring the signs down to an everyday, tangible level by connecting the zodiac signs to an observer's view from Earth.

There are approximately 40 house systems that might be available in an astrology program. House systems can be categorized by different criteria. Two systems of house classification are (1.) by quadrant or by equal divisions, and (2) by equal lunes, unequal lunes, semi-arcs and miscellaneous. The two category systems are described below.

1. House Classification by Quadrant Houses and Equal Divisions

Quadrant Houses. The basic principle of a quadrant system is to take one of the great circles; and divide it equally into 4 quadrants. The ascendant-descendant, and the MC-IC axis define the four quadrants. The first quarter is the ascendant to the IC. The second quarter is the IC to the descendant. The third quarter is the descendant to the MC, and the fourth quarter is the MC to the ascendant. The various house methods subdivide each quadrant into three sections to obtain the 12 house cusps. The great circles most used in the quadrant system are the celestial equator, the ecliptic, and the prime vertical. The measurement on the great circles can be done two ways:

1. *space system*, that measures physical distance, and,

2. *time system*, that measures the amount of time taken to cover distance along the great circle. Time is usually sidereal time.

In all the quadrant house systems the most unanimously agreed upon house cusps are the angles that denote the east (ascendant), west (descendant), overhead (midheaven) and below (IC). These four angles provide the basic grid from which the other houses are derived.

Equal Houses. These house systems simply divide one of the great circles, usually the ecliptic, into twelve equal 30° arcs from the ascendant or midheaven. These points are then projected to the north and south poles of the ecliptic.

2. House Classification by Equal Lunes, Unequal Lunes, Semi-arcs and Miscellaneous.

Another way to classify house systems is described in an unpublished paper by Robert Hand entitled "House Systems: A Summary". This approach uses four categories of houses described below.

House Category 1: Houses that Involve Division of the Sphere into Twelve Equal Lunes. Lunes are the crescent shaped portions created when a sphere is divided by two intersecting planes. *Lune* is also the French word for Moon. House systems in this category are:

Ascendant Equal House System (Equal Houses)
Meridian Equal Houses
Meridian Houses, also called:
- Axial Houses
- Equatorial Houses
- Zariel Houses

Campanus Houses
Horizontal House System

House Category 2: House Systems with Unequal Lunes

Regiomontanus Houses
Morinus Houses

House Category 3. Semi-Arc House Systems

Placidus Houses
Pseudo-Placidus
Koch or Birthplace System

House Category 4: Miscellaneous

Topocentric
Porphyry Houses
Natural Graduation Houses

Which House System is Best to Use?

Obviously, not only are there different ways to categorize house systems, but different astrologers will totally favor one house system over another. The use of different house systems is largely a matter of opinion and preference. There are situations when one house system might be better to use than another, such as casting charts for locations near either of the Earth's poles.

Which house system to use also depends upon what you intend to do in astrology. Astrologer Margaret Meister points out, you must "fit the house system to the method of astrology". For example, in prediction work, Nancy Hastings uses the Placidus House System with secondary progressions as an integral part of the way she practices astrology. The Cosmobiologists find the Koch House System and solar arc directions work well for them.

Even politics can determine the use of house systems. The Regiomontanus House System was widely used in England and France during the 16th through 18th centuries. By the time the Placidus houses were codified, there was a Catholic vs Protestant struggle in England. Placidus was a Catholic monk; the Protestants liked Regiomontanus. During this time, one's political statement was sometimes made by the house system used or advocated.

Regardless which system you use, the end goal of computing house cusps is to identify the areas of specific mundane expressions that the houses symbolically represent in the horoscope. There is not agreement, or conformity, about the significance of the house cusps themselves. In some house systems the cusps mark the center of the houses, while in others the cusps mark the boundaries.

This section describes the most common house systems. Many of the diagrams showing the house systems are from Jerry Makransky's article and book, both entitled *Primary Directions*. These publications are excellent resources for anyone wanting more technical information about house cusp calculations. Table 2 summarizes the major house systems. It is in alphabetical order.

Table 2. House Systems Summary

HOUSE SYSTEM	CLASSIFICATION	COMMENTS
1. Albategnian	Quadrant Divide Prime Vertical	Might have been basis of Placidus Houses.
2. Alcabitius (Alcabitian)	Quadrant Time System Semi-Arc system Divide Diurnal Circle of Ascendant.	Sidereal time division. Only semi-arc system valid for Poles. Also called Classical System.
3. Aries	0° ♈ on Ascendant.	Emphasizes 12 Signs.
4. Campanus	Quadrant Space System Divide Prime Vertical & project onto ecliptic.	Pole distortion. Favored by sidereal astrologers. Equal lunes.
5. Equal Houses	Divide ecliptic into 12 arcs. Equal lunes.	Houses have strong similarity to signs. Valid at poles.
6. Horizontal	Divide horizon into 30° arcs & projects onto ecliptic. Equal lunes.	Emphasizes mundane horizon.
7. Koch	Quadrant Time System Semi-arc houses Can have non-30° houses.	Variation of Alcabiticus. Trisects diurnal semi-arc . Tables available only to 60°. Not valid at Poles.
8. Moon Houses	Not a True House System.	Moon = 10th house cusp.
9. Meridian	Quadrant; Equal lunes Divide Celestial Equator.	Similar to Equal House System. Also called Axial, Equatorial or Zariel houses.
10. Morinus	Divide Celestial Equator. Unequal lunes	Also called *Rational Method*, and *Universal Method*.
11. Placidus	Quadrant Time System. Sometimes called "Semi-arc System".	Time measured distance. Not valid at poles above/below 66°.
12. Porphyry	Quadrant, trisect ecliptic Non-30° houses.	Modification of Equal House System.
13. Regiomontanus	Quadrant Space System. Divide Celestial Equator to 30° arcs & project onto ecliptic.	Not valid at Pole Latitudes. Unequal lunes.
14. Solar Houses	Not a True House System	Natal Sun position (degree) is asc.
15. Sun Houses	Not a True House System	Natal Sun is 4th House Cusp.
16. Topocentric	Quadrant Divides Celestial Equator into 30° arcs and project to ecliptic.	Corrects effects of Placidius Houses at high altitudes. Uses polar axis as a fixed reference point. Mathematically impossible.
17. User Defined Ascendant	Not a house system	The astrologer assigns the ascendant (1st house cusp).
18. Whole Sign Houses	Sign of the ascendant is the first house, etc.	

Albategnian House System
The 10th century Arabian astrologer Prince Muhammed ben Gebir al Batani first introduced this house system. He was called Albategnius in Europe.

According to Fred Gettings in his *Dictionary of Astrology* this method of house division divides the prime vertical into diurnal and nocturnal arcs. The diurnal and nocturnal arcs are then divided into equal parts by two declination circles. The Albategnian system might have been the foundation of the Placidean House System. Gettings gives no citation to verify this statement. This house system is not often used by modern astrologers.

Alcabitian (Alcabitius) House System
There is debate who developed this house system. Was it the first century AD astrologer Alcabitius, or the 12th century Arabian astrologer Alchabitus? Regardless, it is one of the oldest known house systems.

The Alcabitian House System works in a way similar to the Koch system that employs the principle of trisection of the semi-arcs by a time division. You use the length of sidereal time for the ascendant degree to revolve to the cusp of the midheaven. You divide this amount of time into three parts and add the result to the sidereal time of birth. This gives you the 10th, 11th, and 12th house cusps. A similar reverse procedure determines the nocturnal arcs.

In other words, the Alcabitian houses divide the diurnal circle of the ascendant into twelve arcs. The diurnal circle of the ascendant is the small circle parallel to the equator that passes through the ascendant. You trisect the portion of this diurnal circle lying in each quadrant to obtain the houses.

You then divide the diurnal and nocturnal arcs into equal parts by two declination circles. The diurnal semi-arc, or DSA, is the portion of the diurnal circle that lies in the 4th quadrant. The nocturnal semi-arc, or NSA is the portion of the diurnal circle that lies in the first quadrant. The figure below shows the house divisions.

Figure 11. The Alcabitian House System

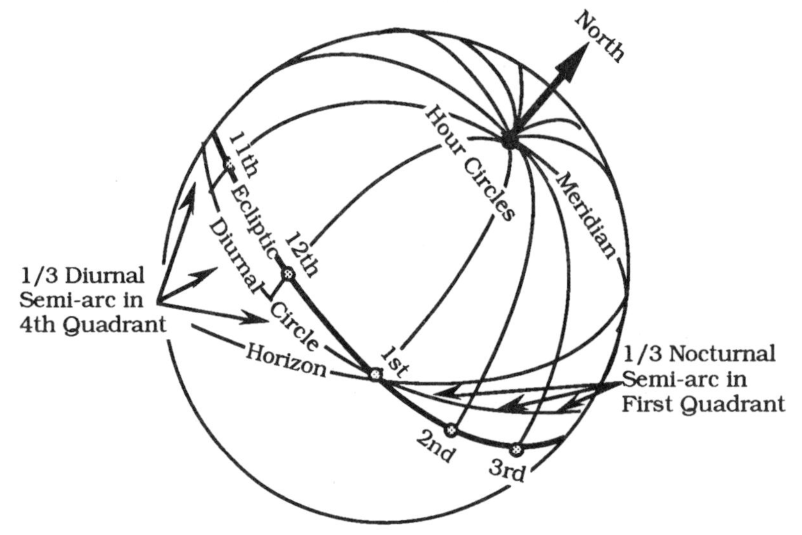

The Alcabitian houses do not lie entirely on one or the other side of the horizon, and the divisions of nocturnal and diurnal semi-arcs are not equal. This causes a sudden change in house size as the ascendant and descendant are crossed.

Some astrologers consider the Alcabitian House System as the only semi-arc system valid for the polar regions. This is because there is always an ascendant. The ascendant is always the first house cusp, and the MC is the cusp of the tenth house.

Aries House System

The Aries House System uses twelve houses of 30° each. Zero degrees Aries (0° ♈) is always on the ascendant (9 o'clock), and zero degrees Capricorn (0° ♑) at the midheaven (12 o'clock). The other house cusps are at 0° of the respective signs.

The planetary positions for the time of birth or event are then placed on the wheel. You also can use the house cusps from another house system, such as Koch, or Placidus, thus giving houses other than exactly 30° each. The Aries House System emphasizes the twelve signs.

Figure 12. Aries House System

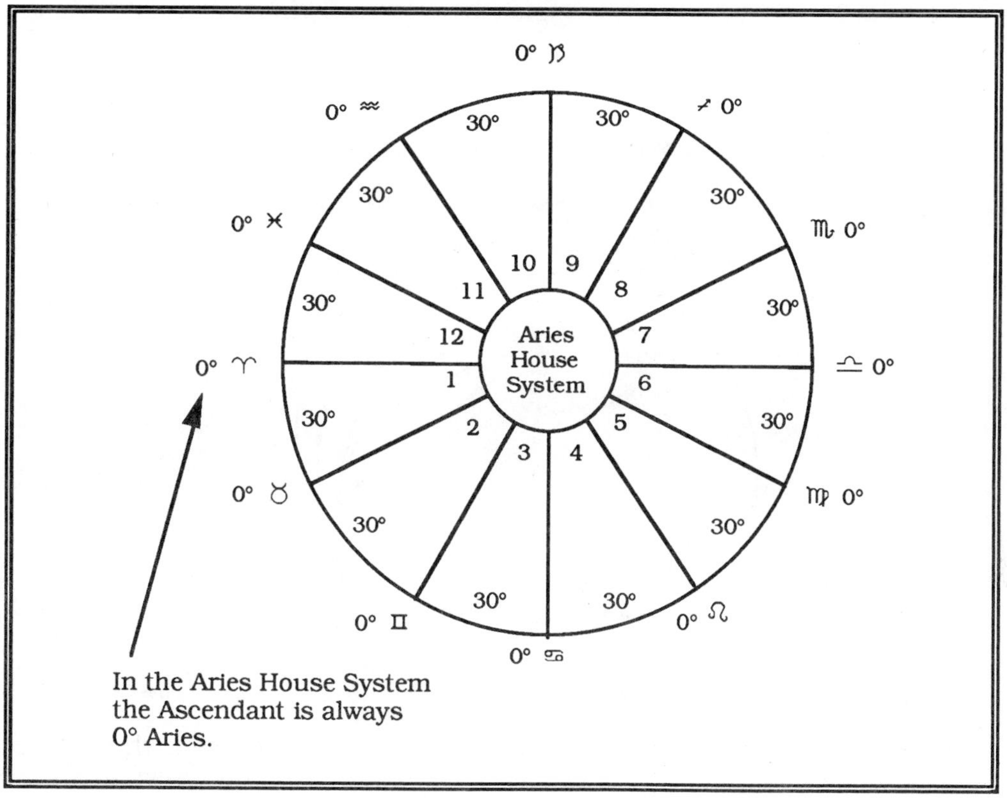

Campanus House System

The Campanus House System was probably adapted from an earlier Arabian system used by the 13th century mathematician/astrologer Giovanni Campano. Historians also credit Johannes Campanus, another astrologer from the 13th century. Sidereal astrologers favor the Campanus House System.

You create Campanus house cusps by dividing the prime vertical into 30° arcs starting at the east point of the horizon. The prime vertical is the great circle that passes through the east point of the horizon. It is the first or "prime" vertical circle. The lunes' poles are the north and south points of the horizon. You then project these divisions of the prime vertical onto the ecliptic by drawing house circles which are lines from the north to the south point of the horizon. The places where these north-south lines intersect the ecliptic are the Campanus house cusps.

Although this system is based upon "equal" lunes, you often get "larger" houses near the horizons. The effect of this is a tendency to place more planets in the horizon houses than would normally be there. The first house cusp is the ascendant, and the 10th house cusp the MC. Houses 1 through 6 lie entirely below the horizon, and houses seven through twelve lie above the horizon. You can find house cusps to the pole regions, unless the ecliptic is on the horizon.

Figure 13. Campanus House System

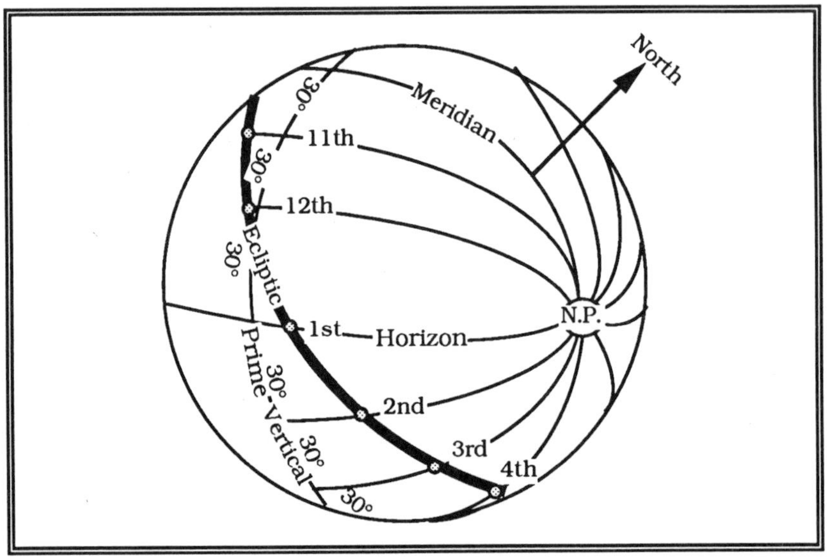

The Campanus House system has favor among astrologers who believe the cusps of the houses mark the center of the house which is the strongest place of influence. One main problem with the Campanus House System is the distortion of the houses for locations near the north or south poles. Charts cast for these locations tend to have many intercepted signs (see *Intercepted Signs* in the Astrological Dictionary, Part 3).

Equal House System

The Equal House System dates from about the first century BC. Some historians credit the early 19th century Australian astrologer Zariel, with this house system, and call it the "Zariel Division". Also, some astrologers call this the Ascendant Equal House System.

You obtain the equal house cusps by dividing the ecliptic into twelve 30° arcs. You then project these points onto great circles that meet at the north and south poles of the ecliptic. Usually the ascendant is the cusp of the first house. The 10th house cusp is the zenith's longitude, called the nonagesimal.

Figure 14. Equal House System

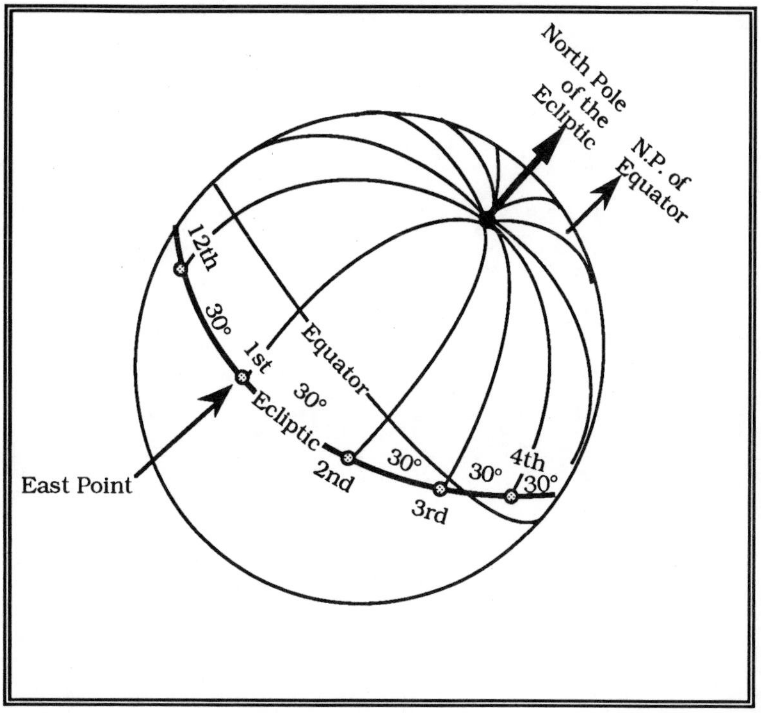

Because this system uses the poles of the ecliptic, the houses strongly associate with the zodiac signs. For astrologers who relate signs to houses this is a strong benefit. Additionally, houses can be calculated in the polar regions, but retrograde ascendants and the definition of the ascendant can be a problem.

Another reference to equal houses is also by the graphic layout of the horoscope that has all houses equal in size. For example, if the ascendant were at 6°6' Libra ♎, then all the other house cusps would be at 6°6' of the respective signs, as shown in the figure below:

Note that the Equal House System is different from an equal house chart that have equally spaced house cusps. Some astrologers use these equal house charts for graphically charting non-equal house systems. The chart form and the house system are two separate and distinctive techniques.

Figure 15. Equal House Chart

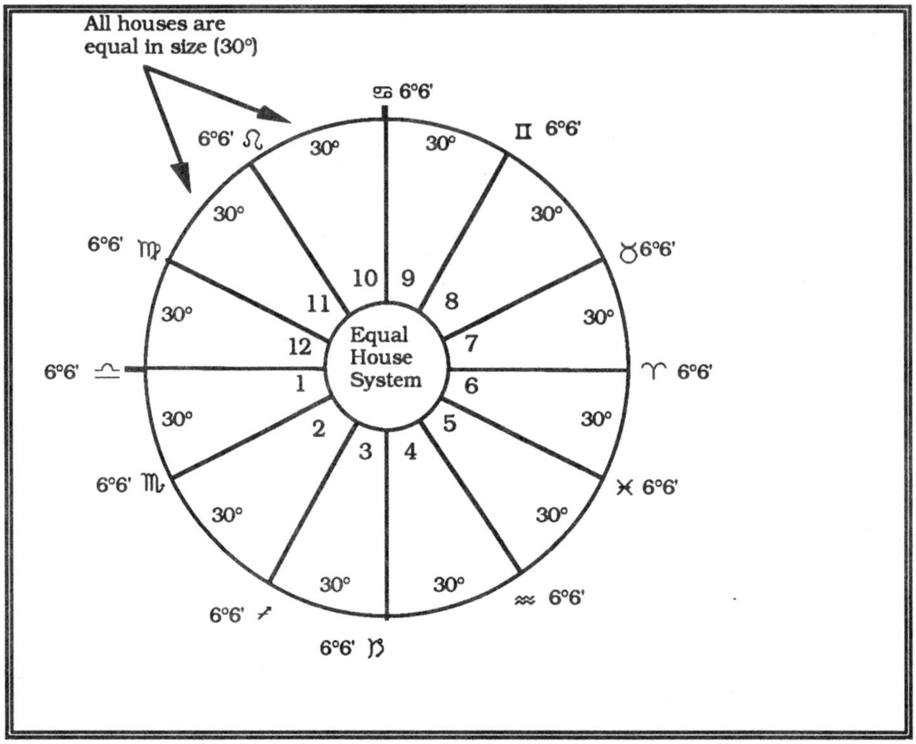

Horizontal House System

In this house system, a specific place on Earth is the reference point. You divide the horizon circle into twelve 30° arcs starting at the east point (the place due east of the observer). You then draw *vertical circle lines* from the zenith (the point directly above the observer) to these twelve points on the horizon. Vertical circles are circles that pass through the zenith and nadir. The intersections of the vertical circles and the ecliptic are the horizontal system house cusps.

In this house system, the cusp of the 10th house is the MC. The cusp on the first house is the anti-vertex, or the point due east on the ecliptic. Therefore, the ascendant is not the cusp of the first house, nor of any house. The horizon is the great circle that is divided into twelve arcs and projected onto the ecliptic. Because of this, the horizon does not form any house cusp as shown below. Many astrologers view this as a serous drawback because the horizon is an important consideration in traditional astrology.

This system is used frequently for local space charts, where the angles are the same as the cardinal points on a compass. For better or worse, this also coordinates planetary positions to the mundane compass directions.

Figure 16. Horizontal House System

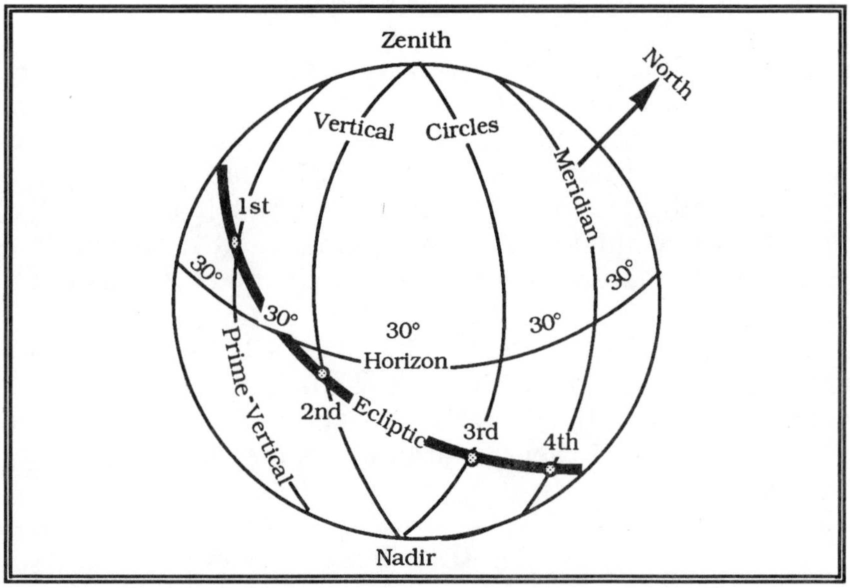

Koch House System

This house system is really a variation of an older system, the Alcabitius House System. Specht and Zanziger, invented this system, but it was made popular by the German astrologer Walter Koch in 1962. The Koch system is also sometimes called the Birthplace System of Houses, and the GOH System, derived from German: *Geburtsortes Hausertabellen.*

The Koch House System trisects the diurnal semi-arc by time division. The method produces a grid that lacks valid application in the polar regions. Interestingly, the older system, Alcabitian, has validity at the poles whereas the Koch system does not.

In the Koch system, you create the house cusps of the first quadrant by trisecting the diurnal circle of the lower meridian. That is, you divide into thirds the nocturnal semi-arc of the midheaven. You form the fourth quadrant houses by trisecting the diurnal circle of the upper meridian.

In other words, you create Koch houses by trisecting the MC semi-arcs from the ascendant to the midheaven and from the IC to the ascendant. You then project these trisected points onto the ecliptic with altitude circles that are parallel to the horizon. Altitude circles, sometimes called ascension circles, are circles tangent to the diurnal circles through the north and south points on the horizon. The intersections of these altitude circles and the ecliptic are the Koch house cusps.

This house system has several odd features. Each house cusp curve is a potential horizon for the birthplace. Thus, it is possible for the tenth house to be on the horizon; this is a little hard to imagine, much less justify. Additionally, the tenth house cusp <u>on</u> the ecliptic is the MC. But the tenth house curve <u>off</u> the ecliptic does not align with (or the same as) the meridian circle. Other house cusps are also not clearly defined off the ecliptic.

The Cosmobiologists prefer the Koch House System. The supporters of Koch houses believe that house cusps on the ecliptic are unusually sensitive to ecliptic transits, directions and progressions. However, similar claims are made for other house systems.

Figure 17. Koch House System

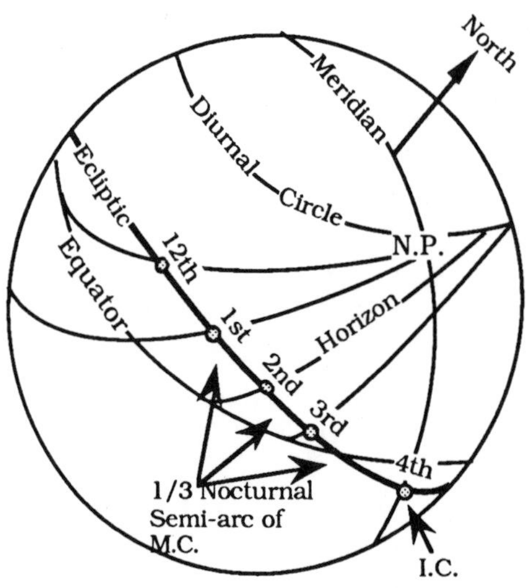

The major disadvantage of the Koch House System is that it produces house divisions that lose validity in the polar regions. The result is many intercepted signs. Tables of the Koch houses are available only to the 60° latitude.

Meridian House System

Australian astrologer David Cope developed this house system in the early 1900s. David Cope's pen name is Zariel. Uranian astrologers frequently use the Meridian House System.

You obtain meridian house cusps by dividing the celestial equator into twelve 30° arcs. Then project these arcs onto the ecliptic with *hour circles*. Hour circles are circles that pass through the north and south celestial poles. The places where these lines intersect the ecliptic are the meridian house cusps. Each house is exactly two sidereal hours long, and the MC is the cusp of the 10th house.

This is similar to other projection house systems, and especially to the Equal House System. The difference is that the house division is from the MC (as the cusp of the 10th house), instead of from the ascendant (as cusp of the first house).

Figure 18. Meridian House System

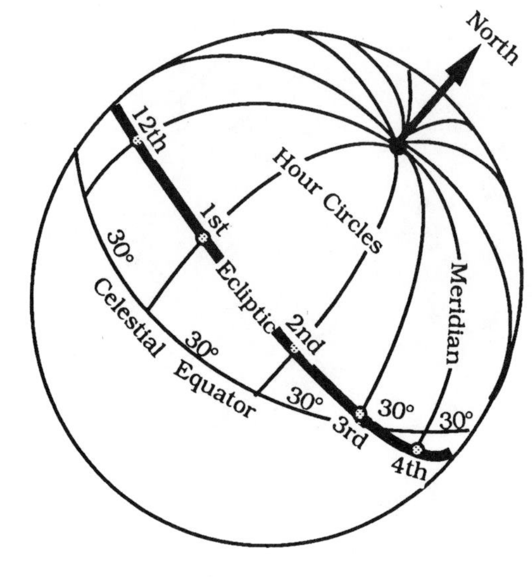

Morinus House System
This system is named after Jean Morin de Villefranche, a 17th century astrologer. This house system is also called the Morinean System, the Rational Method, or the Universal Method. Robert Hand in his paper "House Systems: a Summary", writes that Morin did not invent this house system, and, in fact even criticized it. Morin preferred Regiomontanus houses.

In the Morinus House System, you divide the celestial equator into twelve equal 30° segments starting at 0° Aries. You then draw lines from the north pole to the south pole of the ecliptic through these 12 points on the celestial equator.

The north and south ecliptic poles are perpendicular to the ecliptic in the same way that the Earth's poles are perpendicular to the Earth's equator. These lines are longitude circles and pass through the north and south ecliptic poles. They are perpendicular to the ecliptic. The places where the longitude lines intersect the ecliptic are the house cusps of the Morinus System. The MC and ASC are not necessarily the 10th house and 1st house cusps respectively, but are determined by the intersection of the lunes with the ecliptic.

Figure 19. Morinus House System

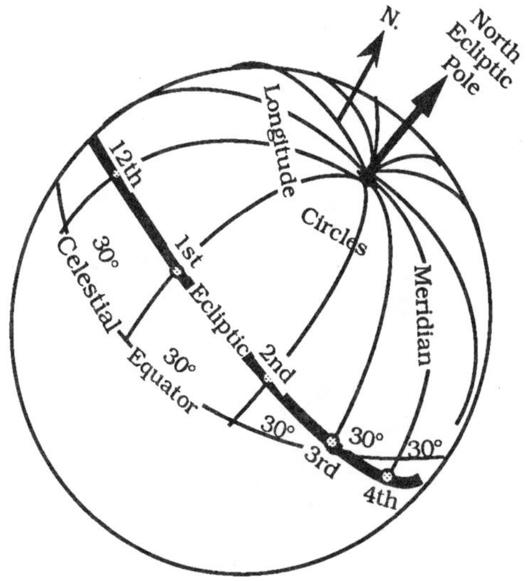

The rationale behind the Morinus House System is somewhat murky in traditional astrological terms as none of the usual points are house cusps. This includes the MC, ascendant, vertex, etc. House cusps can be obtained for the polar regions.

Placidus House System

The Placidus System is named after a monk, Placidus de Tito, who lived from 1603 to 1668. There is much debate among scholars about the origin of the Placidus system. Historians generally agree that this house system was not originated by its namesake, Placidus, but should be accurately accredited to the eighth century Arabian astrologer, ben Djabir.

The Placidus House System is a time system. This is because it is the amount of time taken to cover space that is divided to obtain house cusps. Some astrologers also call this house system the "semi-arc system". This is because the time (in right ascension) is taken for each degree of the ecliptic to rise on its own parallel of declination. This is measured from the IC to the ascendant (nocturnal semi-arc), and from the ascendant to the MC (diurnal semi-arc). The house cusps are points that are 1/3 and 2/3 of the semi-arcs of the ascendant to the MC, and ascendant to the IC. The figure below shows this graphically.

Figure 20. Placidius House System

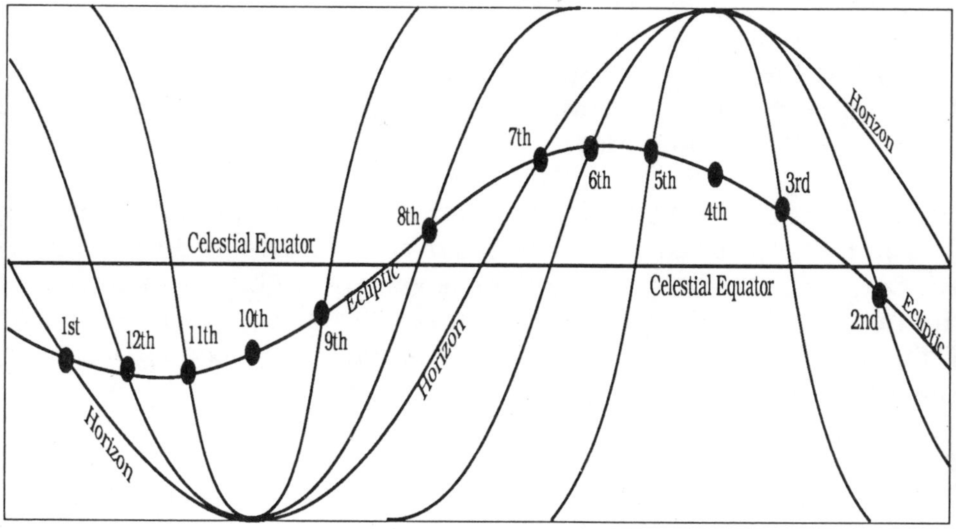

Adapted from an unpublished drawing by Robert Hand

The curves that result from the trisection are not simple arcs or straight lines, but are more like sine waves (remember trigonometry). Astrologer Margaret Hone states that a major problem with the Placidus system is that there should be semi-arcs to trisect. In latitudes greater than 66° 33', there are many degrees that never touch the horizon (circumpolar). These degrees will be either totally diurnal or nocturnal arcs, but not both. In other words, there are no ecliptic house cusps, and charts cast for locations above 66° will not have semi-arcs to trisect.

This literally means that certain degrees can never form house cusps, nor be included in houses. If the Sun, Moon, or other planets were in these degrees, they would not appear in any chart made by this house system. No complete chart could be erected. Astrologer Hone further states that "*some mathematically minded astrologers condemn this system (Placidian) as the least worthy of attention*". (*Modern Textbook of Astrology*, page 138). Additionally, the divisions of the nocturnal and diurnal semi-arcs are not equal. This causes a sudden discontinuity in house size at the ascendant or descendant.

Fred Gettings, in his *Dictionary of Astrology* states that the reason the Placidean system is the most widely used house system today is "*...largely due to historical accident rather than to any particular merit in the system itself*." Gettings points out that since the 19th century most of the available 'Tables of Houses", including the popular "Raphael's Ephemeris", were calculated according to the Placidus method. It is the mass availability of Placidus House Tables that still encourages the wide use of Placidus houses.

On the positive side, the placidian ascendant and MC are the first and tenth house cusps respectively. Houses one through six are below the horizon and houses seven through twelve are above the horizon. Placidian tables of houses are given in the *American Ephemeris, Occidental Tables, American Astrology Tables of Houses* and the *AFA Tables of Placidus Houses.*

Porphyry House System

This system is named after Porphyry, a third century AD astrologer. Hindu astrologers prefer this system and call it the Sripathi House System, after Sripathi Bhatta, who lived about 1000 years ago.

You create Porphyry house cusps by trisecting the ecliptic angular distance between the midheaven and the ascendant and between the IC and the ascendant. This creates the 10th through 3rd houses. Between the ascendant and MC are three equal houses. The houses between the MC and descendant are also equal to each other, but not necessarily equal to the first set of houses.

Opposite houses in the horoscope are equal to each other. That is, the 4th through 9th houses have the same degree of the opposite sign. For example, the 4th house cusp is the same degree and minute of the 10th house cusp, but is the opposite sign. The same is true with the rest of the houses: the 5th and its opposite the 11th, 6th and 12th, etc.

A disadvantage to the Porphyry system is that it creates two different sizes of houses that can change suddenly and without gradation as the angles are crossed. The houses do not lie entirely on one or the other side of the horizon.

Two positive features of Porphyry houses are that cusps can be calculated to the polar latitudes, although they might be a little strange. The ascendant is the opening cusp of the first and the MC is the cusp of the tenth.

In simpler terms, the Porphyry system is a modification of the Equal House System. Natural Graduation Houses is a modern attempt by British astrologer Colin Evans to improve the Porphyry houses. Evans proposed graduating the size of the houses so that there is a constant gradual change in house size. The rationale behind this system is to make more aesthetic looking houses. Whether this is mathematically or astrologically justified is questionable.

Regiomontanus House System

This house system is named after the 15th Century astrologer Johannes Muller, known by his pen name as Regiomontanus. Some astrologers call this system the "*Modus Rationalis*" or rational method. For astrological purposes this house system is a rational division of the celestial sphere.

This system uses the principle of trisection of a quadrant of the celestial equator by 30° arcs using house circles. The first house cusp is the horizon. The degrees at which the circles intersect the ecliptic are the house cusps. Because the Earth's equator is not perpendicular to the north/south axis of the horizon, the projected lunes are not equal. Most other house systems with unequal lunes sometimes have dramatic changes in house size. The Regiomontanus houses change progressively and gradually in size (arc) from house to house.

The ascendant is the cusp of the first house and the MC is the cusp of the 10th house. The first through the sixth houses lie below the horizon, and conversely, houses seven through twelve lie above the horizon.

Figure 20. Regiomontanus House System

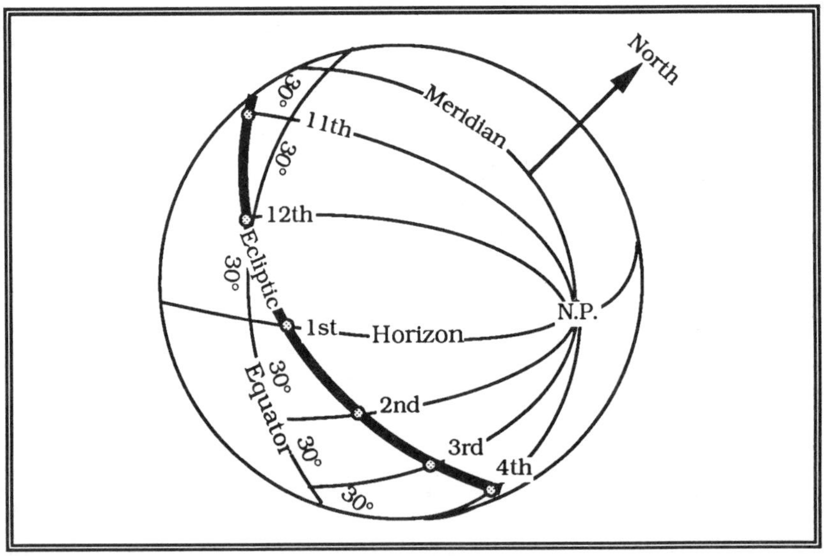

In the Regiomontanus system, the house cusps are considered to be in the middle of the houses, instead of marking the boundaries.

Astrologer Nancy Hastings views this house system not useful for prediction astrology. She uses the Placidus Houses with secondary progressions transits and solar arc directions.

Solar Houses

This house system is useful when casting charts for people with unknown or uncertain birth times. Here you use the Sun's Zodiacal position as the ascendant. You then assign the other house cusps the same degree and minute of each successive sign.

In other words, you use the degree and minute of the natal Sun's zodiacal sign as the first house cusp. For example, if the natal

Sun were at 15°♏33' (Scorpio), then the ascendant would be 15°♏33'. You would assign the eleven other house cusps the same degree and minute as the natal Sun. This is shown in the figure below.

The Solar House System is not a true house system. It is a type of equal house chart. Do not confuse the Solar houses with Sun houses. Both use the natal Sun as a cusp, but the Solar system places the natal Sun as the ascendant. The Sun House System positions the Sun on the cusp of the 4th house.

Figure 21. Solar House System

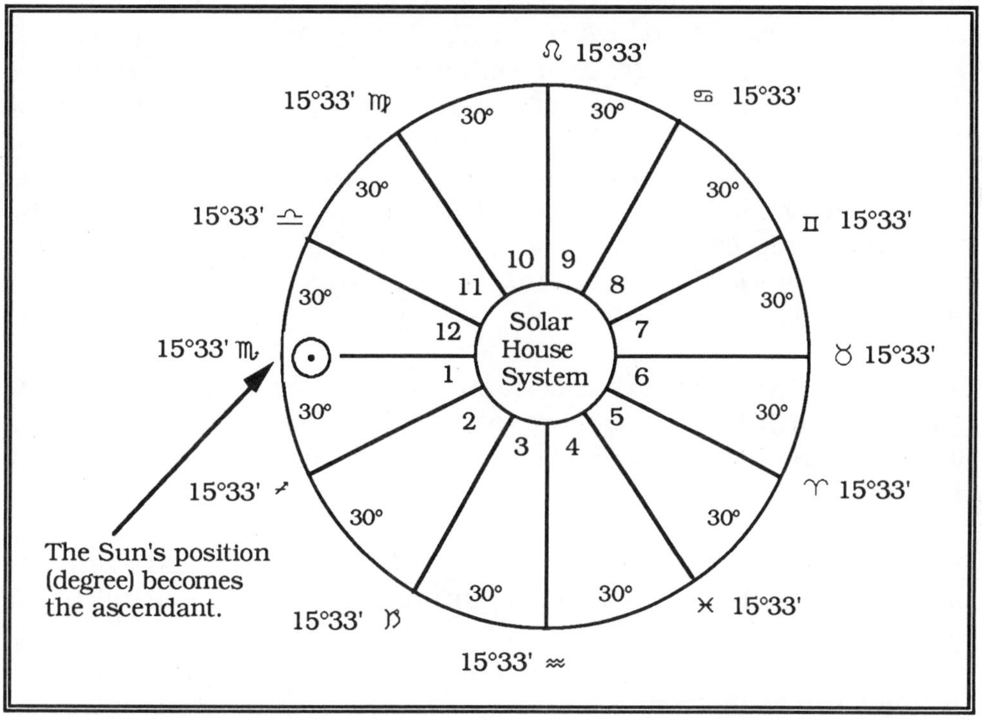

There is another variant of solar houses that places the Sun on the midheaven (MC). Astrologers often use this in mundane work for charts of businesses.

Topocentric House System

The Topocentric House System is named topocentric because it corrects the effects of the distortion of the Placidus house cusps at high latitudes. In this system, the polar axis is a fixed reference point. The basis for house cusp measurements is the rotation of the geocentric horizon around the axis.

To obtain house cusps, you divide the celestial equator into twelve 30 degree arcs. You then project these division points onto the ecliptic. Ascension circles are used for the pseudo (false) latitudes, or those latitudes above 60°. This system gives fewer intercepted signs for those born below -60°, or above 60° latitude.

Robert Hand, in his paper: "House Systems: a Summary", states the rationale behind the Topocentric system is obscure. He states that the Topocentric House System: "*...is accomplished by a series of mathematical misunderstandings, and circular reasoning. The most serious error in the mathematical understanding is that the celestial sphere is not treated as infinite and given a radius of 1 unit. This system rejects the idea of a celestial sphere. Instead cones of ascension are postulated that are supposed to trisect all possible semi-arcs (Placidus), trisect quadrants on the prime vertical (Campanus) and possess houses that represent equal divisions in time (various other house systems). It is a bit of all things to all people. It is also mathematically impossible...(no one) has been able to understand the mathematical reasoning...this system is essentially a mistake.*"

On the positive side, the ascendant and MC are the cusps of the first and tenth house cusps respectively. Houses one through six are below the horizon and houses seven through twelve are above the horizon.

According to Dr. Margaret Millard and Alexander Marr, primary directions in oblique ascension supposedly work well with the Topocentric House System.

Uranian House Options

Uranian astrologers often use an equal house system that places a planet's zodiacal coordinates as one of the house cusps. All the other house cusps are placed 30° further along in the zodiac. Below are two of the more common Uranian House options: the Sun and Moon House Systems. There are many Uranian House Systems that use various planets as different cusp points.

Sun Houses (Uranian)

This Uranian House System takes the position of the Sun as the beginning of the 4th cusp and then assigns all other house cusps at equal 30° houses after that. In other words, the zodiacal position of the Sun becomes the 4th house cusp, with the other 11 house cusps being the same degree and minute of each successive sign. If the natal Sun were at 15°33 ♏, then the opening of the fourth house cusp would be 15°33 ♏. The figure below illustrates this approach.

Figure 22. Sun Houses (Uranian House Option)

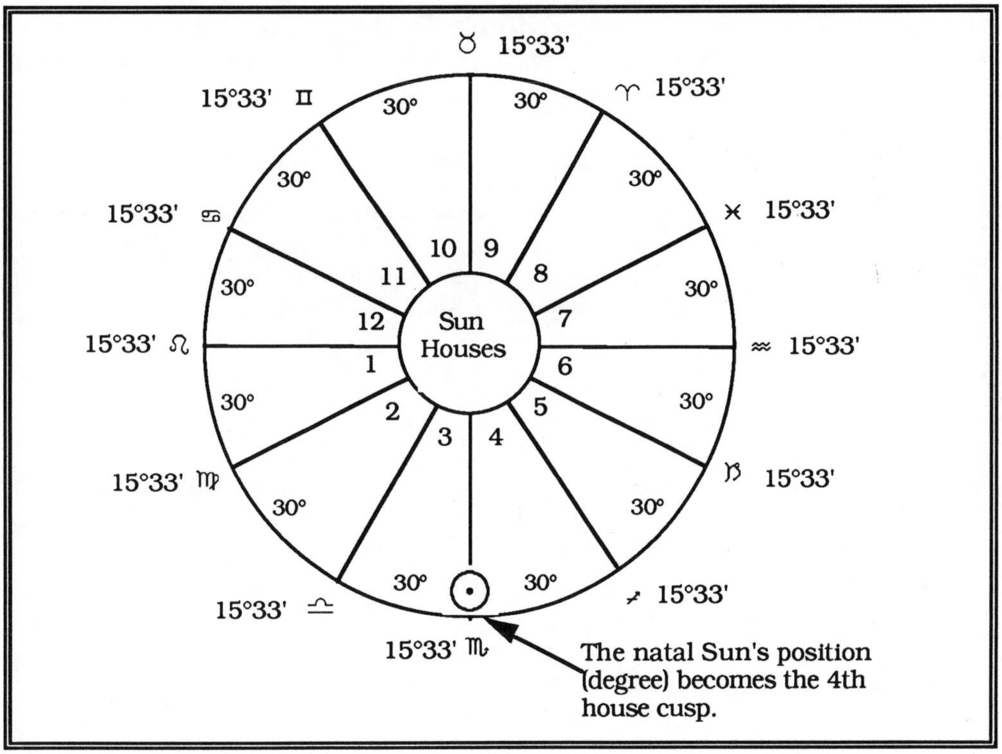

Sun houses are not a true house system that produces house divisions based upon relationships to the celestial sphere or time arcs. You simply use the Sun's position to determine the 4th house cusp.

Moon Houses

This Uranian House System takes the position of the Moon in the chart and assigns that position as the 10th house cusp. All other house cusps are at equal 30° intervals from the Moon's position having the same degree and minute of each successive sign. For example, if the natal moon were at 5° 22' ♋ (Cancer) then the position of the opening 10th house cusp would be placed at 5° 22' ♋. The Moon House System, like the Sun House System, is not a true house system. This is because the position of the Moon determines the cusp of the 10th house.

Figure 23. Moon Houses (Uranian House Option)

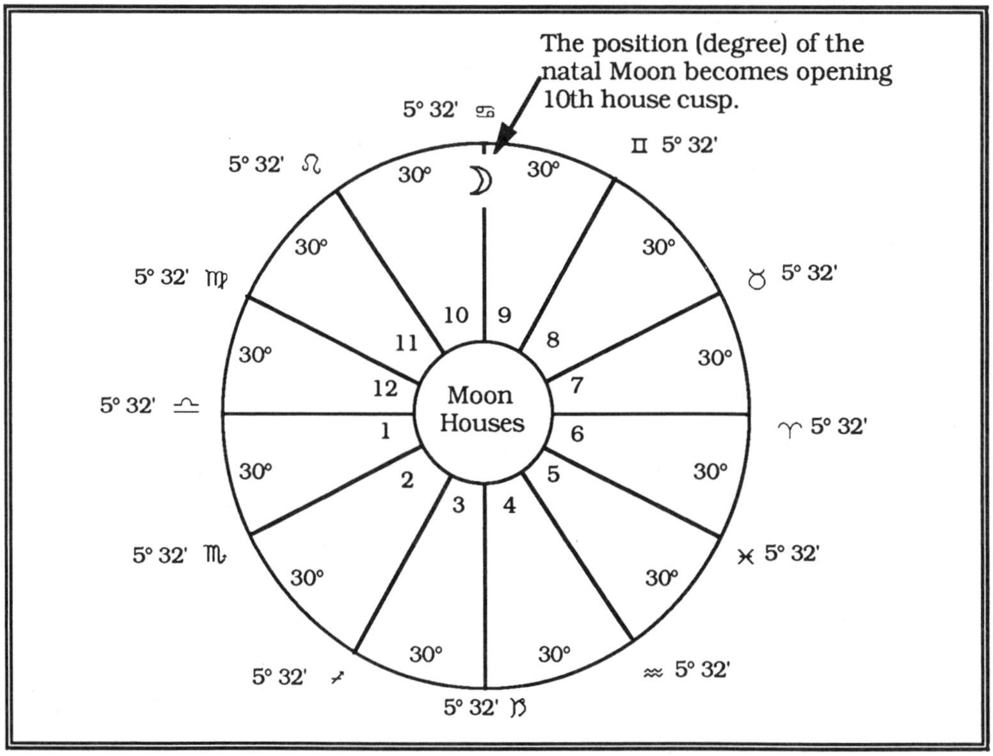

User Defined Ascendant

User defined ascendants are not house systems. The astrologer determines the degree of the ascendant. In other words, you, not the birth time, are the determinant of the ascendant. With this approach you assign the degree and minute of the ascendant to each sign to create the other 11 houses. On the computer you key in the ascendant point, in degrees, minutes and seconds. That point becomes the first house cusp. Often the user defined point is the zero degree of the rising sign (called whole sign houses), or as zero degrees Aries (0° ♈).

Figure 24. User Defined Ascendant

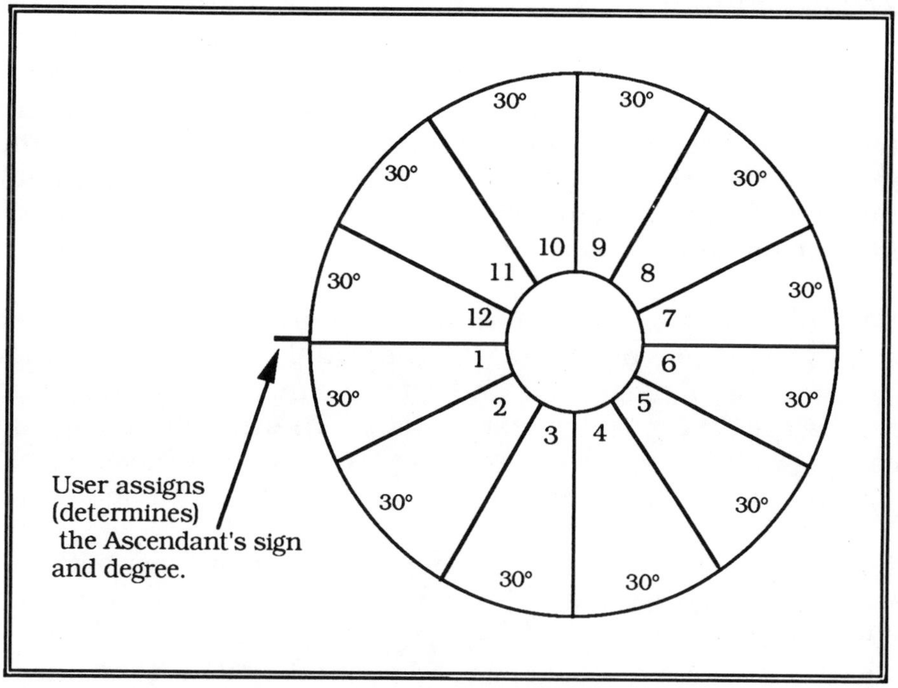

4. CHARTS & TABLES

The chart and table output refer to the various charts and tables that the astrology program can produce. These types include the natal chart, transit searches, harmonic charts, tables, and others. Below are some descriptions.

Natal Chart

The natal chart is a symbolic representation of the sky viewed from the place of birth at the time and date of birth. It is a "freeze frame" of the constantly moving planets. The essential birth data are threefold:

date - year, month, day and second

time - as exact as possible to the minute

location - expressed as geographic latitude and longitude (in degrees, minutes and seconds).

Transit Table

Naturally, planets continue moving after a person is born. The natal chart represents a "snapshot" of the position of the heavens at the exact time of birth (first breath). Astrologers measure the movements of the planets through the sky in reference to the zodiac. Planets move through the signs, and different planets travel at different speeds.

These transiting planets move into certain angular relationships with the position of planets in the natal chart. These angular relationships are aspects, and the moving planet "transits" or crosses over the position natal planet. In other words, a transit search (table) is a list of aspects formed by the passing of the Sun and planets over the points and positions in the horoscope.

The computer program searches its electronic ephemeris to find and list the transits. The transit output can be expressed as a list for the time frame (year, day, etc.). That is, a list of days that transits make aspects to the natal chart. Transits for a specific time can be charted as a bi-wheel with the natal chart on the inside, and the transiting planets on the outside.

Comparing the natal chart with transiting planets can yield information about the passages and cycles a person might be experiencing. The most commonly used aspects in transit searches and tables are:

Symbol	Degrees	Name	Suggested Orb
☌	0 °	conjunction	8° to 12°
✳	60 °	sextile	2° to 7°
□	90 °	square	5° to 8°
△	120 °	trine	4° to 8°
☍	180 °	opposition	6° to 12°

An example of a transit table, adapted from Graphic Astrology, is below.

Table 3. Transit Table Example

Partial Transit Table

Transiting Planets — Aspect Formed — Natal Planets

Date transiting planet enters into orb of natal planet

Date leaves orb of natal planet

Aspect	Enters orb	Exact	Leaves orb	Aspect	Enters orb	Exact	Leaves orb
♂ ⚹ ♃	JAN6	*JAN7*	JAN8	♂ □ ♅	MAY17	*MAY18*	MAY19
♂ □ ♄	JAN7	*JAN8*	JAN9	♂ ☍ ♆	MAY29	*MAY30*	MAY31
♅ ⚹ ♀	JAN9	*JAN25*	FEB13	♃ ⚹ ☽	MAY29	*JUN8*	JUN16
♂ ☌ ♂	JAN12	*JAN12*	JAN13	♂ △ ♇	MAY31	*JUN1*	JUN2
♂ ⚹ ☽	JAN18	*JAN18*	JAN19	♅ ⚹ ☉	JUN4	*JUL1*	JUL25
♂ ☍ ♅	JAN21	*JAN22*	JAN23	♂ ⚹ MC	JUN5	*JUN6*	JUN7
♆ □ ♆	JAN26		JUL25	♇ □ ♇	JUN10	JUL31	SEP18
	FEB25	APR21	*JUN18*	♂ ⚹ ♃	JUN11	*JUN12*	JUN13
♂ ⚹ ♀	JAN29	*JAN30*	JAN30	♂ △ ♂	JUN17	*JUN18*	JUN19
♅ ⚹ ☉	JAN29	*FEB17*	MAR12	♃ ⚹ ♅	JUN21	*JUN28*	JUL4
♂ ⚹ ☉	JAN30	*JAN31*	FEB1	♂ ☍ ☽	JUN23	*JUN24*	JUN25
♂ □ ♆	FEB2	*FEB3*	FEB3	♂ ⚹ ♅	JUN26	*JUN27*	JUN28
♂ ⚹ ☿	FEB5	*FEB6*	FEB7	♂ ☍ ♀	JUL5	*JUL6*	JUL6
♂ △ AS	FEB10	*FEB11*	FEB12	♂ ☍ ☉	JUL6	*JUL7*	JUL8
♂ △ ♄	FEB16	*FEB17*	FEB18	♅ ⚹ ♀	JUL6	*JUL31*	SEP7
♃ ⚹ ♅	FEB25	*MAR3*	MAR11	♄ □ ☉	JUL7	*JUL22*	AUG5
♂ □ ☽	FEB26	*FEB27*	FEB28	♂ □ ♇	JUL11	*JUL12*	JUL13
♂ □ ♀	MAR8	*MAR9*	MAR10	♂ ☍ ☿	JUL13	*JUL14*	JUL15
♅ □ ♆	MAR8	APR22	JUN8	♂ △ AS	JUL18	*JUL19*	JUL20

For a more complete listing of aspects, refer to *Aspects* in the Astrological Dictionary (Part 3).

Derived Charts

The natal chart is the basis for a host of secondary or derived charts. These charts are often cast for the particular time or event. For example, when a transiting Sun is at the same point on the zodiac as the natal Sun. These various derived charts serve as a method to zoom in on a particular part of the natal horoscope. The derived charts tend to add depth and perspective to the study of a person or event.

Remember that a derived chart is an extension of the natal (radix) chart. You can use derived charts to supplement the information gleaned from the natal chart. Below is a short list of derived charts. Refer to the Astrological Dictionary (Part 4) and index for more information about specific derived charts.

Solar Return
Lunar Return
Medical (nodal axis) Charts
Planetary Returns
Relocation Charts
Composite Charts
Progressed Charts
Harmonic Charts
90° Dial Charts
Arc Directed Charts

Astrologers use various methods for examining interpersonal interactions and dynamics. The most commonly used derived charts are the progressions, directions, returns, and the combined charts (composite, synastry and Davison Relationship charts).

Predictive Techniques

There are many methods employed by astrologers to predict future trends and provide insights about the times ahead, or what happened in retrospect. There is not much you can do about a volcanic eruption or an earthquake, but there is much you can do about your reactions to people and events. Predictive techniques can help identify the potentially troublesome times. Knowing this, you can consciously decide what to do about them.

Nancy Hastings wrote an excellent book called: *The Practice of Prediction: the Astrologer's Handbook of Techniques Used to Accurately Forecast the Future.* Below are descriptions of the more common predictive methods.

Progressions
Progressions and directions are two of the many methods of expressing the movement of planets in the chart. In

progressions, you use the movement of the planets during one unit of time to symbolize events over a longer period.

The difference between progressions and directions is that progressions move planets the way the planets themselves move in the sky. Directions use the motion of one point or planet to move all the points or planets including the angles (ascendant and midheaven).

Progressions cast a chart for a specific time, but in doing so substitute one time frame for another. Implied is a link between the first day of life, as a miniature cycle, that is holographically and symbolically reflected throughout the rest of one's lifetime. That is, experience in one type of cycle (day, month, year) also relates to, or lays the foundation for evolving experiences in the other types of cycles.

The formulas for the secondary, tertiary and minor rates below are from the NOVA V 2.10 Documentation (Astrolabe). The formula for the progressed rate is:

$$\text{Rate} = \frac{\text{number of days of progressed time}}{\text{number of days of real time}}$$

As you might guess, substituting one time frame for another can be complex if done by hand. But astrological computer programs are very good at calculating and casting progression charts and tables quickly and accurately. This is especially true for tertiary progressions. Secondary progressions are somewhat easy to calculate and place on a chart by hand.

Secondary Progressions

One widely used predictive technique is secondary progressions. The basis of the technique is simple: you substitute one day for each year of life after birth. For example, if a person is 60 years old, you cast a chart for 60 days after the actual birthday. You examine both the progressed chart and the original natal chart individually, and compare them to each other to gain information and insights.

The formula for the secondary rate is:

$$\text{Secondary Rate} = \frac{\text{1 day}}{\text{365.24219907 days}} = 0.00273790926277$$

More information is in Nancy Hastings excellent book entitled *Secondary Progressions: Time to Remember* .

Tertiary Progression
Tertiary progressions work like the secondary progressions except that each day after birth is equivalent to a month of life. That is, you substitute a day for each lunar month.

The formula for the tertiary rate is:

$$\text{Tertiary Rate} = \frac{1 \text{ day}}{27.32158648147 \text{ days}} = 0.036601096762031$$

(or the Lunar month)

These are known as Tertiary Type I in Europe.

Minor Progression
Minor progressions were developed independently and simultaneously by the Church of Light in the U.S. and Troinski in Europe.

In minor progressions, you substitute a lunar month for a solar year. The formula is:

$$\text{Minor Rate} = \frac{27.32158648147 \text{ days}}{365.24219907 \text{ days}} = 0.074804022419675$$

(or solar year)

As the name implies, these are minor progressions and not used as widely as the secondary and tertiary progressions. Minor progressions are known as Tertiary Type II in Europe.

User Defined Progressions
User defined progressions allow the astrologer to define the progression rate. You choose a ratio of symbolic time to real time to calculate the progressions.

Progressed Angles

Chart angles move forward (counterclockwise) in the chart in a manner similar to that of progressed planets. These angles make aspects to various planets like the transiting and progressed angles. There are different ways to calculate a midheaven degree, and thereby the other angles in the chart. Interestingly, most of the methods arrive within a degree or two of each other.

Most of the more comprehensive (larger and more expensive) computer astrology programs allow you to chose your method of progressing angles. Below are brief descriptions of these methods: the solar arc midheaven, Naibod arc, degree per year arc, user defined arc, ascendent arc, vertical arc, and quotidians.

Solar Arc Midheaven
In the Solar Arc Midheaven system, you add the difference between the natal and progressed Sun to the midheaven. You then derive the progressed ascendant from this progressed midheaven.

True Solar Arc in Right Ascension
This moves the sidereal time, or the right ascension of the *medium coeli* (RAMC) of the natal chart ahead according to the motion of the Sun in right ascension. This gives you the same result as erecting a progressed chart for every year at the solar return. The difference is you do it at the solar apparent time of birth instead of the mean time of birth.

The method behind the true SA in RA is to progress the Sun and find its right ascension. Then subtract the RA of the natal Sun from the progressed Sun and add the result to the RAMC of the birth chart.

True Solar Arc in Longitude
This is a commonly used method of directing the midheaven of a progressed chart. It is exactly like the true SA in RA except that you use the longitudes of the Sun and midheaven rather than their right ascensions. The calculations are: (1.) compute the progressed Sun's position in longitude, (2.) subtract the natal Sun's longitude, and (3.) add the result to the longitude of the natal midheaven.

Astrologers use solar arc because the Sun represents the life arc or the physical body. You also could use a lunar arc, Mercury arc, etc. depending upon what you are looking for.

Naibod Arc in Right Ascension
This is a method used in predictive astrology to get the midheaven. The Naibod arc is expressed as the Sun's mean motion in right ascension.

You calculate the Naibod arc by subtracting Naibod's value of the Sun's mean daily motion in RA from the mean position of the progressed Sun in RA for the date of direction. You then add this value to the right ascensions of other planets and points in the natal chart. The result is the directed positions of all points in right ascension.

Naibod arc in RA moves the sidereal time 3'56.5" for every year of life (or fraction of the year). In other words, you simply recalculate the natal chart using the progressed day's sidereal time, the natal birth time and birth place. The answer is identical with the Naibod Arc in right ascension if you did it for the birthday.

Naibod Arc in Longitude
This method is also know as the mean solar arc because the mean daily movement of the Sun in the zodiac is 59"08" of arc. Here you use the average daily motion of the Sun along the equator, adding about 59' 8" of arc (Naibod rate) measured in time/real day, or progressed year.

For example, for a 40 year old person you would multiply 59 minutes 8 seconds times 40 and then add this sum to the natal midheaven. You then derive the progressed ascendant from this progressed midheaven.

Note that the regular Naibod arc is usually expressed in right ascension and not longitude.

Quotidians
There are two basic different rates used for quotidians, and from these two basic rates, variations are derived. The two basic rates are Q1 and Q2. Both use a day = year substitution. The difference between Quotidian 1 and 2 is the +/- fractions of the 1° per day on the midheaven.

Quotidian-1 (Bija)
Quotidian-1 is also called Bija and often noted as Q1. In the Q1 method, one rotation of the Earth using the fixed stars as markers is equal to one orbital revolution of the Earth around the Sun. For convenience, 24 hours of sidereal time = one civil year or 365.25 days. This represents 360 degrees of apparent solar motion, and a 360° advance of the midheaven in longitude. Therefore, in half a year (about 183 days), the Q1 sidereal time advances 12 hours, and the MC longitude advances 180°.

Only Q1 is based on the sidereal day. Here you take the same day per year system that you used in secondary progressions. That is, a progressed chart for the 35th year of life would use the 35th sidereal day after birth. Also, this type of progression can be calculated in the sidereal zodiac, but often is not.

Quotidian-2
One civil day is taken to be equal to one civil year. This makes one day of sidereal time equal to one civil year + one day. This is 361° of apparent solar motion. In other words, Quotidian-2 revolves the entire chart 361° per year so that there is an approximately one degree difference on the M.C. for each day of the year. Q1 advances 360°; there is approximately a one degree difference between Q1 and Q2.

The NOVA v2.10 (Astrolabe) documentation describes other methods for erecting quotidians. These are summarized below.

Mean Quotidian
This is the quotidian chart you obtained by moving everything in the chart (including house cusps) at a rate of one mean solar day for a year. Interestingly, the mean quotidian for the time and date of the solar return is the same as the Naibod in Right Ascension progressed chart.

Apparent Quotidian
This quotidian chart uses the apparent solar day for a year and is very similar to the mean quotidian.

Neo-Quotidian Rate
Cyril Fagan discovered this quotidian. He based it on the movement of the progressed and transiting Sun in Right Ascension. In normal secondary progressions, 6 hours of a progressed day (1/4 of a day) equals 365.242 divided by 4 days or 1/4 of a year. In neo-quotidians, 6 hours of the progressed day equals 90° of solar motion in RA, this amount might be more or less than 1/4th a solar year. In other words, the neo-quotidian is based on a part of a day. This progressed motion equals the same part of 360° of solar motion in right ascension.

Directions

Directions use the motion of one point or planet to move all the points or planets in the chart backward or forward uniformly. The term "directions" comes from directing the planets and angles to some future position. As with everything in astrology, there are specific rules that dictate how you move or direct the point. Points can be moved by applying an arc of direction for any given time. They also can be moved by measuring the arc between the directed point and another sensitive point, such as a cuspal point.

You do not use arc directions like secondaries. The increment in longitude or right ascension of arc direction value is added to the positions of every planet and point in the natal chart. Thus, the entire chart rotates by the amount of arc added (directed).

You use the directed positions of the points and planets in a way similar to transits, except that directions are used to predict events or happenings with reference to the natal horoscope.

Directions involve studying the future configurations of the planets and angles with the intent to learn something about the future. Cosmobiologists and Uranian School astrologers use directions to time events. Astrologers use a variety of tools for predictive work including progressions, directions and transits.

Primary Directions
This is also known as the primary system. You use primary directions to calculate a specific future time an aspect will take place. Planets are "directed" to precise aspect(s) with other planets. Thus, you can direct Mars to the position of Saturn to calculate when the two planets will be conjunct. The arc in diurnal motion is the basis for the time conversion, with a ratio of approximately four minutes time per year.

Secondary Directions
In astrology there is confusion about the terminology of secondaries and directions. As astrologer Patricia White points out: "in older usage, secondaries were called either 'progressions' or 'secondary directions', but not 'secondary progressions' as this seemed redundant. Progressions meant only secondaries (as in secondary progression) and all other forms of progressions and directions were called 'directions' of one sort or another. This usage is dying away because it is useful to use progressions and directions to distinguish between advancing the horoscope in time (progressions), or by adding the same arc length to each position in the natal chart (directions)."

Thus, in modern terminology, "secondary directions" is somewhat of a misnomer. This is because "secondary" refers to a day/year substitution, whereas "directions" means to move every point and planet according to one measure (arc). According to Nancy Hastings, the term, "secondary directions" is commonly used instead of the correct name: "secondary progressions".

Solar Arc Directions

Solar Arc Directions are based upon the motion of the secondary Sun. In this technique you add the difference (in longitude) between the natal and progressed suns to all positions in the chart (planets, house cusps, etc.). You then compare the directed positions to the natal positions to see if any aspects formed, and interpret these accordingly.

Naibod Arc Directions (in Longitude)

Here you multiply the mean daily motion of the Sun (59° 08') by the age of the person for whom you cast the chart. For example, for a 35 year old person the calculations would be: 59° 08' X 35 = 34° 29' 40". You then add 34° 29' 40" to all positions in the chart including planets, house cusps, nodes, etc. You then use the new values to read the chart. This direction measurement is named after the 16th century German astrologer Valentine Naibod.

<u>Other Arc Directions</u>

There are several other arc directions that a computer program might offer. The NOVA version 2.10 documentation is the reference for the descriptions below.

Degree per Year Arc

In the Degree for a Year Arc, you add one degree to all positions in the chart for every year of life. You then compare these directed positions to the natal positions searching for any aspects between the two sets.

User Defined Arc

Here you, the user, decide the arc direction value. You enter this value into the program in degrees, minutes and seconds that the various points (planets, house cusps, etc.) move forward or backward.

Ascendant Arc

In this technique the progressed ascendant for the solar arc directed midheaven is calculated. You then add the difference between the natal ascendant and progressed ascendant to the natal planets. Note: always use the original place of birth when calculating the ascendant arc.

Vertical Arc and Vertex Arc
The vertical arc is similar to the ascendant arc directions. The difference is you use the arc between the natal vertex and progressed vertex for your calculations.

Return Charts

You cast a return chart for the exact moment a transiting planet "returns" (is conjunct) to its place in the natal chart. For example, transit Saturn's position conjoined natal Saturn (♄☌♄). You usually cast return charts for the current location of the individual, rather than for the birthplace.

Astrologers commonly use solar and lunar return charts. However, you could use any planet to cast a return chart such as Mercury, Venus, Mars, etc. No one will live long enough to experience a Neptune or Pluto return since these two planets take about 165 years and 248 years respectively to revolve around the Sun.

In casting return charts keep in mind that the slower the return planet is moving, the less you can trust the exactness of the house cusps. When a planet is nearly stationary (at station) or moving as slowly as Uranus, it is hard to pinpoint the exact moment that planet will conjoin its natal degree and minute. The actual time of the return chart can be off by hours and perhaps days.

Additionally, subdivisions of the return cycle could be used. That is, cast a chart for the exact time a planet is 90° (quarter-return) or 180° (demi-return) away from its natal position. The astrologer also can use tropical, sidereal or a precession corrected tropical zodiac.

Solar Return
The return of the Sun or planet is the amount of time it takes for one revolution around the solar system. The solar return is when the Sun returns to the same place it was at the time of birth.

You cast a solar return chart for the exact time the transiting Sun reaches the natal Sun's position. The exact transiting Sun position might be a day earlier or later than the actual calendar date we traditionally celebrate as our birthday. Three different locations might be used to cast the solar return chart: the birth location, the current residence location or the present location of the individual. Additionally, solar returns can be precessed (adjusted for the Precession of the Equinoxes) and unprecessed. The solar return is useful for forecasting the events and attitudes a person is likely to experience during the forthcoming year.

Lunar Return
Every month the transiting Moon passes over the natal Moon in the birth chart. This is represented in a transit table by ☽ ☌ ☽ and called the lunar return. There are about 13 lunar months in a calendar year. Therefore, the Moon returns to its natal position about 13 times per year.

Casting a chart for the moment of this occurrence yields the lunar return chart that can be useful in understanding your feelings and emotions. You interpret the lunar return as an "emotions" forecast for that month.

Solunar Returns
This is a chart cast for the time each month when the transiting Moon is conjunct the natal Sun (☽ ☌ ☉). The Solunar Return indicates how an individual feels about events that are happening; it is external event oriented. The transiting Moon conjunct natal Moon (☽ ☌ ☽) is more emotionally oriented about what we feel; it is internally oriented.

Precessed Returns
Due to the Precession of the Equinoxes, many astrologers who use the tropical zodiac prefer to use precessed return charts. Using precessed returns is actually a correction of a planet's position. This correction works by referring the position of the planets in the natal chart to the background of fixed stars. This fixed star background is used to calculate the return chart. The positions of fixed stars are not affected by the Precession.

The time difference between a solar return chart cast in non-corrected, and precession corrected modes is about twelve hours by age 36. This means the house cusps will be approximately 180° apart. For example, if the uncorrected solar return had Aries rising and Capricorn midheaven, the corrected chart might have Libra rising and a Cancer midheaven. This makes for a very different interpretation of the client's return chart.

Precession corrected returns are a way of doing sidereal returns. These are favored by astrologers who are used to the sign symbolism of the tropical zodiac.

Relationship Techniques

Whenever two or more people get together, a third entity representing the relationship is created. Relationship techniques compare how two people interact, react, and what potential issues might arise. The two most commonly used relationship techniques are the composite and synastry charts.

Composite Chart

A composite chart uses the midpoints of planets' locations from the birth charts of two people. The house cusps are usually derived from the composite midheaven and the latitude at which the relationship is taking place.

Astrologers believe the composite chart represents the relationship itself. In other words, the relationship is an entity in its own right. Computers are excellent at calculating and casting a composite chart within seconds. For a description of the calculations, see the *Midpoints* in the Astrological Dictionary (Part 3).

Synastry

Synastry is the branch of astrology that looks at the charts of two individuals to study the harmony or disharmony that might potentially be within the relationship. Astrologers use synastry charts to help assess the compatibility of a couple, or to study the potential outcome between two people.

Astrologers know that relationships between individuals strongly attracted to each other, or who are karmically connected, will have specific horoscope connections between their natal and progressed charts.

One way to cast a synastry chart is by putting two individual charts in a concentric bi-wheel format. This format has one person's chart on the inner wheel and the other person's chart on the outer wheel. You can then easily identify and analyze the aspects and planetary locations between the two charts. Doing this can yield much information about the way the two people affect and interact with each other. The next section on Graphics and Chart Types has an example of a bi-wheel chart.

Davison Relationship Chart
Another chart to describe and understand a relationship was developed by English astrologer Ronald Davison. These charts are cast using a locality and birth time halfway between the natal charts of people involved. In other words, you cast the chart using a midpoint of geographical location, and a date and time halfway between their birth dates and times. It is a form of composite chart.

Harmonic Charts

"There is geometry in the humming of strings.
There is music in the spacings of the spheres."

Pythagoras
Fifth Century BC

Harmonic charts are based in part on numerological theories. They are derived charts produced by multiplying zodiacal longitudes by a harmonic number. A harmonic chart can be defined simply as a chart whose angles (aspects) were defined by the astrologer. You do this by dividing the entire chart circle (360 degrees) by a whole number, such as 360/1, 360/2, 360/3, 360/4...360/N. This is a harmonic series. The various aspects, or harmonics, link the energies of one planet or point to another.

Harmonically defined aspects
According to astrologer Robert Hand aspects among planets and points link energies to energies, thus allowing them to work in pairs or groups. The aspects also identify the areas where the energies manifest. Beyond being just links between and among planets, these energy links display characteristics that are peculiar to the number of degrees involved in the aspect. For example a 90° (square □) aspect has a certain feeling of harshness, whereas a 120° (trine △) aspect is a more fluid link.

Traditionally, astrologers divided a circle into angles obtained by dividing with different whole numbers as shown in the table below.

Table 4. Harmonics and Aspects

Aspect	Symbol	Fraction of a Circle	Degrees
Conjunction	☌	1/1	0°
Opposition	☍	1/2	180°
Trine	△	1/3	120°
Square	□	1/4	90°
Quintile	Q	1/5	72°
Sextile	⚹	1/6	60°
Semi-square or octile	∠	1/8	45°
Semi-sextile	⚺	1/12	30°
Quincunx (inconjunct)	⚻	5/12	150°

Renaissance astrologers experimented with dividing the circle by five, seven, eight and twelve. A division by five gives the quintile, calculated as 360°/5 = 72°.

A division by seven gives the following:

septile calculated as 360°/7 = 51° 25' 42.9"

bi-septile calculated as (2x360°)/7 = 102° 51' 25.7"

tri-septile calculated as (3x360°)/7 = 154° 17' 8.6"

A division by eight gives the following aspects:

semi-square or octile ∠ , calculated as 360°/8 = 45°

sesqui-quadrate or tri-octile, ⚼ (3x360°)/8 = 135°

Hindu astrologers often use the ninth harmonic series and call this the navamsa chart.

Divisions by ten and eleven are rarely used. However, division by twelve (the number of zodiac signs) gives two aspects:

semi-sextile ⚺ calculated as 360°/12 = 30°

quincunx ⚻ calculated as (5x360°)/12 = 150°

Viewing aspects as harmonics implies that astrological phenomena might be associated with the wave theories presented by physics. This implies the cycles of the planets are mathematically linked and associated with waves, such as light, sound, water waves, or even a pendulum.

In wave mechanics, whenever a wave effect occurs, it is accompanied by other waves that are 1/2, 1/3, 1/4, 1/N... (octaves) of the length of the original wave. We also observe this in the cycles of planets with the aspects formed between and among planets. The main difference between the harmonics of astrology and the harmonics of wave theory is the time frame. Planets have a much longer period (wavelength).

Perhaps further studies of the wave mechanics as related to planetary cycles will bring astrology into a new understanding of natural phenomena. Perhaps this phenomena can truly translate the "music of the spheres".

Further explanations of harmonic theory can be found in John Addey's *Harmonic Astrology*, and more recently, Robert Hand's book *Horoscope Symbols*. See also *Music and Astrology* in the Dictionary.

5. GRAPHICS AND CHART STYLES

A chart's visual display and layout format are essential considerations in astrological computing. Why so important? Some programs use the traditional glyphs (♏ ♐ ♒ ♓ ☉ ⚷) in printing charts. Other programs use abbreviations such as JUP, or SAG for Jupiter and Sagittarius respectively. The trade off is that the letter abbreviations (that are harder to read) can print on any printer. Not every printer can print glyphs. Some astrologers are uncomfortable with the abbreviations and thus find the printouts difficult and frustrating to interpret.

The format of tables is also a factor in selecting an astrology program. Some table orientations contain much information, but appear cluttered and busy. Such a layout can make interpretation difficult and detract from the esthetic appeal.

Keep in mind that all printouts are not equal; some are more "user friendly" or "interpreter friendly" than others. We have received comments from several astrologers that they have not used purchased programs simply because they were not happy with the format of charts and tables.

Before purchasing any computer program, request a sample of chart and table printouts to see if they meet your needs and expectations.

Asking the various software companies for samples of their graphic output is one good way of assessing the program's capacity to meet your needs.

The range of graphic choices varies depending on the capabilities of the computer program and your printer. Simple programs sometimes only produce one chart style. Some premium programs offer as many as 80 choices of chart printouts. If you use specific chart types and table displays, then graphics and choices of output styles will be a major factor in selecting your program. Below are a few examples of the chart output styles.

Equal House Wheel (Anglo-American Style)

Do not confuse the equal house wheel with the Equal House System. One is a house system, and the other is a graphic display. This chart has the wheel divided into twelve equal thirty degree segments with the ascendant on the left, and the midheaven overhead. This type of chart is popular among British and American astrologers. An example is below.

Figure 25. Equal House Wheel (Anglo-American Style)

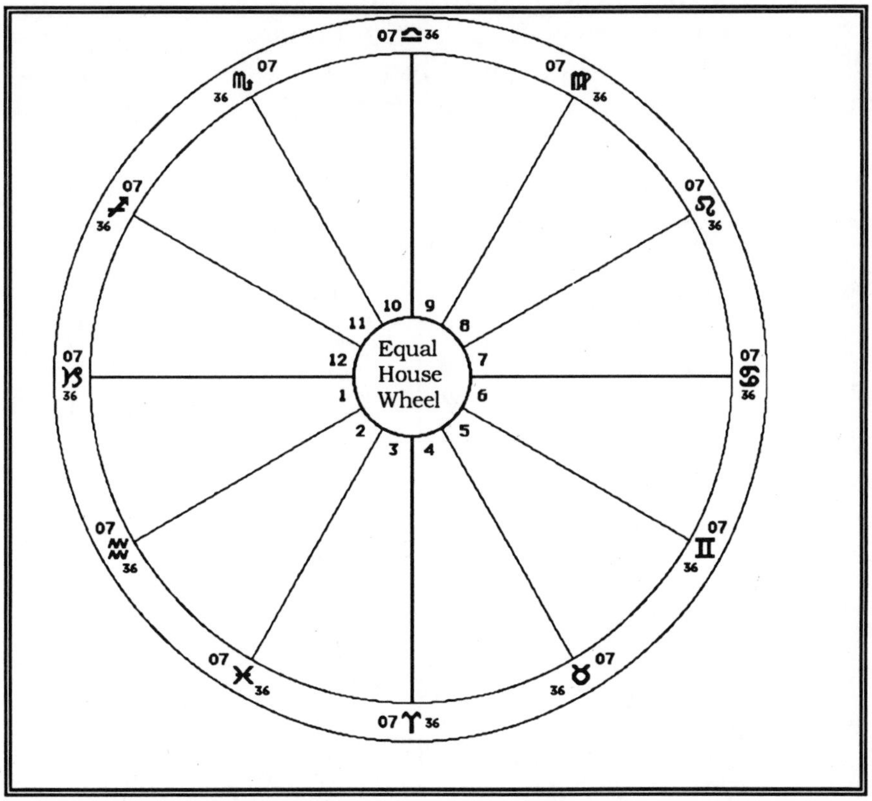

Bi-Wheel

A bi-wheel chart places two horoscopes in a concentric format to compare the relationships between the two charts. You can use a bi-wheel to compare any combination of a person's or entity's charts. A few combinations are:

- natal and progressed planets
- natal and transiting planets
- progressed and transiting,
- any combination of two charts.

Astrologers also use bi-wheels to compare two individual charts, such as in synastry work. Usually the house cusps are those of the inner chart, although some programs allow you to choose which chart defines the house framework of a bi- or tri-wheel.

Figure 26. Bi-wheel Chart

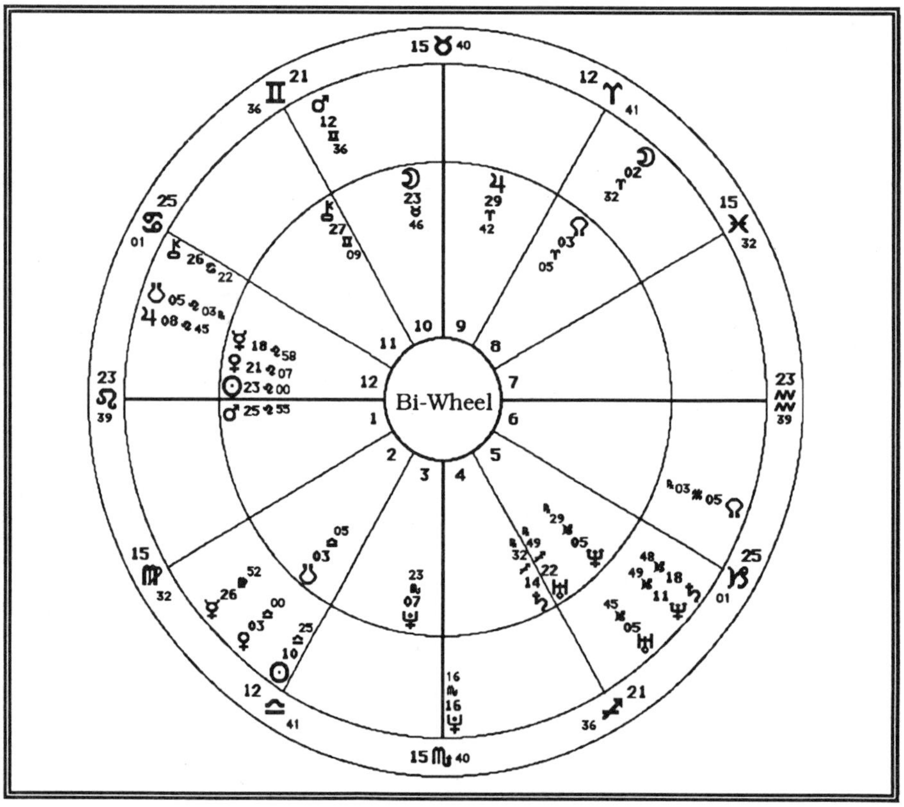

Tri-Wheel or Triple Wheel Chart

A triple wheel places three sets of charts in a concentric ring format to compare the relationship between and among the charts. This inner, middle and outer ring chart is a common method of comparing charts. The basic format is below:

Figure 27. Tri-Wheel or Triple Wheel Chart

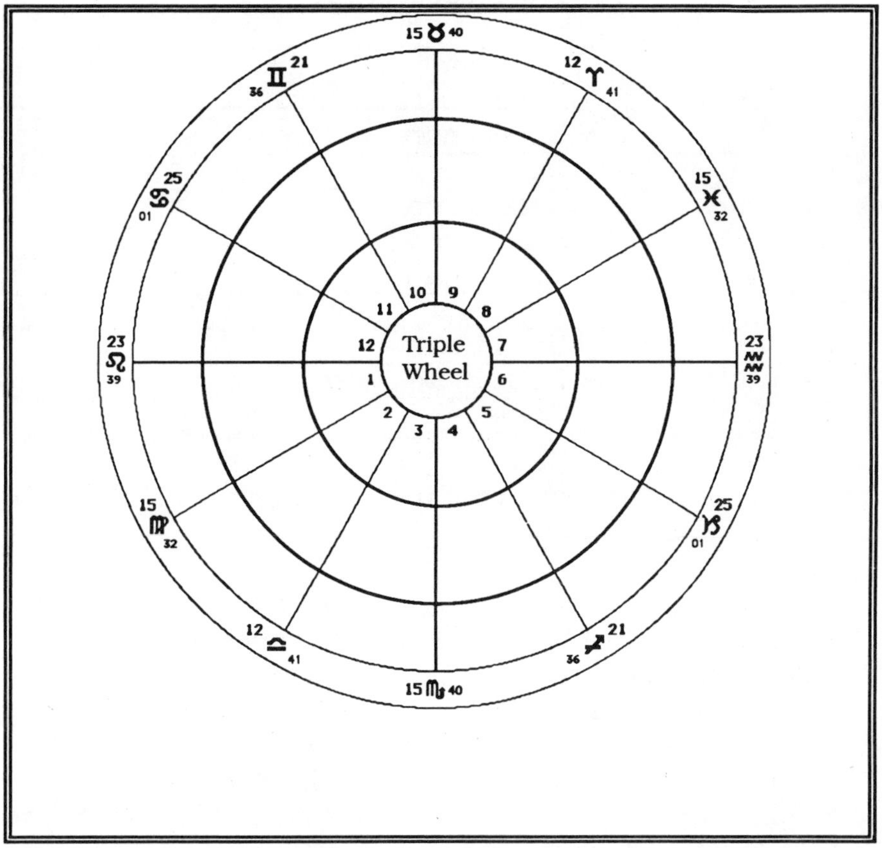

Just as there are many different types of charts, there can be even more combinations of charts in triple wheels. Typical combinations of triple wheel charts are in the table below.

Table 5. Combinations for Tri-Wheel Charts

Wheel Position	Type of Chart
1. Inner	Natal Chart
2. Middle	Progressed Chart
3. Outer	Solar Return
1. Inner	Natal Chart
2. Middle	Transits
3. Outer	Progressed Chart
1. Inner	Composite or Relationship Chart
2. Middle	Natal Chart of Person A
3. Outer	Natal Chart of Person B
1. Inner	Natal Chart
2. Middle	Solar Return
3. Outer	Lunar Return
1. Inner	Natal Chart
2. Middle	Relocation Chart
3. Outer	Transits

Types of charts that you can use in either a bi-wheel, or tri-wheel include:

- Natal Chart
- Progressed Chart
- Relationship Chart
- Relocation Chart
- Moon Phase Chart
- Sunrise Chart
- Solar Arc Directed Chart
- Tertiary Progressed Chart
- Quotidian Progressed Chart
- Transit Chart
- Composite Chart
- Solar Return
- Lunar Return
- Eclipse Chart
- Harmonic Chart(s)
- Minor Progressed Chart
- Other Charts

An advantage of the tri-wheels is that it allows the reader to see the spatial relationships of the various bodies to each other at a glance.

Proportional (European Wheel)

This type of chart places the house cusps and planets in their true positions by degrees. That is, if a house is 37° wide, then that house visually shows 37° of the entire 360° wheel. The advantage to the proportional wheel is that if there is a tight conjunction it is immediately visible without having to look at the numbers showing the zodiacal positions. European astrologers favor the proportional chart hence it is sometimes called the "European Wheel".

Graphic Ephemeris

A graphic ephemeris shows the planets' paths on a printout. You can think of it as a time-line for planetary travel. Interpreting a graphic ephemeris sometimes requires a little detective work because the lines are not always identified. An exception is Astrolabe's Timegraphs program that prints the planet glyphs on the lines.

There are two examples of the graphic ephemeris below, the 45° ephemeris from Timegraphs' and a 45° graphic ephemeris adapted from Graphic Astrology (Time Cycles Research). To help you interpret the 45° ephemeris, planet symbols and explanations were added to the printout.

The format of a graphic ephemeris is very straightforward. Along the bottom (x-axis) is time in months. Along the side (y-axis) are markings for the degrees of the zodiac. By using an ephemeris, you can tell what line belongs to each planet. You do this by looking up the date and degree for each planet and plotting it on the graphic ephemeris. To identify the Sun's path in the 45° chart, find 7° Leo (a fixed sign) on the y-axis and July 9, 1992 on the x-axis.

The faster moving planets (Mars ♂, Mercury ☿, and Venus ♀) have much steeper slopes, whereas the slower moving planets (Pluto ♇, Neptune, ♆ Jupiter ♃, Uranus ♅, and Saturn ♄) have much more level, or horizontal slopes. When a planet's path disappears off the bottom of the graph, it will reappear at the same date on the top of the graph. For example, the Sun's path in the following sample appears four times in the 45° ephemeris and three times in the 90° ephemeris.

Notice that the Moon does not appear on either example. This is because the Moon moves incredibly fast. If Moon lines were drawn for a 6 month period the graph would be practically black. The Moon travels about 90° every week!

A planet's path that curves upward indicates retrograde motion. A horizontal position shows when a planet is at station, and a downward slope is direct planetary motion. When two lines intersect an aspect is formed.

The astrologer can choose graphs illustrating planetary positions over varying lengths of time, usually by six month intervals. The graph can be printed by 30°, 45°, 90° or other moduli. A popular graphic ephemeris is the 45°, recommended by the Ebertin School; the second most common type is 30°.

Figure 28. Graphic Ephemeris - 45° sort

By Astrolabe's Timegraphs Software

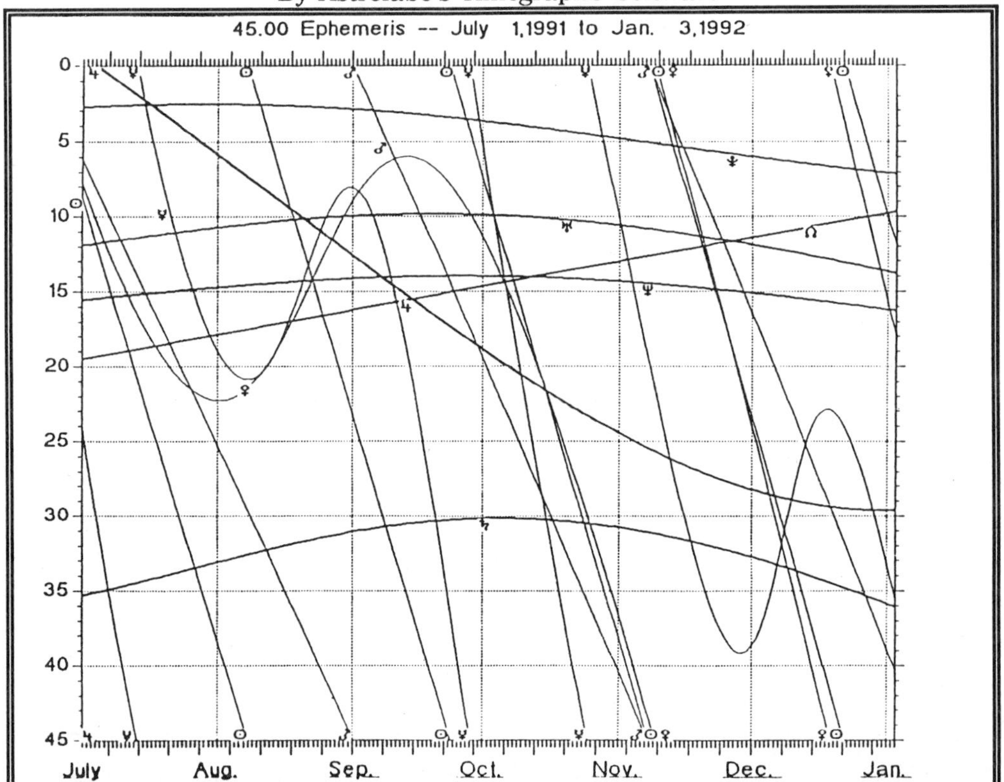

The following is an explanatory paragraph that accompanies Astrolabe Software's Timegraphs program. *"As a planet moves forward in the zodiac, its line travels down and to the right. The degrees of the zodiac are at the left. In a 45-degree graph, only 45 degrees are shown,*

because the zodiac is divided into 8 segments and the segments are laid on top of each other. The 45° represents 0° Aries to 15° Taurus to 0° Cancer to 15° Leo, etc. Whenever two planet lines cross, it means these planets have moved into a 0, 45, 90, 135, 180, or 360 degree angle with each other. Such angles are linked with stress and action."

The 90° ephemeris has along the side (y-axis) three 0° to 30° sections for the cardinal, fixed and mutable signs: a total of 90°. Often a graphic ephemeris will include lines for a natal chart. Here, the positions of natal planets are represented by straight, horizontal lines across the printout. Where lines cross an aspect occurs.

Figure 29. Graphic Ephemeris - 90° Sort

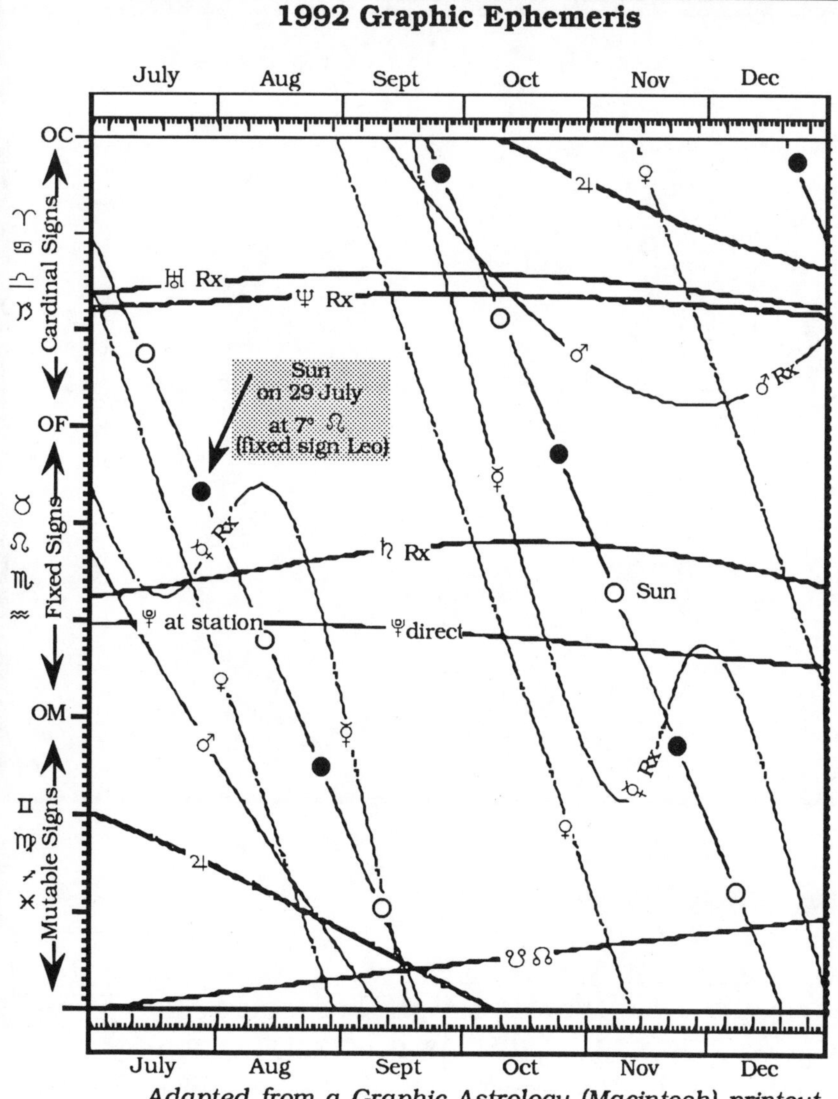

Adapted from a Graphic Astrology (Macintosh) printout

Sidereal Zodiac Chart

A Sidereal Zodiac Chart, shown below, is a constellation chart of the sidereal zodiac. This chart shows the constellations around the outside.

There is debate among modern astrologers regarding how and where to place the house cusps or sign boundaries. The chart below shows an equal arc framework promoted by Robert Powell and other modern sidereal astrologers. More information about the sidereal zodiac charts is in Powell's books entitled *Hermetic Astrology, Volumes I and II.*

Figure 30. Sidereal Zodiac Chart

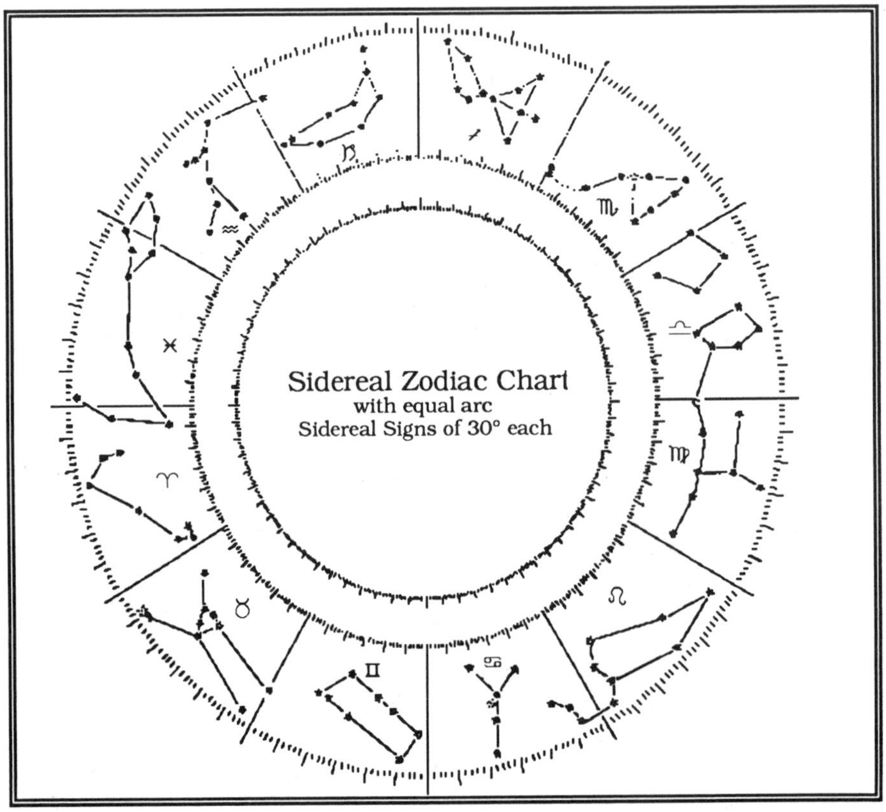

Other Chart Types

Other chart print out designs are variations on a theme. For example the "Ray Wheel" simply has spikes going out of the center. Aspects can be displayed in varying manners, such as inside the inner hub. Many chart types do not show aspects at all, but provide an aspect table printed on the same page.

B. MORE PROGRAM FEATURES

Besides zodiac(s), house systems and coordinates, astrological software will often include other features. This section describes many features an astrological program could offer. These are options that might influence your decision to buy one particular program over another. The *Software Comparison Worksheets* contained in this section list all the features described below (and more) so that you can easily compare programs from different developers.

1. Documentation
2. Points
3. Arabic Parts
4. Astrological Phenomena
5. Adjustable Aspect Orbs
6. Glyphs and Abbreviations
7. Asteroids
8. Uranian Planets
9. Geographic Database (City Coordinates)
10. Auto Time Correction
11. Chart Storage
12. Electronic Ephemeris
13. Calculation Span
14. Precision and Accuracy
15. User's Name and Address on Printouts
16. Screen View of Output
17. Data Entry
18. Batch Processing
19. Interactive Programs
20. Research
21. Desktop Publishing

1. Documentation

User's documentation for programs are sometimes difficult to read and understand. This is especially true for anyone not familiar with many of the computer and astrology terms. In the software review worksheet a line has been included to show approximately how many pages are included in the documentation. Some documentation reviewed for this book was not fully adequate to describe features of the program. Documentation writers often think their readers know and understand more about astrology than is merited.

The most complete program documentations we had access to for this book are NOVA by Astrolabe CCRS by Mark Pottenger and BLUESTAR Level III (v 2.1) by Matrix. These professional programs come with clear, well written documentation, and cost about $300.

2. Points

The horoscope contains several categories of points (or positions). The most important points are the planets and the angles: the ascendant, midheaven, descendant and the IC (*imum coeli* or "lowest heaven").

Other points a program might calculate are asteroids, barycenter galactic center, fixed stars and hypothetical planets. Keeping track and calculating these points by hand can be difficult, but computers are excellent at maintaining and sorting all the data necessary to use this information.

Keep in mind that although some points are places, rather than bodies of mass, they are important. Examples of places are the ascendant, midheaven, descendant, IC, vertex, east point and lunar nodes. Astrologers consider these place points not so much as energies, but places where the energies of other planetary bodies manifest.

3. Arabic Parts

The Arabic Parts, also known as Arabic Points, are calculated points. *Fortuna*, or the *Part of Fortune* (glyph ⊗) is the most commonly known Arabic Point. You calculate the Part of Fortune by adding and subtracting the positions of the Sun, Moon and ascendant. The usual method of calculating this point is to: (1.) convert the longitudes of the planets within the signs to 360°, (2.) do the calculations, (3.) convert the longitude (degree) back into the degrees and minutes within the respective sign.

The validity of the night vs day Part of Fortune has been debated for over 2,000 years. Reportedly, Ptolemy only used the diurnal Part of Fortune. The formula for diurnal (daytime) births is:

Ascendant + Moon - Sun = Part of Fortune.

The formula for nocturnal (night) births is:

Ascendant + Sun - Moon = Part of Fortune

All the other Arabic Parts are calculated using this approach, the basic formula is:

A + B - C = Part of ______

The traditional parts astrologers use in calculations include the Sun, Moon, ascendant, midheaven and sometimes a house cusp. See *Arabic Parts* in the Astrological Dictionary for more details.

4. Astronomical Phenomena

Some programs include information on the time, place, duration and other data for specific celestial phenomena. This phenomena can include eclipses, full Moons, new Moons, equinoxes, solstices, sunrises and sunsets for a range of places.

5. Adjustable Aspect Orbs

An orb is the number of degrees away from exactitude you are willing to allow for an aspect to be significant. A program that offers adjustable aspect orbs lets you define the number of degrees before (applying orb), and after (separating orb) the exact aspect in the zodiac. For example, suppose you define an orb to be 5 degrees. This means that a planet will be in aspect if it is either 5 degrees before, or 5 degrees after the exact placement; a total range of 10 degrees. The applying orb is before the exact aspect forms, and the separating orb is when the two points are moving away, or separating from each other.

Some astrologers use a smaller orb for separating aspects than they do for applying aspects. Consequently, the more sophisticated astrology programs allow you to define the applying and separating orbs individually. Similarly, some astrologers prefer to give the Sun, Moon, ascendant and MC wider orbs than other planets or points.

Traditionally, aspects are classified as major (Ptolemaic) or minor. Major aspects are the conjunction ☌, opposition ☍, square □ and trine △. These aspects are usually given a larger orb from 5 to 10 degrees. The minor aspects, if used, are usually given a smaller orb of 5 degrees or less. Minor aspects include sextile ⚹, semi-square or octile ∠, quintile Q, semi-sextile ⚺, quincunx ⚻, and sesquare, trioctile or sesqui-quadrate ⚼. See *Aspects* in the Dictionary (Part 3), and the table on *Orbs and Aspects* in Useful Casting Information (Part 4).

6. Printed Glyphs and Abbreviations.

Some programs support glyphs, and others use letter abbreviations. Whether printouts have glyphs depends upon both the program and the printer. See *Abbreviations* in the Astrological Dictionary for a list of planet, sign, asteroid and Uranian glyphs and letter abbreviations.

7. Asteroids

More and more astrology programs are including asteroids. There are over 10,000 asteroids orbiting in a ring (or belt), primarily between the orbits of Mars and Jupiter. Astronomers believe the asteroids are either a planet that exploded or one that never formed. Because of their small size, asteroids are easily affected by the gravitational force of other bodies. Thus, their orbits are often unstable and difficult to predict accurately for more than a few hundred years. That is why computer programs usually do not include asteroid positions any earlier than the 18th century.

The asteroids seem to be spread somewhat evenly through the zodiac averaging about 250 per sign at any one time. Demetra George, in her book *Asteroid Goddesses*, believes that the asteroids form a physical and spiritual bridge that links the personal to the social and collective.

The numbers assigned to each asteroid are in the order of discovery. Ceres, the first to be discovered, is asteroid number one. The four most common asteroids included in computer programs are: Ceres ⚳, Pallas ⚴, Juno ⚵, and Vesta ⚶.

Some lesser used asteroids in astrology are: Amor ⊖, Eros ⚸, Hidalgo ♁, Icarus ▽, Lilith ⚸, Pandora ▽, Psyche ⚺, Sappho ♀, Toro ♀, and Urania ⚸. Some astronomers and astrologers include Chiron ⚷ as an asteroid, although current thinking by astronomers is that it is a comet trapped in our solar system.

The common abbreviations and glyphs for the main asteroids that might be used in computers are shown in the Astrology Dictionary under *Abbreviations*.

Most computer services can plot at least four asteroids in a chart. These four are usually Ceres, Pallas, Juno and Vesta. Gamma Graphic Astrology (Time Cycle), CCRS (Astrolabe), and NOVA (Astrolabe) are three programs that include asteroids. Also, Astro Computing Services can provide ephemerides for many asteroids.

Astrologer Mark Pottenger has developed a program that calculates the heliocentric and geocentric positions for over twelve hundred asteroids during the 20th century. This program links with the CCRS program and is available on the MS-DOS computers. A hard disk is required.

There are few computer programs that include the ephemerides for asteroids beyond the four listed above. This will probably change with increased memory capacity and astrological interest in asteroids.

Eleanor Bach first brought asteroids to the attention of astrologers in the early 1970s. The astrological use of asteroids has been promoted by the works of Eleanor Bach, Al H. Morrison and J. Lee Lehman. For more information on asteroids refer to *Asteroids* and the individual names of each asteroid in the Astrology Dictionary, Part 3. Books on asteroids are by Demetra George, *Asteroid Goddesses*, and J. Lee Lehman's book entitled *The Ultimate Asteroid Book*.

8. Uranian Planets

The Uranian planets are also called trans-neptunian planets, and Uranians. The Uranians are hypothetical planets that astronomers and astrologers believe exist to help explain certain forces that act upon other bodies.

The Uranian planets are named after mythological characters: Cupido, Hades, Zeus, Kronos, Apollon, Admetos, Vulcanus, Poseidon. Other hypothetical planets include Vulcan and Lilith. Lilith is also the name of an asteroid, and is different from the hypothetical Lilith.

9. Geographic Database (City Coordinates)

Many programs require you the user to type in the longitude and latitude of the birthplace. However, some programs include a database of geographic coordinates which are the latitudes and longitudes of major cities. These coordinates can be called up, sometimes just by entering a code or by highlighting the desired city in the list.

Additionally, some programs let you add and delete city coordinates. Few of the geographic databases contain foreign listings, so this might be a significant factor if you are working overseas or have clients from other countries. For convenience, Part 4, Useful Casting Information, contains a listing of the coordinates for nearly 1000 principle cities worldwide.

10. Auto Time Correction

Even if your program contains the longitudes and latitudes of major cities, it will probably not automatically link the correct time zone for city and date.

Auto time correction refers to the computer's ability to put local time into Greenwich Mean Time (GMT). This correction requires a knowledge of local time and converting it to GMT. Knowing what local time was used is sometimes difficult because of the differences in how time is, and was, recorded. For example, when daylight saving time was used. Even the use of daylight saving time varies over the decades, by country, and even within counties. Indiana is infamous for the differences and confusion in local times.

In such cases you still have to get out an atlas and look up the locality to find the correct time zone for the year of birth. To avoid looking up place names entirely, you will need a database that stores local time changes by date, in addition to the latitude and longitude.

Why is this so important? Because getting an incorrect time conversion can put an error in the chart of 1 to 2 hours, thus changing all the house cusps. On the other hand, you can get practice in chart rectification. There are three levels of computerized time corrections.

1. The most basic level requires that you determine what standard time (local time) was used and convert this time to GMT. In other words, you must do all the calculations.

2. The most common auto time correction requires you to determine the standard time and enter this as a common abbreviations such as EDT (Eastern Daylight Time), SST (South Sumatra Time), NZT (New Zealand Time). The computer then automatically calculates the time correction. There is a complete list of common time zones and abbreviations in Part 4 - Useful Casting Information.

3. The most sophisticated and user friendly time correction lets you simply put in the location name. The computer then automatically calculates and records the latitude and longitude and time correction. This feature requires a large geographical/time database that needs up to 7 megabytes of memory storage.

The most complete geographic and time-change databases are separate programs. The *ACS PC Atlas* offers comprehensive longitude, latitude and time changes for the United States and the world. As advances in astrology programs and computers evolve, more programs will contain this feature, and more cost effective hardware will have the memory requirements. No doubt, in the next several years, this option will be a standard feature of professional programs.

11. Chart Storage

Most, but not all, programs allow you to store charts so that you do not have to reenter the birth data to see the chart again. Sometimes the only limit on the number of charts you can store is available disk or storage space (in floppy and hard disks, cartridges, tape, etc). Some programs only let you store a limited number of charts, for example up to ten.

A good chart storage system should include a file manager. The file manager allows you to organize groups of charts into separate files or folders, and can easily move charts between and among files.

12. Electronic Ephemeris

In traditional terms, an ephemeris is a set of tables that give the coordinates of the planets and other points at exact times during a specific period. In computer astrology an ephemeris is a database, stored in memory, that contains the same information as in a printed ephemeris in book form. This ephemeris database can be accessed electronically to cast charts and provide transit searches.

13. Calculation Span

The calculation span is the range of the electronic ephemeris. The ephemeris contains the necessary data on points and planets' positions so the computer can cast a chart and do transit searches. Some programs offer only limited ephemerides of a few hundred years. Other electronic ephemerides offer a wider calculation span of 3,000 years ranging from 600BC to 2400AD. CCRS offers a calculation span of 6,000 years! Mark Pottenger has plans for future versions of CCRS that will offer an even broader calculation span. This wide range would be desirable in researching historical events, or Earth geological changes.

14. Precision and Accuracy

Precision is the number of decimal places to which you calculate an answer. For example, pi, or the ratio of the circumference of a circle to its diameter, is approximately 3.14159+. Yasumasa Kanada of the University of Tokyo calculated the famous number pi to a precision of 134 million decimal places. Most astrology programs will compute time, or a planet's position, to a precision of about 10 to 15 decimal places.

Accuracy is how far calculations depart from the actual true position. The accuracy of planets' positions calculated from an electronic ephemeris is expressed in seconds or minutes of arc (segment of a curve). Accuracy is important because the inner planets, Moon, and house cusps, move so rapidly that minor errors in accuracy can cause these positions to be significantly inaccurate. This issue is especially noticeable when using derived charts (solar and lunar charts, etc) that require accurate calculations to be useful.

15. User's Name and Address on Printouts

Some astrology programs allow you to print your name, address, phone number or other customized message on every chart you print. This is desirable if you are planning to cast charts professionally, or cast charts for a fee in your community. It can be an effective, inexpensive way to advertise. In promotional literature this feature is sometimes called customized source.

16. Screen View of Output

The "screen view of output" means that you can see the results of the chart on the computer monitor. In some less sophisticated programs you must print the chart to see it.

On the other hand, some simpler programs only produce a chart on the computer monitor. The only way you can print the chart is with a "screen dump". A screen dump is a computer command that prints only what you see on the monitor. The screen dump will not allow batch processing. Some screen dumps can be attractive printouts. which, for a hobbyist, might be sufficient. Be sure to check that the program you purchase will support the print driver for your specific printer.

17. Data Entry and On Screen Help

Data entry is where the user meets the computer. In every astrology program, a data entry screen will appear on your monitor and allow you to fill the blanks for the required birth data. Many programs will warn you if the data have been entered incorrectly. Be aware that not all programs will give you this warning, thus allowing you to cast an incorrect chart. User proof programs and warning features will become more widely available as programming and programs evolve.

Some astrology programs are more user friendly than others. The use of "Pull Down", "Pop Up", or "Windows" can be of great advantage, especially for beginners.

And then there is the mouse. If you are not a good typist you will love the mouse. A mouse is a device, separate from the keyboard, that lets you move the cursor around the screen much quicker than using the arrow (cursor) keys. The arrow keys only move the cursor up, down or sideways. The mouse will move the cursor in any direction.

Many programs let you use the mouse to select a function or give a command simply by pointing and clicking; no keystrokes are required. Additionally, the mouse really becomes useful if your program lets you manipulate images on the screen such as with interactive programs.

For the expert touch typist, data and commands can often be entered more quickly through the keyboard than with a mouse. This is especially true of mass data entry, where keystrokes can be much faster than reaching for the mouse and moving it around on its little pad.

The use of a mouse is a personal choice. There are experienced computer whizzes who could not live without a mouse, and whizzes who would never touch a mouse though it might be available. Most of us prefer to combine the keyboard entry with selecting options with a mouse.

Whether you have a mouse or are strictly a keyboard user, it is always highly desirable to have "on-screen help". This help is in the form of windows you can turn on, or pull down, when you need assistance. On screen help is usually faster and more convenient than taking time to look up your question in the program documentation.

18. Batch Processing

Some astrology programs let you input data for many charts one after another. Then the computer will do all the computations and printing in the same "batch". The advantage of this is that it lets you do something else while the computer is working. This feature is good if you need printouts of many charts at one time, such as for a chart service or thriving astrology practice.

Other programs only let you input, process and print one chart at a time. Some of these programs are less expensive and sophisticated, but others are designed specifically to be *interactive*, as described next.

19. Interactive Programs

Interactive programs allow an advanced form of data processing. These programs let you interact with the data and the processing simultaneously. You can enter a chart and then play with it on the screen in various ways. For example, you might add charts for comparison, or change times for rectification. Interactive programs are the ultimate "what if" tool for the astrologer and useful for research, rectification, and rapid answering of questions in predictive astrology.

Interactive programs can only be used with the more sophisticated computers that do fast calculations and have advanced graphic capabilities. Astrolabe's Chartwheels II is one such program.

20. Research

Astrology research programs offer query, tally and statistical capabilities. They also should allow you to export or import data for detailed analysis. Currently, in most of the research programs, data must be transferred (exported) to a separate statistical package for more detailed scientific analysis.

The evolution of astrology software within the next few years will offer more powerful research features at cost effective prices. Programs will probably include advanced statistical analysis options and graphic display of research data. With this evolution of programing there needs to be a complimentary evolution of astrologers who are trained in statistical and accepted scientific research methodologies.

We are in an exciting time because of the availability of computers and their ability to handle vast amounts of data. This capability might finally prove what astrologers have been saying for centuries, that the cosmic forces really do affect our world(s).

21. Desktop Publishing

The laser printer is a significant advance in the computer field because these printers produce crisp clear type and graphics that are literally camera ready or typeset quality. In a sense, the availability of inexpensive laser printers to the general public is as revolutionary as the invention of movable type by Johann Gutenberg (1400?-1468?). Before movable type all books had to be hand copied. The *Gutenberg Bible* was the first book printed with movable type.

If you think deskdop publishing is not revolutionary then just consider how printed matter has affected history. Now consider the printed matter around you and who produced it. Look at the local club newsletters, flyers, and small press books on any subject. On a larger scale this means that books that are not considered profitable by major publishers, can still be made available through independent publishers.

Computers and Astrology is an example. The book you are reading was written, edited, formatted and typeset using desktop publishing. Even the line art and glyphs in this book were done (from scratch) using a draw program and a font maker program. This was all done in a small home office.

So why is this so exciting and what does this mean for astrology? Desktop publishing is a tremendously powerful tool for sharing information. We are in the information era. Look in bookstores at the plethora of astrology books made available within the last 5 years. Look at the quality of the local special interest group newsletters, look at the articles in the astrology journals. Look at the professional looking reports you can produce for your clients. Look at the quality of CHARTS as more astrology programs use a laser printer and high resolution graphics.

Additionally, some astrology programs let you import the picture of a chart directly into desktop publishing programs. Then you can change the size, edit the image and incorporate the chart into an article, newsletter, or book without doing an expensive pastup or having to hire a graphic artist. This is invaluable if you do astrological writing or editing. Most of the horoscopes in this book were typeset by transferring them from Graphic Astrology to a paint program for modifications, and then into a desktop publishing program.

PART TWO: ASTROLOGY SOFTWARE

A. Software

1. Quality Control
2. For Consumers from Developers: Bugs
3. Pirating (Unauthorized Copying)
4. Software Companies
5. Computer Assisted Interpretation
6. Programs in Foreign Languages
7. Hardware Requirements
8. Color Reports

B. Casting Services

1. Services in the United States
2. Finding Local Services

C. Astrology Software Review Methodology

1. Software Comparison Worksheets

A. AVAILABLE PROGRAMS

To prepare this book, information on over 30 horoscope programs was collected and reviewed from internationally known software developers. These developers are: A.I.R., Astrocalc, Astrolabe Software, Electric Ephemeris, Matrix Software and Times Cycles Research. You can purchase programs directly from these companies. Contact the software developers or distributors directly to answer specific program questions, and request program descriptions.

Astrological software and computers are rapidly evolving. Because of this, completed software comparison worksheets of individual programs have not been included in this text, but will be available as a separate publication. Contact Good Earth Publications for information about current software comparison worksheets.

1. Quality Control of Astrology Programs

As far as we could assess, quality control of astrological software is entirely the domain of the software developer. You should report grievances or errors directly to the software developer. This is also true of the rest of the software industry. Unless the developers are uncooperative, they will attempt to correct the bugs in subsequent versions of their programs. Usually a program either evolves and gets better and better, or it becomes obsolete and fades away.

Yet on several occasions, we were told about errors in programming that produced false, or inaccurate charts. Reporting and correcting programming errors is where cooperation between users and developers is essential. To this extent, the market forces should prevail in assuring that accurate and quality software is available for the general public.

For Consumers From Developers: Bugs

There is a reality faced by all software developers, regardless of the program type. That reality is the possibility of bugs. No matter how much a developer pre-tests a program before releasing it, there can still be bugs. What are bugs? You might be visualizing insects crawling over your disks. No, not those kind of bugs. Bugs in the computer world mean programming errors.

The more complex and sophisticated the program, the harder it is to test all the permutations and combinations of possible inputs. This is especially true in astrology, where there are so many methods and choices available.

Complex computer programs are like spider's webs. Try touching one part of a web and observe how the other parts move and are affected. Because it is interconnected in a complex interlinked design. The same is true for computer programs.

An analogy between programs and a web might help you conceptualize the situation. In a spider's web (program), a bug (programming error) might appear in one part of the web. Though that particular bug is eliminated from the web, somehow other parts of the web also can be affected. Even more subtle, this change might not be immediately apparent, and could possibly even create more bugs (gasp!). Bugs in seldom-used parts (options) of a program might go undetected for years, *yet the basic integrity of the program or web is intact and can function.* Ask any local spider.

Also problems with programs can be caused by influences other than programming. Problems can be generated by faulty data input, hardware incompatibility, different DOS or system versions, damaged disks, sunspots and gremlins.

What to do? If you have a problem, contact the developer and be as specific as you possibly can about what happened. What data did you enter? What happened on the screen? Has the problem happened before? The technical support person will try to reproduce your problem and figure out what caused it. It if is a programming error, the programmer might easily correct it. They might even send you a new version without charge. This change would then be made available to others with the same problem and included in the next release (upgrade version) of the program.

But what if the bug is difficult to identify, or it does not greatly detract from the usefulness of the program? If this is the case, programmers prefer to fix a whole batch of bugs at one time and release a new version of the program. As a properly registered user, you will have the opportunity to get version updates at a moderate cost. Lets face it, some minor bugs we can live with, at least for a while.

Despite a developer's best efforts and intent there is always the possibility of bugs. When you buy a program, part of what you pay for is the technical support and software maintenance. Both of which are necessary, not only for your questions, but also for the development of future software and supporting materials.

3. Pirating (Unauthorized Copying of Astrology Software)
Developing truly accurate and professional astrology programs takes thousands of person-hours and even more investment capital. Like all businesses, software companies must make a fair return on their investment to stay in business. Astrolabe estimates that the seemingly harmless copying of their programs reduces legitimate software sales by over 50%. It is obvious that in a field as specialized as astrology software, this can be the kiss of death to small companies. To date, all astrology software developers can be classified as small companies.

When you purchase your software everyone involved benefits. *Software companies* benefit by being able to stay in business and develop better programs. *You*, the user, benefit by (1.) having better programs available, (2.) from the technical support offered by the company, and (3.) from reasonable prices of software. *Your clients or non-astrologers* benefit from improved high-quality report programs.

This is why the pirating, or unauthorized copying of programs has the potential to undermine current and future astrology program availability and support. The choice is yours.

4. Software Company Addresses
Below is a list of software developers, distributors and programmers. The list is not exhaustive; no doubt there are more. The list will be updated in future editions of *Computers and Astrology*. Contact the publisher for information about updated lists, or to be included in the next edition.

UNITED STATES ASTROLOGY SOFTWARE COMPANIES

Company	Programs
* **AIR Software** 115 Caya Avenue West Hartford, CT. 06110 Phone (800) 659-1AIR Fax: (203) 233-6117	Star-Trax (Time Search) ARP (Astrological Research Package) Nostradamus (Horary) Father Time (Electional) Zeus (Cast Charts) High resolution on all programs
* **Astrolabe Software** Box 1750 350 Underpass Road Brewster, Mass. 02631 Orders: 800-843-6682 Business (508) 896-9567 FAX (508) 896-5289	NOVA Chartweels, Timegraphs CCRS Astro Star I (CP/M) StarTrack (Apple II)
Astrologic P.O. Box 220182 Chantilly, Virginia 02631	
AstroResearch 1500 Massachusetts Ave NW #746 Washington, D.C. 20005, USA	
Gerald Baron 2733 Country Club #180 Stockton, California 95204, USA	
* **Cosmic Patterns** P.O. Box 14605 Gainsville, Florida 32604 Phone: (904) 373-1504	Kepler

*** Electric Ephemeris** — PCA (Personal Computer Astrology)
Astrological Software
396 Calendonian Road
London, N1 1DN, U.K.
Phone: 071-700-0666/0999
FAX: 071-794-2467

*** Full Phase Software**
P.O. Box 17045
Seattle, Washington, 98107

Richard Gozdal
P.O. Box 56513
Chicago, Illinois 60656 USA

Hettigers
315 Hrmony Court
San Antonio, Texas 78217, USA

RK West Consulting
P.O. Box 8044
Mission Hills, California 91346 USA

John Halloran
P.O. Box 75713
Los Angeles, California 900075, USA

Lambert/Gann Publishing
P.O. Box 0
Pomeroy, Washington 98347, USA

*** Matrix Software** — Blue*Star, M65, Quick Charts
315 Marion Avenue
Big Rapids, Michigan, USA
Phone: (800) PLANETS
FAX: 616-796-3060

Pathfinder
3848 Mentone #405
Culver City, California 91346, USA

Mark Pottenger — CCRS Horoscope, FAR, Asteroids
838 5th Avenue
Los Angeles, CA 90005
Phone: (213) 487-1000

*** Time Cycles Research**
Dennis Haskell
27 Dimmock Road
Waterford, Connecticut 06385
Phone: (203) 444-6641

Graphic Astrology (Mac)
IO Series
High resolution on all programs

Unique Computing Services
P.O. Box 3310
Tallahassee, Flordia, 32315 USA

* Companies that advertise routinely in U.S. national publications

EUROPEAN ASTROLOGY SOFTWARE COMPANIES

Astrocalc
British Astrological Software
67 Peascroft Road
Hemel Hempstead
Herts HP3 8ER
Phone: 0442-251809

Many programs and modules

Astron/Europe
Peter-Marquard Str. 4A
D-2000 Hamburg 60
Germany

Astro Polarity
Alberstrasse 6
D-1000 Berlin 62
Germany

Editions Tesla
La Haiac de Pan
35170 Bruz., Belgium

Francisco Publi
Caja Postal de Correos
#90427206, de Barcelona, Spain

L'espace Blue
91 Rue de Seine
75006 Paris, France

Le Meridien
11,Rue Leandri
83100 Toulon, France

Additionally, there are two companies that manufacture hand held or pocket calculators that are excellent for the traveling astrologer. These companies are:

Aureus La Informatique
189 Avenue de Choisey
75013 Paris, France
Phone: 45-821819

Pocket Astro Computers

Logister
Maison Rue de Rosicrucienne
Editeur, Michelle de Boulonge
07200 Au Benas
Phone: 75-871050

Pocket Astro Computers

Software Distributors
You can purchase software directly from developers, but there are also distributors that carry a wide range of astrological software and computer supplies. Two of these are:

American Federation of Astrologers
P.O. Box 22040
6535 South Rural Road
Tempe, Arizona 85285-2040, USA
Phone: (602) 838-1751
FAX: (602) 838-8293

Astron/US Distributor
P.O. Box 1545
Solana Beach, California, USA

Microcycles
P.O. Box 78219
Los Angeles, California 90016-0219
Phone 800-829-2537

5. Computer Assisted Interpretation (Report Generators)
More and more computer programs are available that offer chart interpretation. Electronic chart interpretations are really simple

cook book delineations that look up pre-written interpretations for each chart factor and produce a printed report.

This type of linear interpretation is controversial. How can a computer account for all the complex factors that go into interpreting a chart? How can a computer replace the personal insights of a qualified astrologer? Can computer generated interpretations become surrogate astrologers? It is a current topic of much debate.

Nevertheless, computer assisted interpretation of charts is available and can provide supportive material for individuals. Contact the software developer directly for more information about report generation programs.

6. Programs in Foreign Languages

Personal computers are available and used worldwide. Computer applications are now available in multilingual versions. This is also true with astrology. Currently there are a few astrology programs in languages other than English. No doubt there will be many more, especially in French, German and Spanish.

In 1977, Matrix was the first developer to offer software specifically for astrologers. Since then, they have developed a worldwide network of astrologers who know matrix programs offer user assistance. Matrix has made many of their programs available in German, French, Spanish, and several other languages. Astrolabe Software has chart interpretation programs available in French, German, Spanish and other languages.

Although astrology and the symbols used are universal, there are language considerations in the data entry screens, output reports and computer assisted interpretations. For more specific information, we suggest you contact the software developer, or distributor.

7. Hardware Requirements

As computers and programs evolve there are different hardware specifications required to run specific programs. Matching programs to your individual hardware and operating system can be a frustrating experience. Sometimes, the only way to know if a program will work on your particular computer and printer is to install and run the program. Perhaps eventually, computer hardware and operating systems will evolve to be standardized for universal compatibility. That time has not yet arrived.

Also, keep in mind that as programs become more sophisticated and do more functions, there is usually a corresponding greater requirement for Random Access Memory (RAM). On MS-DOS computers, the newer programs work best with the full 640K of RAM that can be addressed directly by DOS. If your computer has extended or expanded (EMS) memory, check to see if the program you are buying can make use of it. On a Macintosh or Amiga, most astrological programs require at least 1 megabyte of RAM, and preferably 4 Megabytes or more.

In general, MS-DOS compatible and IBM PC (386 clones) are functionally the same. When MS-DOS first came out, there were some incompatible brands of MS-DOS machines, but these have almost disappeared. Also, generally speaking, the XT, 286, 386, and 486 clones are functionally similar. However the newer faster machines are necessary for advanced programs that require graphic capabilities and math co-processors. For these reasons there is only one MS-DOS compatible category in Table 6: *Astrology Programs and Hardware Requirements.*

CP/M is now almost completely obsolete. According to the staff at Astrolabe, no new CP/M astrology software is being written and hardly any CP/M machines are being sold. A partial list of computers supported by commercially advertised astrology software is in Table 6.

8. Color Reports (Plotter or Color Ribbon).
A few programs offer the option of color printing using colored ribbons or a plotter. Developers sometimes offer color printing as an “add-on” module that can be purchased separately. There are few programs that do color reports. This is because there has been very little standardization in color printers or plotters.

This has meant that a developer had to do a separate program for each brand of color printer or plotter. The option of color reports has been economically feasible for only the most mass marketed programs. Newer programming tools and the less expensive color laser or inkjet printers will potentially change this over the next decade. Professional computer casting services are increasingly offering color reports as an option to consumers.

B. Casting Services

1. Casting Services in the United States

There are many services available in the United States that offer a variety of options. We suggest you write to these services directly to obtain costs and types of outputs available. The costs for such services range from $1.00 per chart to over $35 for printed reports ranging from 2 to over 50 pages. Listed below are a few of the larger casting services that advertise nationally.

Casting Services Addresses

Astro Computing Services, Inc. Great Catalog!
P.O. Box 16430
San Diego, California 92116-0430
Phone: (800) 888-9983

Astro Numeric Service Astro*Carto*Graphy Maps
Trigon Systems Corporation
P.O. Box 425
San Pablo, California, 94806
Phone: (800) 627-7464

Great Bear Astrological Center
P.O. Box 5164
Eugene, Oregon 97405
Phone: (503) 683-1760

2. Finding Local Casting Services.

As computers become widely available there will be more astrologers in your locality that personally own or have access to a computer. This means you might be able to have charts cast for you in your own town. This can provide a quick turn around time to obtain charts. To locate local services, contact your area bookstores, check the yellow pages, and ask local astrologers. You probably will be surprised by the number of individuals who are willing to cast charts for you on their computers.

Table 6: Astrology Programs and Hardware Requirements

HOROSCOPE CASTING PROGRAMS OVER $200

	GRAPHIC ASTROLOGY Gamma Edition	IO Series	MacAstrologer Version 1.0	NOVA 2.0	CCRS HOROSCOPE PROG. 90	BLUE*STAR 512K	BLUE*STAR 2.1	M65 & M65A RESEARCH	PCA V. 2.6	A.R.P.
DEVELOPER	**TIME CYCLES**	**TIME CYCLES**	**FULL PHASE SOFTWARE**	**ASTROLABE**	**ASTROLABE**	**MATRIX**	**MATRIX**	**MATRIX**	**ELECTRIC EPHEMERIS**	**A.I.R.**
COST	$200	$250	$180	$295	$250	$300	$300	$300	£ 113	$249
HARDWARE & RAM REQUIREMENTS										
Macintosh	YES		YES		YES					
MS-DOS Compatible				DOS 2.1	YES	YES	DOS 2.1	YES	YES	YES
Apple II Computers								YES		
CP/M Compatable				"core"					AMSTRAD	
Amiga					YES					
Commodore 128 & 64								YES		
TRS-80										
RAM Requirements	512K RAM	1 MB	128K	256K RAM	1 Mgb 640K RAM	512K RAM	512	Many add-on		256K
Disk Drives				2 Drives		2 Drives	Harddisk			2 Drives
Disk Memory	800K	Hard Disk		360K	Hard Disk	360K	3.5 MB	Modules		360K

HOROSCOPE CASTING PROGRAMS UNDER $200

	ASTROSTAR I and C-STAR	CHART-WHEELS I and II	STAR TRACK SERIES	NOVA CORE	BLUE*STAR 64	BLUE*STAR LEVEL 1 (Junior)	BLUE*STAR LEVEL 2	A1 Versons 1 - 20	Star-Trax	Kepler
DEVELOPER	**ASTROLABE**	**ASTROLABE**	**ASTROLABE**	**ASTROLABE**	**MATRIX**	**MATRIX**	**MATRIX**	**ASTROCALC**	**A.I.R.**	**COSMIC PATTERNS**
COST	$195/$65	$75/$150	$195	$150	$100	$50	$100	£18 - £150	$149	$100
HARDWARE & RAM REQUIREMENTS										
Macintosh										
MS-DOS Compatible		YES	NO	NO				SOME	YES	YES
Apple II Computers			Apple DOS 3.3					YES		
CP/M Compatible	ASTRO STAR I			CP/M				AMSTRAD		
Amiga								Version 7		
Commodore 128	C-Star				ONLY			YES		
TRS-80										
RAM Requirements	64K RAM	512K RAM	48K RAM	64K RAM	64K or 128K	256 RAM	256 RAM		560K RAM	560K RAM
Number of Disk Drive	2 Drives Rec.		2 Drives	2 Drives	1 Drive	1 Drive	2 Drives		2 Drives	
Disk Memory		Hard Disk		160K					560K	Hard Disk

Information Deemed Reliable But Not guaranteed.

C. How to Choose Software

Because of the rapidly changing technology in both hardware and software, a review of current programs would be obsolete as soon as it was completed. For this reason, this section provides a methodology and checklist for doing your own software review.

The first thing to look for in software is not the number of features vs price. Look for the features you are likely to need and use.

Once you have determined your needs you will be in a better position to asses how well different software packages can serve you. If you have a specialty field in astrology, find out if the software developer is known for expertise in the particular techniques you use.

For example, suppose you are a Uranian astrologer and want a program that specifically offers the Uranian techniques. A program can include the Uranian planets and house systems, but these are only the basics. If the programmer or the programmer's advisors actually practice Uranian astrology, then the program they write will fully and authentically do Uranian astrology.

It is possible to include the basics of an astrological technique in a program and advertise its availability. But in actual use, the programming might not provide what you really need.

Recommendation: first go through the astrology software comparison worksheets and *mark the features that are most important to you.* Then do a more in-depth investigation of these features with the developers or suppliers.

Unless you already have your computer, choose the software that best meets your needs, then purchase the appropriate computer and printer to match the software.

A five page worksheet is provided that allows you to compare up to six programs side by side. The User's Guide (Part 1) explains most of the features listed in the worksheet.

The recommended steps for conducting your review are simple.

1. Go through the check list and mark the features you need or desire. Also keep your future needs in mind.

2. Contact the software companies and ask them to send information on their programs. **Be sure to request sample printouts.**

3. Once you receive the information, scan and identify the features you want. Then mark the appropriate box on the worksheet to show that feature is available.

4. Call the software company if you have any questions about what they offer.

5. Once you have chosen a software package, purchase the computer and printer that will run the program and print your reports. If you already own your computer, make sure the software will run on the model you have. Be sure to ask about such requirements as RAM, disk drive requirements, printer compatibility, math co-processor, and other specific hardware requirements.

Completed Astrology Software Comparison worksheets for many software programs are available from Good Earth Publications. Contact the publisher for information about the latest update.

ASTROLOGY SOFTWARE COMPARISON

Worksheets

ASTROLOGY SOFTWARE COMPARISON WORKSHEET					
	Program 1.	Program 2.	Program 3.	Program 4.	Program 5.
Program Name					
DEVELOPER					
COST					
ZODIAC					
Tropical					
Sidereal (Fagan-Allen)					
Sidereal (other)					
HOUSE SYSTEMS					
Campanus					
Placidus					
Koch					
Albategnian					
Alcabitian (Alcabitius)					
Aries (Natural)					
Equal (from any point)					
Horizontal					
Meridian					
Morinus					
Porphyry					
Regiomontanus					
Solar Houses					
Topocentric					
Uranian Houses					
Sun Houses					
Moon Houses					
Other					
Whole sign					
User Defined Ascendant					
Any Planet Ascendant					
Geodetic M.C.					
Other					
COORDINATE SYSTEMS					
Centers of Reference					
Geocentric					
Heliocentric					
Planetocentric					
Horizon Coordinates					
Altitude/Azimuth					
Equator Coordinates					
Right ascension/declination					
Hour Angle Coordinates					
Ecliptic Coordinates					
Celestial Latitude/Longitude					
Local Space Coordinates					
Altitude/Azimuth					
Campanus Mundoscope					
Amplitude/Longitude					
Prime Vertical					
Relocated Horizon					
Galactic					

ASTROLOGY SOFTWARE COMPARISON WORKSHEET					
	Program 1.	Program 2.	Program 3.	Program 4.	Program 5.
Program Name					
DEVELOPER					
COST					
CHARTS & TABLES					
Natal Chart					
Transit Table/Search					
Derived Charts					
Composite (Midpoint)					
Synastry (Relationship)					
Davison Relationship					
RETURN CHARTS					
Solar Return					
Kinetic Solar					
Lunar Return					
Kinetic Lunar					
Precessed Returns					
Fractional Returns 1/2,1/4 etc.					
Planet Returns					
Helio					
Geo					
Synodic Return					
Metonic Return					
Solunar					
PROGRESSIONS					
Secondary Progression					
Tertiary Progression					
Minor Progression					
User Defined Progressions					
How Many?					
PROGRESSED ANGLES					
Solar Arc Midheaven					
Naibod Arc					
Degree per Year Arc					
User Defined Arc					
How Many?					
Quotidian-1 (Bija)					
Quotidian-2					
DIRECTIONS					
Primary Directions					
Solar Arc Directions					
Naibod Arc Directions					
Ascendant Arc					
Vertical Arc					
User Defined Arc Direction					
Planet Arcs					
Harmonic Charts					
Johndro Locality Charts					
Arc Charts					
Arc Harmonics					
Other Charts					

ASTROLOGY SOFTWARE COMPARISON WORKSHEET

	Program 1.	Program 2.	Program 3.	Program 4.	Program 5.
Program Name					
DEVELOPER					
COST					
GRAPHICS/CHARTS AND TABLES					
Printed Glyphs					
Equal House Wheel					
Proportional Wheel					
Bi-wheel					
Tri or Triple Wheel					
Aspect List (grid or sort)					
Graphic Ephemerides					
Sidereal Zodiac (Constellational)					
90° Dials					
Whitney Graphics					
Custom House Tables					
Transit Table (Search)					
Other Charts or Tables					
POINTS INCLUDED					
Sun, Moon, 8 Planets					
Chiron					
Asteroids					
How Many?					
Fixed Stars					
Uranian Points					
Part of Fortune					
Other Arabic Parts					
Vertex/Anti-vertex					
Trans-pluto					
Aries Point					
East Point/Equatorial Asc.					
Barycenter of Solar System					
Galactic Center					
Other Points					
ASTRONOMICAL PHENOMENA					
Moon Phases					
Eclipses (solar, lunar)					
Sunrise, Noon, Sunset,					
Solstice & Equinoxes					
Tropical Ingresses					
Adjustable Aspects & Orbs					
Applying Orb					
Separating Orb					

ASTROLOGY SOFTWARE COMPARISON WORKSHEET					
	Program 1.	Program 2.	Program 3.	Program 4.	Program 5.
Program Name					
DEVELOPER					
COST					
OTHER PROGRAM FEATURES					
Documentation					
Import/Export Data					
Configurable Data Storage Options					
Changable default settings					
House					
Zodiac					
Orbs					
Other					
Address/Phone in Chart File					
Auto. Time Corrections					
Calculation Speed					
Screen view of output					
Output to File					
Computer Interpretation					
Chart Storage (limits)					
City Storage (Atlas)					
Customized Source of Chart					
# Lines for Your Name & Address					
Batch processing					
Pull Down Menus (Pop-Up)					
Other Features					
Ease/Flexiblity of Data Input					
Ease to Create Multiple Files					
Research Features					
Predefined Tallies					
User defined Tallies					
User Defined Queries					
Stastical Functions					
File Sorting					
Rectify Assist					
Electional Assist					
Astroclock					
Ephemeris Calculation Span					
Accuracy (in min. or sec. of arc):					
this Century					
at 500 years					
at 2000 Years					
Accuracy For:					
Sun & Planets					
Moon					
Others (House Cusps)					
Return Times					
Station Times					
Event/Ingress/Aspect Times					
Macros					

ASTROLOGY SOFTWARE COMPARISON WORKSHEET					
	Program 1.	**Program 2.**	**Program 3.**	**Program 4.**	**Program 5.**
Program Name					
DEVELOPER					
COST					
DEVELOPER SUPPORT					
Phone Support					
800 number					
Bug Fixes					
Notification to Licensed Users					
Version Updates Discounted to Licensed Users					
Other					
LANGUAGES OTHER THAN ENGLISH					
French					
German					
Spanish					
Other					
HARDWARE & RAM REQUIREMENTS					
Macintosh					
MS-DOS Compatible					
Apple II Computers					
CP/M Compatible					
Amiga					
Commodore 128 & 64					
TRS-80					
RAM Requirements					
Hard Disk Required					
Memory Required (Megabytes)					
Graphics Card Required					
Math Co-processor					
PRINTERS SUPPORTED					
Dot Matrix					
Laser					
Color Printer					
Color Plotter					
PROGRAMMING					
Source Code Available?					
Program Language					
Programmer					

PART THREE: ASTROLOGICAL DICTIONARY

While researching this book we found many bits of information that might be useful to an astrologer, but not readily accessible in books found in libraries or most bookstores. Some of this information is not directly applicable to computers, but is useful in a broader reference context.

This section contains definitions and articles on many facets of astrology, arranged in alphabetical order. The information here is not exhaustive. It is intended to simply define and explain common terms used in astrology, past and present. It also illustrates some technical points you might find while studying the astrological sciences. At the very least, there are many curious and quaint facts and lore that could be used in a game of astrological "trivial pursuit".

A

Abbreviations: From the earliest times astrologers have used abbreviations and sigils to denote specific principles or data. Currently, there are many international schools of astrology and entire texts have been written on all the abbreviations, symbols, glyphs and notations in existence. Below are the common abbreviations that astrologers use in the 20th century. A list of the time zone abbreviations is in Part 3: Information Useful in Casting Charts.

Table 7. Common Abbreviations Used in Astrology

A	Amplitude	m	minute(s)
A	Ascendant	M	Midheaven
Ap	Solar Apex	MC	Medium Coeli
AS	Ascendant	MH	Midheaven
AS	Asteroid	MK	Mondknoten (Dragon's Tail)
Asc	Ascendant	N	Harmonic Number
AU	Astronomical Unit	NN	North Node
AV	Antivertex	OA	Oblique Ascension
AX	Solar Apex	OR	Orion
B	Birth (place/time)	p	progressed
BQ	Biquintile	p	progression
Bi	Biquintile	P	Persephone
CU	Cupido	P	Phase
d	day (s)	PF	Part of Fortune
d	declination	PG	Pegasus
d	dexter	Q	Quintessence
d	died	Q	Quintile
D	Direct	r	radical
D	Dragon's Head	r	radix = natal
DH	Dragon's Head	R	Retrograde
DR	Dragon's Head	RA	Right Ascension
DS	Descendant	s	second(s)
Dsc	Descendant	s	sign(s)
DT	Dragon's Tail	s	sinister
EC, ECL	Ecliptic	s	solar arc directions
EH	Equal House	s	stationary
EP	East Point	SA	Semi Arc or Solar Arc
EQ	Equator	Sd	Stationary, going direct
FS	Fixed Star	sh	speculative horoscope
GC	Galactic Center 	SN	South Node
GMT	Greenwich Mean Time	Sr	Stationary, going retrograde
GST	Greenwich Sidereal Time	SUr	Sunrise
h	hour(s)	SVP	Synetic Vernal Point
H	Harmonic	Sx, SXT	Sextile
H	Heliocentric	SZ	Sidereal Zodiac
H	Hermes (Mercury)	t	transit
H	Horizon	ta	time approximate
H	Horoscopus (Ascendant)	TE	Terra (Earth)
HA	Hades	TNPs	Transneptunian Planets
IC	Imum Coeli	TP	Transpluto
IMC	Imum Coeli	TZ	Tropical Zodiac
JO, JN	Juno	V, VL	Vulcan
KR	Kronos	VP	Vernal Point
L	Luna (Moon)	VX	Vertex
LMT	Local Mean Time	y	year(s)
LST	Local Sidereal Time	ZE	Zeus
LY	Light Years		

Abbreviations for Planets, Signs, Asteroids and Imaginary Bodies. Some computer programs and printers are not capable of printing glyphs. If you usually interpret charts with glyphs, then trying to interpret with abbreviations can be frustrating. Additionally, some astrologers think abbreviations make a chart look cluttered and unattractive. Below are tables containing the abbreviations and glyphs for planets, signs, asteroids and Uranian planets.

Table 8. Planet Glyphs and Abbreviations

PLANET	COMMON 3 LETTER ABBREVIATION	COMMON TWO LETTER ABBREVIATION	GLYPH
Sun*	SUN	SU or SN	☉
Mercury	MER	MR or ME	☿
Venus	VEN	VN or VE	♀
Earth	EAR	ER OR EA	⊕
Moon*	MON or MOO	MN or MO	☽
Mars	MAR	MR or MA	♂
Jupiter	JUP	JP or JU	♃
Saturn	SAT	ST or SA	♄
Uranus	URA	UR	♅ or ⛢
Neptune	NEP	NP or NE	♆
Pluto	PLU	PL	⯓ or ♇

* Not planets, but traditionally listed with the planets

Table 9. Zodiac Signs, Glyphs and Abbreviations

SIGN	COMMON THREE LETTER ABBREVIATION	COMMON TWO LETTER ABBREVIATIONS	GLYPH
Aries	ARI	AR	♈
Taurus	TAR or TAU	TR or TA	♉
Gemini	GEM	GM or GE	♊
Cancer	CAN	CN , CA or CR	♋
Leo	LEO	LE	♌
Virgo	VIR	VR , Vi or VG	♍
Libra	LIB	LI or LB	♎
Scorpio	SCO	SC	♏
Sagittarius	SAG	SA or SG	♐
Capricorn	CAP	CP	♑
Aquarius	AQU	AQ	♒
Pisces	PIC or PIS	PI	♓

There is confusion about glyphs for aspects, asteroids and the imaginary bodies. To help address this, Mark Pottenger is developing a character set intended to serve as a central repository for glyphs. This character set is a PostScript font. It includes glyphs for signs, planets, aspects, asteroids and other astronomical events. Mark says some astrologers are inventing glyphs, especially for asteroids. This has already caused some conflicts and confusion. Mark is the programmer for CCRS and FAR programs and Research Director of the International Society for Astrological Research. For more information about the central repository character set contact Mark Pottenger at 838 5th Avenue, Los Angeles, California 90005.

Table 10. Asteroid Glyphs and Abbreviations

ASTEROID	GLYPH	COMMON ABBREVIATION	ASTEROID NUMBER
Aesculapia			1027
Amor		AMR	1221
Apollo			1862
Arachne			407
Ariadne			43
Astraea	or		5
Atlantis			1198
Bacchus			2063
Ceres	⚳	CER, CE or CR	1
Chiron	⚷	CHI or CI	2060
Circe			34
Cupido			763
Daedalus			1864
Dembowska			349
Demeter			1108
Diana			78
Dike			99
Dudu			564
Eros		ERO	433
Eurydike			75
Frigga			77

Table 10. Asteroid Glyphs and Abbreviations (continued)

ASTEROID	GLYPH	COMMON ABBREVIATION	ASTEROID NUMBER
Hebe			6
Hera			103
Hidalgo		HIG	944
Hopi			2938
Hybris			430
Hygiea	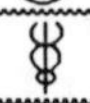		10
Icarus		ICR	1566
Industria			389
Isis			42
Juno		JNO, JO or JN	3
Kassandra	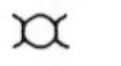		114
Lilith		LIL	1181
Minerva			93
Nemesis			128
Niobe			71
Orpheus	 or 		3361
Pallas		PAL, or PA	2
Pandora		PAN	55
Persephone			399
Pittsburghia			484
Proserpina			26
Psyche		PSY	16
Sappho		SAP	80
Sisyphus			1866
Siva			1170
Terpsichore			81
Themis			24
Toro		TOR	1685
Urania		URI	30
Vesta		VST,VS or VT	4

Table 11. Names and Glyphs of Imaginary Bodies

Imaginary Planet	GLYPH	COMMON ABBREVIATION
Admetos		AD
Apollon		AP
Coda		
Cupido (also an asteroid name)		CU
Dido (also an asteroid name)		
Hades		HA
Hercules		
Hermes		
Horus (also an asteroid name)		
Isis (also an asteroid name)		
Jason		
Kronos		KR
LaCroix		
Lilith (also an asteroid name)		
Lion		
Loki		
Melodia		
Midas (also an asteroid name)		
Minos		
Moraya		
Osiris (also an asteroid name)		
Pan (also an asteroid name)		
Persephone (also an asteroid name)		
Polyhymnia (also an asteroid name)		
Poseidon (also an asteroid name)		PO
Shanti		
Transpluto		
Vulcan		
Vulcanus (Vulkanus)		VU
Wemyss-Pluto		
Zeus		ZE

Active Influence: The result of an aspect between two or more points in the chart, producing the energy or influence that can trigger an event.

Admetos: Symbol ♆, one of eight hypothetical planets of Uranian astrology. Admetos is linked with raw materials, circulation and death. Its presence in the horoscope indicates something that is potentially blocked, limited or stuck.

AFA: See *American Federation of Astrologers, Inc.*

Affliction: A planet in a difficult aspect with another body is "afflicted" or "in affliction".

Agricultural Astrology: See *Astrology Specialties.*

Air Signs: Gemini ♊, Libra ♎, and Aquarius ♒.

Altitude: A Horizon System coordinate that measures the elevation of a body above, or below, the plane of the horizon. This is measured positively above the horizon from 0° to 90°, and negatively below the horizon 0° to -90°. See Figure 7: Horizon System Coordinates.

American Federation of Astrologers, Inc.: The AFA is an astrological membership organization and a publisher and distributor of books, tapes, videos, software and other related astrological supplies. It is also an educational organization that gives examinations and awards certificates that acknowledge certain levels of astrological competence. The highest level of achievement AFA awards is the Gold Card Astrologer. AFA maintains a roster of professionally accredited astrologers and will be pleased to help you locate accredited astrologers in your area. AFA holds a week long international convention every two years in the even numbered years, usually in July or August. The address for the AFA is: P.O. Box 22040, 6535 South Rural Road, Tempe, Arizona 85285-2040, Phone (602) 838-1751, FAX (602) 838-8293.

Amor: Symbol ⏀, an asteroid. Amor was the Roman God of Love, and synonymous with Cupid. Unlike Eros, the love of Cupid is innocent. It is the love of everything including friendships, family, and nature. In this context Amor represents the type of love found in a true friendship or among family members where the connections and feelings are so deep that no ulterior sexual motives could destroy that love. Thus, Amor in a chart might represent the potential for intimacy and love without the motive of passionate desires. The asteroid Amor, discovered in 1931, is the 1,221st asteroid listed. See also *Asteroids.*

Angles, the Four: The four angles represent major points on an astrological chart. These are the ascendant, descendant, MC and IC. The *ascendant* and *descendant* are the points of intersection of the ecliptic to the horizon. The other two points are the midheaven, also called *Medium Coeli* (MC), and the *Imum Coeli* (IC) or lowest heaven. The midheaven and IC are the points of intersection of the ecliptic and the meridian. See the figure below.

Figure 31. The Four Major Angles in a Horoscope

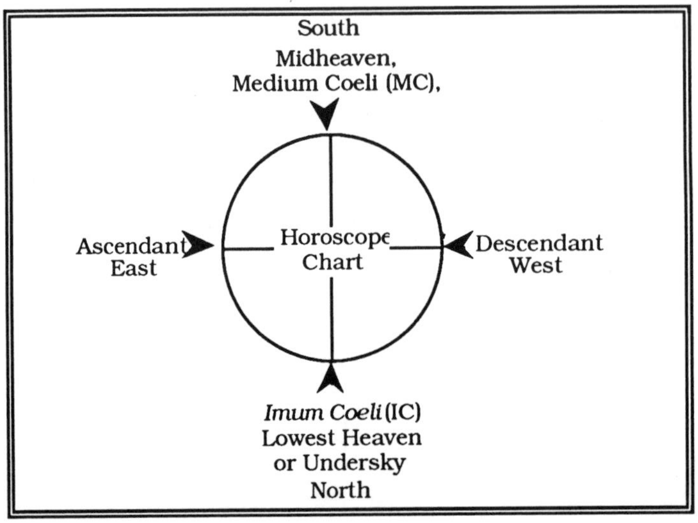

Notice East appears at the left of the diagram instead of at the right. This is because astrology "originated" in the northern hemisphere where, to look at the noonday Sun (represented by the midheaven) you must face south. This places the east on your left and the west on your right.

Angular Houses: See *Houses, Kinds.*

Angular Planets: Any planet in the first, fourth, seventh or tenth house is angular. Traditionally, astrologers consider these houses to be where planets exert their greatest effect. See also *Houses, Kinds.* Angular also indicates a planet or point is conjunct ☌ the ascendant, descendant, MC, or IC.

Aphelion: The point in an orbit where the body is at its greatest distance from the Sun. The Earth's aphelion is approximately 94.5 million miles. The Earth's perihelion is only 91.4 million miles away.

Figure 32. Aphelion and Perihelion

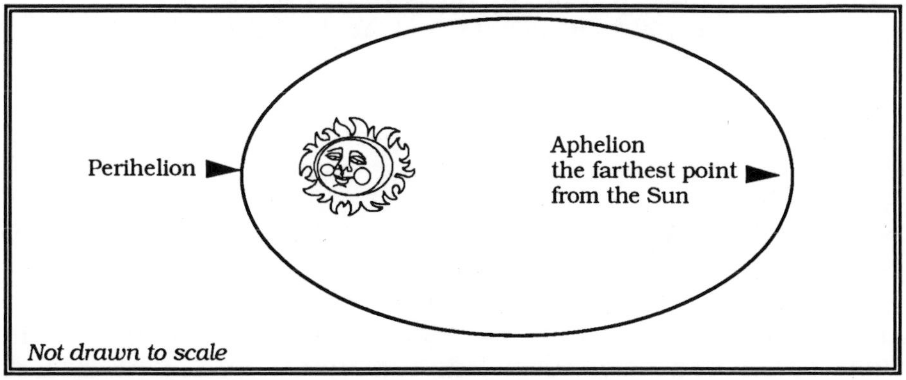

Apogee: The point in an orbit where the Moon or satellite is at its greatest distance from the Earth. It is opposite of perigee where the object is closest to the Earth. The full Moon will look smaller at the apogee and larger at the perigee when it is closest to the Earth. Derived from Greek *apo-*, away from + *gaia, ge*, Earth. See also *Perigee*.

Figure 33. Apogee and Perigee

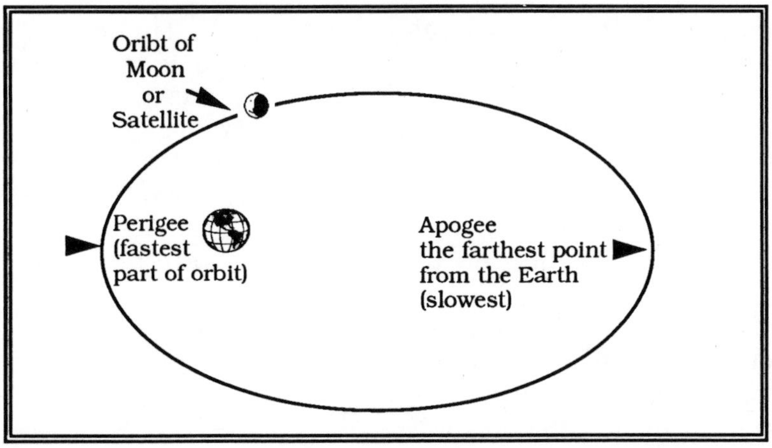

Apollon: Symbol ♃, one of eight hypothetical planets in Uranian astrology. Apollon is linked with success, expansion, science, commerce and peace.

Aquarian Age: One of twelve great ages, each lasting approximately 2,160 years and caused by the Precession of the Equinoxes. We are now on the cusp of the Aquarius Age and leaving the Pisces Age, which we have been in since around the time of Christ. Astrologers do not agree on the exact date the Age of Aquarius begins ranging from hundreds of years. See also *Precession of the Equinoxes*.

Aquarius: The eleventh sign of the zodiac, it is a masculine, air, fixed sign ruled by Uranus. Its older ruler was Saturn ♄. The Sun travels through Aquarius from about 20 January to 19 February.

The glyph for Aquarius ♒ symbolizes the flow of water. As Aquarius is an air sign, the sigil can be interpreted as a flow of spiritual knowledge, or the pouring of knowledge from the river of life.

Characteristically, Aquarians prefer to express themselves through groups or causes. They are friendly, but detached and more concerned about humanity as a whole than with single individuals. Aquarians love freedom, in all its forms, which is why they sometimes find close personal relationships too restrictive. In a similar theme of freedom, Aquarians are the reformers, or rebels of the zodiac, often insisting upon change from the *status quo*.

Positive Aquarian traits: original, humanitarian, independent, friendly, reformist and idealistic.

Negative Aquarian traits: erratic, unpredictable, eccentric, rebellious, contrary, impersonal, stubborn and perverse.

Arabic Parts: Also known as Arabic Points (AP). These are calculated points on a birth chart. They can also be found by placing a specific planet on the ascendant. Solar and Lunar Houses are determined by placing the Sun's or the Moon's position respectively as the ascendant, and assign the same cusp degree to each consecutive house cusp. See Solar and Lunar Houses in the User's Guide, Part 1.

Using the Solar Houses (Sun on the ascendant), you obtain:

Moon = Part of Fortune
Mercury = Point of Commerce
Venus = Point of Love
Mars = Point of Passion or Sword
Jupiter = Point of Increase
Uranus = Point of Catastrophe
Neptune = Point of Treachery
Pluto = Point of the Gavel

Placing the Moon on the ascendant yields the following points:
Sun = Point of Spirit (Fortune by night)
Mercury = Point of Faith
Venus = Point of Female Children
Jupiter = Point of Male Children
Cusp of Eighth House = Point of Death

Mercury on the ascendant gives:
Moon = Point of Servants
Mars = Point of Understanding

Venus on the ascendant gives
Moon = point of Mother
Saturn = Point of Fortune in Husbandry
Cusp of Seventh House = Point of Marriage.
Conversely, with the Cusp of the Seventh House as the ascendant, Venus becomes the Point of Divorce.

Mars on the ascendant gives:
Venus = Point of Plays
Jupiter = Point of Discord

Saturn on the ascendant
Sun = Point of Father
Moon = Point of Magistracy and Possessions, or the Point of Inheritance
Mars = Point of Sickness
Jupiter = Point of Brothers and Sisters

You can also calculate the above points from the natal chart without revolving the chart to place the Sun, Moon or another planet's position to the ascendant. A common example is *Fortuna*, or the *Part of Fortune*. You calculate Fortuna by adding and subtracting the positions of the Sun, Moon and ascendant. The usual approach is to (1) convert the longitudes of the planets (in signs) to degrees of a circle, (2) apply the formula. (3) convert your answer in degrees of a circle back into the degrees and minutes within the respective sign.

The formula for a Part of Fortune daylight (diurnal) birth is:

Part of Fortune = ° Ascendant + ° Moon - ° Sun

The formula for a Part of Fortune nighttime (nocturnal) birth is:

Part of Fortune = ° Ascendant + ° Sun - ° Moon

You can calculate other Arabic Parts using this same formula, that is:

Point of _______ = A + B - C

The traditional positions used in calculations are the Sun, Moon, ascendant (Asc.), midheaven and sometimes a house cusp. Other commonly calculated parts are:

Catastrophe = Uranus + Asc. - Sun.

Children (Female) = Venus + Asc. - Moon.

Children (Male) = Jupiter + Asc. - Moon.

Commerce = Mercury + Asc. - Sun.

Death = Eighth House Cusp + Asc. - Moon.

Discord = Jupiter + Asc. - Mars.

Divorce = Venus + Asc. - Seventh House Cusp. (the point opposite Venus in the natal chart.)

Faith = Mercury + Asc. - Moon.

Fatality = Saturn + Asc. - Sun.

Father = Sun + Asc. - Saturn.

Husbandry = Saturn + Asc. - Venus.

Inheritance and Possessions = Moon + Asc. - Saturn

Journeys by Water = 15° Cancer + Asc. - Saturn.

Point of Increase = Jupiter + Asc. - Sun.

Life = Moon + Asc. - Full Moon before birth.

Play = Venus + Asc. - Mars.

Love = Venus + Asc. - Sun.

Marriage = Seventh House Cusp + Asc. - Venus.

Merchandise, Sorrow and Imprisonment = Fortune + Asc. - Spirit.

Mother and Friends = Moon + Asc. - Venus.

Organization = Pluto + Asc. - Sun.

Passion = Mars + Asc. - Sun.

Servants = Moon + Asc. - Mercury.

Siblings (Sisters and Brothers) = Jupiter + Asc. - Saturn.

Sickness = Mars + Asc. - Saturn.

Spirit = Sun + Asc. - Moon. (Fortune by night)

Sudden Advancement = Sun + Asc. - Saturn.

Treachery = Neptune + Asc. - Sun.

Understanding = Mars + Asc. - Mercury.

Other systems to calculate the Arabic Parts use oblique ascension and right ascension.

There are approximately 200 Arabic Parts. Some additional Parts names are in the table below. More information on the Arabic Parts is in Robert Hand's excellent book, *Horoscope Symbols*, and in Nicholas deVore's book: *Encyclopedia of Astrology*.

Table 12. Arabic Parts Names

Assassination	Love *
Bondage	Male Children *
Brethren	Marriage *
Catastrophe *	Merchandise *
Commerce *	Mother *
Death/Delay *	Organization *
Discord *	Peril (Dangerous Year)
Divorce *	Passion *
Faith and Trust *	Play *
Fate (Brotherly Love) *	Possessions (Goods)
Father *	Secret Enemies
Female Children *	Servants *
Find Lost Objects	Sickness *
Friends	Spirit *
Frugality (Husbandry)	Sudden Advancement *
Homosexuality	Suicide
Honor	Surgery
Honorable Acquaintance	Travels (Long)
Hopes & Wishes	Travels (Short)
Hopes and Imagination	Travels (by air)
Husbandry *	Travels (by water) *
Imprisonment and Sorrow	Treachery *
Increase *	Understanding *
Inheritance *	Widowhood
Legal Affairs	
Life *	

** Formula for part given above table.*

Arc: Part of the circumference of a circle, or a segment of a curve.

Aries: The first sign of the zodiac. The Sun travels through Aries from about 21 March to 20 April. Aries is a fire, cardinal, masculine sign, ruled by the planet Mars.

The glyph ♈, might represent the horns of the ram. Some astrologers claim it is a drawing of the human eyebrows and nose, because Aries rules the face and head. Others claim it represents the fountain of life, or a young plant springing up from seed.

Astrologically, Arian people are very aware of themselves and very action oriented. Their basic nature is that of a warrior or pioneer. There also might be a strong element of selfishness because the Arian type tends to be insensitive to the needs of others.

Positive Arian traits: pioneer, initiatory, courageous, enthusiastic, independent, enterprising, loving freedom.

Negative Arian traits: Selfish, rash, impulsive, impatient, aggressive and head-strong, over bearing, dictatorial, egotistical.

Array: A general pattern or spread of planets in a chart. An array considers the placements of the planets in a general shape, without necessarily considering aspects. Some array names are: bundle or cluster, locomotive or open angle, hemispheric or bowl, bucket or wedge, seesaw, tripod, splash, splay and star. Figure 34 suggests models for the overall shapes of the arrays. Further information on planetary arrays is in Palden Jenkins' book, *Living in Time.*

Ascendant: The ascendant is the point or degree on the east horizon at birth (first breath) or when an event takes place. It is the degree of the opening cusp of the first house. The sign of the zodiac on this point is the rising sign.

In more technical terms, the ascendant is the point of intersection of the horizon and the ecliptic nearest the east point. The ascendant moves quickly, approximately 1° every 4 minutes, or one sign every 2 hours, depending whether it is in a sign of long or short ascension. Two people born simultaneously on opposite sides of the Earth will have completely opposite house orientations, but the same planetary positions and aspects.

The ascendant is not synonymous with the rising sign although astrologers often use these terms interchangeably. The ascendant is a specific degree, whereas the rising sign is an entire sign of 30 degrees. Early astrologers, called the ascendant the *oriens.* See also Figure 31, *The Four Major Angles in a Horoscope.*

Ascending: A general term referring to any planet or point positioned in the eastward portion of a chart. One definition of ascending is anything located between the cusps of the fourth and tenth houses. A more precise description would be if a planet is within the orb of the ascendant itself, usually within 7.5° to 10° either side of the first house cusp.

Figure 34. Planetary Array Patterns

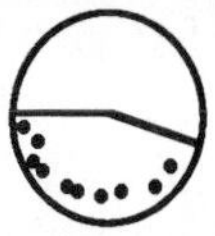

Bundle or Cluster Pattern

All planets are arrayed within 120° of each other.

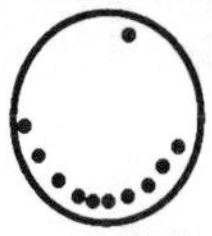

Bucket or Wedge Pattern

All but one planet occupies up to half the chart, with one planet as singleton or a handle.

Bowl or Hemispheric Pattern

All planets are in half of the zodiac.

Locomotive or Open-angle Pattern

All planets occupy up to two thirds of the chart leaving 120° empty.

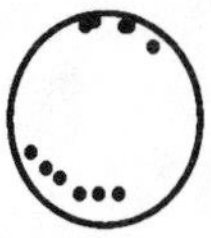

Seesaw Pattern

There are two distinct clusters of planets, opposite to each other with at least two signs on either side separating the clusters.

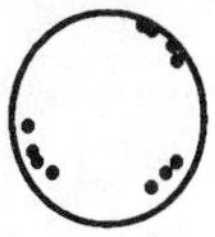

Tripod Pattern

There are three distinct groupings of planets, preferably forming a trine.

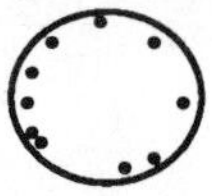

Splash Pattern

There is no particular pattern, planets are randomly arrayed.

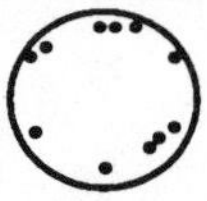

Splay Pattern

There are distinct clusters of conjoined or grouped planets.

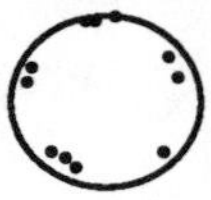

Star Pattern

Symmetrical patters with 4 or 5 points of a highly aspected array.

Aspect(s) The angular separation or positions of two or more planets with respect to each other. It is also the distance between two points on a horoscope (circle). The major aspects are found by subdividing the chart by divisors such as 2, 3, 4, 6, 8, and 12. Minor aspects are calculated by dividing the zodiac by 5, 7, and 9. See also *Orb* and *Harmonics*. A circle showing common aspects is below:

Figure 35. Cycle of the Main Aspects

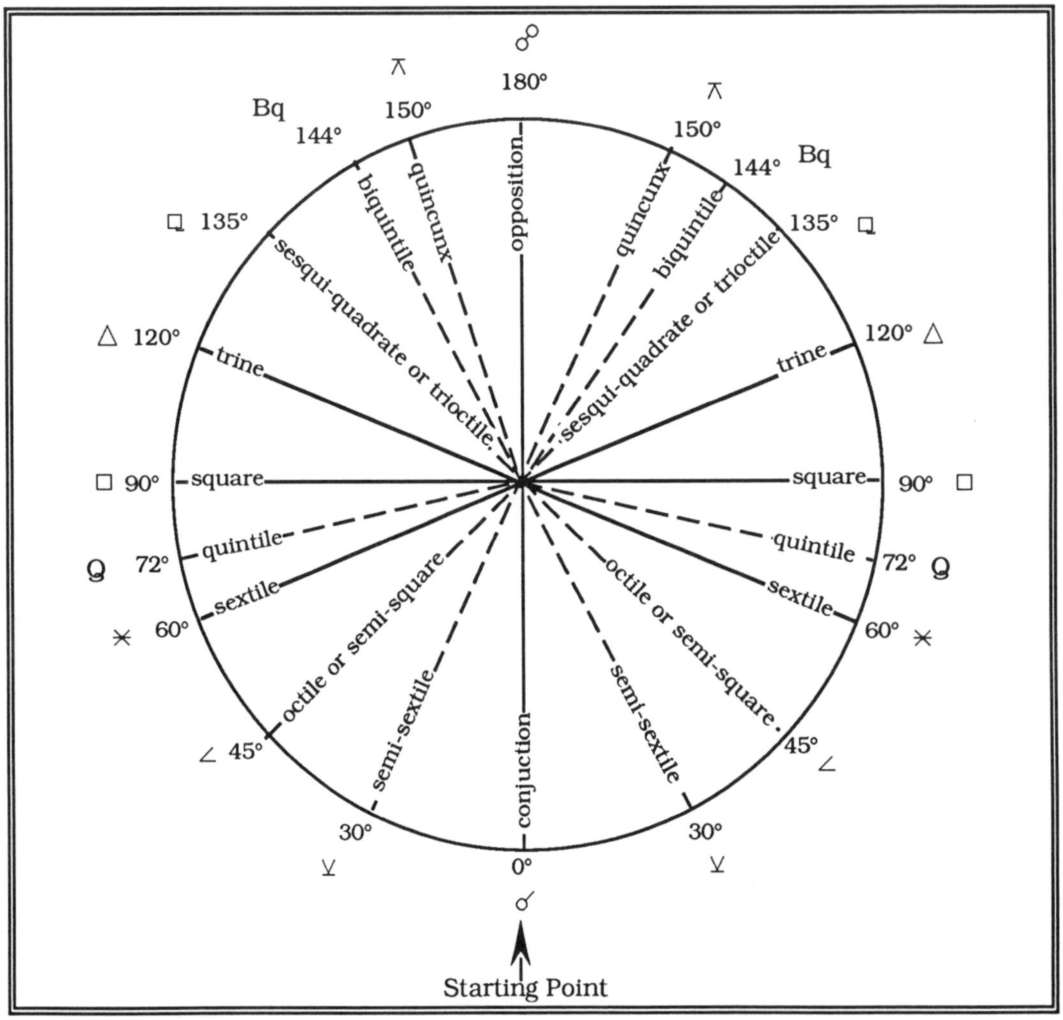

Aspectarian: A table or list of aspects formed between planets, the Moon and Sun for a given period.

Asteroids: The asteroids comprise over 55,000 small heavenly bodies whose orbits are primarily between Mars and Jupiter. The largest asteroid is approximately 620 miles in diameter and the smallest is less than one mile.

Figure 36. Asteroid Belt

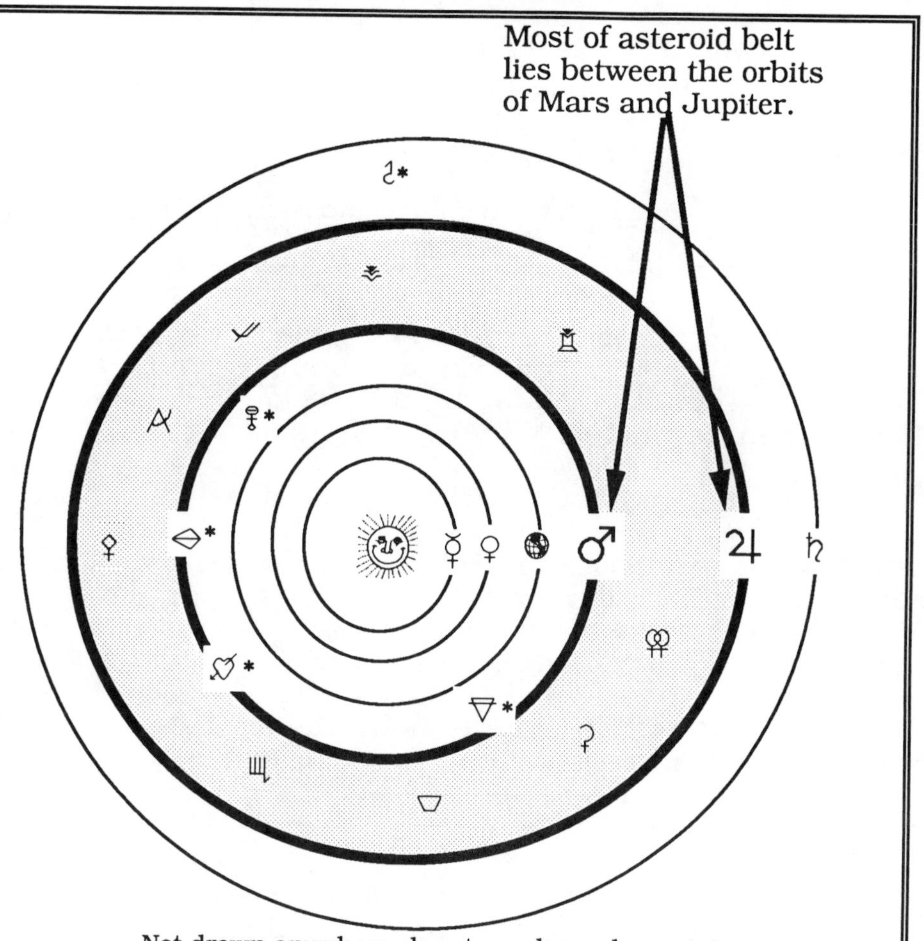

Most of asteroid belt
lies between the orbits
of Mars and Jupiter.

Not drawn anywhere close to scale or placement.
* Asteroids not within the main asteroid belt.

The first asteroid was discovered on January 1, 1801. It was named Ceres and assigned the number 1. Three more asteroids were discovered in a relatively short time: Pallas in 1802, Juno in 1804, and Vesta in 1807. The discovery rate of other asteroids was slow until the development of photographic methods. In only 50 years, from 1890 to 1940, the number of known asteroids increased from less than 300 to almost 1,500. Astronomers currently estimate there are about 55,000 asteroids bright enough to be photographed on a 100-inch telescope.

The discoverer of the asteroid traditionally has the honor of naming it. At first, asteroids were named after gods and goddesses of Greek and Roman mythology. Once these were assigned, astronomers turned to other sources including opera heroines, Knights of the Round Table, flowers, Muses, pets, cities, countries, and deserts.

Some were named after specific people, including friends and lovers of the discoverer. One is even named after a computer: NORC.

The New York Chapter of the National Council for Geocosmic Research Asteroids Subcommittee has acknowledged that the name of an asteroid might be significant and perhaps there is a link between the asteroid name and meaning.

The five principle asteroids used in astrology are Chiron ⚷, Ceres ⚳, Pallas ⚴, Juno ⚵ and Vesta ⚶. Other asteroids sometimes used are Amor ⊖, Eros ♡, Hidalgo ⚹, Icarus ▽, Lilith ⚸, Pandora ▽, Psyche ↙, Sappho ♀, Toro ?, and Urania ⋏. Some astrologers suggest the asteroids form a physical and spiritual bridge from the personal plants (Mercury, Venus and Mars) to the social and collective planets (Jupiter, Saturn, Uranus, Neptune and Pluto).

For further reading and interpretations of asteroids, see Demetra George's book *Asteroid Goddess*, and J. Lee Lehman's book: *The Ultimate Asteroid Book*. Dr. Lehman discusses almost 60 asteroids and their meanings in astrology. See also *Glyphs for Asteroids* and individual descriptions of *Ceres, Pallas, Vesta, Juno, Amor, Eros, Hidalgo, Icarus, Lilith, Pandora, Psyche, Sappho, Toro, and Urania*.

Astro*Carto*Graphy®: A registered brand name of a program that generates printouts of a natal chart against a map of the world. Astrological maps, or geographical astrology is a technique that, in the words of its developers:

> *"...enable a person to determine which parts of the natal chart potential will be accented, highlighted, or brought into consciousness in a new location."*

The Astro*Carto*Graphy Book of Maps, page 1.

The computer program, Astro*Carto*Graphy, is not commercially available, but printouts can be ordered from Astro Numeric Service, Trigon Systems Corporation, P.O. Box 425, San Palo, CA 94806.

Astrolabe: From old French (*astrelabe*), middle Latin (*astrolabium*), and Greek (*astrolabon*); liberally meaning *astron* = star + *lambanein* = take; an instrument for taking (measuring) the stars. Probably a Greek invention of about 100BC, the astrolabe accurately calculates the motions of the Sun, stars and the observer's latitude. It also can determine time and was used for determining the degrees of the four cardinal points of a horoscope. A portable astrolabe is the armillax. Today, an astrolabe is sometimes called a planisphere.

Because it can show the positions of the stars, it was an invaluable tool for navigation and astronomical observations for nearly 2,000 years.

Astrolabe is also the name of a company, headed by Robert Hand, whose mission is: "*To improve the tools of astrology, and thus to advance astrology beyond what it is today.*" Astrolabe has developed 17 major software programs for the astrological arts that run on a variety of computers. More information about Astrolabe Software is in Part Two, *Astrological Software.*

Astrological Associations: There are many astrological organizations that offer educational programs, conferences, reference services and other supportive materials. Several larger ones are listed below.

Australia
Federation of Australian Astrologers
c/o Kevin Barrett
94 Blaxland Road
Wentworth Falls NSW 2782
Fax 011-61-47573912

United Kingdom
Astrological Association (of Great Britain)
Subscriptions: c/o Kim Farnell
396 Caledonian Road
London, N1, 1DN

Faculty of Astrological Studies
Registrar
BM 7470
London WC1N 3xx
Phone 0444 453 504

United States
See *American Federation of Astrologers* (AFA)

International Society for Astrological Research (ISAR)
P.O. Box 38613
Los Angeles, California 90038, USA

See *National Council for Geocosmic Research* (NCGR)

Astrology: Astrology is an art and science that studies the cycles of planets and other heavenly bodies, and the affairs of people on Earth. The word, "astrology" is from Greek *astron* (star), and *logos* (word or speech) -logy is often the ending of a topic of science or knowledge. Astrology literally translates to science of the stars, or "star talk".

As a language of symbolism, astrology ascribes 12 archetypes that correspond to twelve basic personality types of the total human personality. Archetype refers to a model, primal or pure form. The archetypical symbolism also correlates to the yearly seasonal cycles that Dane Rudhyar describes as the "Pulse of Life". The cosmic forces manifest and influence living beings within the context of cycles of time and space. Astrology is an ancient science dating back to pre-history. It is a unique field of study that combines certain elements of science, art and intuition.

Astrology Specialties: There are many branches or specialties of astrology. The major ones are briefly described below:

Agricultural Astrology was probably the first use humans ever made of the planetary cycles. This branch of astrology deals with the best times for planting, cultivating and harvesting crops. The Moon plays a great role in agricultural astrology.

Astro-Economics is a new term and branch of astrology that forecasts the stock and commodity markets and other economic trends. Among the methods used are Gann techniques, cycles, Fibonaci ratios, and planetary angles. The World Conference of Astro-Economics holds annual meetings. For further information about the conferences contact Grace K. Morris, 4931 W. 95th Street, Oak Lawn, Illinois, 60453.

Constellational Astrology is a branch of astrology that expands from the traditional 12 sign zodiac to all recognized constellations and other heavenly bodies or celestial phenomena.

Electional Astrology attempts to determine the best time to initiate a project, such as establish a business, or hold a wedding. A good reference on electional astrology is *Perfect Timing* by Gregory Szantos, and *The Timing of Events* by Bruce Scofield.

Esoteric Astrology, promoted by Alice A. Bailey, suggests that space is an entity that has a universal consciousness and will. In this philosophy, the universe in its entirety is the body of the Creator and even the smallest atom or cell contains an intelligence that can respond to currents that flow from the Universal Mind.

This approach is similar to the ancient doctrine *hylozoism* which emphasizes that matter is inseparable from life. It also finds a close cousin in the new physics that theoretically proves the existence of a multidimensional universe that has multiple realities happening simultaneously (the Ring Theory). In other words, the entire universe is interconnected as one.

Esoteric astrology proposes that the purpose of astrology is to trace the evolution of consciousness, that is, to remember and connect with our primal source. Dr. Rupert Sheldrake referred to this universal consciousness as the "Hundredth Monkey" phenomenon. The Hundredth Monkey Theory proposes that when a critical mass of individuals have an awareness of something (an idea, process or feeling), then all the individuals, as a group, become aware, or conscious of it. In esoteric astrology, the twelve signs of the zodiac represent powerful thought forms within the cosmic, or universal mind.

Horary Astrology seeks to answer a question by consulting a chart cast for a specific moment. The term horary pertains to an hour or occurring hourly. In astrology, horary refers to propitious or specific times.

Horary astrologers believe that asking a question is in itself a significant event that plays a part in the manifesting of the situation. The astrologer only looks for answers to the question in the chart. In other words, the question is "born" when first articulated and its birth chart is cast like any other horoscope. The ascendant represents the person asking the question, the planet ruling the ascendant is the querent's primary significator. A.I.R. Software has a horary program called *Nostradamus*. CCRS has a tabular information page for classical horary astrology.

Medical Astrology focuses on the health of an individual and uses the premise that each planet and sign relates to specific body parts and the psyche of an individual. The astrologer uses the natal chart to determine the most vulnerable, and the strongest parts of a person's physical, mental and spiritual health.

Meteorological or Natural Astrology deals with forecasts of weather conditions. This branch focuses on such natural events as weather patterns, earthquakes, tidal waves, storms. See also *Geological Changes and Astrology.*

Mundane or Judicial Astrology views countries and populations as having a similar birth-life-death cycle as an individual. Astrologers cast a chart for the time of creation of a nation. Judicial astrology predicts and tracks economic and social trends, events and even wars.

Natal or Genethliacal Astrology is the best known branch of astrology that uses the birth time and place of an individual to cast the natal chart (horoscope). Genethliacal astrology studies the astrological links of family traits and interactions. Genethliacal is an archaic term derived from Greek that generally refers to natal astrology. Genethliaci is an ancient term for astrologers.

Uranian Astrology is the name of a modern system of astrology derived from theories developed by the Hamburg School, under the direction of Alfred Witte. Uranian astrology differs from traditional astrology in three ways:

1. Planetary aspects are found using mathematical calculations that emphasize numerical divisions. Some Uranian astrologers use a special "Degree Dial" to identify aspects and important chart patterns.

2. In addition to the standard planets, Uranian astrology includes 8 hypothetical planets, all trans-Neptunian. The planets are Cupido ♃, Hades ⚸, Zeus ⚵, Kronos ⚶, Apollon ⚷, Admetos ⚸, Vulcanus ⚹, and Poseidon ⚺. The existence of the planets is based on the observation that energies seem to come from places where there are no known planets.

3. There is much reliance upon midpoints, and a limited number of aspects.

The Uranian astrologers claim that their system, after over 50 years of use, is accurate, empirical and valid.

Vocational Astrology is the branch of astrology that suggests occupational possibilities that might be suitable for the individual based upon the natal chart. The primary focus of astrology is to help individuals know who they are and to develop self-awareness. Once a person is more aware, their interests become clearer and the direction of their life work should become apparent. As a tool for enhancing self-knowledge vocational astrology helps clarify and direct vocational choices.

Astronomy: The objective study of the heavens through observation. The scientific measurement of the positions and motions of the celestial bodies.

Astronomical Coordinates: Reference values used to define the position of a body in the celestial sphere. The three major systems are horizon, equatorial and ecliptic. Refer to User's Reference under *Coordinate Systems* for more detailed descriptions and graphics.

Astronomical Unit: A unit of length used in measuring astronomical distances. It is equal to the mean distance of the Earth from the Sun, approximately 93 million miles.

Autumnal Equinox: The point where the Sun crosses from north to south on the intersection of the celestial equator and the ecliptic. This occurs on, or about, 23 September, and is the fall equinox. It is the beginning of Libra (0° ♎). See Figure 1: Seasons, Solstices and Equinoxes.

Ayanamsa: An ancient Sanskrit term meaning "yearly degree", it describes the difference in distance (arc) between the beginning points of the tropical and sidereal zodiacs. It is expressed in degrees, minutes and seconds.

Azimuth: The primary angular measurement of the horizon coordinate system, the azimuth is measured around the horizon (clockwise) from the north point to the vertical circle containing the body or point. It is sometimes measured from the south point (north to south). See Figure 7: Horizon System Coordinates.

Aztec Signs: The Aztecs of ancient Mexico were deeply involved in astrology. Aztec astrology has twenty days (signs) as listed below:

Table 13. Aztec Signs and English Equivalents

1. Cipactli	Crocodile	11. Ocamatli	Ape
2. Eecatl	Wind	12. Malinalli	Twisted
3. Calli	House	13. Acatl	Reed
4. Cuelzpalin	Lizard	14. Ocelotl	Jaguar
5. Couatl	Snake	15. Quauhtli	Vulture
6. Miquiztli	Death	16. Cozcaquauhili	Eagle
7. Macatl	Deer	17. Olin	Sun's Motion
8. Tochtli	Rabbit	18. Tecpatl	Flint Knife
9. Atl	Water	19. Quiauitl	Rain
10 Itzcuintli	Dog	20. Xochitl	Flower

Bruce Scofield and Barry Orr have written a program that does Aztec charts. It is available from Astrolabe Software.

B

Beltane: See *Fire Festivals.*

Bestial Signs: Aries ♈, Taurus ♉, Leo ♌, Capricorn ♑, and Sagittarius ♐ are the beasts of the zodiac.

Bi-Corporal Signs: Gemini ♊, Virgo ♍, Sagittarius ♐ and Pisces ♓ are bi-corporal (two body) because each contains two animals: twins, half man/half horse, and two fish respectively.

Bi-Wheel Chart: A chart type that displays two concentric circles. These two circles contain two charts that the astrologer wants to compare. Bi-wheels are especially useful for synastry charts and to show transits. See also the User's Guide under *Graphics and Chart Styles* for an example of a bi-wheel.

Birth, Moment of: The accepted moment of birth of a person or animal is its first breath during delivery. The valid starting time of a venture or event is the first moment it can be definitely said to have started as a real event. This can be "real" in physical terms, such as moving into a house, convening a meeting, getting into a car for a journey, or definitely making a decision. For weddings, the astrologer usually casts a chart for the time the vows are stated.

Birth data: The information necessary to cast a chart. The data includes the time of first breath (as precise as possible to the hour, minute, and second), city, with district or hospital if known (expressed as latitude and longitude), and date (day, month, year including time zone and time changes).

Blue Moon: A blue Moon is the second full Moon that occurs in a single calendar month. This happens every few years as the date of one full Moon falls at the beginning of the month, and the second full Moon just at the end of the month.

Blue Moon also refers to a Moon that actually appears bluish, which is caused by atmospheric conditions. Sometimes a moon can appear blue or blue-green just before sunrise or just after sunset if there is a large amount of particulate matter (smoke or dust) in the atmosphere. These particles can act as filters for certain wavelengths to change temporarily the color of the moon's appearance.

C

Cadent Houses: See *House, Kinds.*

Cancer: The fourth sign of the zodiac, Cancer is a feminine water cardinal sign ruled by the Moon. The Sun is in this sign from about June 21 to July 22.

The glyph ♋, is the image for the crab after which Cancer is named. It also could represent cradling arms and protected space from which one can grow.

Cancers are the worriers of the zodiac, and their faces often show it, with pronounced worry lines. There are often expressions of patience, sympathy and motherliness, especially as they sentimentally remember the good old days. The typical Cancerian loves the home and family, and might have trouble letting go or releasing whatever they cherish or control. Symbolically, Cancer represents the mother in the horoscope.

Positive Cancerian traits: sympathetic, industrious, sociable, thrifty, protective.

Negative Cancerian traits: moody, over emotional, a hard exterior hiding a weak character, unforgiving, unstable.

Candlemas: See *Fire Festivals.*

Capricorn: The tenth sign of the zodiac, it is a feminine, cardinal earth sign ruled by Saturn. The Sun travels through Capricorn from about 23 December to 19 January.

The glyph for Capricorn ♑ represents the twisted horns of a goat, or the tail of a fish. It also might represent the winding path to a mountain peak.

Capricornians are characteristically ambitious, and are often looking for a raise, or concerned about keeping up with the neighbors. They are practical with the daily necessities of life. Capricorn rules bureaucracies, protocols, contracts, and procedures. Just like big bureaucracies, Capricorns can tend to be cold, rigid, unchangeable, and conventional. But also like bureaucracies, they can be practical and efficient. Capricornians usually have a good but dry sense of humor.

Positive Capricornian traits: reliable, systematic, disciplined, patient, practical, process oriented.

Negative Capricornian traits: rigid, miserly, cold, bureaucratic, and pessimistic.

Cardinal Ingresses: The entry of the Sun into one of the four cardinal signs or quadruplicities. The four signs are Aries ♈, Cancer ♋, Libra ♎ and Capricorn ♑, that mark the beginning of the four seasons. These are the vernal equinox, summer solstice, fall equinox and winter solstice, respectively.

Cardinal Points: The four directions on a compass: north, east, south and west. Cardinal means "of foremost importance or pivotal".

Cardinal Signs: Aries ♈, Cancer ♋, Libra ♎, and Capricorn ♑ are the cardinal signs and associated with the cardinal houses - the 1st, 4th, 7th, and 10th. These signs fall on the "cardinal angles", East (Aries), North (Cancer), West (Libra) and South (Capricorn). These are signs of action and initiation and are the pioneers, activists and reformers of the zodiac. See also *fixed* and *mutable.*

Positive cardinal traits: enterprising, aggressive, creative, assertive, self-conscious, and independent.

Negative Cardinal traits: self-seeking, total dominance, impatient, self-centered, ruthless and opportunist.

Cayce, Edgar: The 14,256 readings done by Edgar Cayce are among the most renowned prophetic passages available in the 20th century. Many books are available about the Cayce readings. The Association for Research and Enlightenment (ARE) mission is to preserve and further the Cayce work. Cayce was a profoundly religious man and one of his favorite activities was teaching Sunday school at the Christian church he attended. He never studied astrology, yet in many of his readings, Cayce referred to astrological influences and conditions. Juliet Brooke Ballard's describes these in her book: *The Hidden Laws of Earth: Edgar Cayce's View of Astrology.*

Interestingly, Cayce named two planets in addition to those already known in 1930. These two planets were Septimus and Arcturus. Septimus is the Latin word for seventh and Pluto is the seventh planet outward from the Earth. Pluto was discovered after Cayce identified Septimus. Students of Cayce assume that Pluto and Septimus are the same planet. Arcturus is the name of a star.

Celestial Equator: An great circle on the celestial sphere that is mid-way between the celestial poles. It is in the same plane as the Earth's equator. See Figure 5: Horizon System: Observer at North Pole.

Celestial Globe: A model of the celestial sphere that shows the relative positions of planets and other heavenly bodies to the Earth. The Earth is usually at the center of the model.

Celestial Poles: The points in the sky that are directly overhead at the mundane Earth's poles. In other words, it is the Earth's rotational axis extended into space.

Celestial Sphere: An sphere that extends infinitely with the Earth as the center. The stars, planets and other bodies' positions can be plotted on this sphere.

Ceres: Symbol ⚳. One of four asteroids most used in astrological readings. In Roman mythology, Ceres was the mother and goddess of agriculture. As Demeter, she is the Greek goddess of Grain. Demeter relates specifically with the Earth's fertility. Discovered 1801, Ceres is asteroid #1 and is the largest.

Astrologically, Ceres symbolizes the parental bonding within families, agriculture and fertility. See also *Asteroids.*

Chandra Symbols: The Chandra Symbols are a series of 360 images, one for each degree of the zodiac. Like the Sabian Symbols, the Chandra Symbols were channeled. On April 11, 1839, John Sandbach received the information from his spirit guide Chandra, which is the Sanskrit word for Moon. For more information refer to John

Sandbach's book: *Degree Analysis Part II: Chandra Symbols in the Horoscope*. For other degree systems, also see *Sabian Symbols* and *Dwadeshamsas*.

Chart Rectification: See *Rectification*.

Chiron: Glyph ⚷, Chiron is a small planetoid (asteroid) or a large comet. Charles Kowal of the Hale Observatory discovered Chiron in 1977. Chiron orbits eccentrically between the orbits of Saturn and Uranus and crosses the orbits of both. Chiron crosses outside the orbit of Uranus where it stays in Aries for about 8 years. Chiron is within the orbit of Saturn when in the constellation of Libra, which it speeds through in about 1 year. Chiron spends most of its time beyond Saturn's orbit. Chiron's orbit is about 51 years. It has a diameter of about 300 km. Some astronomers believe that Chiron is a trapped comet and not an asteroid.

Mythologically, Chiron was the wise centaur (half man, half horse), son of Cronos (Saturn) and Philyra. Chiron's teachers were Apollo and Artemis (Diana). He was famous for his skills in hunting, medicine, music and the art of prophecy. He tutored all the great Greek heros: Peleus, Diomedes, Achilles, Hercules and Asclepius, the great physician.

One version of the myth was that a poisoned arrow from Hercules mortally wounded Chiron. Because he was immortal, Chiron could neither die or recover. Another interpretation is that he could not heal himself because it was not his wound; it was the wound (and pain) of the society that separated itself through discrimination, fear and ignorance.

Being immortal, yet mortally wounded is a difficult situation. Not wanting to be on Earth any longer, Chiron bargained for the release of Prometheus and in exchange, gave up his immortality to take his place among the stars as Sagittarius.

Prometheus, also an immortal god, was chained to a rock and had his liver eaten by an eagle as punishment for giving fire to humanity and for keeping a secret from Zeus. Thus, Chiron, because of his wound and pain inflicted by society, helped to free Promethius who was unjustly tortured and imprisoned for aiding humanity. Prometheus' name has since the time of ancient Greece stood as the great rebel against injustice and false authority of power.

The astrological rulership of Chiron is still being determined. Does Sagittarius the knower, rule Chiron, or is the ruler Virgo the server? Regardless, Chiron is a powerful point in the chart. Perhaps it represents the healer and knower within each of us that can be activated to heal not only ourselves, but also heal on a universal level.

Through Chiron, we can know and heal ourselves while at the same time help to heal others and the world. Chiron represents the principle of holistic knowledge, healing and education.

Chiron's glyph, ⚷ represents a key to universal knowledge and healing, which is rising up from the eternal spirit (circle). In a birth chart, Chiron is an indicator of the individual's holistic perceptions of healing and education, and where healing needs to take place.

Positive Chiron traits: healing, teaching, knowing, holistic views.

Negative Chiron traits: misunderstanding, reliance on dogma, wounded, suffering, beastly, spiritual unrest.

For further reading, two good references on Chiron are: *The Continuing Discovery of Chiron*, by Erminie Lantero, and *Chiron: Rainbow Bridge Between the Inner and Outer Planets* by Barbara Hand Clow.

Circumpolar Stars: Those stars that are always above the horizon in high northern or low southern latitudes, including the seven stars of Ursa Major that form the outline of the big dipper.

Civil Day: The 24 hour Mean Solar Day; the standard 24 hour day from midnight to midnight. Civil day also could be defined as the time between two successive transits of the mean Sun.

Combustion: In astrology, any planet within 8° 30' of the Sun is subject to combustion; considered by some to be an unfortunate position, especially for the Moon. This is supposedly "undesirable" because the Sun "burns up" the planet thus destroying its individual function in the chart.

Composite Chart: A chart cast using the midpoints of planets in two peoples' charts to create a chart for the relationship itself. The relationship becomes an entity in its own right by virtue of being a blending of the two individuals energies. See the User's Guide (Part 1) for more information and examples of how to calculate midpoints. An authoritive reference on composites is Robert Hand's *Planets in Composite: Analyzing Human Relationships.*

Configuration: Three or more planets linked together by aspects form a specific shape or pattern. Some configurations are Grand Trine, Grand Cross, Grand Sextile, Grand Octile and the most common, the T-Square. See the names of the individual configurations for more detailed descriptions.

Conjunction: Symbol ☌. An aspect formed when two or more planets are close to each other. Some astrologers consider conjunctions to be influential within an 8° orb, and expand the orb to 10° up to 17° if the Sun or Moon are involved. A conjunction of the Sun and Moon shows a person was born on, or close to, the new Moon (☉ ☌ ☽).

Grammatically, note that conjunction is a noun and not a verb. As an astrologer, do not show your illiteracy by using 'conjuncted'. The verb is *to conjoin* and is conjugated as conjoin(s) (present tense), conjoined (past tense), and conjoining (present participle). The adjective is conjoint.

Constellations: Star groupings and patterns which have been assigned symbols and identities. Astronomers acknowledge 88 constellations that were made official during the Astronomical Congress of 1928. The description of each constellation, and its boundary, was published in 1930 in a book titled *Atlas Cele'ste.* The International Astronomical Union endorsed Eugene Delporte's work *Delimination Scientifique des Constellations*, which, for the first time, mapped the heavens accurately and yet was flexible enough to consider the Precession of the Equinoxes. The 88 constellations fit perfectly together on the celestial sphere.

Astronomers and astrologers named constellations after perceived shapes and patterns that the stars form in the sky. These names are passed to us through tradition, primarily because it is easier to refer to a star in Pegasus, or in Taurus, than to give its geometrical position (coordinates). The following table lists the 88 official constellations.

Table 14. The 88 Recognized Constellations

Latin Name	English Version	Where	Latin Name	English Version	Where
Andromeda	Andromeda	north	Lacerta	Lizard	north
Antlia	Airpump	south	Leo	Lion	zodiac
Apus	Bird of Paradise	south	Leo Minor	Small Lion	north
Aquarius	Water Bearer	zodiac	Lepus	Hare	south
Aquila	Eagle	north	Libra	Scales	zodiac
Ara	Altar	south	Lupus	Wolf	south
Aries	Ram	Zodiac	Lynx	Lynx	north
Auriga	Charioteer	north	Lyra	Lyre (Harp)	north
Boetes	Herdsman	north	Memsa	Table (Mountain)	south
Caelum	Sculptors Tool	south	Microscopium	Microscope	south
Camelopardalis	Giraffe	north	Monoceros	Unicorn	south

The 88 Recognized Constellations (continued)

Latin Name	English Version	Where	Latin Name	English Version	Where
Cancer	Crab	zodiac	Musca	Southern Fly	south
Canes Venatici	Hunting Dogs	north	Norma	Straight edge	south
Canis Major	Great Dog	south	Octans	Octant	south
Canis Minor	Little Dog	south	Ophiuchus	Serpent-Bearer	north
Capricornus	Goat (Sea goat)	zodiac	Orion	Orion (the Hunter)	south
Carina	Keel (of Argo)	south	Pravo	Peacock	south
Cassiopeia	Cassiopeia	north	Pegasus	Flying Horse	north
Centarus	Centaur	south	Perseus	Perseus	north
Cepheus	Cepheus	north	Phoenix	Phoenix	south
Cetus	Whale	south	Pictor	Painter or Easel	south
Chameleon	Chameleon	south	Pisces	Fish	zodiac
Circinus	Compasses	south	Piscis Austrinus	Southern Fish	south
Columba	Dove	south	Puppis	Poop (of Argo)	south
Coma Berenices	Berenices's Hair	north	Pyxis	Mariner's Compass	south
Corona Australis	Southern Crown	south	Reticulum	Net	south
Corona Borealis	Northern Crown	north	Sagitta	Arrow	north
Corvus	Crow (Raven)	south	Sagittarius	Centaur Archer	zodiac
Crater	Cup	south	Scorpius	Scorpion	Zodiac
Crus	Southern Cross	south	Sculptor	Sculptor	south
Cygnus	Swan	north	Scutum	Shield	north
Delphinus	Dolphin	north	serpens	Serpent	north
Dorado	Swordfish Goldfish	north	Sextans	Sextant	south
Draco	Dragon	north	Taurus	Bull	zodiac
Equuleus	Filly	north	Telescopium	Telescope	south
Eridanus	River	south	Triangulum	Triangle	north
Fornax	Furnace	south	Triangulum Australe	South Triangle	south
Gemini	Twins	zodiac	Tucana	Toucan	south
Grus	Crane	south	Ursa Major	Big Dipper (Bear)	north
Hercules	Hercules	north	Ursa Minor	Little Dipper (Bear)	north
Horologium	Clock	south	Vela	Sail (of Argo)	south
Hydra	Sea Serpent	north	Virgo	Virgin	zodiac
Hydrus	Water Snake	south	Volans	Flying Fish	south
Indus	Indian	south	Vulpecula	Fox	north

South shows the constellation is south of the zodiac band; north means it is north of the zodiac band.

Contraparallels: See *parallel.*

Cosmobiology: A school of astrology that uses a completely different mathematical approach to the natal horoscope. Cosmobiology uses very little or no house systems, but relies heavily upon angles, aspects and midpoints. Dr. Reinhold Ebertin, with his associates, founded the Cosmobiology Institute in West Germany.

Cross-quarters: These are the midpoints between the solstices and equinoxes. These points represent when the seasons go through definite changes and are times of energy manifestations. They mark discrete stages in the annual cycle of the life-force.

In Hindu mythology the cross quarter points are the "Four Gates of Avataric Descent". An avatar is a deity who has ascended to Earth in human or animal form. Avatar is also the generic term for the incarnations of Vishnu. The Four Gates represent the creative powers and four corners of the universe. These four gates are guarded by the bull, the lion, the eagle, and the angel. Astrologically, these points are at 15° Taurus, Leo, Scorpio and Aquarius respectively.

The ancient British pagans and others celebrated the quarter points as the fire festivals. These festivals are *Beltane* in early May (15° Taurus ♉), *Lammas* in early August (15° Leo ♌), *Samhain/Halloween* in early November (15° Scorpio ♏), and *Candlemas/Imbolc* in early February (15° Aquarius ♒). These are all "fixing" or "fixed" signs that carry through the purpose of the season. See also *Fire Festivals* for a diagram.

Culmination: The arrival, or crossing of a planet at the mid-heaven, the highest point in the chart.

Cupid(o): Symbol ⚳, one of eight hypothetical planets of Uranian astrology, Cupido represents matters of art and small groups such as family or community associations. Cupido is also asteroid #763.

Cusp: An imaginary line that separates one sign of the zodiac from another. The point of division between signs or houses. The transitional first or last part of a house or sign. The lines that divide the houses. See also *House Systems* in the User's Guide.

Cycles: Because the cosmos is ever changing in often predictable ways, cycles play a key role in astrology. Astrologers believe that planetary cycles reflect in human life and history. The ceaseless changes of the universe influence changes on living beings. Many vaster cycles have time frames beyond a human life-span. These influence epoches of human history such as changes in climate, social, cultural and religious revolutions, conflicts and wars, etc. Below are a few cycles. Also see *Planet Returns.*

***Diurnal Cycle* :** The daily cycle of day/night.

Sidereal Cycle : One complete rotation (cycle) of the Sun, Moon or a planet using the positions of the fixed stars as reference points.

Synodic Cycle: The interval of one conjunction to the next of two planets. Synodic cycles also measure the cycle of aspects between two heavenly bodies, especially the interval between two successive transits of the Moon and planets with the Sun. The synodic period for:

Jupiter - Saturn ♃☌♄ = 19.86 years
Saturn - Uranus ♄☌♅ = 45.363 years
Uranus - Neptune ♅☌♆ = 171.403 years
Uranus - Pluto ♅☌♇ = 127.28 years
Neptune - Pluto ♆☌♇ = 493.28 years.

Lunation Cycle: The synodic cycle between the Sun and Moon, creating the moon's phases.

Metonic Cycle: The almost exactly 19 year (235 lunar months) cycle, after which the phases of the Moon recur in the same order and on the same days as in the preceding cycle. That is, the return of a cycle of solar eclipses to a specific degree of the zodiac. The Metonic Cycle is named after the Athenian astronomer Meton.

Sarconic or Saros Cycle: The oldest records describing the sarcos cycle were by Chaldean astrologers around 2,100 BC. Every 18 years 11 days and 8 hours (18.03 years, or 223 lunar months), the Sun/Moon eclipses occur in the same point in the sky. When an eclipse happens on the winter solstice it will be 18.03 years before it occurs again. The ancient Chaldeans call this period *saros* and believed it had magical powers that could cause the end of the world.

D

Day: The measurement of time it takes the Earth to rotate once on its axis. It can be measured as a Sidereal Day, a Solar Day, or a Mean Solar Day.

Davison Relationship Chart: Casting a chart for a locality, date and time halfway between the birth dates, times and places of two people will yield another type of chart useful for describing and understanding their relationship. In other words, you cast a chart using a midpoint of the date, time and geographical location. English astrologer Ronald Davison. developed and made this technique popular.

Decanate or Decan: Each sign can be trisected into three 10 degree segments called *decanates*, or *decans*. The first decan is 0°0'0" to 9°59'59", the second is 10°0'0" to 19°59'59", and the third is 20°0'0" to 29°59'59". The result is the division of the 12 zodiac signs into 36 equal arcs of 10 degree each. These divisions are the first, second and third decans respectively.

One interpretation of the decans is they represent (in a minor way) the signs of the same element. That is, the first decan emphasizes the nature of the sign and element it is in. The second is governed by the following sign of the same element. The third decan is ruled by the last sign of the same element. The planetary ruler of the decan is the same as the sign governing the decan. For example, a Scorpio decan would be ruled by Pluto, a Pisces decan would be ruled by Neptune, etc.

It would take you a long time to analyze the decanates of all the planets. Usually astrologers interpret the decans of the ascendant, Sun and Moon.

Figure 37. Decans

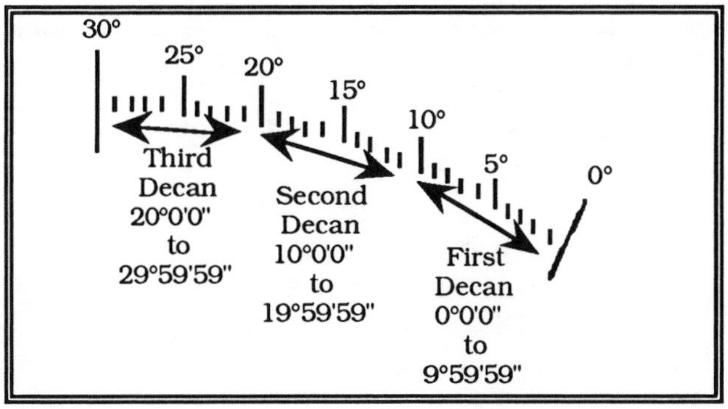

Ancient astrology attached great importance to the decans, especially the early Egyptians, mediaeval European, and Arabian astrologers.

It takes about four sidereal minutes for the MC (and other angles on average) to move 1° of the zodiac belt, so a decanate (10°) moves approximately every 40 minutes.

Declination: The distance of any planetary body (point) north or south of the equator, measured in degrees, minutes and seconds. The measurement of angular distance of a body from the celestial equator. If north of the equator the number is positive (+), if south of the equator the number is negative (-). See Figure 9: The Equator Coordinate System.

Decreasing in Light: When a planet has passed opposite the Sun (opposition) it is decreasing in light. That is, when a faster moving body moves toward a conjunction ☌ from the opposition ☍. Considered by some in astrology as a condition of weakness.

Degree: Symbol °, One thirtieth part of any zodiac sign or the three hundred and sixtieth (1/360) part of any circle.

Derived Charts: The natal chart is the basis for a host of secondary or derived charts. These charts are cast for the particular time an astrological event occurs, for example, when the transiting Sun is at the same point on the zodiac (ecliptic) as the natal Sun.

These various derived charts serve as a method to focus on a particular part of the basic horoscope. As an extension of the basic chart, derived charts tend to add depth and perspective to the study of a person or event. Astrologers use derived charts to supplement information gleaned from the natal chart. Below is a short list of derived charts.

Table 15. Derived Charts

Solar Return
Lunar Return
Lunation Charts
Medical (nodal axis) charts
Planetary Returns
Relocation Charts
Synastry Charts
Composite Charts
Progressed Charts
Harmonic Charts
Ingress Charts
90° Dial Charts
Arc Charts (Directed)

Descendant: The sign and degree that is setting on the western horizon at the time and place of birth, or event. The descendant is always the point opposite the ascendant. On a chart, the descendant is usually on the right of a chart and is the opening cusp of the seventh house, the house of relationship. Early astrologers called the descendant *occidens*. See *Angles, the Four* and corresponding Figure 31: The Four Major Angles in a Horoscope.

Detriment: A planet is in detriment when it is in a sign opposite its rulership (sign). The energy of a planet in detriment is in some sense hampered or repressed from harmonious release. Therefore the effects might be either weak or negative.

Direct motion: This is the forward motion of a planet through the zodiac as viewed from the Earth. It is also one day's motion (in longitude).

Directions: A system of re-calculating a natal chart whereby all positions' points move forward or backward by the same degree of arc. Two of the most commonly used directions are the Solar Arc Directions, and the Naibod Arc Directions. See also the Users Guide under *Directions* for more information.

Diurnal Arc: The measurement of a planet from its rising to its setting, in degrees.

Diurnal Charts: Diurnal is another word for "daily". Quotidians or "diurnals" also refer to charts erected daily at the same GMT as the original birth chart. You literally cast a chart daily.

Diurnal Circle: The apparent path or arc of a celestial body across the sky during the daylight hours.

Diurnal Motion: The apparent motion of a celestial body across the sky from east to west as seen from Earth.

Diurnal Semi-Arc: The path from the rise (of the Sun, planet or point) to the upper meridian and from the upper meridian to set (of the Sun, planet or point). Nocturnal semi-arc is from set to the lower meridian, and from the lower meridian to rise.

Dragon's Head: Symbol ☊. It is the north node of the Moon. The north node is a point in space where the Moon crosses the ecliptic of Earth's orbit on its journey northward. The term "Dragon's Head" was originally *Caput Draconis*, and is from the connection between the Moon and the celestial dragon forces. A dragon was imagined to circle the Earth. One legend is that eclipses happened when the celestial dragon swallowed the Sun, and then regurgitated it. Regarded in astrology as the direction for personal growth or development in a birth chart. Some astrologers ascribe to it a nature similar to Jupiter and Venus. See also *Nodes of the Moon.*

Dragon's Tail: Symbol ☋. The Dragon's Tail is the south node of the Moon (or south node). The Dragon's tail comes from the traditional astrology term, *Cauda Draconis.* The south node represents the place of most comfort or experience in the birth chart. See also *Nodes of the Moon* and *Dragon's Head.*

Dwadeshamsa: A degree analysis system of the horoscope that uses 2 1/2 degree segments of the zodiac. Sometimes called *dwads*. The exact origin of the dwadeshamasas has been lost in history. But dwads are significant in Hindu astrology. There are four systems of determining the dwads The oldest system is from the Chaldeans which combines sign rulerships with numerology. The dwads are significant because each 30° sign can be divided exactly 12 times by 2.5 degrees (30/2.5 = 12). Since the zodiac has 12 signs, this allows for each sign to have a subrulership within the primary sign.

In other words, as with the decans, the sequence of the dwads is according to planetary rulership. Degree analysis uses the concept that each zodiac sign has within it expressions of the other zodiac signs. That is, a sign does not express the same quality throughout its entire 30°. This is not a new idea, and there are also other systems that explore meanings by degree, for example, the *Sabian Symbols*, and the *Chandra Symbols.*

In the Dwadashamsas the meaning of each dwad comes from combining the primary sign with modifying influence of the subsign. For example, the Scorpio dwad of the sign Virgo would have an effect of combining the archetype of Virgo with the influence of Scorpio (i.e. service and healing, discrete transformation, etc.).

There are two methods for determining the subrulership of the dwads, one always uses the sequence of Aries through Pisces, and the second begins with the first dwad equal to sign of the dwad. Further information on the dwads can be found in John Sandbach's books *Degree Analyses: Dwadeshamsas and Deeper Meanings*, and *Degree Analysis Part II: Chandra Symbols in the Horoscope.* Part II contains interpretations of the dwads, and the Chandra Symbols.

E

Earthquakes: *See Geological Changes and Astrology.*

East Point: The east point has several definitions. (1.) The equatorial ascendant as the eastern intersection of the ecliptic with the great circle through the celestial poles and the east and west points of the horizon. (2.) Where the prime vertical and the horizon intersect in the east. (3.) In terms of ecliptic longitude the anti-vertex, is the degree of the ecliptic that is due east of the birth place. This point is commonly (and mistakenly) called by astrologers the eastern point on the horizon, or the symbolic point of sunrise in a horoscope.

Easter: The reason we celebrate Easter on so many different dates is because it is on the first Sunday following the full Moon that occurs on, or after, the spring equinox (about March 20 or 21). The ecclesiastic (calender) definition is different from the standard astronomical definition.

Earth Signs: Taurus ♉, Virgo ♍, and Capricorn ♑.

Eccentric planetary orbits: The orbits of the planets are not circular, but slightly elliptical and the degree of ellipticity is the orbit's eccentricity that varies from 0 (a perfect circle) to 1. In our solar system, the eccentricity of orbits varies from Venus at 0.007 to Pluto at 0.246. The planets Mercury (☿), Pluto (♇ or ♇), and the planetoid Chiron (⚷) have elliptical (egg shaped) orbits and are inclined to the ecliptic. These are explained in greater detail below.

Because *Mercury* is closest to the Sun, its small, eccentric orbit does not pass outside other planets' orbits. From the Earth, Mercury appears to hover around the Sun and is always within 27° ahead of, or behind the Sun in the zodiac. The inclination of orbit to ecliptic for Mercury is 7°0'.

Pluto's eccentric 248.4 year orbit takes it inside Neptune's ♆ orbit for 12 years from November 1983 to November 1995. During this time Pluto is in Scorpio ♏. This is when Pluto is closest to the Sun and Earth. When Pluto is in Taurus ♉, it is furthest away from the Sun. Pluto remains in Taurus for about 36 years. The inclination of orbit to Ecliptic for Pluto is 17°10'.

Chiron's orbit is between Saturn ♄, and Uranus ♅, and eccentrically crosses the orbits of both. Chiron crosses and is outside the orbit of Uranus for about eight years when it is in the constellation of Aries. It crosses and is within the orbit of Saturn for about one year when it is in the constellation of Libra. Much of the symbolism of this newly discovered planet is still being revealed.

Eclipse: The total or partial obstruction from view of one celestial body concealed by another celestial body, or its shadow. Solar and lunar eclipses are the visible result of the Moon and Sun being in alignment with the Earth. An eclipse of the Sun occurs when the Sun's light is partially or totally cut off by the Moon passing in front of it at the new Moon.

The eclipse at the full Moon is the Earth's shadow passing over the Moon. These eclipses are known as "meta-transitions" and can occur only when a new, or full Moon is within 15° of the lunar nodes. Eclipses tend to happen in twos or threes, and can be predicted from the *metonic cycle.* Since ancient times great attention is given to the eclipses and there is much symbolism associated with the event.

There are three kinds of Moon-Sun (Lunar-Solar) eclipses.

1. *Partial eclipse* where the Moon is conjoin the Sun, but the moon's orbit does not take it directly across the center of the Sun.

2. *Annular eclipse* where the Moon is conjoin the Sun, but is at the far point in its orbit around the Earth. Because the Moon is at its farthest point, its image is too small to cover completely the sun's disk shape. Thus a ring of sunlight is visible around the edges of the Moon.

3. *Total eclipse* where the Moon is conjoin with the Sun and at a close enough point in its orbit around the Earth. In this eclipse, the Moon's image is large enough to totally block out all sunlight from the Sun.

Eclipse Rules of Thumb: There are several constants in eclipses that are worthy of note:

- The only time a lunar eclipse occurs is during a full Moon.
- The only time a solar eclipse occurs is during a new Moon.
- Solar eclipses occur at least twice a year, but never more than five times in one year.
- There can at most be four lunar eclipses in a year.
- The most both solar and lunar eclipses can happen within one year is seven times.
- Solar and lunar eclipses occur in pairs within 14 days of each other.
- Total solar eclipses can last for as long as 7 minutes 40 seconds. Annular eclipses can last up to 12 minutes 24 seconds.

- Lunar eclipses can last up to 3 hours 40 minutes, with the period of totality lasting for as long as 1 hour and 40 minutes.
- The *Saros Cycle* repeats every 18 years, 11 days, 8 hours.

Ecliptic: The path of the Sun across the celestial sphere is the ecliptic. It is on this path that eclipses occur. The ecliptic is a great circle on the celestial sphere inclined at an angle of about 23 degrees and 27 minutes to the equator. You can also think of the ecliptic as the plane of the solar system, as seen from Earth.

As seen from the Sun, the ecliptic is the plane that passes through the Sun's center that contains the orbit of Earth and the other planets (except Pluto). All the planets except Pluto move around the Sun in orbits that are in almost the same plane (within about 3°) as the ecliptic, and keeping to the narrow band we call the zodiac, which extends about 8° either side of the ecliptic.

Figure 38. Planets in the Plane of the Ecliptic

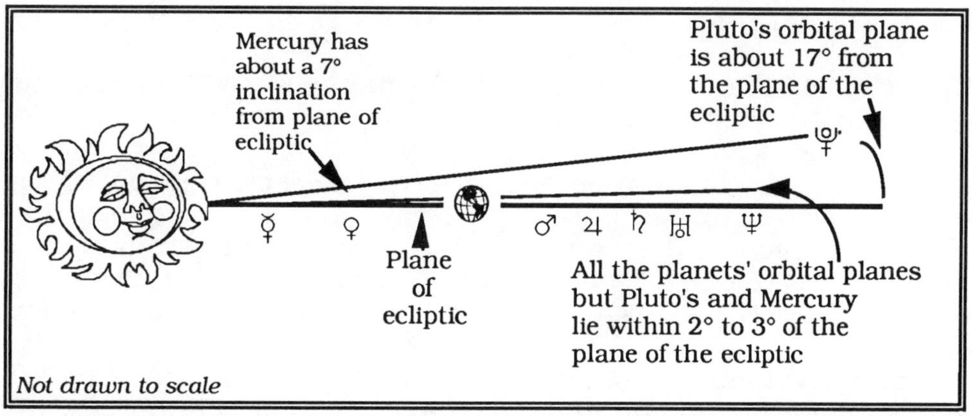

Ecliptic System: A coordinate system that uses the plane of the Ecliptic as the primary reference plane.

Electional Astrology: See *Astrology Specialties.*

Electional chart: A chart cast to help make choices or the selection of the best times for planned activities. Some astrologers call this an "*event chart*". See also *Electional Astrology* under *Astrology Specialties.*

Elements, the four: Fire, earth, air and water, characterize different energies that manifest though the zodiac signs. There are three signs for each element:

Fire	Aries ♈, Leo ♌, Sagittarius ♐
Earth	Taurus ♉, Virgo ♍, Capricorn ♑
Air	Gemini ♊, Libra ♎, Aquarius ♒
Water	Cancer ♋, Scorpio ♏, Pisces ♓

Ellipse: An oval-shaped curve and the orbital shape of most planets.

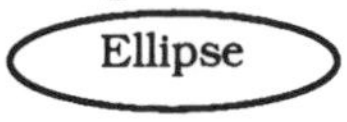

Elongation: The angular eastward or westward distance of a celestial body from the Sun.

Ephemeris: A book of tables, or database, that contains astrological and astronomical data on the motions of the planets. The plural of ephemeris is ephemerides. In casting charts it is essential to find the positions of the planets. An ephemeris is usually published in noon and midnight Greenwich Mean Time (GMT) editions. A computer ephemeris database contains the same information, but the computer can make the adjustments in time, usually automatically, for a given birth or event time.

Equation of Time: The difference in time between the Apparent Solar Time and the Mean Solar Time.

Equator: There are two equators: terrestrial and celestial. *Terrestrial equator* is 0° latitude and is an imaginary great circle around the planet (diameter). The terrestrial equator is perpendicular to the poles of the Earth's rotation. The celestial equator is the Earth's equator projected out into space inclined at a 23° from the ecliptic.

Equator System: A coordinate system whose main plane of reference is the plane of the equator. See Figure 9: *The Equator Coordinate System.*

Equatorial Ascendant: Also called the "east point", this is the eastern intersection of the ecliptic with a great circle through the celestial poles and east and west points of the horizon.

Equinoctial Signs: Aries ♈ and Libra ♎ are the equinoctial signs because these are the signs of the zodiac the Sun enters when the spring and fall equinoxes occur. See Figure 1: *Seasons, Solstices and Equinoxes.*

Equinoxes: At the equinoxes, the Sun crosses the equator, causing sunrise to be at due east and sunset to be due west. There are equal light and dark hours; that is, day and night are of equal length. The spring (vernal) equinox occurs around March 21 when the Sun is at

0° Aries ♈. The autumn (fall) equinox occurs around September 23 when the Sun is at 0° Libra ♎.

The equinoxes happen twice a year and are the midpoints between the solstices. The equinoxes are times of energy-transition. In more technical terms, an equinox happens when the Sun reaches the point of intersection between the ecliptic and equator. See also *Solstices* and the User's Guide (Part 1) under *Tropical Zodiac* for more information.

Eros: Symbol ⚵; an asteroid. Eros was the God of Love and the son of jealous Aphrodite in Greek mythology. Eros fell in love with and became one with Psyche. Eros has the element of sexual passion. In modern psychology Eros has the meaning of self-preserving instincts (as opposed to self-destructive). In Greek, *Eros* means love or desire. The asteroid Eros in a chart might represent that area where the possession or attachment of passion and fantasy elements manifest. It is asteroid number 433. See also *Asteroids*.

Even Signs: The even numbered signs: (2) Taurus ♉, (4) Cancer ♋, (6) Virgo ♍, (8) Scorpio ♏, (10) Capricorn ♑, and (12) Pisces ♓. See also *Feminine Signs*.

Evening Stars: A bright planet visible in the west just after sunset; especially applied to Venus and Jupiter, also called *hesperus* and *vesper*. When Venus and Mercury are at their greatest elongation, as in the Spring, and when they are north of the celestial equator, they are well placed to be visible in the sky just after sunset. Venus especially is very bright and sets about 4 hours after sunset. Mercury sets about 2 hours after sunset. In the Fall these planets are south of the celestial equator and neither is at a very high altitude. In the Fall they set before the Sun. In Winter they rise before the Sun and are morning stars.

Event Charts: When a chart is cast for a specific event it is an event chart. It is sometimes called an *electional chart*.

Exaltation: A term to describe the places of greatest influence of the Sun, Moon and planets. Each planet has a sign where it is exalted. That is, where its energy is pure and elevated to the archetypical level of perfection. It is the complementary sign where the planet's energy is positively expressed. This is the sign of exaltation. In this placement, the planet is operationally strong and most actively creative. When a planet is the sign opposite its exaltation, it is in its *fall* or *dishonor*.

> The Sun ☉, exalted in Aries ♈, is the emanating source where creation originates. Energy begets action.

The Moon ☽, exalted in Taurus ♉, measures the rhythms instinctual in nature and matter. Feelings begin with reactions.

Mental Mercury ☿, exalted in Virgo ♍, gives the facility of discrimination. Intellect begins with analysis.

Venus ♀, exalted in Pisces ♓, enhances the idealism of love and beauty. Love begins with sensitivity.

Mars ♂, the initiator, is exalted in Capricorn ♑. This gives the activating force and determination or it organizes the material world. Activity begins with ambition.

Jupiter ♃, the planet of expansion, is exalted in Cancer ♋ the sign of birth, early growth and nurturing. Expansion begins with growth and accumulation.

Saturn ♄, lord of Karma, compliments the Libran ♎ goal of balanced action and reaction. The Law begins with relationships.

Uranus ♅, the radical transformer, draws power from the depths of Scorpio ♏. Transformation starts with regeneration.

Neptune ♆ originates in the maternal Cancer ♋ who gives rebirth nurturing to transcend into a higher state of being. Transcendence begins with growth.

Pluto ♇ is at home in Pisces ♓ where it effects the transition between old and new cycles. Resurrection begins with dissolution.

F

Feminine Signs: These represent the female energy (yin), and are also the even, earth and water signs. Seasonally, winter is yin and summer is yang. See also *masculine signs*, and *Even Signs*.

Figure 39. The Feminine, Even, Yin Signs

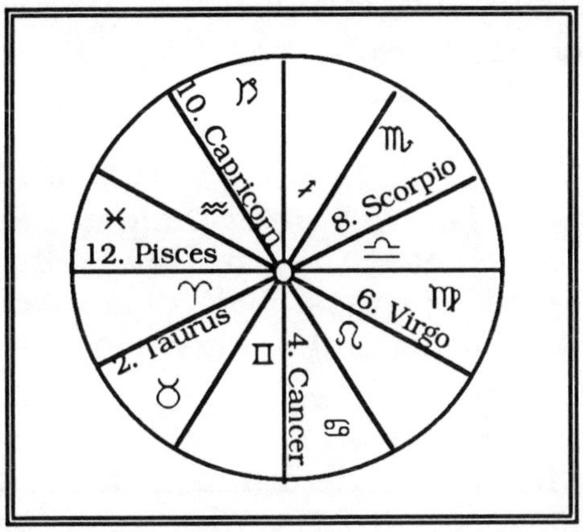

Finger of God: See *Yod.*

Fire Festivals: or Cross Quarters There are eight great festivals of European Paganism and other ancient peoples. These celebrations are on the four festivals of the quarter days, and the four festivals of the cross quarter days.

Figure 40. Quarter and Cross Quarter Festivals

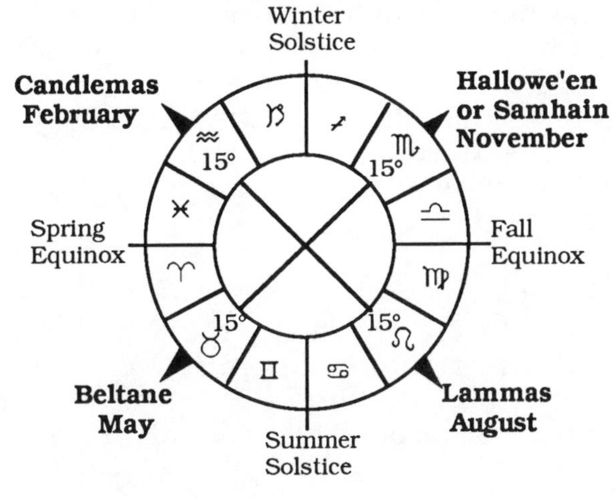

The Fire Festivals or Cross Quarters are in Bold

The Quarter Days are the solstice and equinox celebrations; the Cross Quarter days are the fire festival sabbats considered by the ancients to be the gateways to manifestation and the seasonal shift. The quarter and cross-quarter points are approximately 45° from each other on a horoscope chart shown in Figure 40.

The Fire Festivals are all in the fixed signs that astrologically and traditionally occur around the 2nd to 8th of May (15° ♉), August (15° ♌), November (15° ♏), and February (15° ♒) respectively. Below is a summary of the intent of the four fire festivals of the cross quarters:

> *Beltane*: The spring cross-quarter from 2nd to 7th May when the Sun is at 15° ♉. This is the great fertility festival that celebrates the return of the life force through the uniting of God and Goddess. Beltane is exactly opposite Halloween in the horoscope. May Day is the modern celebration of Beltane.
>
> *Lammas* or *Lugnasadh*: The summer cross-quarter when the August Sun is at 15° ♌. This is the festival of first fruits; a harvest festival that celebrates the bread that can be made from the season's first ripe grain.
>
> *Samhain* or *Halloween*: The Fall cross-quarter when the November Sun is at 15° ♏. This is also the Celtic New Year. This day is when the wall, or veil, between the physical world, and the spirit world is the thinnest. At this time, contact with dead ancestors can take place more easily, so that loved ones can easily join in joyous celebration. In this context, the festival celebrates the concept of eternal life and the transcendence of physical death. This festival also recognizes that the solar light is dying and it is a time for death of the old. Yet the new light is born within and has the promise for rebirth. Halloween is the third and final harvest festival of the year. The other two harvest festivals are (1) Lammas, and (2) the Fall Equinox.
>
> *Candlemas Oimelc* or *Imbolc*: The winter cross-quarter when the Sun is at 15° ♒. This is the Feast of the Waxing (increasing) Light or the winter purification festival that celebrates being, and the first stirring of life beneath the Earth. In modern terms this roughly corresponds to "Groundhog's Day".

In summary, the Fire Festivals renew the sense of living in communion with the natural cycles: being in tune with and celebrating the changes of season and land.

Fire Signs: Aries ♈, Leo ♌ , and Sagittarius ♐ .

First Order Cycle: The duration of time between two consecutive points of conjunction between two planets. With every astrological cycle there is a small difference in the next cycle or conjunction. A

Second Order Cycle is when conjunctions occur in the exact original starting point. For example, Saturn conjoins Neptune twice in 90.73 years (first order cycle). When Saturn conjoins Neptune at the same degree or point as the first conjunction, the second order cycle is completed. In this case, in 26 conjunctions or 1,179.4 years.

First Point: Refers to 0° Aries. From this point longitude is measured along the ecliptic, and right ascension along the celestial equator.

Fixed (fixing) Signs: Taurus ♉, Leo ♌, Scorpio ♏ and Aquarius ♒ are fixed, conservative and resistant to change signs. These signs also have the characteristics of persistence and a resourcefulness that usually makes them reliable. The fixed signs carry through the tone, or theme of the season. There are three modes of signs: cardinal, fixed and mutable.

Fixed positive key words are: consistent, loyal, reliable, traditional, patient, powerful and purposeful.

Fixed negative key words are: opinionated, inflexible, fanatical, habitual, hoarder, and resistant to change.

Focal Planet: A planet by virtue of its position in the chart, or rulership pattern. It is the focus of energy in the chart.

Fortitude: An ancient astrological term referring to the strength or quality possessed by a planet when it is in its own sign, or in the sign of its exaltation.

Fortuna, Pars Fortune: Also known as the *Part of Fortune*. An Arabic Part that is a place in the birth chart where "good things" will happen. Its symbol, ⊗ is close to the glyph used by astrologers to represent the Earth ⊕. This symbol in ancient Chinese is the *Tien*, that signifies "a field", and the Egyptian hieroglyph for territory. See also *Arabic Parts*.

Four-Footed Signs: Sometimes termed the "animal signs", these are Aries (the ram ♈), Taurus (the bull ♉), Leo (the lion ♌), Sagittarius (the half man/horse centaur ♐) and Capricorn (the sea goat ♑). In ancient astrology, a person whose ascendant is in one of these signs was presumed to possess the qualities of that particular animal. For example: "brave as a lion", "strong as a bull", etc.

G

Galactic equator: The great circle of the celestial sphere that lies in the plane bisecting the band of the Milky Way, inclined at an angle of about 62° to the celestial equator.

Galaxy: A large scale aggregate of stars (stellar system), dust, and other parts that have an overall definite structure. The galaxy our solar system is in is the Milky Way.

Galilean Moons: Four of Jupiter's fifteen moons that are visible with a small telescope. Discovered by Galileo in 1610 with the newly invented telescope, the moons are Ganymede, Callisto, Io, and Europa.

Gemini: The third sign in the zodiac, is an air mutable masculine sign ruled by Mercury. The Sun is in this sign from about May 22 to June 21.

The glyph for Gemini ♊ represents a human twin holding hands with the immortal twin. Another interpretation is the twins represent a dual mind, one that sees all sides of a question and jumps with interest to new ideas. The glyph also could represent a swing, and ideas swinging back and forth.

The Geminians view themselves as usually being right and will not change their minds, until asked again at a different time, when they might take a totally different stand. Gemini is the butterfly of the zodiac because they quickly flit from one subject or experience to another. They are good at changing topics quickly, usually speaking more than doing. Gemini is mental, intellectual, and versatile and has a strong need to relate to others. One of Gemini's lessons is to learn to slow down, be patient and listen.

Positive Geminian traits: adaptable, versatile, intellectual, witty, busy, spontaneous, talkative, and eloquent.

Negative Geminian traits: contradictory, restless, two-faced, critical, impatient, superficial, and a gossip.

Geocentric Charts: This is the view of the planets from the Earth and the most common way of expressing the planets' positions in an astrological chart. It is also the perspective of most ephemerides. Geocentric is the perspective of the solar system from the center of the Earth. Heliocentric charts view the planets (including Earth) from the center of the Sun.

In astrology, the Geocentric chart represents an individual or micro view of solar system because it relates all the solar system movements to the Earth itself. The Heliocentric chart provides insights into the macro or greater universal energies and suggests the deeper, profound nature of the individual's relationship to the universal plan.

Astrologers can work simultaneously with both the heliocentric and geocentric charts to obtain complementary insights and enhanced information about an individual or an event. Other systems that can be used are *Mundane Space* and *Local Space*. Thus, each chart can represent a different level and perspective of life. See *Coordinate Systems* in the User's Guide (Part 1).

Geological Changes and Astrology: The idea that positions of the planets have an effect on geological changes is ancient. With available computer and programming technology becoming widespread, more research capability will be available to greater numbers of astrologers. Computers can be used for researching the effects of the cosmos on the physical Earth.

There were increasing Earth changes in the 1980's and will probably be even more in the 1990s. The few brief observations outlined below were gleaned from various sources, of which the primary source is Joseph F. Goodavage's book: *Astrology, the Space Age Science.* An additional reference is in *The Astrology of the Macrocosm* in the chapter written by Diana K. Rosenberg entitled "Stalking the Wild Earthquake".

Uranus
In 1953 Dr. Rudolf Tomascheck studied 134 severe earthquakes and found Uranus was close to the overhead position at the times and places of the major disasters. In five cases out of six, Uranus was directly or almost directly overhead when a major earthquake took place. A statistical check of critical earthquakes projected odds of 10,000 to one against the quakes occurring when Uranus was directly over the stricken areas.

Neptune
The mythology of Neptune suggests that it has much to do with earthquakes and weather. Earthquakes have happened at, or immediately after, conjunctions or oppositions of Uranus, Mars and Neptune. There is also a critical period when Neptune crosses Uranus, especially if in a hard aspect to Mars that can act as the trigger.

Moon
John J. O'Neill, Pulitzer Prize winner, Science Editor of the *NY Herald Tribune* wrote: *"...the Sun and Moon exert maximum forces when they are on a line with the Earth at New and Full Moons, which take place alternatively at 14 day intervals. The Sierra region is more*

sensitive to the New Moon, the San Andreas and other parallel fault regions respond to the Full Moon situation."

To quote from the *1991 Old Farmer's Almanac*, page 30: "*When the Moon "rides high" or "runs low", the date of the high begins the most likely five-day period of earthquakes in the northern hemisphere. The date of running low suggests a similar five day period in the southern hemisphere. The Moon on the equator occurs twice each month. At this time in both hemispheres, there is a two day earthquake period.*"

The Moon riding, or running high literally means the Moon is high in the sky; as it is when in Gemini or Cancer. If the Moon appears to skim along the horizon then it is "running low" and is in Sagittarius or Capricorn in the northern hemisphere.

Sun and Moon Eclipses
An eclipse of the Sun or Moon conjoined with Mercury, might generate an atmosphere of turbulent, variable winds, and storms that could accompany earthquakes.

Equinoxes and Solstices
At the solstices, new forces seem to activate the full length of the great mountain ranges. This strain, plus the forces of the Sun and Moon and the New and Full Moon, provides a most likely situation for the release of an earthquake.

Signs
Sir Isaac Newton experimented with Johannes Kepler's (1571-1630) theory that the new or full Moon in configuration with certain planets that "*take place in the first degrees of Taurus, and especially the Pleiades, will produce earthquakes...*".

In summary, we need more research about the correlations between geological changes and planetary movements. There appear to be links between geological changes and planetary configurations that involve multiple hard aspects (conjunctions, oppositions and squares) of the planets, Sun and Moon in our solar system.

Geographic Coordinates: A way of identifying a precise location on Earth using an imaginary system of lines that grid the globe. These lines are called latitude and longitude. Latitude measures north-south distance from the equator. The *Parallels of Latitude* run east-west, parallel to the equator. *Meridians of Longitude* run along north-south lines and measure the distance east or west of Greenwich. See also *Coordinate Systems* in the User's Guide.

Glyphs: Sigils or symbolic figures that represent the meaning or spirit behind a work. In astrology, glyphs represent archetypical energies.

See *Abbreviations* for the glyphs for planets, signs, asteroids and Uranian planets.

Grand Aspects: Configurations of three or more planets that have specifically defined aspects between them are Grand Aspects. The most common is the *T-square*. Other grand aspects are the *Grand Trine, Grand Cross, and Grand Sextile.* See the individual names of each of these configurations.

Grand Cross: A configuration of at least four planets in a mutual square aspect □ (90° angles) to one another, with two opposite ☍ across the cross. This is more intense than a T-square. Like a T-square, the planets involved are usually of the same mode. Considered a very powerful and challenging pattern, there is tremendous spiritual power in a grand cross if the individual faces and resolves the issues. It is a breakthrough aspect and appears when profound choices must be made and things can change radically.

Figures

41. Grand Cross **42. Grand Sextile** **43. Grand Trine**

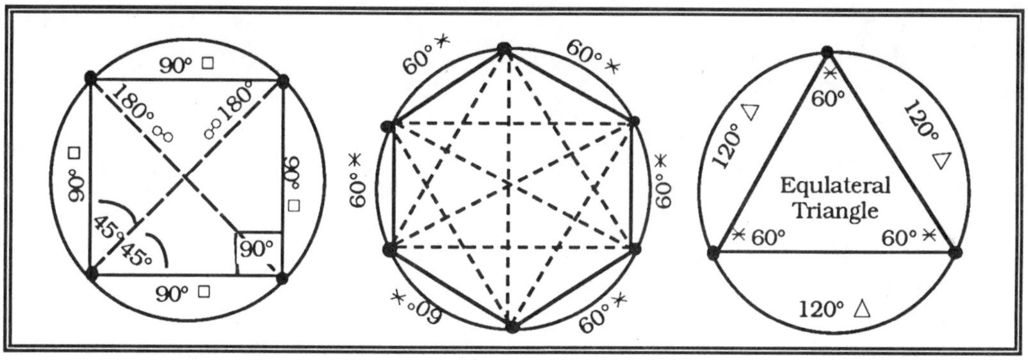

Grand Sextile: A configuration of six planets sextile (✶) 60° to each other. Many individual aspects are at work in this pattern, including many oppositions. A grand sextile can make so much energy flow that it can be purgative and cleansing. This configuration is very rare and extremely powerful. See Figure 42.

Grand Trine: A configuration where three planets form a triangle △ (60° angles) with planets 120° arc apart. This is a very strong, stable and harmonious alignment of planets. The energy flows freely and events seem to happen in a positive way, as if they had always been intended. Considered a very powerful and beneficial pattern.

Graphic Ephemerides: Shows the zodiac positions of the planets on a graphic printout. See the User's Guide under *Graphic Ephemerides* for examples.

Greenwich Mean Time: Mean solar time for the 0° Earth longitude meridian at Greenwich, a borough of London. GMT is the basis of calculating time throughout the world.

Gregorian Calendar: The calendar that superseded the Julian calendar starting in 1583. It is the calendar used throughout most of the world. It was named after its sponsor Pope Gregory XII.

H

Hades: Symbol ♇, one of eight hypothetical planets of Uranian astrology. This trans-neptunian planet deals with the underworld, but it also has to do with antiquity, the ancient past and secrets. Because of life and death dealings, health professionals often have a strongly placed Hades.

Halloween: See Fire Festivals.

Harmonic Chart: A name given to a chart designed to present data according to the system of "Harmonics" developed by John Addey. In this system, zodiacal longitudes are multiplied by the harmonic number. If necessary, you subtract 360 repeatedly to bring the answer back under 360°.

Harmonic Conjunctions: Occurs when a planet pair is conjunct. This can be listed for any harmonic. Mark Pottenger, in the documentation for the CCRS Horoscope program, suggests "the effective orb in the original charts is 10.8 degrees for harmonic 1, 5.4° for harmonic 2, 3.6° for harmonic 3 and so forth."

Harmonics: A branch of astrology based upon statistical methods connected with numerological and wave theory. John Addey found that when he statistically analyzed large numbers of birth data, the planetary and nodal positions exhibited wave-like fluctuations. This could not be accounted for by traditional astrological interpretation. Further research showed that numerical harmonic relationships seemed to apply in various groups of charts. The conclusion was that all whole number divisions (harmonics) of the 360 degree circle might have special implications or meanings to astrological sciences.

Derive the various harmonics by dividing the entire chart circle (360 degrees) by a whole number, such as 360/1, 360/2, 360/3 ...360/N. This is a harmonic series. The aspects, or harmonics, link the energies of one planet or point to another. Astrologers are still researching harmonics and the meaning of each harmonic series. An excellent description of harmonics is in Robert Hand's book: *Horoscope Symbols*. See also *Harmonics* in the User's Guide (Part 1).

Harmonic of Return: This is somewhat new to astrology and is described in detail in the NOVA 2.1 Program documentation by Astrolabe. A return is when a planet or point orbits around and "returns" to its starting position. A return can be calculated for any angle, including conjunctions. That is, a return can be for a square, trine, opposition, or any aspect you want to study.

The following general rules on harmonic returns are from the Nova documentation (Section 7 Pages 5-6).

- A conjunction return has an effect through the entire 360° of the cycle.

- An opposition return has an effect for the second 180° of the cycle.

- A square return has an effect for the second 90° (waxing square) or 90° forth (waning square) of the cycle.

Using the Moon for an example: a conjunction return has an affect for 27+ days. An opposition return has an affect for less than 14 days; a square return for less than 7 days. Keep in mind that an opposition is two squares and a conjunction is four squares. To set up quarti-lunars, which are for less than seven days, you will want to look at the square returns and the opposition and conjunction returns. In other words:

- the first quarti-lunar = conjunction return
- the second quarti-lunar = first square return (waxing square)
- the third quarti-return = opposition return
- the fourth quarti-lunar = second square return (waning square)

Ninety degrees of arc is the fourth harmonic of the circle.

In the table below, the denominator of the fraction identifies the harmonic of the circle. Note that a conjunction (1) represents all harmonics. In using harmonics, what you must specify is the 1/n of 360. If an aspect does not divide evenly into 360, then you have either a multiple of a valid harmonic, or a completely invalid number.

Astrolabe recommends the harmonic number of the return not be very high. This is because higher numbers relate brief time periods and might not be very meaningful. The table below shows the harmonic number and the fraction of the circle that results.

Table 16. Harmonics and Aspects

Aspect	1	2	3	4	5	6	7	8	9	12
Conjunction ☌	1/1	2/2	3/3	4/4	5/5	6/6	7/7	8/8	9/9	12/12
Opposition ☍		1/2		2/4		3/6		4/8		6/12
Quincunx ⚻										5/12
Bi-quintile Q					2/5					
Sesqui-quadrate ⚼								3/8		
Trine △	1/3	2/6							3/9	4/12
Square □				1/4				2/8		3/12
Quintile					1/5					
Sextile ⚹						1/6				2/12
Semi-square or octile ∠								1/8		
Semi-sextile ⚺										1/12

The bottom number (denominator) is the harmonic of the circle

Heliocentric: The view of the positions of planets from the vantage point of the Sun. See also *Geocentric Planets.*

Hidalgo: Symbol ♁. An asteroid. Hidalgo was the lowest Spanish rank of nobility and similar to the title "*don*". The asteroid Hidalgo was discovered in 1920 by Walter Baade. Except Chiron, Hidalgo has the longest orbit of all the asteroids: 13.7 years. Hidalgo's orbital path takes it from slightly inside the orbit of Mars almost to the orbit of Saturn as shown below:

Figure 44. Hidalgo's Orbital Path

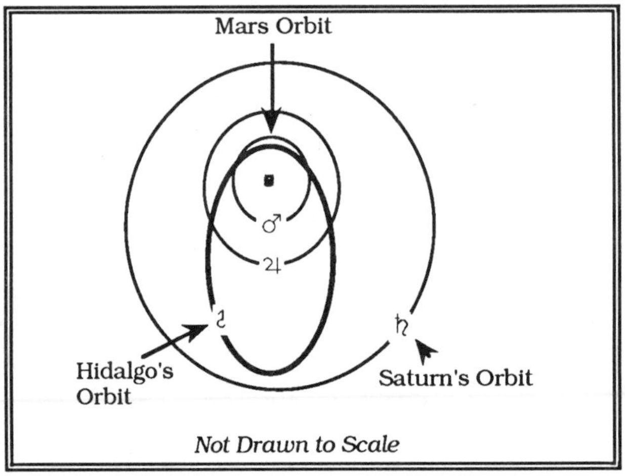

Astrologer Lee Lehman suggests Hidalgo might represent control over people by force of will and rebellion. Therefore Hidalgo could represent the ego directed to control others, or the need to dominate. In this sense, it is a macho asteroid. Its number is 944. Also see *Asteroids* .

Horary Astrology: The branch of astrology that seeks to resolve a question asked at a specific moment. This is one of the predictive, or oracular, branches of astrology. See also *Astrology Specialties.*

Horary Charts: Are cast to answer a question. The time the questions is asked is the time used to cast the chart. See also *Horary Astrology.*

Horizon: The ascendant - descendant line, horizontally drawn across a chart. The apparent intersection of the Earth and sky, as seen by an observer is the "apparent" or "visible" horizon.

Horizon, Celestial or Rational: The great circle of the celestial sphere whose plane is perpendicular to the local vertical and passes through the center of the Earth.

Horizon System: A coordinate system that uses the horizon plane as the primary reference. See *Coordinate Systems* in the User's Guide (Part 1).

Hour Angle: The arc measured westward (clockwise) along the celestial equator. From the observer's point, this measurement is from the celestial meridian to the hour circle passing through a celestial body. See also *Hour Circle.*

Hour Circle: A great circle passing through the poles of the celestial sphere and a celestial body. It intersects the celestial equator at 90° or right angles. The angle between the hour circle through the object and the observer's meridian is the hour angle. See also *Hour Angle.*

Figure 45. Hour Circle and Hour Angle

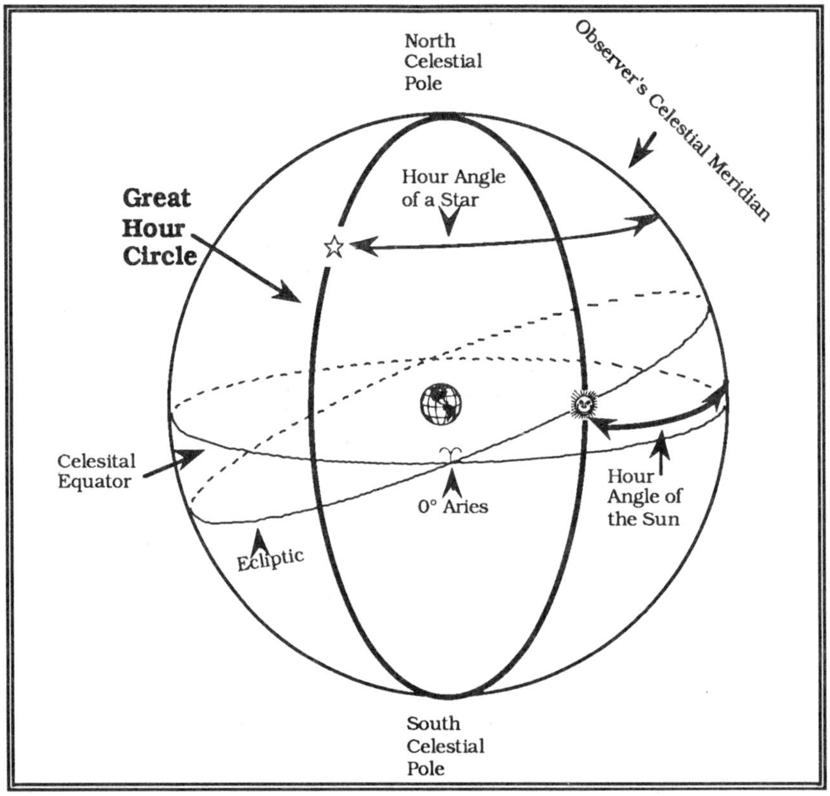

House System: The methodology for the division of a chart into twelve sections is a house system. There are many different systems used to calculate the cusp of each house. The more sophisticated computer programs offer up to 40 different house systems. Three of the most common house systems are Campanus, Koch, and Placidus. For a detailed description of the main house systems, see User's Guide under *House Systems*.

Houses: The houses are twelve divisions of a chart that relate to the zodiac, and symbolically represent different parts in our lives (home, career, associations, etc). Houses indicate where the energy of the planets and signs are experienced in tangible form though human activity on Earth. The houses relate specifically to the Earth's daily rotation on its axis. There is a shift of one house about every 2 hours. You number the houses beginning at the ascendant in a counterclockwise direction.

Figure 46. Sun in the Houses

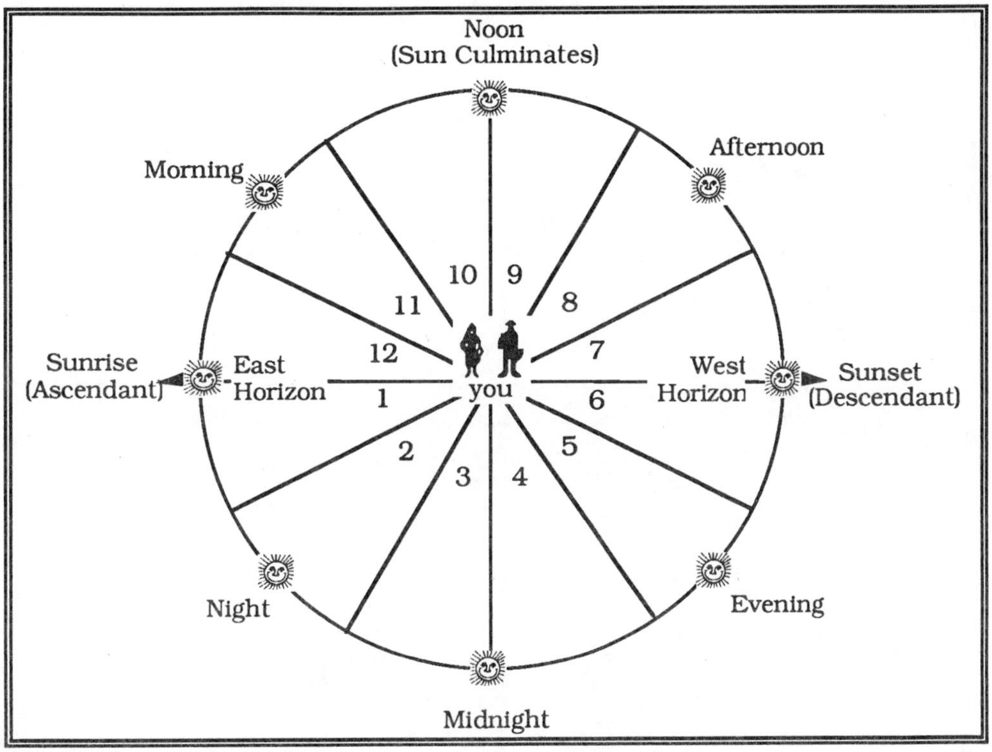

Additionally, the astrological houses symbolically represent fields of experience in a human life. These are the departments of life where the planetary energies translate into action. Like the twelve signs, the houses can represent the cycle of existence, beginning with the birth of self awareness in the first house, and ending with the dissolving of the ego in the twelfth house. Houses can also represent the seasons, or as Dane Rudhyar entitled one of his books, *The Pulse of Life.*

The following figure shows the structure of the twelve houses with the thematic keywords and associated zodiac sign.

Figure 47. The Wheel of the Astrological Houses

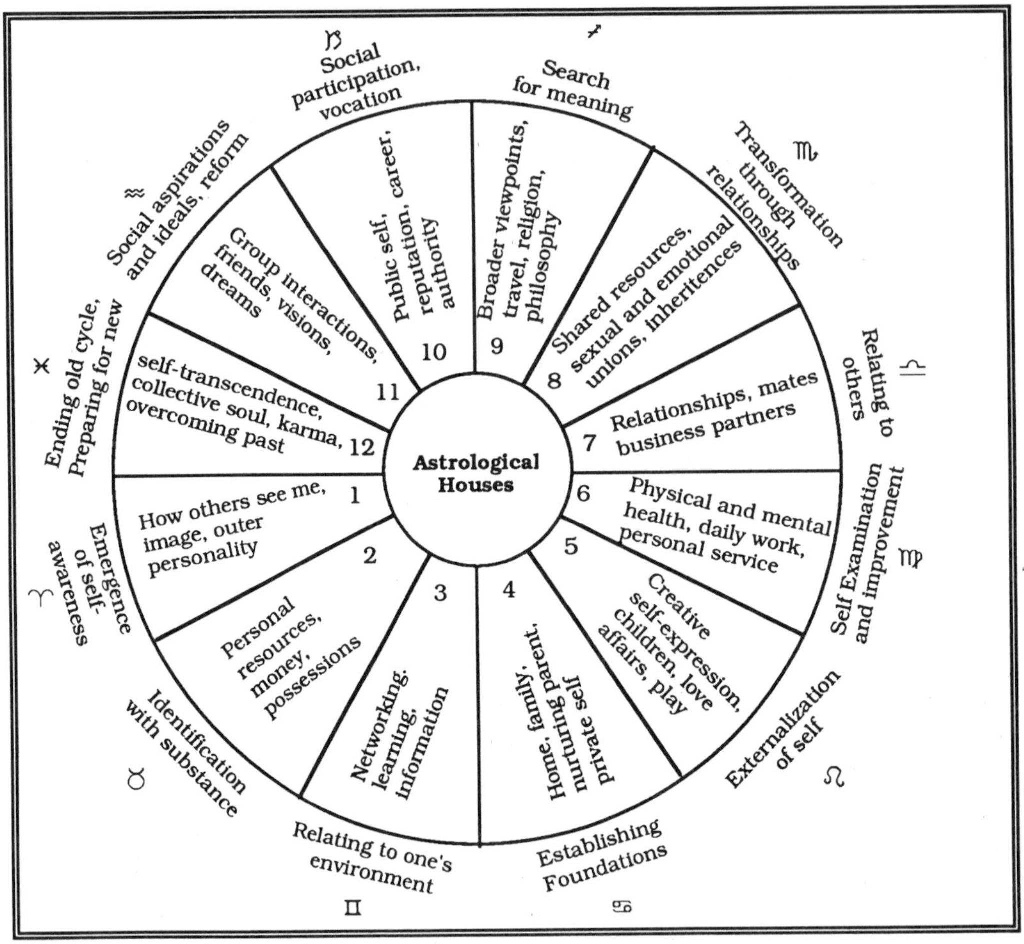

Houses, Kinds: There are three kinds of houses that relate to the three modes of operation, or phases of each season:

Figure 48. Kinds of Houses

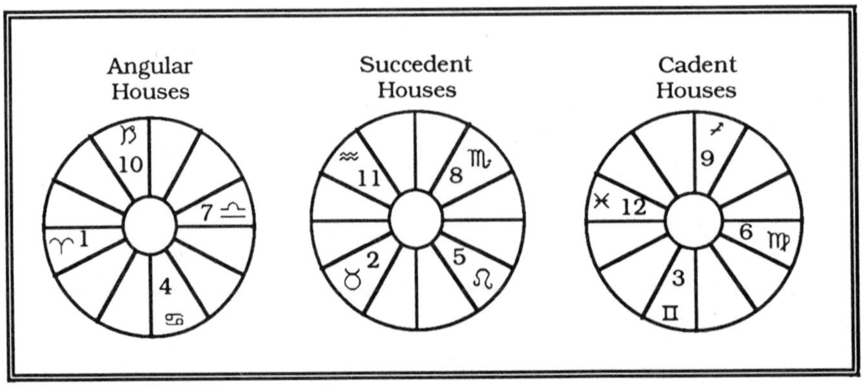

Angular houses (1, 4, 7 and 10) correspond to the cardinal signs (Aries, Cancer, Libra and Capricorn) that represent activity in physical matters.

Succedent Houses (2, 5, 8, and 11) are named because they succeed the angular houses (going clockwise around the chart). They correspond to the fixed or fixing signs (Taurus, Leo, Scorpio and Aquarius). These represent stable qualities that involve inner emotions. Planets in these houses tend to give a strong will and fixed purpose to the individual. The succedent houses are second in strength to the angular houses as places where the planets express their influence.

Cadent Houses (3, 6, 9 and 12) correspond to the mutable signs (Gemini, Virgo, Sagittarius and Pisces). These are very important because they signify faith and belief. They also represent mental expression, variable conditions and communications. Note that "Cadent" means rhythmic beat or motion to and fro. Cadent Houses are where planets exert the weakest effects. From Latin *cadere* "to fall". However, Michel Gauquelin has statistically shown that the maximum significance of a planet occurs in the 15° before the angles, which fall in the cadent houses.

Human or Humane Signs: Gemini ♊, Virgo ♍, Aquarius ♒, and the top half of Sagittarius ♐. The symbols for these signs include human bodies in some form. These signs on the ascendant bestow a humane and kind nature.

Hypothetical Planets: Some astrologers, especially of the Uranian school, maintain that, although no planet has been sighted, there is an observed effect on the orbital behavior of other bodies. This suggests the existence of "hypothetical planets".

Table 17. Hypothetical Planets

Admetos	Kronos	Persephone*
Apollon	La Croix	Polyhymnia*
Cupido*	Lion	Poseidon*
Dido*	Melodia	Transpluto
Hades	Midas*	Vulcan
Hercules	Minos	Vulkanus
Hermes	Moraya	Wemyss-Pluto
Horus*	Osiris*	Zeus
Isis*	Ov	
Jason	Pan*	

* Also asteroid names

These planets or forces exist but have not been discovered by current technology. At least 25 of the hypothetical planets have ephemerides including data on position, revolution and supposed influences. Sometimes some asteroids and hypothetical moons of some planets are among the over 1,000 hypothetical planets. The more referenced hypothetical planets are listed above. Many hypothetical planets bear the same name as asteroids. See also *Uranian Planets*.

I

IC or Imum Coeli: Latin for "lowest part of the skies". The IC is the lowest point in the horoscope and the opening cusp of the fourth house. It is also the north vertical. See also *Angles, the Four* for a diagram.

Icarus: Symbol ∇, an asteroid. The name for the asteroid that passes closest to the Sun. In Greek Mythology, Icarus escaped from Crete on artificial wings made for him by his father. Soaring high, he flew so close to the Sun that the wax used to fasten the wings melted, and he fell into the Aegean Sea.

The asteroid Icarus passes closer to the Sun than any other known asteroid. Only some comets pass closer to the Sun. At its closest point (perihelion), Icarus is only 17 million miles from the Sun, compared with 28.6 million miles for Mercury, the innermost planet. At its aphelion (furthest point from the Sun), Icarus is 183 million miles. Because of its wide orbit, Icarus also passes close to the Earth, as close as 4 million miles in 1949 and 1968. The figure below shows Icarus's orbit.

Figure 49. Icarus Orbital Path

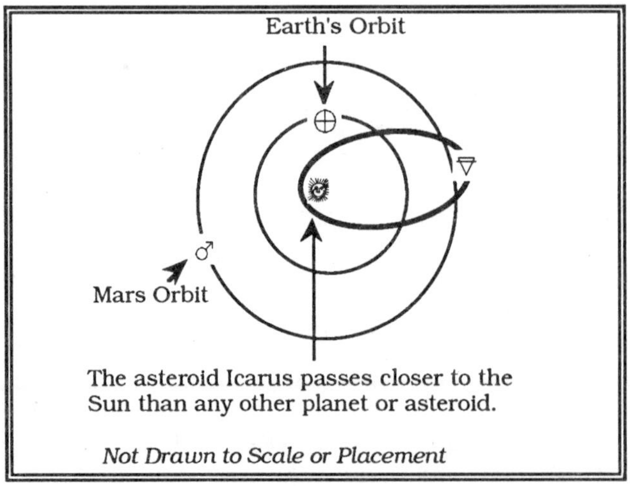

Some astrologers associate Icarus with the hypothetical planet Vulcan. Astrologer J. Lee Lehman suggests Icarus shows that area of life where you are willing to risk everything. Whether it is wise to do so would be a matter of judgement, maturity, and perhaps even evolution. Icarus is asteroid number 1566. See also *Asteroids* .

Ingress: The entry of a planet into a new sign. In astrology, the ingress can indicate a change of theme or direction.

Ingress Chart: In mundane astrology an ingress chart is cast for the moment the Sun enters 0° of each cardinal sign (Aries ♈, Cancer ♋, Libra ♎ and Capricorn ♑). This also correlates to the solstices and equinoxes. According to astrologer Judy Johns, the ingress chart is the primary tool for political astrology, and can be used in combination with the natal chart for the nation (the date a nation was founded), and the natal chart of the leader. More details of ingress charts can be found in *The Astrology of the Macrocosm: New Directions in Mundane Astrology.*

Inclination (of an orbit): The angle between the ecliptic and the plane of an orbit. These vary from 0° 46' (Uranus) to 7° (Mercury), while Pluto is 17° 10'. See Figure 38: Planets in the Plane of the Ecliptic.

Inferior Planets: Not referring to quality, but to those planets that have an orbit closer to the Sun than the Earth. Specifically, the inferior planets are Mercury ☿ and Venus ♀.

Infortunes planets: An obsolete term applied to Mars and Saturn. It means malefic.

Intercepted signs: Signs that do not cross any house cusps are intercepted. Intercepted signs occur in pairs opposite one another. These occur more often in charts cast for locations close to the poles, or when a solstitial sign is rising (Capricorn ♑ and Cancer ♋).

Figure 50. Intercepted Signs

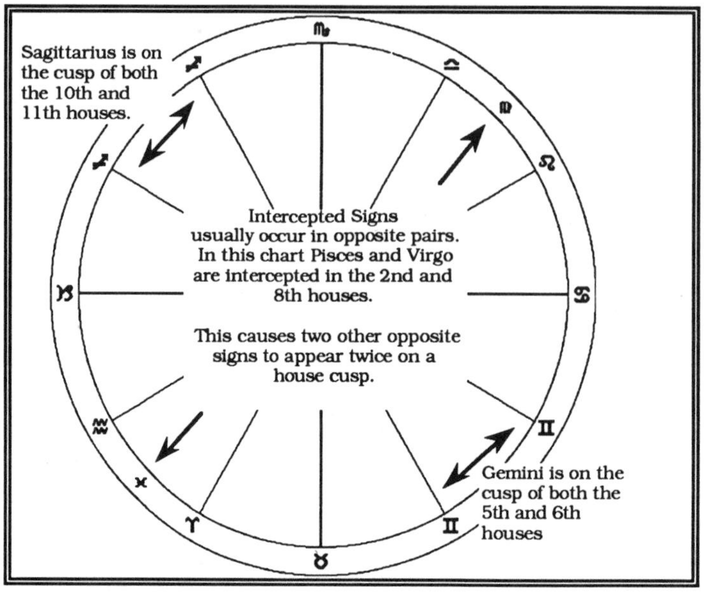

Sagittarius is on the cusp of both the 10th and 11th houses.
Intercepted Signs usually occur in opposite pairs. In this chart Pisces and Virgo are intercepted in the 2nd and 8th houses.
This causes two other opposite signs to appear twice on a house cusp.
Gemini is on the cusp of both the 5th and 6th houses

International Date Line: The 180th meridian of longitude (+ or - degrees in certain places) where the date officially changes.

International Society for Astrological Research: ISAR is an organization dedicated to astrological research. One research project is the development and maintenance of the Rodden/ISAR Database (RID). This database contains over 12,500 sets of birth data and events. Specific fields include vocational categories, family members, and other items of interest in astrological research.

Another ISAR research project began in 1985 by Scott Vail. This project led to the 1986 book *Tables for Aspect Research*, that gives decade by decade totals of angular separations of planets for this century. The book complements the program *Frequencies for Aspect Research (FAR)*, which extends the time range beyond the century limit of the book and allows more flexibility in picking time periods. Direct inquires about ISAR and FAR to Mark Pottenger at 838 5th Avenue, Los Angeles, California 90005, USA.

Ishtar: An ancient Assyrio-Babylonia goddess who was the daughter of the Moon God, Sin. She was the goddess of love, ruling over fertility. Her myth parallels Aphrodite; roughly corresponding to the present day Venus.

J

Joined in or to: Showing that a body is within the orb of any aspect to any other body, especially refers to a conjunction.

Judicial Astrology: See *Astrology Specialties.*

Johndro Locality Chart: Created by astrologer Johndro, this chart uses the locality of the birth place to determine the angles. Also called "locality angles".

Juno: Symbol ⚵, one of four asteroids most used in astrology. Juno represents the wife or divine consort. Juno was the wife of Jupiter and patroness of marriage and the well-being of women. She is also the Greek goddess, Hera. Juno was the third asteroid discovered.

Astrological archetype of Juno shows the need for personal relationships and our capacity to make commitments to those relationships. See also *Asteroids.*

Jupiter: The fifth planet from the Sun, Jupiter is the largest and most massive in the solar system, with a diameter approximately 11 times that of Earth. Its orbit is between Mars and Saturn. Jupiter takes about 12 years to circle the Sun, and has 16 moons.

In Roman mythology, Jupiter was the supreme god patron of the Roman State. He also was the Greek god Zeus.

Jupiter rules Sagittarius, and in older astrology, Pisces. It is exalted in Cancer, its detriment is in Gemini and its fall is in Capricorn.

The glyph for Jupiter ♃ represents a semi-circle of spirituality that is lifting the heavy cross of the material world. Whereas the glyph for Mars is pointedly in one direction ♂, the glyph for Jupiter is expanding in many directions, up, down, sideways and across. It signifies the part of you that needs to reach out and overcome limitations. Notice that the glyph for Jupiter ♃ is almost the opposite of Saturn ♄; just as the planets, in many ways, represent opposite energies.

Astrologically, Jupiter is expansive, and expresses itself on the physical plane through activities demanding thought, speculation, growth and study. The Jupiter archetype has a philosophical outlook and deals with advanced studies such as religion, law, languages, and publications. Jupiter types delight in a rich and varied life that includes travel or exploration. As a jovial planet, Jupiter instills faith and hope within the human soul. Throughout time Jupiter has been "*the Great Benefic*", and represents the bringer of good fortune, abundance and prosperity; it is the "Santa Claus" of the planets.

Positive Jupiter traits: benevolent, generous, optimistic, jovial, sense of justice and compassion, visionary, and philosophical.

Negative Jupiter traits: excessive, exaggerative, misjudging, pompous, wasteful, self-indulgent, unbalanced beliefs, and blindly optimistic, and insensitive to other's needs.

K

Kite: If in a grand trine, there is a another planet that forms two sextile ⚹ aspects to the remaining planets, with an opposition ☍ to one the of planets, then a kite exists. This is shown in the figure below. A kite has a flowing energy, channeled through the opposition toward a specific task. The planet at the bottom of the kite often has a focal role.

Figure 51. Kite

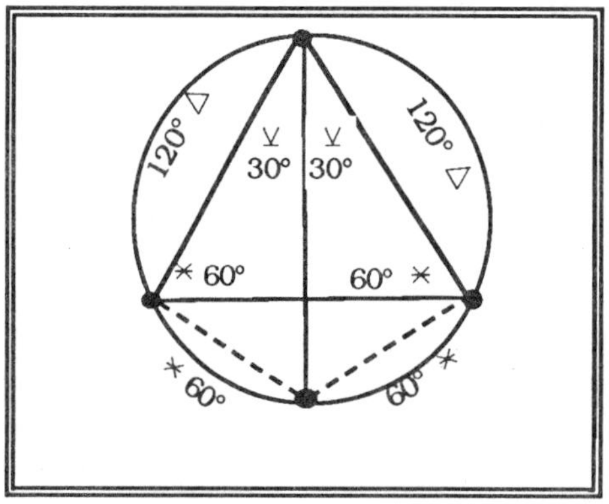

Kinetic Solar Return: A chart cast for the date and time the transiting Sun returns to the position of the secondary progressed Sun. A kinetic lunar return is when the transiting Moon returns to the position of the secondary progressed Moon.

Kronos: Symbol ♆, one of eight hypothetical planets of Uranian astrology. Kronos is linked with authority. Astrologer Maria Kay Simms proposes that Kronos is everything that is above average, or is physically high, such as airplanes or mountains.

L

Lammas: See *Fire Festivals.*

Latitude: The position or distance of any place that is north or south of the Earth's Equator. The angular distance north or south of the equator, measured in degrees along a meridian usually on a map or globe. Also known as the terrestrial latitude. Derived from Latin, meaning wide or broad. See Figure 4: Earth Coordinates: Latitude and Longitude.

Latitude, Celestial: The angular or perpendicular distance north or south of the ecliptic.

Leo: Leo is the fifth zodiac sign. It is a masculine, fire, fixed sign ruled by the Sun. The Sun is in Leo from about July 23 to August 22.

Leo's glyph ♌ could represent the heart with its two valves, or the tail of a lion. Leo is king, the boss, the leader. Leo knows how to organize everyone's life better than they do. Once understood, there will be little trouble with Leo. Leo loves being the center of attention, preferably on stage. Leo can be interfering, intolerant and pompous. As with all fire signs there is a strong element of selfishness, but the Leonine is rarely insensitive to the needs of others. They also can be affectionate, enthusiastic, cheerful and optimistic. Leo can literally "brings sunshine" into other people's lives.

Positive Leonine traits: self-expressive, creative, dignified, inspirational, magnanimous, theatrical, hospitable and a showman.

Negative Leonine traits: selfish, vain, demanding, ostentatious, snobbish and power-mad.

Libra: The seventh sign of the zodiac, Libra is a masculine, air, cardinal sign ruled by Venus. 0° Libra heralds the fall equinox around September 23, and the Sun leaves Libra approximately 22 October.

The glyph for Libra ♎ can symbolize a pair of scales, as balance is a key Libra trait. It also could represent a bridge. Another interpretation comes from an Egyptian hieroglyphic that represents the setting Sun. An appropriate image for the sign associated with the descendant in a natural horoscope (a chart with 0° Aries as the ascendant).

Librans have a natural charm and enjoy being with people. Libra is such a social sign that they sometimes find it difficult to be alone. They have a need to share their lives and "love to be in love". Libra is very romantic and sentimental. Librans tend to want peace at any price, and have a hard time remaining emotionally stable if there is discord or conflict around them. Sometimes, wanting a natural resolution, Librans will put off any action waiting to "see what happens." Some might interpret this as lazy.

Positive Libran traits: diplomacy, cooperative, idealistic, gregarious, charming, romantic, the peace maker.

Negative Libran traits: lazy, indecisive, dependent, insincere, frivolous, flirtatious, gullible and resentful.

Libration: An astronomy term indicating the irregularities of the Moon's motions on its axis.

Lights or Luminaries: Generic terms often used for the Sun ☉ and Moon ☽ to distinguish them from the planets.

Light Year: The distance light particles travel in one year of Earth time. This is 5.88 x 10 to the twelfth miles, 63,280 astronomical units, or 9.46 x 10 to the twelfth kilometers. Light travels at a speed of about 186,000 miles per second.

Lilith: Symbol ⚸, an asteroid. According to an ancient Semitic legend, Lilith is an evil feminine spirit or demon alleged to haunt lonely, deserted places. In Hebrew folklore Lilith was the first wife of Adam believed to have been in existence before the creation of Eve. She was expelled from Eden and the more docile and subservient Eve was created from Adam's rib.

Lilith in Jungian terms represents the "Feminine Shadow". She represents independence and autonomy, the subconscious issues of self that should be dealt with on the conscious level. Perhaps she represents areas where the irrational ego comes to light though the rational consciousness and the acceptance of self and self love. Lilith is asteroid number 1,181. Also see *Asteroids* .

Longitude, Celestial: The distance of a body from 0° Aries ♈ as measured along the ecliptic toward the east (counter clockwise). It is expressed as degrees and minutes and seconds, or in a sign's degrees and minutes. See Figure 10: The Ecliptic Coordinate System.

Longitude: The position and distance of any place either east or west of the Prime Meridian at Greenwich. Also called terrestrial longitude. Expressed in degrees, or in terms of hours, minutes and seconds.

Lugnasadh: See *Fire Festivals.*

Lunar Month: There are different ways to measure a lunar month. The average time between successive new or full Moons, equal to 29 days, 12 hours and 44 minutes (29.5306 days). This is also the "synodic month". Other ways to measure a lunar month are:

- The tropical lunar month (equinox to equinox) is 27.3216 days.
- The sidereal lunar month (fixed star to fixed star) is 27.3217 days.
- The anomalistic lunar month (perigee to perigee) is 27.5546 days,
- The draconic lunar month (node to node) is 27.2122 days.

Lunar Return: Every month the transiting Moon passes over the natal Moon in the birth chart. This monthly transit is the Lunar Return and is symbolically shown as ☽ ☌ ☽. Since there are 13 lunar months in a calendar year, the Moon returns to its natal position 13 times per year. Casting a chart for the moment of this occurrence yields the lunar return chart which can be useful in understanding feelings and emotions based outlook on life; in effect it is an emotions forecast for that month.

Lunation: The time elapsing from a new Moon to the next new Moon, averaging 29 days, 12 hours, and 44 minutes. Sometimes used as a synonym for the new Moon. Technically, it is the precise moment the Moon is conjoin the Sun. This is also a Syzygy. Some astrologer's believe the affect of the new Moon falling upon sensitive points in a chart has significance for events for the forthcoming month.

Lune: A portion of the sphere's surface contained within two semi-circles ☽. Lunes also describe the moon shaped divisions that define the houses on a sphere. *Lune* is the French word for "Moon".

M

Mars: The fourth planet from the Sun, Mars is the first "superior" planet because it's orbit is outside (beyond) the orbit of Earth. Mars takes about 1.88 sidereal years to travel around the Sun, and remains in each zodiac sign just under two months. Mars has two moons, Phobos and Deimos.

Astrologically, Mars rules Aries, is exalted in Capricorn, in its detriment in Libra and has its fall in Cancer.

In Roman mythology, Mars was the God of War, identified with the Greek god, Aries. The glyph ♂ could represent a shield and spear. Another view is the symbol ♂ represents the masculine phallic nature and an erect penis. An old and not often used glyph for Mars is ⚴, which is the reverse of Venus ♀. In modern scientific notation, the symbol of Mars represents the male.

Mars represents the physical energy in a chart; the planet bestows great energy. It is the masculine influence in both sexes. Mars is how you assert yourself and defend your ego. A strong Martian type usually finds expression through the physical, and activities that demand the physical exertion of energy. Mars rules all forms of physical and manual labor including building, construction, athletics. All work involving iron and steel belongs to Mars, including sharp tools and weapons of war. Mars is the warrior of the planets.

Positive Martian traits: courageous, assertive, initiative, enterprising, decisive, freedom-loving, a pioneer.

Negative Martian traits: aggressive, violent, selfish, coarse, irate, brutal, rude, selfish, boisterous, lacking forethought or planning.

Masculine Signs: These signs represent male energy (yang) and are the odd numbered signs: (1) Aries ♈, (3) Gemini ♊, (5) Leo ♌, (7) Libra ♎, (9) Sagittarius ♐, and (11) Aquarius ♒. These signs are fire and air signs. See also *Feminine Signs.*

Figure 52. Masculine, Odd, Positive Signs

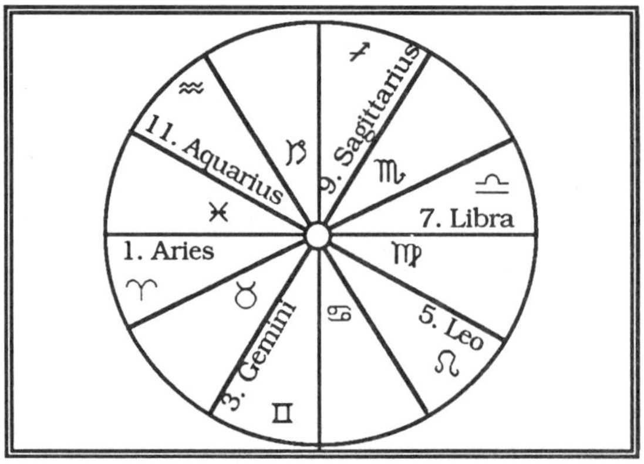

Mean Solar Day: The time between two successive transits (returns) of the mean Sun. Our standard 24 hour day, measured from midnight to midnight. Also called "Civil Day".

Mean Sun: The Sun is our timekeeper, and hypothetically defined as moving at a uniform speed along the celestial equator so that it completes its orbit in the same period as the apparent Sun. Used to compute the mean solar day, and mean time.

Mean time: Time measured giving equal 24 hour days throughout the year. Also called "civil time", and "mean solar time". The Mean Sun is a measurement of time.

Medical Astrology: See *Astrology Specialties.*

Medium Coeli: Latin for "middle of the skies", it is also the MC and midheaven. The highest point in the chart is the intersection of the ecliptic and meridian directly overhead at the time of birth. This is the cusp of the 10th house. It is sometimes wrongly called the "zenith" or grossly applied to the whole of the 10th house. Technically, these points do not always correspond. Another term is the south vertical.

The midheaven archetypically represents obligations, duties, social standing and acknowledgement from others; one's role in the social contract. Other MC phrases and key words include fitting in, being seen, rules, authority and maturity. Planets forming an aspect with the midheaven enhance or inhibit the type and choice of profession, public standing, and the ability to make a contribution to society. See also *Angles, the Four* for a diagram.

Mercury: Mercury ☿ is the smallest of the inner planets and the one nearest to the Sun. Pluto is the smallest of all our solar system planets. Mercury is always within 28° of the Sun and has no satellites. Its diameter is less than half of Earth. Mercury and Venus are inferior planets.

Mythologically, Mercury is the Greek god Hermes, serving as a messenger to the other gods and presiding over commerce, travel and thievery. He often carries the *caduceus*, a staff with two snakes intertwined around a rod, which is a symbol of the power of knowledge. Besides being a messenger, Hermes was a skilled orator, writer and teacher.

Mercury rules over Gemini, and traditionally, Virgo. Mercury is in its detriment in Sagittarius. There is some debate whether Mercury is exalted in Aquarius or Virgo, and if its fall is in Pisces or Leo. It rules the nervous system.

The glyph for Mercury ☿, the messenger of the gods with his winged helmet, can be interpreted different ways. The union of the circle, crescent and cross could be interpreted as symbolic of Mercury's ability to bring things together and unify. Its upper crescent could be thought of as antennae, for air communications.

Mercury relates to the intellect, co-ordination, local transportation, computers and details, day-to-day problems. Profound metaphysical and philosophical thought is the domain of Jupiter.

Positive Mercurial traits: communicative, intelligent, rational, clever, learning, logical, Jack-of-all-trades.

Negative Mercurial traits: over intellectual, restless, too talkative, gossip, cunning, critical, unfocused, cynical, hyper.

Mercury Hour: The *Mercury Hour* is a quarterly magazine written by and for astrologers. Its purpose is to provide an open channel of communication for astrologers worldwide. This astrological magazine is unique because it consists primarily of correspondence between and among astrologers who discuss, challenge, review, teach and learn from each other on anything and everything astrological. It has no organizational affiliation and has survived the test of time being in circulation for almost 20 years. Each issue is about 70 pages. For more information contact Edith Custer at 3509 Waterlick Road, C-7, Lynchburg, Virginia, USA, 24502, phone: (804) 237-4011.

Meridian, Celestial: An imaginary line that passes through the center of the Earth from the point directly overhead (zenith) to a point below the Earth (nadir). In astronomy, the meridian is a great circle on the celestial sphere that passes through the poles of the horizon (the top zenith and the bottom nadir). It corresponds to the terrestrial longitude.

Meteorological or Natural Astrology: Terms that denote both astronomy and astro-meteorology (meteorological astrology). See *Astrology Specialities*.

Metonic Cycle: See *Cycles*.

Midheaven: The uppermost point in a chart. Also see *Medium Coeli*, and *Angles, the Four* for a diagram.

Midpoint: The degree halfway between any two planets. Some astrologers believe the midpoint is where the combined energy of the two plants is the strongest. Sometimes the midpoint will form a strong aspect to another planet that can give underlying meaning to a chart or situation. An example of how to calculate a midpoint between two planets is below.

Assume A's Sun is at 25° 47' Taurus ♉, and B's Sun is at 16° 19' Scorpio ♏. The steps in how to calculate a midpoint are as follows:

Step 1. Change the longitude of each pair of points from the zodiac notation to a 360° circle. To do this, count all chart positions from 0° Aries, not from 0° of their signs. For each sign, add the number of degrees given below:

Table 18. Changing Signs to Degrees (of Arc)

Aries ♈	0°	Libra ♎	180°
Taurus ♉	30°	Scorpio ♏	210°
Gemini ♊	60°	Sagittarius ♐	240°
Cancer ♋	90°	Capricorn ♑	270°
Leo ♌	120°	Aquarius ♒	300°
Virgo ♍	150°	Pisces ♓	330°

A's Sun	**B's Sun**
25° ♉ 47' + 30° = 55° 47'	16° ♏ 19' + 210° = 226° 19'

Step 2. Add the longitudes of each pair of planets or points. Using the two Suns above you get:

55°47' + 226° 19' = 281° 66' divided by 2 = 140.5° 33' converted to 141° 3'.

Step 3. Convert the longitude notation back to the sign notation.
141° 3' - 120° (for Leo) = 21° ♌ 3' as the midpoint for the couples composite Sun.

Do the same procedure for each pair of planets and other pairs of points in the chart, including the nodes, and ascendant. Only calculate the midpoint of each pair of the same planets or points. Two midpoints are possible. Usually astrologers use the nearer (smaller) midpoint. For example, the midpoint between 15° ♒ Aquarius and 15° ♈ (Aries) is 15° ♓ (Pisces), not 15° ♍ (Virgo).

Minor Planet: The asteroids are sometimes called minor planets or planetoids. See also *Asteroids.*

Modern Planets: Planets discovered since the development of advanced telescopes are the modern planets. These are Uranus (♅), Neptune (♆) and Pluto (♇ or ♇). Some astrologers also include the asteroids as modern planets. Early astrologers used only the seven visible planets.

Modes, the three: Sometimes called the *quadruplicities*, because there are four signs within each mode. The modes represent the three basic qualities of life. See also *Houses, types.*

Cardinal Signs (creation) that initiate and set the tone for a season. Aries ♈, Cancer ♋, Libra ♎, and Capricorn ♑.

Fixed or Fixing Signs (preservation) that carry through the purpose of a season, Taurus ♉, Leo ♌, Scorpio ♏, and Aquarius ♒.

Mutable Signs (endings, completion) that conclude and assimilate a season. Gemini ♊, Virgo ♍, Sagittarius ♐, and Pisces ♓.

Moon: See also *Satellite.* The natural satellite of the Earth, it is visible by the reflection of sunlight. Astrologers often call the Moon a *light, luminary.*

Mythologically, the persona of the Moon is the Goddess in three changing forms: Artemis the new Moon, Selene the full Moon, and Hecate the dark Moon.

Next to the Sun, the Moon is the most important body in the birth chart. The Moon rules over the sign of Cancer, is exalted in Taurus and has its fall in Scorpio. The metal of the Moon is silver, but some astrologers also link it with aluminum. The Moon does not have retrograde direction.

The glyph ☽, a crescent moon or radar dish, represents the part that reflects sunlight or other abstract energy. But even more important is the part of the Moon that remains in darkness. This is the part not seen, including the subconscious and hidden aspects.

In a birth chart the Moon represents the imaginative, reflective characteristics, and is linked with the subconscious and instinctive behavior. It also represents motherhood, home, family, ancestors, memory and the masses. Characteristics inherited from past generations are related to the Moon and its position.

Positive Lunar traits: nurturing, receptive, providing, protective, sensitive, intuitive, patient, imaginative, maternal, and good memory.

Negative Lunar traits: over-emotional, insecure, easily hurt, fearful, worried, moody, clannish, changeable, unreliable and gullible.

Moonrise and Moonset: The Moon rises and sets at a different time every day. This is because we use a calendar based upon a solar day, not a lunar day. Moonrise and Moonset are about one hour later on each succeeding day, but this varies by latitude. In the northern latitudes above 60° there are many days when the Moon does not set at all, and others when the Moon does not rise at all.

The new Moon ● always rises with the sunrise in the east to begin a new lunar month. The Sun usually obscures the new Moon as it rises, but a few days after the new Moon, it can often be seen as a thin crescent setting in the west at sunset.

The first quarter Moon is increasing in light (waxing) and always rises about noon in the east approximately seven days after the new Moon. It looks like a pale half-moon ◐. The full Moon ○ always rises in the east at sunset approximately 14 days after the new moon. The full Moon shines throughout the night. The third or last quarter Moon always rises about midnight and is a half Moon ◑.

The waxing or increasing moon can be remembered by the "right-hand Moon" ◐. The curve of the right hand has index finger and thumb following the curve of the increasing crescent. Similarly, the waning or decreasing Moon, can be remembered as the "left-hand Moon" ◑. The instant of Moonrise or Moonset is when the upper crest of the Moon is exactly even with the horizon.

Morning Star: Any planet visible in the east, just before sunrise. This can include Jupiter ♃, Mars ♂, Saturn ♄, Mercury ☿ and especially Venus ♀, depending on the time of year. See also *Evening Star.*

Mundane or Judicial Astrology: This branch of astrology studies countries and populations. Mundane astrologers believe that nations and their people go through a similar birth-life-death cycle and individual. Mundane astrology can put into context wars, economic changes and social trends. See also *Astrology Specialties.*

Mundane Position: The mundane position shows which planets are above and which are below the Earth's horizon at any one time.

Mundoscope: A chart that places the planets along the prime vertical for a given time. The time can be the ingress of the Sun or Moon into a certain sidereal sign. Astrologer Fagan used this type of chart in his research on ancient sidereal astrology. It is rarely used today.

Muses: The muses were the daughters of Mnemosyne (Goddess of Memory) and Zeus (god of the heavens). There were nine muses all relating to some form of art or field of knowledge. The muses are viewed as very inspiring. Asteroids are named after the nine muses. The muses and the asteroid numbers are:

Table 19. Muses and Asteroids

Muse	Subject	Asteroid Number
Calliope (Kalliope)	Epic Poetry	22
Clio (Klio)	History	84
Erato	Lyric and poetry	62
Euterpe	Song and Music	27
Melpomene	Tragedy	18
Polyhymnia	Sacred Song	33
Terpsichore	Dancing	81
Thalia	Comedy	23
Urania	Astronomy/Astrology	30

Also see *Asteroids* and the specific Muse name for more information.

Music and Astrology: In 1766 a German mathematician Johann D. Titius (1729-1726) observed that all the planets had orbits that became progressively greater by a ratio of 2 to 1 as their distance increased from the Sun. In other words, the Earth is twice as far from Mercury's orbit as Venus. Mars is twice as far as Earth, etc. In music, an octave is the interval of eight diatonic degrees between two tones. One tone has twice as many vibrations per seconds as the other. The ratio of 2:1 is the octave. Do the planets form a set of octaves? There is evidence they do.

When Voyager 2 was close to Saturn it recorded noises (frequencies) of the magnetosphere. Voyager sent this information back to Earth. When this data was played quickly through a synthesizer, a kind of melody could be heard. If the planets do "sing" to each other then their physical characteristics such as orbit, distance and speed might be important in harmonic results.

Johann Elert Bode (1747-1826), a German astronomer drew attention to Titius' discovery of the 2:1 ratio of the distances of planets from the Sun. This became known as Bode's Law. But, according to this Law, there was a gap between Mars and Jupiter. In 1801, Guiseppe Piazzi discovered Ceres, a planetoid whose orbit was almost exactly where Bode's Law predicted a planet should be. Astronomers discovered more planetoids orbiting between Mars and Jupiter. Today over 10,000 have been identified. This is the asteroid belt believed to be the remains of a destroyed planet. The discovery of Uranus, Neptune and Pluto showed their mean orbits were close to the exact distances required to complete two further octaves. Neptune is halfway between Uranus and Pluto thus filling the half octave. The table below shows the close relationship of Bode's Law and the planets' orbits.

Table 20. Bode's Law and Planetary Orbits

Planet	Perfect Octaves (Units of distance from Mercury)	Mean Orbits (Actual units of distance from Mercury)	Diatonic Scale
Mercury	0	0	do
Venus	1	1.1	re
Earth	2	2	mi
Mars	4	3.7	fa
Asteroid Belt	8	about 8	so
Jupiter	16	16	la
Saturn	32	30.5	ti
Uranus	64	62.6	do
Neptune	96	98.9	
Pluto	128	130.1	

Adapted from Earth Mother Astrology, page 104

Each planet's orbital speed on the harmonic level could represent the planet's pitch. It is somewhat difficult to find information on the ancient doctrine of the "music of the spheres". Pythagoras correlated the seven ancient planets to the notes of the musical scale.

It is interesting that Pythagoras did not know about Uranus, Neptune and Pluto. Thus these planets contributed nothing to the celestial scale. It is also interesting that Venus, Uranus and Pluto rotate on their axis in a opposite direction of the other planets. Who knows what this might mean to musicians or the symphony of the stars?

Pythagoras divided the solar system into intervals corresponding to the octave as follows:

Table 21. Planets and Octaves

Earth to the Moon ☽	=	1 tone
Moon ☽ to Mercury ☿	=	1/2 tone
Mercury ☿ to Venus ♀	=	1/2 tone
Venus ♀ to Sun ☉	=	1 1/2 tones
Sun ☉ to Mars ♂	=	1 tone
Mars ♂ to Jupiter ♃	=	1/2 tone
Jupiter ♃ to Saturn ♄	=	1/2 tone
Saturn ♄ to fixed stars	=	1/2 tone

The sum of the above is 6 whole tones. You can find more information about planets and octaves in: *Music of the Spheres* by Guy Murchie.

Musical tones are based on harmonics and the mathematical division of a vibrating string. The string is divided into halves, thirds, fourths, fifths, sixths, sevenths, eighths, etc.

There are several systems that relate planets to notes. One system assigns the Sun to C, Saturn to D, Mercury to E, the Moon to F, Mars to G, Venus to A and Jupiter to B.

Johannes Kepler (1571-1630) a mathematical genius and mystic, wrote that "*the belief in the effect of the constellations derives in the first place from experience, which is so convincing that it can be denied only by people who have not examined it*".

Kepler also believed that the planets resonated as musical notes in their travels around the heavens. He created a paradigm whereby the planets' orbits are linked in motion by means of five geometrical shapes, each touching its neighbor within the celestial sphere as shown in the model below:

Figure 53. Kepler's Celestial Geometry

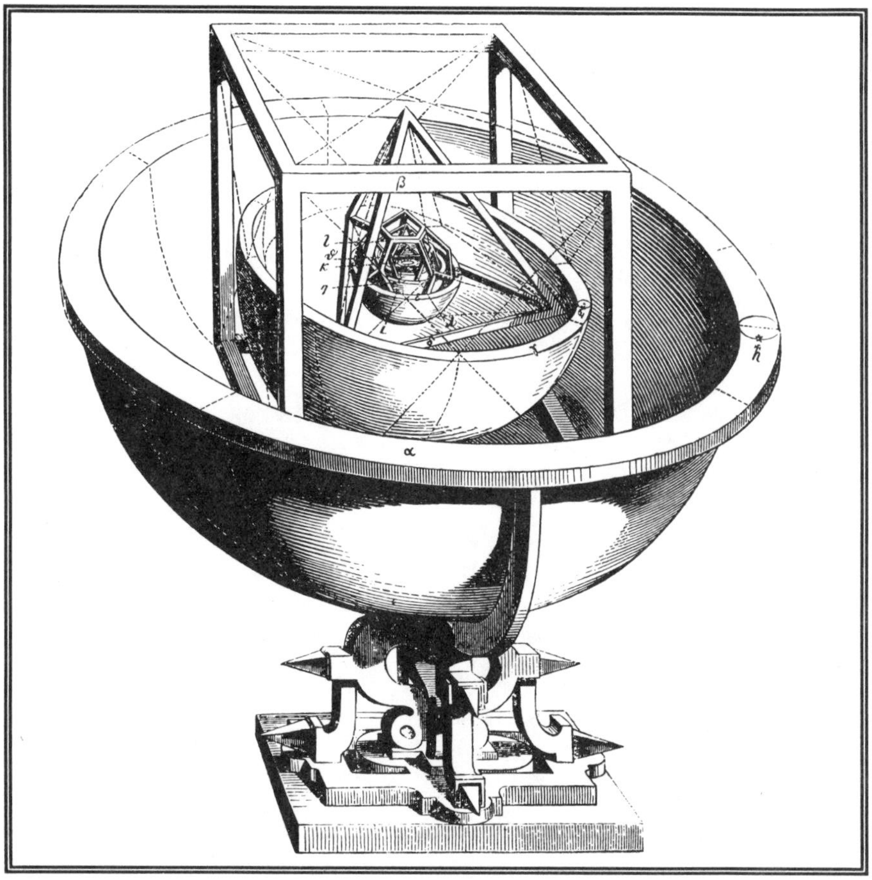

New York astrologer Gerald Jay Markoe created a way to translate any astrological chart into a musical composition. His system is described in an article called "The Musical Correlations of a Natal Chart", *NCGR Bulletin* Vol 8, #34, Fall-Winter 1982.

In summary, harmonics in music relates to a tone whose vibratory rate is an exact multiple of a given primary tone. Harmonics in mathematics is supported by wave theory and the numerical relationships between vibrations of a same fundamental tone. Harmonics in astrology gains credibility with the orbit spacing of the planets and Bode's Law. There must be correlations between the harmonics of music, wave theory, and planetary orbits but we have much yet to discover and understood.

Mutable signs: Gemini ♊, Virgo ♍, Sagittarius ♐, and Pisces ♓, so called for their mutable (flexible) nature. These are the conciliators and compromisers of the zodiac. They are also sometimes called the "common signs". The mutable nature is changeable and adaptable, but under pressure there is a tendency to be unfocused and unstable.

There are three modes of signs: cardinal, fixed and mutable. See also *Modes*.

Mutability positive tendency key words are: adaptable, flexible, and equitable.

Mutability negative tendency key words are: exaggeration, indiscriminate, lack perseverance, unfocused, and loss of self and purpose.

Mute Signs: So called from the inability to make sounds or speak, at least as heard from human ears: Cancer ♋, Scorpio ♏, and Pisces ♓.

N

Nadir: The lowest point on the celestial sphere directly underfoot and directly opposite the zenith.

Natal Chart: A chart cast for the moment of birth, usually the first breath. The natal chart represents a snapshot of the positions of planets in the solar system at the moment of birth. The data needed to cast a natal chart are the birth date, time (zone from GMT and time changes), and city (in latitude and longitude).

Natal or Genethlical Astrology: See *Astrology Specialties.*

National Council for Geocosmic Research: The NCGR is a United States based nonprofit educational and research organization. The NCGR has a complete educational program with certifying exams for competency in the astrological arts. The educational curriculum is intended to give structure to astrological studies and raise quality standards for students and teachers. There are four levels designed to provide the basis of a four year college degree with a major in astrology. NCGR local chapters and the national conferences conduct classes and testing.

NCGR also supports special interest groups, and holds local and national conferences. A monthly newsletter, the *NCGR Journal* is published four times a year. There are many NCGR chapters around the United States, and a chapter in Mexico. As a benefit to members NCGR offers a reciprocal discounted membership in the Astrological Association of Great Britain.

Information about membership can be obtained through Margie Herskovitz, Membership Secretary, 5826 Greenspring Avenue, Baltimore, Maryland, USA.

Natural Astrology: See *Astrology Specialties.*

NCGR: See *National Council for Geocosmic Research.*

Neptune: The eighth planet from the Sun, Neptune takes 164.8 years to revolve around the solar system. It remains in each sign about 14 years making it one of the planets that affects an entire generation of people. Neptune's orbit is between Uranus and Pluto. It has eight moons, Triton and Nereid are the largest.

Neptune rules Pisces, is exalted in Leo, has its detriment in Virgo, and its fall in Aquarius.

Mythologically, Neptune was the equivalent of Poseidon, God of the sea. Neptune can also represent the sea of unconsciousness. Poseidon was the brother of Zeus and Pluto. The Romans and Greeks believed that when Neptune was angry he could cause severe storms, earthquakes, tidal waves and great destruction.

The glyph ♆ is from the trident, or long, three-pronged fork of Neptune, God of the Sea that dissolves everything. Another interpretation is the glyph symbolizes matter piercing the personality to free it from selfish endeavors.

Neptune has a dissolving influence, bestowing nebulousness and confusion. There can be emotional chaos and self-deception. The personality function of Neptune is the slow dissolving of old ruts so that new patterns can be experienced. Neptune is mystical, and the Neptunian type often finds being "earthbound" difficult. Skilled use of Neptune allows you to reach the highest consciousness. Unskilled use of Neptunian energies can plunge you to the lowest depths, often through escapist means such as drugs, alcohol and even suicide.

Physiologically, Neptune is associated with the pineal gland, also known as the "third eye". According the Eastern spiritual teachings the opening of this center gives you access to psychic and clairvoyant abilities.

Positive Neptunian traits: idealistic, intuitive, psychic, inspirational, visionary, spiritual wisdom, compassion, sacrifice, communion with everything, selfless service to others, and universal love.

Negative Neptunian traits: chaos, confusion, delusion, fear, escapism, ungrounded, self-deceiving, and impractical.

Neptune/Pluto Cycle: The synodic cycle (return of conjunctions) for these two planets is about 493 years, which is the first order cycle. The second order cycle is about 73,372 years involving 147 synodic cycles.

Nocturnal Semi-Arc: The nocturnal arc is the distance a point travels between setting and rising. A nocturnal semi-arc is half the nocturnal arc. The path from set (of any planet) to the lower meridian (below the Earth) and from the lower meridian to rise. The diurnal semi-arc is from rise to the upper meridian (above the Earth) and from the upper meridian to set.

Nodes: The points of intersection where the orbit of a planet or celestial body cross the ecliptic when moving northward (north node) or southward (south node).

Nodes, Lunar: The lunar nodes are the points in space where the Moon crosses the ecliptic (the Earth's orbit). The ascending (north node ☊) is where the Moon in its orbit moves from the south of the Earth's ecliptic to the north of it. The descending (south node ☋) is moving from the north to the south.

The two nodes are axial and are always at opposite ends of the zodiac. The nodes move retrograde (backward) through the zodiac, completing the cycle every 18.6 years, which is about every generation. The nodes transit a sign about every 19 months. Sometimes the north node is called the Dragon's Head and the south node as the Dragon's Tail.

When a new or full Moon moves to within 10° to 12° of the lunar nodes there will be an eclipse. Therefore, people born on the day of an eclipse will have the Sun and/or Moon conjoin the lunar node.

In astrology, the north ☊ and south ☋ nodes are important points on a chart. The north node of the Moon indicates the direction for growth, intake, or dharma. The south node represents areas of release and past life experiences, or karma. See also *Dragon's Head* and *Dragon's Tail.*

Nonagen: An aspect of 40° between 2 planets, it is also the *novile.* The orb should be no greater than 2°. The 40° results from dividing a circle by 9 (the 9 series harmonics). In Hindu astrology, the nine series represents completion and the end products of life. It also includes close relationships and especially marriage. Astrologer Myrna Lofthus interprets the nonagen as representing bondage or restriction in the houses and planets involved because of a need for reevaluating past-life attitudes that the placement represents.

Nostradamus: A 16th century French physician and astrologer whose full name was Michel de Notre-Dame or Notredame (1503 - 1566). His name was Latinized to Nostradamus. In 1555 he published a book of rhymed prophecies titled *Centuries* that contains over 1000 quatrains or cryptic paragraphs that are arranged in ten groups of 100 paragraphs. All the quatrains were future predictions. *Centuries* has been in print continuously for over 450 years. Astrologer Steve Cozzi identified about 60 quatrains that have obvious astrological references. More about this fascinating subject is in the *Astrology of the Macrocosm: New Directions in Mundane Astrology*, in the chapter entitled: "The Astrological Quatrains of Michel Nostradamus".

Novile: See *Nonagen.*

O

Obliquity of the Ecliptic: Obliquity is the deviation from a vertical or horizontal line, plane, or position, and the angle or extent of deviation. The present obliquity of the ecliptic is a 23.5° angle between the Earth's celestial equator and the ecliptic.

Occultation: When a planet or celestial body is hidden from view. Normally, occultation describes the Earth's Moon passing in front of a star or planet. This is similar to an eclipse. This also represents two bodies conjoined on two planes, longitude and latitude.

Octile: Symbol ∠ a 45° aspect, also called the semi-square. One aspect of the harmonic series with the division of 8. (360°/8 = 45°). Other aspects in this series include the square □ 90°, conjunction ☌ 0°, tri-octile or sesqui-quadrate ⚼ 135° and opposition ☍ 180°.

Odd Numbered Signs: See *Masculine Signs.*

Opposition: Symbol ☍, this aspect forms when two planets or bodies are 180° apart. Sometimes called the "aspect of separation", this 180° separation places the planets directly opposite each other. The angle crates tension or stress between the planets involved. An opposition can also intensify the planets' actions and influences.

Oimelc: See *Fire Festivals.*

Orb: The arc (area) before and after a planet's position where an aspect is operative or influential. Orbs can be closely defined (within a few degrees) or widely defined (many degrees). Orbs do not have a definite cut-off point. See *Orbs and Aspects Table* in Part Four for suggested aspect orbs.

Orbit: The path of any heavenly body traveling through space when under the influence of the gravitational force(s) of another body. This path may have the shape of an ellipse, parabola, or hyperbola. In astrology, one complete orbit of a planet or Moon is the "return time". Thus, Saturn Return refers to one complete orbit of Saturn around the Sun.

Orbital Inclination: The angle that a body's orbit is inclined to the Ecliptic. See Figure 38: Planets in the Plane of the Ecliptic.

P

Pallas: Symbol ⚴. The second largest asteroid and the second asteroid discovered. German astronomer H. W. Olbers discovered Pallas in 1802. Mythologically, Pallas Athene, or Pallas, was born fully grown and armed, from the head of Zeus (Jupiter). Like her father, she threw thunderbolts, but as the daughter of Athena, she is the goddess of wisdom and the arts (handicrafts). She was the Roman Goddess Minerva.

Astrologically, Pallas rules the ability of the mind to create reality (and illusions) and how we formulate and attain goals. Astrologer Zipporah Dobyns associates Pallas with the sign Libra ♎. Also see *Asteroids.*

Pan: In mythology, Pan is the horned god of woods, fields, flocks and nature spirits. His father was Hermes or Apollo. Pan was half human and half goat with goat's horns, ears and legs, including hoofs instead of feet. He is portrayed as a merry, musical fellow who is impulsive and amorous.

Pan is also the name given to a hypothetical planet. See also *trans-pluto planets* and *hypothetical planets.*

Pandora: Symbol ▽, an asteroid. Entrusted with a box that contained all the ills and woes that could plague humankind, she opened it, and thus brought misery to the world. But, Pandora's box also contained one essential ingredient: hope. Astrologically, the asteroid Pandora might be interpreted as the area where a decision or process opens up an entire new pathway. This is similar to the new physics' "many worlds", or ring theory that hypothesizes a single moment or decision can open an entire decision tree, or life-time line. Additionally, the ring theory postulates that many life-time lines can exist simultaneously. Thus, Pandora might represent the areas and moments when a chain of events alters our lives, for better or worse. See Also *Asteroids.*

Parallel and Contra-parallel: Symbols ॥ and ⧺ These have the same nature as a conjunction or opposition. It refers to two planets being within an orb of about 1 degree of each other either north or south of the celestial equator. At these positions they are in *parallel of declination.* If one planet lies north and the other south of the celestial equator (within 1° of the same declination), they are contra-parallel: a form of opposition.

Part of Fortune: See *Arabic Parts*

Part of Love: = Venus + Ascendant - Sun. See also *Arabic Parts.*

Part of Divorce: = Venus + Ascendant - 7th House Cusp. In effect, what you are doing is rotating the descendant to the ascendant's position. Then the position of Venus is the part of divorce. See also *Arabic Parts.*

Part of Marriage: = Ascendant + Seventh House Cusp - Venus. As Zip Dobyns observed, this symbolically represents the self (Asc) + other (7th house cusp) - love or pleasure (Venus): what a marriage! See also *Arabic Parts.*

Part of Spirit: = Ascendant + Sun - Moon. See also *Arabic Parts.*

Partile Aspect: Refers to an aspect that is exact to the degree and minute.

Perigee: The point in orbit where the Moon, satellite, or planet is closest to the Earth. From Greek *perigeios*, near the Earth: *peri* = near + *ge* = Earth. See also *Apogee* for diagram.

Perihelion: The point in a planet's orbit where it is closest to the Sun. Latin, *peri* + Greek, *helios* (Sun). Opposite to aphelion, when a planet is furthest from the Sun. See also *Aphelion* for a diagram.

Persephone: Astrologer Dane Rudhyar suggested there is another planet, beyond Pluto, which he dubbed Persephone or Proserpina, after Pluto's wife. In Greek Mythology, Persephone was the only daughter of Demeter (Ceres). Her father was Zeus. Persephone was the Maiden of the Spring. Pluto abducted her and made her Queen of the Underworld. Demeter was totally distraught with her daughter's kidnapping and vowed not to let the Earth be fertile until her daughter returned to her. A compromise was made, so that Persephone could return to her mother and the world of light for all but a third of each year. Those four months she would spend with her husband, Pluto, in his dark kingdom, also symbolic of winter. Persephone, Proserpina and Demeter are asteroids #399, #26, and #1108 respectively.

Phases: The routine periodic changes in the visible amount of light (illumination) of an astronomical body. The Phases of the Moon are the most commonly used.

Phenomenon: Something seen or observed. In astrological terms, this refers to celestial events such as solar and lunar eclipses, sunset/sunrise times, lunar phases, stations, ingresses, planet aspects, void-of-course Moon data, etc.

Pisces: The last of the twelve signs of the zodiac, Pisces is a feminine, water, mutable sign ruled by Neptune (and Jupiter in older astrology). The Sun sign period for Pisces is about 20 February to 20 March.

The glyph for Pisces ♓ represents two fish joined by a silver cord. The two fishes face in different directions in the constellation with one up and one on the right. This arrangement might symbolize the quarrel between the human spirit and soul or between of the esoteric and mundane.

As a mutable water sign, Pisces is the most fluid sign of the zodiac and often is emotional, sensitive, impressionable and insecure. Pisceans sometimes retreat within themselves. The archetypical Pisces is unworldly and operates on an intuitive level that cannot be understood through logic, analysis or pressure. They sometimes have difficulty with mundane reality, and seek escape through drugs and alcohol. Counselor Troi of Startrek has many archetypical Piscean qualities.

Positive Piscean traits: intuitive, sympathetic, receptive, humble, compassionate, imaginative, sensitive and self-sacrificing.

Negative Piscean traits: vague, indecisive, impressionable, confused, escapism, hypersensitive and self-pity.

Planets: The larger bodies that orbit around the Sun and form our Solar System. To date, there have been 9 planets identified: Mercury ☿, Venus ♀, Earth ⊕, Mars ♂, Jupiter ♃, Saturn ♄, Uranus ♅, Neptune ♆, and Pluto ♇ or ⯓.

In astrology, the Planets symbolically have different functions as outlined in the table below:

Table 22. Planetary Functions

Personal Planets:	Mercury, Venus, and Mars
Social/Group Identity:	Jupiter and Saturn
Transformative:	Uranus, Neptune, Pluto
Existential Planets:	Sun and Moon.

Planting by the Moon: Many gardeners claim they obtain a larger harvest and better plants by planning their gardening activities according to the Moon's phases. There are many sayings about planting by the dark or the light of the Moon, but this idea is summarized most appropriately by Llewellyn George:

> *"No astrologer ever claimed anything for the mere light of the Moon. It is not the light given or reflected by the Moon, its quality or intensity that is concerned with planting, but it is the quality of the rays that the Moon transmits which is so significant of its influence according to astrology."*
>
> Llewellyn George
> *Powerful Planets*

Below are the basic rules of Moon phase gardening.

• Plant annuals that produce above ground yields during the increasing light (from new Moon to the full Moon). Annuals are plants that complete their life cycle within one year and must be seeded anew each season. Most vegetables are annuals.

• Plant biennials, perennials, bulb and root plants when the Moon is decreasing in light. Biennials include crops that you plant one season to winter over and harvest the next season, such as winter wheat and garlic. Perennials, bulb and root plants are those that grow from the same root year after year.

• An even more basic rule is to plant crops that produce above ground when the Moon is increasing (waxing) in light; and crops that produce below ground when the Moon is decreasing (waning) in light.

More detailed information on lunar gardening can be obtained from *Astrological Gardening* by Louise Riotte, and annual publications: *Llewellyn's Moon Sign Book* and The *Kimberton Hills Agricultural Calendar.*

Pluto: Glyph ♇ or ♇. The ninth, smallest and farthest known planet from the Sun is Pluto; it has a sidereal revolution period of about 248.5 years. Because of its eccentric orbit, Pluto stays in a zodiac sign between 13 and 32 years. Pluto has one moon, Charon, discovered in 1978. In mythology, Charon is the ferryman who escorts the dead across the rivers of the lower world.

Pluto's discovery was March 12, 1930. Pluto's diameter is approximately one fifth that of Earth. At its furthest point (aphelion), Pluto is about 4.6 billion miles from the Sun, at its closest point (perihelion), about 2.8 billion miles. Pluto's eccentric orbit is inclined at a 17° angle from the ecliptic or orbital plane of the Earth. This eccentric orbit can bring Pluto inside the orbit of Neptune, most recently from 1979-1999. During this time, Neptune, not Pluto, is the outermost known planet. Also at this time, Pluto is closest to the Earth.

Figure 54. Pluto's Orbit inside Neptune's Orbit

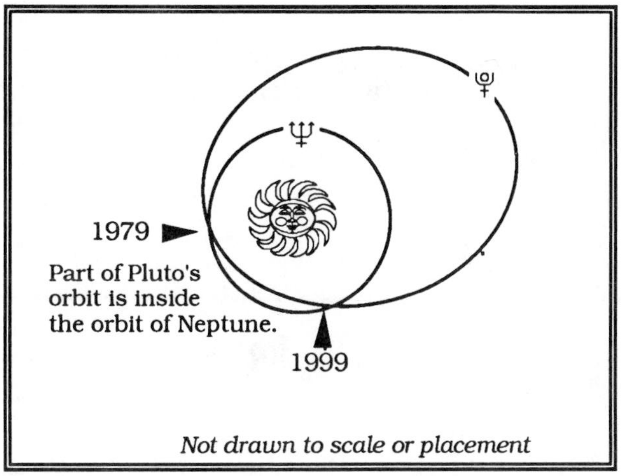
1979
Part of Pluto's orbit is inside the orbit of Neptune.
1999
Not drawn to scale or placement

The Latin translation of *Plouton* is "Rich One". Mythologically, Pluto is rich; he rules all that is below the Earth's surface. He is God of the Underworld who receives and regenerates souls. Pluto is also the Greek God, Hades.

Pluto is the planetary ruler of Scorpio; it is in its detriment in Taurus. The exaltation and fall have yet to be determined. In the natal chart, Pluto indicates where changes and transformations are going on.

Pluto's glyph ♇, resembles a crucible, the vessel used for melting and separating materials (especially metals) at high temperatures. Another interpretation is that it represents matter (the cross) overcome by an uplifted personality or soul (the semi-circle) with the eternal spirit above them both (the circle).

The symbol ♇ is a combination of P for Percival and L for Lowell. The Lowell Observatory discovered Pluto in 1930. Percival Lowell was the astronomer whose calculations led to the discovery of Pluto.

Astrologically, Pluto represents the destructive and regenerative forces. Pluto penetrates into the core of an object and permanently transforms it. Metaphors for such dramatic transformation include the caterpillar into a butterfly, and the alchemical transmutation of lead into gold. In penetrating into the deep secrets of the cosmos, Pluto uncovers both creative and destructive forces. Depending upon the level of evolution, the Plutonic individual can become either a black magician, or a spiritual healer, the underground gangster or the religious saint. Pluto in a birth chart shows how and where you may undergo transformation, for better or worse.

Physiologically, Pluto governs birth and death. Pluto rules the sexual organs, and Plutonic types tend to be highly sensuous and magnetic. Pluto is the only zodiac sign not afraid of death and the archetypical sign of a shaman.

Positive Plutonic traits: transforming, renewing, regenerating, healing, psychic, shaman, can make a fresh start.

Negative Plutonic traits: destructive, manipulative, controlling, vindictive, revengeful, cruel, and sadistic.

Points: The horoscope contains several categories of points, or positions on the chart. The most important points in a chart are;

- Planets, Sun and Moon (lights).
- Angles:
  Ascendant,
  Midheaven (MC *medium coeli*),
  Descendant and
  IC *Imum coeli* or "Lowest heaven"
- Nodes of the Moon
- Arabic Parts

Other points are the asteroids, and hypothetical planets (Uranians). Keep in mind that even though some points are places, instead of bodies of mass, they can be significant. Examples are the ascendant, midheaven, descendant, IC, and lunar nodes. These place points are not necessarily energies themselves, but are where the energies of the planetary bodies can be expressed.

Point (Part) of Love: An Arabic Part. See *Arabic Parts*.

Point of Transformation: A calculated point that focuses the activities of Uranus, Neptune and Pluto. It might provide a clue to the process of world transformation. You get the Point of Transformation by adding the longitudes of the three planets and dividing by three to get the average. The point of transformation is not an Arabic Part. Dane Rudhyar developed this point and describes it in his book: *The Galactic Dimension of Astrology*.

Polarity: Signs directly opposite (across from) each other in the zodiac: Aries ♈ - Libra ♎
Taurus ♉ - Scorpio ♏
Gemini ♊ - Sagittarius ♐
Cancer ♋ - Capricorn ♑
Leo ♌ - Aquarius ♒
Virgo ♍ - Pisces ♓

Porphyry: Original name was Mal'chus Porphyrius who lived about 232 to 304AD. A Greek scholar and neoplatonic philosopher/astrologer, Porphyry was a prolific writer and wrote an introduction to *The Tetrabiblos*, Ptolemy's astrological treatise. Porphyry also applies to purple colored stones or crystals, especially feldspar.

Poseidon: Symbol ♆, one of eight hypothetical planets of Uranian astrology. This planet embodies the qualities of mind, spirit and ideas. Poseidon is also the Greek God of Waters and earthquakes. He was the brother of Zeus and identified with the Roman god, Neptune. Poseidon is also asteroid #4341.

Precessed Returns: Due to the Precession of the Equinoxes, many astrologers who use the tropical zodiac prefer to use precessed return charts. Using precession returns is a correction that works by linking the position of planets in the natal chart to the background of fixed stars. You then calculate returns for the planetary position according to the fixed background.

The positions of the fixed stars are not affected by precession. This is useful because the time difference between solar returns cast in non-corrected and precession corrected modes is twelve hours by age 36. This means the house cusps will be approximately 180° apart. For example, if the uncorrected solar return had Aries rising and Capricorn midheaven, the corrected chart might have Libra rising and a Cancer midheaven. This makes for a very different interpretation of the return chart.

Precession: **Precession of the Equinoxes**: The Earth not only rotates on its axis daily, but also wobbles, like a spinning top, rotating the axis about every 26,000 years. The effect of this wobble is the "Precession of the Equinoxes".

The Precession causes the equinoctial points to move clockwise (backward) through the zodiac at a rate of about 1° every 72 years. This means a shift of 1 sign every 2,160 years (72 years/degree x 30°/sign = 2160 years/sign).

About 1,700 to 2,000 years ago, the vernal equinox could be projected onto the ecliptic at a point corresponding to the beginning of the constellation Aries (0°♈). This point has since moved backward into the arc of the constellation of Pisces, creating the period known as the Age of Pisces.

Astrologers are in a debate about when (by hundreds of years) the vernal equinox will be leaving the constellation of Pisces, and entering the constellation of Aquarius. Because of movement of the vernal equinox caused by the Precession of the Equinoxes, we are now on the cusp of the Age of Aquarius, and leaving the Age of Pisces. Currently, the Precession is about 24° to 26° from the beginning of the cycle. See Figure 3: The Difference Between the Sidereal and Tropical Zodiacs.

Figure 55. The Precession of Equinoxes and the Winter Solstice

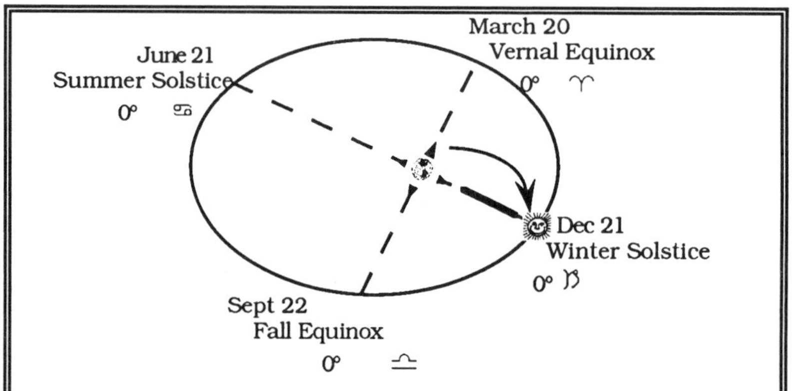

Adapted from *Sun Reflections*, page 83.

Not drawn to scale or placement

Because of the Earth's altered orbit (wobble), the distance from the Sun to the Earth on the solstices and equinoxes changes slightly each year, as does the drift of the signs and constellations. Currently, the Earth is closest to the Sun in northern winter at the winter solstice. This has not always been so. The eccentricity also changes over time.

The Precession does not affect the cardinal directions on Earth. It only affects the orientation of the Earth's axis to the celestial sphere. Therefore it affects the positions of the stars at the celestial poles and the points where the extensions of the Earth's axis intersect the celestial sphere.

For example, in the 20th century, the celestial north pole is very near Polaris, the "North Star". This was not, and will not always be so. Unless the Earth's axis shifts, in about 12,000 years, the celestial pole will be close to the bright star, Vega and Vega will be our new "North Star" as shown below.

Figure 56. North Star Orientation in the Precession of the Equinoxes

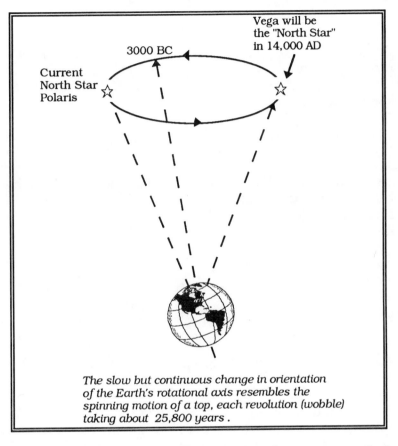

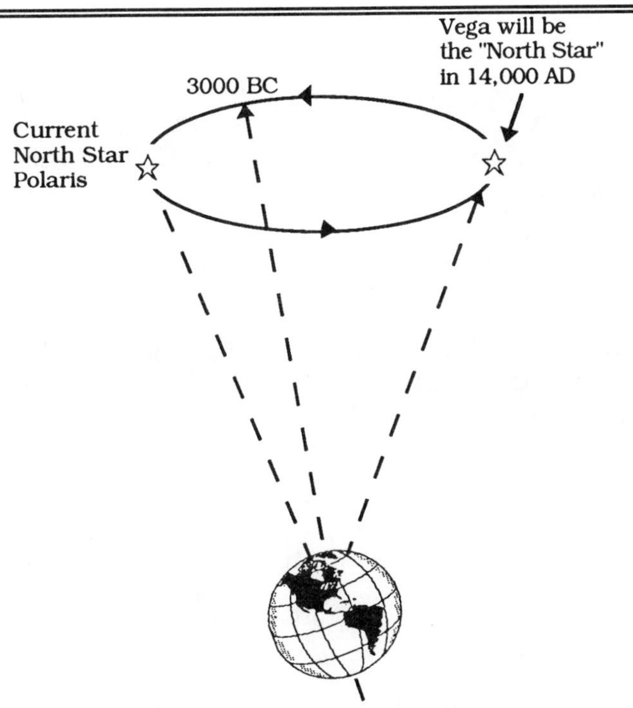

The slow but continuous change in orientation of the Earth's rotational axis resembles the spinning motion of a top, each revolution (wobble) taking about 25,800 years .

Primary Directions: A study of future configurations of planets and angles with the purpose of learning something about the future. Planets are "directed" to the precise aspect with another planet. For example, Venus can be directed to the place of Jupiter in the natal chart to figure out when that conjunction will take place. Primary Directions are based upon the diurnal rotation of the Earth on its axis. See also Part 1 - User's Reference.

Prime Meridian: The meridian at Greenwich which is the zero longitude point for measurements on Earth.

Prime Vertical: The great circle that intersects the horizon at the east and west points passing through the zenith at right angles to the meridian.

Progressed Angles: Chart angles move forward (counterclockwise) in the natal chart in a manner similar to the progressed planets. These moving angles form aspects to the various planets and points in the natal chart. Some examples of progressed angles are:

- Solar Arc Midheaven
- Naibod Arc
- Degree per Year
- Mean Quotidian
- Apparent Quotidian
- User Defined Arc
- Ascendant Arc
- Vertical Arc
- PMD in Longitude

See also the User's Guide under *Progressed Angles* for more information.

Progressions and Directions: These are two of the many methods of relating the movements of the planets in the natal chart against a current or reference time-frame. In progressions and directions, one unit of time substitutes for another another unit of time. Types of progressions are:

- Secondary Progression
- Tertiary Progression
- Minor Progression
- User Defined Progressions
- Quotidian-1
- Quotidian-2

See also the User's Guide under *Progressions and Directions* for more information.

Proper Motion: Proper motion is the movement of a star across the celestial sphere over time (years or centuries). You measure proper motion relative to other stars.

Psyche: Symbol ✓, an asteroid. Psyche was the maiden loved by Eros. One condition of their marriage was that Psyche could not see the face of Eros. Because he was a God, his appearance would be too much for her. Still, curiosity could not be contained. One night, by candlelight, Psyche looked upon the face of Eros and knew his secret. Eros left his wife only to be imprisoned by his jealous mother, Aphrodite. Meanwhile, Aphrodite sent Psyche on impossible missions. On the final mission, Eros who had escaped from his mother's house, rescued Psyche. Because of her love for Eros and her bravery, Psyche obtained immortality and remained his wife.

In psychology, and perhaps astrology, the "psyche" has come to mean the personification of the soul and the search for individuality. In the myth, Psyche took control of her situation by looking at her divine husband's face although it was forbidden. Through the impossible trials set by the jealousy of Aphrodite, Psyche might have been destroyed. But her love helped her succeed in the search for her husband, and ultimately reunite with him and become divine. Her love literally transformed her (Sigh). The asteroid Psyche was the 16th one to be discovered. See also *Asteroids.*

Ptolemy: Claudius Ptolemaeus of Alexandria (120 - 180 AD), was the author of the famous book *Tetrabiblos* that summarized the astrological findings of the Chaldeans. In book 1 of *Tetrabiblos* he stated his belief about the physical effects of the planets. He was the foremost astronomer and geographer of his time. He catalogued over 300 new stars and described the refraction of light.

Q

Quadruplicities: The 12 signs are organized into three qualities of cardinal, fixed or mutable. These three groups (each with four planets) are:

Cardinal:	Aries ♈, Cancer ♋, Libra ♎ , Capricorn ♑
Fixed:	Taurus ♉, Leo ♌, Scorpio ♏, Aquarius ♒
Mutable:	Gemini ♊, Virgo ♍, Sagittarius ♐, Pisces ♓

Quadrature: A square aspect of 90° distance.

Quadrants: The four quarters of the horoscope are quadrants. Many different adjectives distinguish the four quadrants and the cycles they symbolically represent. Some are of the descriptive terms are below.

Quadrant Characteristics

1. Spring, vernal, infantile
2. Summer, festival, youthful
3. Autumnal, mature
4. Winter, wintery, old, dying

Quarter phases: The Moon has four principle phases, these are the new Moon ●, waxing half Moon ◐ (first quarter), full Moon ○, and waning half-Moon ◑ (third quarter).

Quarter points: The opening cusps of the cardinal signs (Aries, Cancer, Libra and Capricorn) are the quarter points. These are also the solstice and equinox points. See also Figure: 1 Seasons, Solstices and Equinoxes (Part 1), and *Fire Festivals* in the dictionary (Part 3).

Querent: From Latin *quaerere*, to seek or ask. In horary astrology, the querent is the person asking the question.

Quincunx: Also called inconjunct, symbol ⚻. An aspect of 150°, the two points separated by 5 zodiac signs. See also *Aspects.*

Quindecile: An aspect of 24°, derived from dividing the zodiac (360° circle) into fifteenths. See also *aspects.*

Quintile: Symbol Q. An aspect of 72°, derived from dividing the zodiac into fifths. Some astrologers view the quintile as giving a quality of single-mindedness that enhances the energies of those planets in the aspect. It also indicates talent. See also *aspects.*

Quotidians: Sometimes called diurnals, they are rates to advance the midheaven. See *Quotidians* in the User's Guide (Part 1) under *Progressed Angles.*

R

Radix: Refers to the birth chart that is the "root" or *radix* of astrological arts. Astrologers often call the birth chart a radical chart.

Radix System: A method of progressing a birth chart by the addition of the symbolic direction of 59'8" for each year of life to all positions on the chart. See Part 1 *Naibod Arc Directions.*

Rays, the Seven: In esoteric astrology there are certain qualities or energies embodied in the planets, signs, houses and other astrological factors. Alice A. Bailey wrote a five-volume *Treatise on the Seven Rays.* These books, and especially the third volume, *Esoteric Astrology,* describe in great detail the theoretical and practical basis of the seven rays. A brief summary of the rays is in the table below.

Alan Oken wrote a book describing the rays and esoteric astrology entitled: *Soul-Centered Astrology: A Key to Your Expanding Self.*

Table 23. The Rays, Signs and Planets

Ray	Signs	Esoteric Planets
1. Will or Power	Aries Leo Capricorn	Mercury Sun Saturn
2. Love - Wisdom	Gemini Virgo	Venus Moon
3. Active - Intelligence	Cancer Libra Capricorn	Neptune Uranus Saturn
4. Harmony through Conflict	Taurus Scorpio Sagittarius	Neptune Uranus Saturn
5. Concrete Science	Leo Sagittarius Aquarius	Sun Earth Jupiter
6. Idealism and Devotion	Virgo Sagittarius Pisces	Moon Earth Pluto
7. Ceremonial Order	Aries Cancer Capricorn	Mercury Neptune Saturn

Adapted from Esoteric Astrology, Tabulation X, page 590.

Rectification: A process of adjusting the birth chart to obtain or verify the exact birth moment, or ascendant. It is the correction of the supposed time of birth to the true birth time. The process involves adjusting the chart to fit references of known events or characteristics of the individual.

Regiomontanus: A system of determining house cusps. Regiomontanus was a pen name assumed by Johann Muller (1436-1470), a German mathematician, astronomer and astrologer.

Relocation Charts: The recasting of a chart for a different location. That is, same birth time, but different latitude and longitude for the new place in question. Astro*Carto*Graphy® charts are sometimes advertised as relocation charts.

Retrograde Motion: Differences in orbits of planets around the Sun cause the illusion of backward motion. This is the apparent westward (clockwise) motion of a body as seen from Earth. Retrograde motion appears opposite from the usual or direct motion. A retrograde planet itself does not change direction and go backward. The table below shows the approximate retrograde and stationary periods.

Table 24. Planetary Retrograde and Stationary Periods

Planet	Retrograde	Stationary
Mercury ☿	24 days	1 day before and after
Venus ♀	42 days	2 days before and after
Mars ♂	80 days	3 days before and after
Jupiter ♃	120 days	5 days before and after
Saturn ♄	140 days	5 days before and after
Uranus ♅	155 days	6 days before and after
Neptune ♆	157 days	7 days before and after
Pluto ♇ or ♇	160 days	7 days before and after

Adapted from *Astrology, the Divine Science* by Marcia Moore, page 738.

Retrograde Planets: A retrograde planet appears to move backward in its orbit as viewed from Earth. In astrology, retrograde planets represents something happening within an individual. This something may not have an outward expression that is apparent in outer life. The retrograde planet and its placement in the chart determine the area of life affected and the introspective effects.

Return Charts: Refers to a chart cast for the exact moment a transiting planet "returns" or is conjoin its natal place. Solar (birthday or yearly) and lunar (monthly) return charts are the most commonly used. However, any planet within a lifetime can be used in a return chart. See also *Planet Return Times.*

Return (Times): A planet return is the amount of time it takes a planet to revolve around the Sun, and return to its original position in the zodiac. In a transit search, a return would occur when a transiting planet is conjoin with a natal planet. For example, transiting Saturn conjunct natal (radix) Saturn (♄☌♄) is the "Saturn return". Naturally, in a Solar return (a birthday), it is the Earth revolving around the Sun and not vice-versa.

The heliocentric and geocentric returns are approximately within the same time length of time, but there also can be a +/- difference in times due to the irregular planet orbits. The approximate return times for planets are below. See also individual planet returns and *Return Charts.*

Table 25. Return Times (Heliocentric)

Moon	27.3 days	Lunar Return (Geocentric)
Mercury	87.9 days	Mercury Return
Venus	244.7 days	Venus Return
Earth	365.5 days	Solar Return (Geo/Helio)
Mars	1.88 years	Mars Return
Jupiter	11.9 years	Jupiter Return
Nodal Cycle	18.6 years	Moon's Nodal Return (Geocentric)
Saturn	29.5 years	Saturn Return
Chiron	50 to 51 yr	Chiron Return
Uranus	84 yr	Uranus Return
Neptune	164.8 years	Not in the human life-span
Pluto	248.5 years	Not in the human life-span

Right Ascension (RA): Just as latitude and longitude are coordinates of Earth, right ascension and declination are the coordinates of the celestial sphere. These are often abbreviated RA and Dec. Right ascension is a coordinate of the equator system that begins measurement at the first point of Aries (0° ♈) eastward along the equator. See Figure 9: The Equator Coordinate System.

Rising Sign: Applies to the zodiac sign containing the ascendant. The rising sign is not synonymous with the ascendant. The ascendant is a specific degree, whereas the rising sign is an entire sign of 30°. Also see *Ascendant.*

Ruminant Signs: Refers to the cud-chewing ruminant animals in the zodiac: Aries ♈ (the ram), Taurus ♉ (the bull), and Capricorn ♑ (the goat).

S

Sabian Symbols: In astrology, the Sabian Symbols are a cyclic series of 360 images that are linked with the 360 degrees in the zodiac. Elsie Wheeler, a clairvoyant, described the Sabian Symbols and Marc Jones recorded them. This was done in 1925 in Balboa Park in San Diego, California. In 1953, Marc published the results in his book: *Sabian Symbols in Astrology*. In 1974 Dane Rudhyar reinterpreted the symbols in his book: *An Astrological Mandala: the Cycle of Transformations and its 360 Symbolic Phases.*

The Sabian Symbols provide insights into the individual meaning of the degree or point they represent in the zodiac. Sometimes the Sabian symbols are used as an oracular means, like the I Ching.

The Sabians (Sabeans) were an ancient sect of the first millennia BC in Mesopotamia who had a deep interest in all phases of astrology and the influence of the zodiac on the individual. There are no apparent links of the ancient Sabians and the modern Sabian Symbols.

Sagittarius: The ninth sign of the zodiac, it is a masculine, fire, mutable sign, ruled by Jupiter. The Sun period for Sagittarius is about 23 November to 22 December.

The glyph of Sagittarius ♐ represents the arrow of desire shot from a sacred bow. Some occultists interpret the symbol as a cross, with an arrow uplifting materialism into the upper spiritual worlds. It is an excellent sigil for the philosophical, spiritual, expansive nature of Sagittarius. Characteristically, Sagittarians are the travelers and philosophers who aspire to great heights. They are especially good at sports and languages and attach a great importance to freedom.

Positive Sagittarius traits: philosophical, idealistic, generous, versatile, open-minded, freedom-loving and sporty.

Negative Sagittarius traits: extremists, tactless, careless, blindly optimistic, indolent, boisterous, capricious, righteous, and restless.

Samhain: See *Fire Festivals*.

Sappho: Symbol ⚢, an asteroid. Sappho was a Greek lyric poet of Lesbos who lived about 600 BC. Sappho's lyrics were mostly about love and even more explicitly, about sex. Of her nine books of lyric poems, all were lost except one ode to Aphrodite and a few other fragments. Among the ancient writers, Sappho ranks with Homer and Archilochus. Plato, in *Phaedrus*, called her the "tenth muse". The story that she threw herself from the Leucadian rock because of her unrequited love for Phaon, a boatman, is legendary. This woman believed in sex and its expression in all forms, poetic and physical.

Astrologically, Dr. Lehman suggests that Sappho relates to both sex and work. Powerful sexual energies also can be directed toward, or shared with work. The poet Sappho did exactly this, her work involved writing lyrics about sexual activities. In Sappho's view, she had the best of both worlds. Where Sappho appears in the natal chart might indicate dedicated activity to either work or play. This active energy would be directed primarily in creating life (sex) or preserving life (work). See also *Asteroids* .

Saros: See *Cycles*.

Satellite: A small body that orbits around another body, such a Moon around a planet. The satellites of planets in our solar system are below.

Table 26. Planets and Their Satellites

NAME OF PLANET AND SATELLITES	DISCOVER	YEAR DISCOVERED	NAME OF PLANET AND SATELLITES	DISCOVER	YEAR DISCOVERED
EARTH					
Moon	?	?			
JUPITER					
Metis	Synnott	1979	Leda	Kowal	1974
Adrastea	Danielson	1979	Himalia	Perrine	1904
Amalthea	Barnard	1892	Lysithea	Nicholson	1938
Thebe	Synnott	1979	Elara	Perrine	1905
Io	Galileo	1610	Ananke	Nicholson	1951
Europa	Galileo	1610	Carme	Nicholson	1938
Ganymede	Galileo	1610	Pasiphae	Melotte	1908
Callisto	Galileo	1610	Sinope	Nicholson	1914
SATURN					
Atlas	Terrile	1980	Calypso	Smith et al	1980
Prometheus	Collins et al	1980	Dione	Cassini	1684
Pandora	Collins et al	1980	Helene	Laques Lecacheux	1980
Epimetheus	Walker	1966	Rhea	Cassini	1672
Janus	Dollfus	1966	Titan	Huygens	1655
Mimas	Herschel	1789	Hyperion	Bond	1848
Enceladus	Herschel	1789	Iapetus	Cassini	1671
Tethys	Cassini	1684	Phoebe	Pickering	1898
Telesto	Smith et al	1980			
URANUS					
Cordelia	Voyager 2	1986	Belinda	Voyager 2	1986
Ophelia	Voyager 2	1986	Port	Voyager 2	1985
Bianca	Voyager 2	1986	Miranda	Kuiper	1948
Cressida	Voyager 2	1986	Ariel	Lassell	1851
Desdemona	Voyager 2	1986	Umbriel	Lassell	1851
Juliet	Voyager 2	1986	Titania	Herschel	1787
Portia	Voyager 2	1986	Oberon	Herschel	1787
Rosalind	Voyager 2	1986			
NEPTUNE					
1989 N 6	Voyager 2	1989	1989 N 2	Voyager 2	1989
1989 N 5	Voyager 2	1989	1989 N 1	Voyager 2	1989
1989 N 3	Voyager 2	1989	Triton	Lassell	1846
1989 N 4	Voyager 2	1989	Nereid	Kuiper	1949
PLUTO					
Charon	Christy	1978			

Saturn: The sixth planet from the Sun and the second largest in the solar system (Jupiter is the largest). Saturn takes about 29.5 years to travel through the zodiac. It has 17 moons, and a system of rings. It is the last planet that you can see easily with the naked eye.

Saturn rules Capricorn, is exalted in Libra; detriment in Cancer and in its fall in Aries. The glyph of Saturn ♄ actually looks like a seat (Saturn). Saturn's glyph has the same two elements as Jupiter ♃, but the two parts are inverted. One interpretation is the semi-circle represents human imagination, that must be harmonized with the cross representing the immediate circumstances in one's life. Another interpretation is that it symbolizes the personality held down by matter.

Mythologically, Saturn is identified with the Greek god, *Chronos*. Archetypal Saturn rules time, and is the great structurer of human life experience. It represents the ability to create order, form and discipline in one's life. However, taken to excess, Saturn also can repress life, or even snuff it out. The Saturnine type usually expresses itself physically through activities demanding control and organization. For this reason, they make excellent accountants. On the social level, Saturn rules over bureaucracies and bureaucratic organization, which is where strongly placed Saturn types are likely to be found. There is an urge to set rigid structures and exercise control over life. The very rings of Saturn symbolically represent limitation. Saturn also rules old age and represents the father.

Positive Saturnian traits: life's teacher, father, responsible, disciplined, grounded, thorough, patient, practical, constructive, thrifty, the citadel.

Negative Saturnian traits: inhibited, pessimistic, controlling, mean, selfish, dogmatic, cruel, severe, and hardship.

Scorpio: The eighth sign of the zodiac, Scorpio is a feminine, water, fixed sign, ruled by Pluto, and by Mars in older astrology. The Sun travels through Scorpio from the 23rd of October through the 22nd of November. The glyph for Scorpio ♏ might represent the tail and stinger of the scorpion, or it could be a serpent bisected by Virgo's harvest sickle.

Scorpio is the most misunderstood and maligned sign of the zodiac. The essence of Scorpio is transformation. The many aspects of Scorpio reflect its multiple images: the scorpion, the eagle, the snake and the phoenix. These multiple images symbolically represent the evolutionary levels of the Scorpio archetype.

The *scorpion* is a cunning, earthbound creature that is ready to strike and will sting itself rather than surrender to an enemy. In this sense, Scorpio is the first sign to acknowledge ego death. The scorpion lives in dark crevices under the ground, and lower Scorpio rules crime, espionage and the underworld.

The *eagle* represents the power to rise above worldly difficulties and soar away from earthbound limits. Thus, Scorpio is aware of both the depths and heights (the best and the worse) of the world.

The *serpent* is a traditional symbol of the healer, Scorpio has tremendous healing and regenerative capabilities, also the power to destroy. Chemicals can be used as medicines or as poisons, depending upon intent.

The *phoenix* represents death and rebirth; rising from one's own ashes to a new life. Scorpio rules reproduction and feels an intense need to connect with others at a soul level. Scorpio is the only sign not afraid of death; the archetypical shaman who travels to other worlds and returns to the Earth plane with new information and experiences.

Positive Scorpio traits: intense, passionate, healer, psychic, transformation and rebirth.

Negative Scorpio traits: revengeful, stubborn, secretive, possessive, vindictive, jealous, controlling and manipulative.

Second Order Cycle: See dictionary under *First Order Cycle.*

Secondary Progressions: A widely used technique in predictive astrology, also called progressions. The method is to cast a chart by substituting one day for each year of life after birth. Thus, if a person is 20 years old, a chart will be cast for the birth day plus 20 days. You examine the progressed chart on its own, and compare it with the natal chart. See User's Reference under *Progressions and Directions.*

Semi-octile: An aspect of 22 1/2°.

Semi-Quartile or Semi-Square An aspect of 45° written ∠, interpreted as causing tension or misalliance. Also called an *octile.* A minor aspect, equal in importance to the sesqui-quadrate.

Septile: Symbol S, an aspect of 51.4°, resulting from the division of the zodiac circle by seven.

Sesqui-quintile: An aspect of 108°. See also *Quintiles* and *Aspects.*

Sesqui-quadrate or sesquare: An aspect of 135° written as ⚼. A minor aspect, sometimes interpreted as having stress or strain. Also called a tri-octile.

Sextile: An aspect of 60° glyph: ⚹ . Interpreted as an easier aspect that enhances creativity and cooperative energy.

Sidereal: Measurements of the stars or constellations.

Sidereal Day/Hour: The time of a complete rotation of the Earth, measured as the interval between two successive meridian transits of the vernal equinox. This is 23 hours, 56 minutes and 4.09 seconds in units of mean solar time. A sidereal hour is 1/24th part of a sidereal day.

Sidereal Month: Using a fixed star as a reference, a sidereal month is the average time for the Moon to revolve around the Earth: 27 days, 7 hours, and 43 minutes, 11.5 seconds.

Sidereal Period: The amount of time the Sun, Moon or a planet takes to make one complete circuit around the celestial sphere, returning to the same star (*sider*) in the zodiac where it began. It takes the Sun 1 year to make a full circuit of the celestial sphere. One sidereal orbit takes the Moon 27 1/3 days, Mercury 88 days, Venus 225 days, Mars 1.9 years, Jupiter 11.9 years, Saturn 29.5 years, Uranus 84.01 years, Neptune 164.79 years and Pluto 248.7 years.

Sidereal Time: Sidereal time is based upon the axial and orbital rotation of the Earth using the fixed stars as a reference point. Sidereal time is the scientifically and astronomically accurate time. The astronomical clocks show 23 hours, 56 minutes and 4 seconds in a period we normally call 24 hours, or one day. This is about a 3 minutes 56 second difference. In this respect, sidereal time is different from the ordinary clock time we use in our daily routines that divides the day into am and pm. Ephemeris tables for sidereal time are usually at noon or midnight.

Sidereal Year: The time for one complete revolution of the Earth around the Sun, relative to the fixed stars. Measured as 365 days, 6 hours, 9 minutes and 9.54 seconds (units) of Mean Solar Time (MST).

Sidereal Zodiac: See User's Guide under *Zodiac*, Part 1.

Sigil: A seal, signature, mark, glyph or sign that supposedly has occult or magical powers.

Sigma Point: The intersection of the observer's celestial meridian and the celestial equator.

Signs of Long Ascension: The signs that take a longer time in ascending (rising) than the other signs. In the northern hemisphere these signs are Leo ♌, Virgo ♍, Libra ♎, Scorpio ♏, Sagittarius ♐, and Capricorn ♑. The Southern hemisphere signs of long ascension are opposite those in the northern hemisphere.

Signs of Voice: These are the signs that can make sounds, as heard by human ears: Aries ♈, Taurus ♉, Gemini ♊, Virgo ♍, Libra ♎, Aquarius ♒, and Sagittarius ♐. See also *Mute Signs.*

Singleton: This is the sole planet in an otherwise empty hemisphere of a chart, especially in the *bucket configuration.* The singleton planet is the handle and becomes a strong focal planet. Also refers to the only planet in a sign.

Solar Day: The time between two successive meridian passages of Sun. The average value of the apparent solar day is the Mean Solar Day.

Solar Return: The solar return is when the Sun returns to the same place it was at the time of birth. In a transit search this would be represented by the Sun conjunct Sun (☉ ☌ ☉). Every year, everyone has a solar return - your birthday. The solar return is useful for forecasting the events and attitudes someone is likely to experience during the upcoming year. A solar return cast for an individual's birthday on 1 January 1999 will provide information about the issues and events that are likely to be prominent to their next birthday at 1 January 2000. See also User's Guide under *Return Charts.*

Solar Time: The time we use for practical purposes. Its basis is the apparent daily motion of the Sun.

Solar Year: The time between two successive transits of the Sun through the vernal equinox (solar return to the vernal equinox). It is the calendar year we use consisting of 365.2422 mean solar days. It is also commonly called the "tropical year". A solar month is one twelfth of a solar year.

Solstices: *Sol* = Sun; *stice* = make stand. When the Sun is at its greatest northern or southern declination and appears to stand still. This occurs about 22 to 23rd of June (0° Cancer ♋,) and December (0° Capricorn ♑). At these points, the Sun is furthest from the Equator and appears stationary. These are the longest and shortest days of the year respectively. See also *equinoxes* and User's Guide (Part 1) under *Tropical Zodiac* for diagram.

Square: Symbol □, an aspect of 90°. See *Aspects.*

Standard Meridian: The meridian system adopted for time zones. Standard meridians are in increments of 15° longitude beginning from the Prime Meridian (0°) at Greenwich, England.

Standard Time: The local civil time of a standard meridian. The difference between the time zones is usually (but not always) 1 hour, and 15° longitude.

Station: When a planet appears stationary (from Earth) and is changing either from direct to retrograde, or from retrograde to direct, it is "at station". Astrologically, when a planet is at station, it is possible to feel the planet's energy clearly or more intensely. See also *Retrograde.*

Stellium: A grouping of at least three planets whose position is about the same degree in the horoscope; these planets are in a multiple conjunction.

Succedent Houses: See *Houses, Kinds.*

Sun: A star that is the basis of our solar system and that, being the source of light and heat, sustains life on Earth. A sun also can be any star that is the center of a planetary system. Astrologers sometimes call the Sun a planet because of traditional nomenclatures established by the geocentric perspective.

The glyph for the Sun ☉ suggests a target, just as the Sun represents your center. Symbolically it also represents the circle of spirit containing the essential seed, or soul. Another interpretation of the glyph is that the circle represents the infinite and unlimited potential of the spirit; the dot is the point where the infinite transforms into finite form. It allows you to be aware of your central being.

The Sun sign represents individuality, will and power. The metal of the Sun is gold. The Sun rules over the sign Leo ♌, is exalted in Aries ♈, and has its fall in Libra ♎.

Positive Solar traits are: purposeful, integrated, creative, self-confident, generous, big-hearted, affectionate, and dignified.

Negative Solar traits are: pompous, arrogant, domineering, extravagant, condescending, unintegrated, timid, and self-centered.

Superior Planets: Not reflecting quality, but location. The superior plants are those whose orbits lie outside Earth's orbit: Mars ♂, Jupiter ♃, Saturn ♄, Uranus ♅, Neptune ♆, and Pluto ♇.

Super Moon: This is a new term coined by Richard Nolle to describe what is technically a perigee-syzygy, of a new or full Moon (syzygy) that occurs when the Moon is at its closest point to the Earth (perigee). Astrologer Nolle proposes there is ample evidence to suggest that a super Moon alignment can be a major cause of upheavals in geophysical activity (including earthquakes and weather), and mass psychology (including social and economic disruptions). Super Moon alignments for the 90s are below:

Table 27. Super Moons

DATE	GMT	SIGN	SUPER MOON TYPE
1990 April 25	04:27	at 04°43 ' ♉ Taurus	New Moon
1990 May 24	11:47	at 03°03 ' ♊ Gemini	New Moon
***1990 Dec. 2**	**07:50**	**at 9°52' ♊ Gemini**	**Powerful full Moon**
1990 Dec 31	18:35	at 09°50' ♋ Cancer	Full Moon
1991 June 12	12:06	at 21°02 ' ♊ Gemini	New Moon
***1991 July 11**	**19:06**	**at 18°59' ♋ Cancer**	**New Moon eclipse**
***1991 Dec. 21**	**10:23**	**at 29°03' ♊ Gemini**	**Full Moon eclipse**
***1992 Jan. 19**	**21:28**	**at 29°04' ♋ Cancer**	**Powerful full Moon**
1992 Feb 18	08:04	at 28°55 ' ♌ Leo	Full Moon
1992 July 29	19:35	at 06°54 ' ♌ Leo	New Moon
1992 Aug 28	02:42	at 05°03 ' ♍ Virgo	New Moon
1993 Feb 6	23:55	at 18°13 ' ♌ Leo	Full Moon
***1993 March 8**	**09:46**	**at 17°50' ♍ Virgo**	**Powerful full Moon**
1993 April 6	18:43	at 16°58 ' Libra	Full Moon
1993 Sept 16	03:10	at 23°16' ♍ Virgo	New Moon
1993 Oct 15	11:36	at 22°08' ♎ Libra	New Moon
1994 March 27	11:10	at 06°33 ' ♎ Libra	Full Moon
1994 April 25	19:45	at 05°22' ♏ Scorpio	Full Moon
***1994 Nov 3**	**13:35**	**at 10°54' ♏ Scorpio**	**New Moon eclipse**
1994 Dec 2	23:54	at 10°35' ♐ Sagittarius	New Moon
1995 May 14	20:48	at 23°35 ' ♏ Scorpio	Full Moon
1995 Jun 13	04:04	at 21°42' ♐ Sagittarius	Full Moon
1995 Dec 22	02:22	at 29°45' ♐ Sagittarius	New Moon
1996 Jan 20	12:51	at 29°45' ♑ Capricorn	New Moon
1996 July 1	03:58	at 09°36 ' ♑ Capricorn	Full Moon
1996 July 30	10:35	at 07°32' Aquarius	Full Moon
1997 Feb 7	15:06	at 18°53' ♒ Aquarius	New Moon
***1997 Mar. 9**	**01:15**	**at 18°31' ♓ Pisces**	**New Moon eclipse**
1997 Aug 18	10:55	at 25°32' ♒ Aquarius	Full Moon
***1997 Sep. 16**	**18:51**	**at 23°56' ♓ Pisces**	**Full Moon eclipse**
1998 Mar 28	03:14	at 07°15' ♈ Aries	New Moon

1998 April 26	11:41	at 06°03' ♉ Taurus	New Moon
1998 Oct 5	20:12	at 12°23 ' ♈ Aries	Full Moon
1998 Nov 4	05:18	at 11°35 ' ♉ Taurus	Full Moon
1991 May 15	12:05	at 24°14' ♉ Taurus	New Moon
1999 Jun 13	19:03	at 22°20 ' ♊ Gemini	New Moon
1999 Nov 23	07:04	at 00°23 ' ♊ Gemini	Full Moon
1991 Dec 22	17:31	at 00°25' ♋ Cancer	Full Moon

*Super Moons that will be part of eclipses or exert unusually strong forces

Detailed description of the super Moon phenomena is in *The Astrology of the Macrocosm: New Directions in Mundane Astrology*, in the chapter entitled "The Super Moon Alignment" by Richard Nolle.

Synastry (Relationship) Chart: A synastry chart compares the birth charts of two people in a bi-wheel form (concentric bi-wheel). The astrologer can then compare the interrelated aspects between the two charts. A synastry reading can yield much information about the way the two people affect and interact with each other. See also *Synastry Chart* in the User's Guide.

Synodic Cycle: See *Cycles, Synodic*

Synodic Month: The average time between two successive full moons, equal to 29 days, 12 hours, 44 minutes and 2.8 seconds. This is also the "Lunar Month".

Synodic Period: See *Synodic Month.*

Syzygy: Derived from Greek *suzugia*, and Latin *syzygia*, meaning union, coupling or yoking together. Syzygy often describes Sun-Moon conjuctions ☽☌☉, and sometimes for oppositions of the lights ☽☍☉. Technically, you should only use the term with the Sun and Moon. Sygygy is also when the Sun, Moon and Earth align in a straight line, as during total eclipses.

T

Taurus: The second sign of the zodiac ruled by Venus. It is a feminine, earth, fixed sign. The Sun is in Taurus from about 20 April to May 21.

The symbol of Taurus ♉, represents a bull's head and horns, or a pot of earth that contains the Aries seedling. Like a bull, Taurus types tend to be strong-willed, conservative, slow, practical and sensuous. Taurus gives the Aries energy an earthy grounding, it is like the baby discovering the physical world, seeing, seeking comfort and sensual pleasure. Security is important. Taurus does things a little slower than other signs, but it consistently plods along until it gets what it wants.

Positive Taurus traits: persevering, reliable, compassionate, loyal, trustworthy, steady, earthy, practical, and patient.

Negative Taurus traits: possessive, lazy, self-indulgent, a potential bore, inflexible, stubborn, obsessed with routine, and tyrannical.

Thoth: In Egyptian mythology Thoth (Mercury) was the inventor of astrology. He was in charge of the "Merkhet", or "instrument of knowing", a tool used to detect the direction of the stars for the orientation of temples and pyramids.

Toro: Symbol ⚴, an asteroid. The asteroid Toro is not associated with mythology, but appears to have the characteristics of a bull on a rampage. The orbit of Toro is one of the strangest. Toro orbits the Sun with resonance to both Venus and Earth. What this means astrologically is still being determined. See also *Asteroids.*

Transit: A transit occurs when the current position of a planet forms an aspect to a planet, Sun, Moon, house cusps, or any other point in the natal chart. In astrology, transits are a useful way to understand personal life changes, including mood shifts. See Table 33: Major Life Transits by Age.

Transiting Planets: Whenever a planet passes through the part of the zodiac occupied by a house in the natal chart it is transiting through that house.

Trapezium: A pattern of planets consisting of a parallelogram, or a four sided figure with two sides parallel. This configuration has many variations on a theme.

Figure 57. Trapeziam

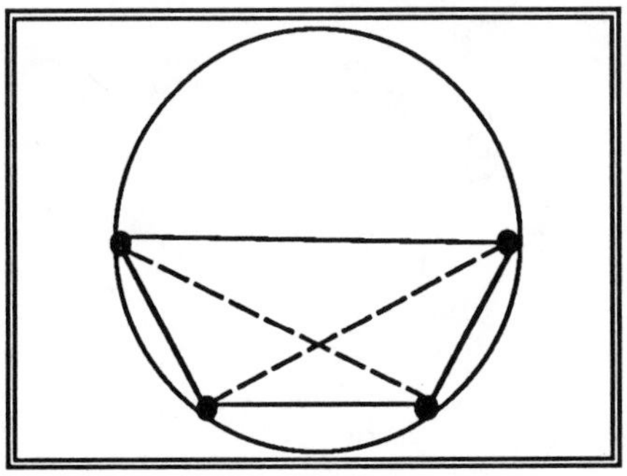

Astrologer Palden Jenkins, in his book *Living in Time*, interprets the trapezium structures as:

- The two aspects linking opposite corners show the main issues.
- The shorter of the two parallel sides suggests the energy source.
- The longer of the two parallel sides indicates the means of expression.

Trigon: See *Triplicity.*

Trigonocrators: See *Triplicity.*

Trine: Symbol △, an aspect of 120° considered a strong and favorable aspect. Trines suggest an ease or complimentary flow of energies. See also *Aspects.*

Triplicity: The division of the zodiac signs into the four elements, earth, air, fire and water. Although there are four elements, it is a triplicity because there are three (*tri*) signs within each element. That is, the 12 signs are each divided into four elements (12 signs / 4 elements = 3 signs per element). See also *Elements.*

Another ancient form of triplicity is trigon which specifies a group of three signs linked with the same element; it is basically equivalent to triplicity. Similarly, *trigonocrators* is a Greek term meaning "rulers of trigons". This relates to a doctrine developed by Ptolemy that gives planetary rule over the four groups of triplicities as shown below.

Table 28. Trigonocrators

Triplicity	Signs	Day Planet Ruler	Night Planet Ruler
Fire	Aries ♈ Leo ♌, Sagittarius ♐	Sun ☉	Jupiter ♃
Earth	Taurus ♉ Virgo ♍ Capricorn ♑	Venus ♀	Moon ☽
Air	Gemini ♊ Libra ♎ Aquarius ♒	Saturn ♄	Mercury ☿
Water*	Cancer ♋ Scorpio ♏ Pisces ♓	Mars ♂ Venus ♀*	Mars ♂ Moon ☽*

**The water tripicity has the single rule of "negative Mars", but with the two co-rulers of Venus and Moon as indicated.*

According to Fred Gettings in his *Dictionary of Astrology*, many modern astrologers misunderstand the idea behind the trigonocrators and are using the planetary rulerships of the individual zodiac signs instead of the older rulerships of their elemental natures.

Tri-Wheel (Triple Wheel) Chart: Sometimes also called a triple wheel because it displays three concentric circles with the positions of points in a chart displayed inside each wheel. See Figure 27: Tri-Wheel or Triple Wheel Chart.

Tropic of Cancer: The parallel of latitude 23 degrees, 27 minutes north of the equator (equal to the obliquity of the ecliptic). This is the most northern latitude the Sun reaches at its greatest declination (height or distance from the equator) at an altitude of 90°. When the Sun reaches the Tropic of Cancer (in June) it is the summer solstice and the longest day (daylight) of the year in the northern hemisphere. At this time the Sun appears to stand still in the sky as it enters the sign of Cancer (0° ♋).

Tropic of Capricorn: The parallel of latitude 23 degrees, 27 minutes south of the equator (equal to the obliquity of the ecliptic). This is the most southern latitude the Sun reaches at its greatest declination (height or distance from the equator) at an altitude of 90°. When the Sun reaches the Tropic of Cancer (in December) it is the winter solstice and the shortest day (daylight) of the year in the northern hemisphere. At this time, the Sun appears to stand still in the sky as it enters the sign of Capricorn (0° ♑).

Tropical Month: The time equal to 26 days, 7 hours, 43 minutes and 4.7 seconds.

Tropical Year: The time between two successive transits of the Sun through the vernal equinox. It is the calendar year we use consisting of 365.2422 mean solar days. It is also commonly called the "solar year".

Tropical Zodiac: See User's Guide - Part 1 under *Tropical Zodiac.*

T- Square: A pattern of planets with a square opposition square aspect structure. It is a challenging aspect with energy striving to release to overcome limitations. The issue and choice in this arrangement is either work and breakthrough, or avoidance and breakdown.

Figure 58. T-Square

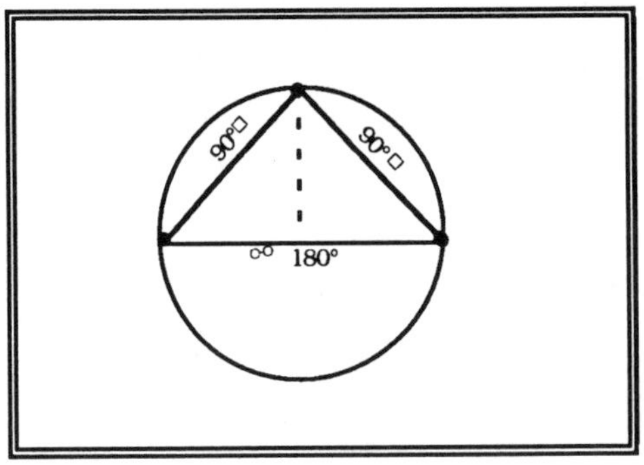

U

Umbra: A dark area, and specifically, the blackest part of a shadow where all light is cut off; the full shadow cast by an object.

Umbral Eclipse: The Moon is in umbral eclipse when it touches the Earth's shadow. A total umbral eclipse of the Moon is when the Moon is completely within the Earth's shadow.

Under The Sun's-Beams: A term showing that a point or planet in a chart is within 17° orb of the Sun.

United Astrology Congress (UAC): An international conference sponsored jointly by Association for Astrological Networking (AFAN), International Society for Astrological Research (ISAR), and the National Council for Geocosmic Research (NCGR). UAC is held biannually on even numbered years. Contact any of the sponsoring organizations for information about the next conference.

Universal Time: Mean Solar Time derived from mean midnight on the meridian of Greenwich.

Uranian: Uranian is an adjective describing an erratic or independent nature. These descriptions extend to the planet Uranus that has the archetypal characteristics of being original and unorthodox.

Uranian School: A modern branch of astrology derived from the Hamburg School of Alfred Witte. The Uranian School approach uses midpoints and a variety of formulas that combine the various points in a chart. Planetary pictures can consist of natal, progressed, and transiting points. Uranian astrology also uses 8 hypothetical planets, whose influences, or energies have been measured, but whose physical presence has not been discovered. See also *Uranian Astrology* under *Astrology Specialities*.

Uranian Planets: Hypothetical planets that Uranian astrologers assume exist. Their presence explains forces that act on other bodies. The eight Uranian planet's names are: Cupido ♃, Hades ⯓, Zeus ⯔, Kronos ⯕, Apollon ⯖, Admetos ⯗, Vulcanus ⯘, and Poseidon ⯙. See also name of the individual Uranian Planets.

Urania: Symbol ⚸, an asteroid. Urania was the Muse of Astronomy from Greek Mythology. From Greek *Ourania* meaning "the heavenly one". In Greek times, astronomy and astrology were not so clearly delineated. Urania might symbolize the process by which the universe translates into intelligible form that humans can understand. See also *Asteroids* and *Muses*.

Uranus: The seventh planet from the Sun, Uranus orbits between Saturn and Neptune. It has 15 satellites and a ring system like Saturn. Uranus takes about 84 years to travel around the Sun and remains in each zodiac sign about 7 years. Compared with other planets, Uranus is unorthodox in its movements. We do not know why its orbit is different from the mathematically predictable orbit, or why it has an extreme axial tilt. Its axis has a radical 98° tilt, compared to the Earth's tilt of 23.5°.

Uranus rules Aquarius, is exalted in Scorpio, has its detriment in Leo and fall in Taurus. Mythologically, Uranus was a personification of the sky. He was the son and consort of Gaea, and the father of the Cyclopes and Titans.

The glyph ♅ symbolizes two personalities of the physical and spiritual, joined by the cross of matter with the Sun or ego breaking through Saturn's confining shell to higher realms. The little circle might represent the energy and vital force ready to explode. The symbol also might suggest the initial of its discover, Herschel.

Uranus symbolizes the capacity to free ourselves from past limitations. It is the planet of change, including social and personal revolutions and disruptions. This change is usually original and can manifest as genius or madness; it is reformative and unconventional. In the birth chart, Uranus shows how and where we can create meaningful change in our lives, and express our unique individuality. Physiologically, Uranus rules electrical impulses that travel through the nervous system. Uranian types usually have highly sensitive nervous systems and are prone to nervous tension, if not breakdowns.

Positive Uranian traits: brilliant, original, inventive, progressive, innovative, independent, versatile intuition.

Negative Uranian traits: erratic, unreliable, rebellious, deviant, antisocial, cranky, abnormal.

V

Venus: As the second planet from the Sun, Venus is an "inferior" planet because its orbit is inside that of Earth's. Venus is always close to the Sun, never traveling more than 48° from it along the ecliptic. In a birth chart, Venus either occupies the same sign as the Sun, or falls within two signs either side of Sun.

Mythologically, Venus was the goddess of Love and beauty, identified with the Greek goddess Aphrodite. She is the embodiment of grace, harmony and loveliness. Venus rules over Taurus and Libra, is exalted in Pisces, detriment in Aries and has its fall in Virgo. Many esoteric astrologers view Venus as the twin sister of Earth.

Scientifically, the glyph for Venus ♀ is the symbol for female. It is even like a flower, whose purpose of beauty, the colors and scents, is to attract pollination so that the plant can bear fruit and support life.

Astrologically, Venus represents the power to love. It is the feminine influence in both sexes and represents the ability to enjoy beauty, feelings, and to co-operate with others. Venus symbolizes how we draw to ourselves what we love and value.

Positive Venusian traits: adept in love and the social arts, appreciation of beauty in life, refined, graceful, artistic,

Negative Venusian traits: self-indulgent, vain, over sensuous, lazy, indecisive, excessively romantic, impractical, too dependent on others.

Vernal Equinox: The beginning of the tropical zodiac at the first point of Aries (0° ♈) where the Sun crosses the equator around 21 March each year. It is the point from which you measure the right ascension and the tropical celestial longitude. See Figure 1: Seasons, Solstices, and Equinoxes.

Vespertine: Relates to appearing in the evening. In astronomy, vespertine refers to a planet that sets in the west after Sunset. In botany and zoology, it applies to plants that bloom in the evening, or animals that become active in the night. The opposite of vespertine is *matutine.*

Vesta: Symbol ⚶; one of four asteroids most used in astrology readings. Vesta represents the sister, and in Roman mythology, she was the goddess of the hearth or home. She is the Greek goddess, Hestia, who was worshiped in the ancient Temple of Vesta. This ancient temple also housed the sacred fire tended by the six vestal virgin priestesses. Vesta is the third largest asteroid with a diameter of approximately 310 miles. Vesta was discovered in 1807.

Astrologically, Vesta in a birth chart shows where there is a need for personal commitment to work and ideals. See also *Asteroids*.

Virgo: The sixth sign of the zodiac, Virgo is a feminine, earth, mutable sign ruled by Mercury. The Sun is in Virgo from about 21 August to 23 September.

The glyph for Virgo ♍ might be a contracted drawing of the serpent severed by Virgo's harvesting scythes. A similar interpretation is true for Scorpio and this implies that the symbols for Scorpio ♏ and Virgo ♍ involve serpents. Both signs involve health and healing. Another interpretation is that the glyph symbolizes the feminine sexual parts, as Virgo comes from Virgin.

One European astrologer who has intensely studied the *Bible* for astrological inferences, believes the reference to Virgin Mary did not mean that she was a "virgin" in our modern definition. He believes this means she was born under the sign of Virgo. As a deeply religious man, he also believes that this does not affect the purity or holiness of the mother of the Christ. He thinks that the meaning of Virgo to virgin changed with the fall of the Roman Empire that began the Dark Ages (476AD) and continued during the Inquisition (1237-1834AD). During that time, the Catholic church considered astrology to be a pagan activity and the work of the devil. Anyone who believed in, or used astrology was a "heretic", for which the punishment was often torture and death.

In modern astrology, Virgo is sometimes a synonym for purity and perfection. A Virgo keyword is service. Characteristically, Virgos are hard workers, extremely practical and have a love for detail, analysis and learning. Health is a concern of Virgo. Precision and neatness are naturals for a Virgo.

Positive Virgo traits: service, health concerned, analytical, meticulous, modest, tidy, industrious, considerate, reliable.

Negative Virgo traits: aloof, finicky, hypercritical, and hypochondriac.

Vocational Astrology: See *Astrology Specialties*.

Void or Elemental Void: The absence of an element in the horoscope represents a void. This suggests a need to compensate for that element. The four elements are fire, earth, air and water. For example, a person with no planets in earth signs might need to focus on connecting with the earth (dirt) and staying grounded. This person might use gardening as a grounding influence.

Void of Course Moon: "Void of course" literally means "moving toward nothing". The Moon is void between the time it forms its last major aspect to any other planet, and its ingress (entry) into the next sign. The last major aspects are the traditional Ptolemaic aspects: conjunction ☌, sextile ⚹, square □, trine △, and opposition ☍. The duration of a void of course Moon can be seconds, or hours.

In astrology, the void of course Moon is when you might feel disconnected and without direction. It is an inauspicious time to make decisions, and a difficult time to begin any new venture, because there is no energy to support the effort. It is also a bad time to have surgery or operations of any kind. Void of Course is a good time to get centered, take time off from business, let life flow, and be concerned with spiritual, non-materialistic efforts.

Vulcan: Symbol ⚴, this intra-mercurial planet symbolizes an explosive nature of great energy, power and force. This is probably the most famous hypothetical planet and has been discussed since mid 1850. Some astrologers think Vulcan is the asteroid Icarus. There is some association of Vulcan with sunspots and atmospheric changes. See also *Icarus*.

Alice A. Bailey, in her system of "intuitional astrology", concludes that Vulcan is a "sacred planet" connected with the "First Ray". See *Rays, the Seven*. In Roman mythology, Vulcan is the God of Fire and craftsmanship, especially metalworking.

Vulcanus: A Uranian astrology term that has several meanings in astrology. Vulcanus is a hypothetical planet of Uranian astrology.

Vulcan Period: An esoteric astrology term to describe a future and perhaps final condition of humanity and Earth. This period will be when humanity has reached its highest spiritual evolution and consciousness. The Vulcan Period has no relationship with Uranian Astrology.

W

Wane: When something is decreasing in light, it is waning. The Moon wanes as it goes from the full Moon ○ through the third quarter ◑ to the new Moon ●. Opposite of waxing, which is to increase in light. The waning Moon can be easily remembered as the "left-hand Moon" as the index finger and thumb of the left hand form the crescent of a decreasing Moon. See also *Moonrise*.

Water Bearer: Glyph ♒, the symbol of the water bearer 

is of a man pouring water from a vase or urn. Aquarius is a zodiac sign, and a constellation.

Water Signs: Cancer ♋, Scorpio ♏, and Pisces ♓.

Waxing: To increase in light, as from the new Moon ●, through the first quarter ◐, to the full Moon ○. The waxing Moon can remembered by the "right-hand Moon" by using the index finger and thumb to form a crescent of the Moon's increasing light. Opposite of waning.

Week Days and Planets: In everyday modern languages traditional astrology appears in the week days. Some examples are below:

Table 29. Week Days and Planets

Planet	English	French	Italian	Spanish
Moon	Monday	Lundi	Lunedí	Lunes
Mars	Tuesday	Mardi	Martedí	Martes
Mercury	Wednesday	Mercredi	Mercoledí	Miércoles
Jupiter	Thursday	Jeudi	Giovedí	Jueves
Venus	Friday	Venredi	Venerdí	Viernes
Saturn	Saturday	Samedi	Sabado	Sábado
Sun	Sunday	Dimanche	Domenica	Domingo

West Point: The west point has several definitions. (1.) The equatorial descendant as the western intersection of the ecliptic with the great circle through the celestial poles and the east and west points of the horizon. (2.) The point where the prime vertical and the horizon intersect in the west. (3.) In terms of ecliptic longitude, the vertex is the degree of the ecliptic that is due west of the birth place. This point is commonly (and mistakenly) called by astrologers the western point on the horizon, or the symbolic point of sunset in a horoscope.

Whole Signs: An unexplained term sometimes applied to Gemini ♊, Libra ♎, Aquarius ♒, Taurus ♉, Leo ♌, Scorpio ♏ and Sagittarius ♐.

Y

Yod: A pattern of three planets with two planets forming a sextile with each other. Both planets are in a clockwise and counterclockwise 150° quincunx (inconjunct) to the planet at the tip of the apex.

Figure 59. Yod

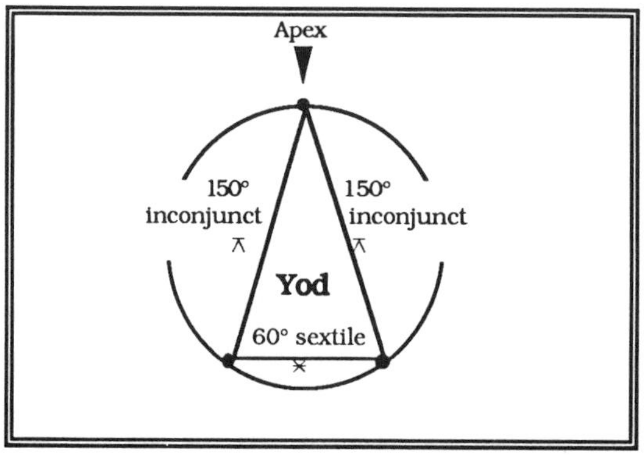

The Yod is sometimes called the "Finger of God", " Hand of God", and the "Finger of Destiny". It is type of "do or die" scenario, with the apex being the critical factor in determining the outcome.

Astrologer Myrna Lofthus feels the purpose of the Yod is to bestow upon the individual a special blessing, if the conscious mind can remember its divinity and seek spiritual riches. In this sense, Lofthus describes the Yod as a form of "dowsing rod" that draws the positive vibrations from the planets and signs involved. Through these positive vibrations, the person can "find" their higher self(s).

Yod is a Hebrew name for the letters I, J and Y. With Pluto ♇ and Neptune ♆ forming a sextile over the past few decades the Yod has been a relatively common configuration.

Z

Zadkiel: The name of the spiritual being ruling the sphere of Jupiter.

Zazel: The name from ancient cabbalistic sources given to the Daemon of Saturn.

Zenith: The point directly above the observer on the celestial sphere. It is always 90° above the horizon and is geometrically the pole of the horizon. In popular speech, the Sun is sometimes said to reach its zenith, which refers to the highest point in the diurnal arc relative to a given place on Earth. Sometimes, astrologers erroneously call the cusp of the 10th house the zenith. See *Midheaven* and *Angles, the Four* for diagram. The zenith is opposite the Nadir (see also).

Zero Degree: 0° is within the first degree of a sign from 0°0'0" to 0°59'59". The first point would be a more astute term, such as the first point of Aries.

Zeus: Symbol ⚵ one of eight hypothetical planets of Uranian astrology. Zeus is the upper octave of Uranus and relates to physical leadership and creativity.

Zodiac: An 8° band on both sides of the Earth's Ecliptic, (16°) that contains the constellations (12 signs) of the zodiac. See section 1 for more details.

Zodiac Metals: The metals of the planetary rulers:

Table 30. Zodiac Metals and Planetary Rulers

Zodiac Sign	Metal	Planetary Ruler*
Aries/Scorpio	Iron	Mars ♂
Taurus/Libra	Copper	Venus ♀
Gemini/Virgo	Mercury	Mercury ☿
Cancer	Silver	Moon ☽
Leo	Gold	Sun ☉
Sagittarius/Pisces	Tin	Jupiter ♃
Capricorn/Aquarius	Lead	Saturn ♄

** Note, all pairs of signs are old rulerships of planets.*

Zodiac Symbols: There are many pictures depicting the zodiac. Below are simplistic drawings of the twelve zodiac figures.

Table 31. Zodiac Symbols

Symbol	Sign	Common Name	Glyph
	Aries	Ram	♈
	Taurus	Bull	♉
	Gemini	Twins	♊
	Cancer	Crab	♋
	Leo	Lion	♌
	Virgo	Virgin	♍
	Libra	Scales	♎
	Scorpio	Scorpion,	♏
	Sagittarius	Archer, Centaur Archer	♐
	Capricorn	Goat, Sea Goat	♑
	Aquarius	Water Bearer	♒
	Pisces	Fish	♓

PART FOUR:

USEFUL CASTING INFORMATION

When casting or interpreting charts, you might need information that would be time saving to have in one handy reference. This is especially true when using programs that do not offer features such as auto time correction and geographic databases. Additionally, included in this section are other concise bits of data and information not often found in consolidated tables or convenient sources.

A. Orbs and Aspects

B. Major Life Transits

C. Major Planetary Conjuctions

D. Rising Sign Table

E. Data on the Sun, Moon and Planets

F. Astronomical Constants

G. World Time Zones

H. Major World City Coordinates and Time Zones

Listed by City

Listed by Country

Listed by Region

A. Orbs and Aspects

There are many different opinions regarding the proper orb, or how many degrees to either side of a planet's position should be allowed. Since orbs do not have a fixed or definite cut-off point, they can be defined closely or widely. A wide orb is 10° to 12° and usually reserved for the lights (Sun and Moon). A close orb would be 1°, often used for transits. Below is a table summarizing the aspects and orbs recommended by various astrologers.

Table 32. Orbs and Aspects

Symbol	Degrees	Name	Orb Range	Signs Apart	Harmonic Divisions or comments	Interpretive Meaning
☌	0°	Conjunction	8°-12°	0	1/1	Blended power United Energy
⩚	18°	Vigintile or Semi-decile			1/20	
	22.5	Semi-octile			1/16	
√	24	Quindecile			1/15	
⊻	30°	Semi-sextile	2°	1	1/12	Continuity, Sympathetic or flowing energy
	32.73°	Undecagon			1/11	
⊥	36°	Decile or Semi-quintile			1/10	
	40°	Nonagen or Novile	up to 2° orb		1/9	
∠	45°	Semi-square, or Octile	2° - 4°	1.5	1/8	Tension or Strain, misalliance
S	51.4°	Septile			1/7	
⚹	60°	Sextile	2° - 7°	2	1/6	Creativity, cooperative energy
Q or ☆	72°	Quintile	2°	2.4	1/5	Artistry, elevation
⋈	80°	Bi-novile			2/9 or novile x 2	
□	90°	Square	5°-8°	3	1/4	Strain or Stress, Challenges, Dynamic Tension

Orbs and Aspects (continued)

Symbol	Degrees	Name	Orb Range	Signs Apart	Harmonic Divisions or comments	Interpretive Meaning
✳	102.8°	Bi-septile			2/7 septile x 2	
¥	108°	Tredecile or Tresile			1.5 quintile or 3 signs +18°	
△	120 °	Trine	4°-8°	4	1/3	Ease or Complementary flow of energies
⚼	135 °	Sesquiquadrate, Sesquare or Tri-octile	2°	4.5		Stress or Strain
± or ☆	144 °	Bi-quintile	2°		2/5	Intellectual function, fundamental energies of change
⚻	150 °	Inconjunct or Quincunx	2°	5	5/12	Adjustment, Uncertainty, Fluxation of energies
	154.3°	Tri-septile			3/7 A septile x 3	
⋈	160°	Quatri-novile			4/9	
☍	180 °	opposition	6°-12°	6	1/2	Awareness, Challenges, Objectivity
ǁ or ‡	-	parallel, contraparallel	1°	-		Emphasis

According to Mark Pottenger there are conflicts regarding symbols for aspects. Mark is assembling a central repository for glyphs and has been surveying astrologers for glyphs they use. Some astrologers use the symbol for biseptile ⁎ to also represent the septile and tri-septile. Some astrologers use the symbol ☆ to represent both the quintile and bi-quintile. In the set above we used ☆ to represent a bi-quintile.

The use of hyphens in aspects is not standard. We used hyphens for any aspect that has a bi-, tri-, semi- or quatri-. For example, semi-decile rather than semidecile and quarti-novile rather than quatrinovile. We believe hyphens make the aspect easier to read and comprehend.

B. Major Life Transits

Often, when interpreting transits, it helps to be aware of the major life transits a person might be experiencing. Below is a table that gives a generalized idea about the timing of major transits. Refer to an ephemeris or transit search for exact times and other transits.

Table 33. Major Life Transits by Age

About Age	Major Transit
7 years	1st Waxing square of Saturn to its natal place ♄ □ ♄.
11.9 years	1st Jupiter return (to its natal place) ♃ ☌ ♃.
14 -15	1st Saturn opposite natal Saturn ♄ ☍ ♄
17 - 18	2nd Jupiter opposition ♃ ☍ ♃.
19 years	2nd nodal cycle begins (moon) ☊ ☌ ☊ and ☋ ☌ ☋.
21 - 22	1st Waning square of Saturn to its natal place ♄ □ ♄.
23 - 24	2nd return of Jupiter ♃ ☌ ♃.
25 - 26	1st Chiron opposition ⚷ ☍ ⚷.
27 - 28	Progressed Moon returns to natal place ☽ ☌ ☽. Uranus trine natal Uranus ♅ △ ♅. 2nd inversion of the moon's nodal positions ☊ ☌ ☋.
28- 30	1st Saturn return (to natal position) ♄ ☌ ♄. 3rd Jupiter opposition ♃ ☍ ♃. Natal Sun/Moon aspect repeats in progressions.
35 - 37 +	2nd waxing square of Saturn to Natal position ♄ □ ♄. 3rd return of Jupiter ♃ ☌ ♃.
38 +/-	3rd nodal moon cycle begins ☋ ☌ ☋.
41 - 42	4th Jupiter opposition natal Jupiter ♃ ☍ ♃. Neptune in waxing square to natal Neptune ♆ □ ♆.
38 - 42	Uranus opposition ♅ ☍ ♅.
43 - 44	2nd Saturn opposition to natal position ♄ ☍ ♄.
47 - 48	3rd inversion of the Moon's nodes to natal nodes ☊ ☌ ☋. 4th Jupiter return ♃ ☌ ♃.
50 - 51	2nd waning square of Saturn to natal place ♄ □ ♄. 1st Chiron Return ⚷ ☌ ⚷
53 - 54	5th Jupiter opposition natal Jupiter ♃ ☍ ♃.
55	Progressed Moon 2nd return to natal position ☽ ☌ ☽.
56	Uranus in waning trine to Uranus ♅ △ ♅. 4th nodal moon cycle begins ☋ ☌ ☋.
56- 58	2nd Saturn return ♄ ☌ ♄.

Major Life Transits by Age (continued)

About Age	Major Transit
59 - 60	5th Jupiter return ♃☌♃. 2nd Natal Sun/Moon aspect repeats in progressions.
63 +/-	Waning square of Uranus to natal position ♅ □ ♅.
65 - 66	3rd waxing square of Saturn to natal position ♄ □♄. 6th Jupiter opposition natal Jupiter ♃☍♃. 4th inversion of the moon's nodal positions ☊☌☋.
72 - 73	3rd Saturn opposition ♄ ☍♄. 6th Jupiter return ♃☌♃.
75 - 76	5th nodal moon cycle begins ☋☌☋. 2nd Chiron opposition ⚷ ☍ ⚷.
76 - 84	1st Uranus return ♅ ☌ ♅.
77 - 78	7th Jupiter opposition natal Jupiter ♃☍♃.
79 - 80	3rd waning square of Saturn to natal position ♄ □♄.
82 +/-	Neptune opposite natal Neptune ♆☍♆.
83 - 85+	7th Jupiter return ♃☌♃. 5th inversion of the Moon's nodal positions ☊☌☋
87 - 88	3rd Saturn Return ♄ ☌♄.
89 - 90	8th Jupiter opposition natal Jupiter ♃☍♃.
94 - 95	4th waxing square of Saturn to natal position ♄ □♄.
95 - 96	8th Jupiter return ♃☌♃. 6th nodal moon cycle begins ☋☌☋.
100 - 101	9th Jupiter opposition natal Jupiter ♃☍♃.
101 - 102	4th Saturn opposition ♄ ☍♄. 2nd Chiron return ⚷☌⚷.
104 +/-	6th inversion of the moon's nodal positions ☊☌☋.
107 +/-	9th Jupiter return ♃☌♃.
108 - 109	4th waning square of Saturn to natal position ♄ □♄.
112 - 113	10th Jupiter opposition natal Jupiter ♃☍♃.
114 +/-	7th nodal moon cycle begins ☋☌☋.
116 - 117	4th Saturn return ♄ ☌♄.
119 +/-	10th Jupiter return ♃☌♃.
123 +/-	11th Jupiter opposition natal Jupiter ♃☍♃. 1st Neptune waning square to natal Neptune ♆ □ ♆.

C. Major Planetary Conjunctions

Conjunctions happen when two planets occupy the same degree in the zodiac. They are one of the most powerful aspects that can be formed. Conjunctions between the outer planets can signify major shifts or events individually, nationally, and across cultures. Below is a list of the major outer planetary conjunctions listed in order of decreasing interval between conjunctions.

To estimate other aspects within each cycle, divide the length of the cycle by four to obtain approximately the first 90° (waxing) square □, 180° opposition ☍, and waning square □. This would respectively place the faster moving planet three signs ahead, six signs apart, and three signs behind the slower moving planet. Check an ephemeris for exact dates. More information about planetary cycles can be found in Vivian B. Martin's book: *Astrocycles*.

1. **Neptune/Pluto** ♆☌♇. About every 492 years.
There can be a change of ideals and psychological shifts through altered awareness.

2333-2334
1891-1892

2. **Uranus/Neptune** ♅☌♆. About every 172 years.
Strange things can happen with this conjunction. New ideas and influences can be subtle but powerful, and perhaps revolutionary.

1992-1993	in Capricorn
1820-1821	

3. **Uranus/Pluto** ♅☌♇. About every 115 to 125 years.
Forces that have been gathering slowly in the environment (individual and collective) can break loose in a sometimes devastating and transforming way. Much growth and social restructuring can occur during this time.

1965	in Virgo
1850	
1710	

4. **Saturn/Uranus** ♄☌♅. About every 45 years.
Reformation of bureaucracies and power structures can take place, possibly extremely suddenly. Progressive urges and internal forces for change can clash with resistance to maintain the status quo. The stage is set for tension and sudden release.

2032	in Gemini
1988	in Sagittarius and Capricorn
1942	in Taurus

5. **Saturn/Neptune** ♄☌♆. About every 36 years.
Saturn rules apparent reality and Neptune rules other realities. These two together are likely to lead to dogmatic fundamentalism vs spiritual conflicts.

2025	in Aries	1952	in Libra
1989	in Capricorn	1917	in Leo

6. **Saturn/Pluto** ♄☌♇. About every 33 years
There can be a change of individual and social structures through evaluating and a cleaning out of obsolete and redundant anything.

2053	in Pisces	1947-1948	in Leo
2019-2020	in Capricorn	1914-1915	in Cancer
1982	in Libra		

7. **Jupiter/Saturn** ♃☌♄. About every 20 years
Societies and individuals are inclined to examine inhibitions and restructure the self. This is a restless time with change vs constrictive forces.

2040	in Libra	1960-1961	in Capricorn
2020	in Capricorn & Aquarius	1941	in Taurus
2000	in Taurus	1921	in Virgo
1980-1981	in Libra		

8. **Jupiter/Uranus** ♃☌♅. About every 14 years.
This transit can bring surprises and sudden opportunities. Situations are seen from a different perspective.

2038	in Cancer	1983	in Sagittarius
2024	in Taurus	1969	in Libra
2010	in Aries	1955	in Cancer
1997	in Aquarius	1941	in Taurus

9. **Jupiter/Neptune** ♃☌♆. About every 13 years.
This is an idealistic and compassionate time with an increased interest in spiritual, religious and mystical philosophy.

2024	in Taurus	1984	in Capricorn
2010	in Aries	1971	in Sagittarius
1997	In Capricorn	1958	in Scorpio

10. **Jupiter/Pluto** ♃☌♇. About every 12 years.
Lots of interest in self-improvement. Energy is available to make great things happen, or totally destroy what is. Power issues can be intense.

2033	in Aquarius	1955-1956	in Leo
2019	in Capricorn	1943	in Leo
2007	in Sagittarius	1931	in Cancer
1994	in Scorpio	1919	in Cancer
1981	in Libra	1907	in Gemini
1968	in Virgo		

D.

Table 34. RISING SIGN TABLE

Hour of Birth

	12 Mid Night	1 AM	2 AM	3 AM	4 AM	5 AM	6 AM	7 AM	8 AM	9 AM	10 AM	11 AM	12 NOON	1 PM	2 PM	3 PM	4 PM	5 PM	6 PM	7 PM	8 PM	9 PM	10 PM	11 PM
JAN	♎	♎	♏	♏	♐	♐	♑	♑	♒	♒	♓	♈	♉	♉	♊	♊	♋	♋	♌	♌	♍	♍	♍	♎
FEB	♏	♏	♐	♐	♑	♑	♒	♒	♓	♈	♉	♉	♊	♊	♋	♋	♌	♌	♍	♍	♍	♎	♎	♎
MAR	♐	♐	♑	♑	♒	♒	♓	♈	♉	♉	♊	♊	♋	♋	♌	♌	♍	♍	♍	♎	♎	♎	♏	♏
APR	♑	♑	♒	♒	♓	♈	♉	♉	♊	♊	♋	♋	♌	♌	♍	♍	♍	♎	♎	♎	♏	♏	♐	♐
MAY	♒	♒	♓	♈	♉	♉	♊	♊	♋	♋	♌	♌	♍	♍	♍	♎	♎	♎	♏	♏	♐	♐	♑	♑
JUNE	♓	♈	♉	♉	♊	♊	♋	♋	♌	♌	♍	♍	♍	♎	♎	♎	♏	♏	♐	♐	♑	♑	♒	♒
JULY	♉	♉	♊	♊	♋	♋	♌	♌	♍	♍	♍	♎	♎	♎	♏	♏	♐	♐	♑	♑	♒	♒	♓	♈
AUG	♊	♊	♋	♋	♌	♌	♍	♍	♍	♎	♎	♎	♏	♏	♐	♐	♑	♑	♒	♒	♓	♈	♉	♉
SEPT	♋	♋	♌	♌	♍	♍	♍	♎	♎	♎	♏	♏	♐	♐	♑	♑	♒	♒	♓	♈	♉	♉	♊	♊
OCT	♌	♌	♍	♍	♍	♎	♎	♎	♏	♏	♐	♐	♑	♑	♒	♒	♓	♈	♉	♉	♊	♊	♋	♋
NOV	♍	♍	♍	♎	♎	♎	♏	♏	♐	♐	♑	♑	♒	♒	♓	♈	♉	♉	♊	♊	♋	♋	♌	♌
DEC	♍	♎	♎	♎	♏	♏	♐	♐	♑	♑	♒	♒	♓	♈	♉	♉	♊	♊	♋	♋	♌	♌	♍	♍

Adapted from *Astrology, The Divine Science* by M. Moore, page 740

Note: These ascendant times correlate approximately with a 40° latitude and standard time. Births closer to the equator show less difference in rising signs between winter and summer births. Conversely, births at either of the poles will have a greater difference in rising signs. At latitudes greater than 60° north or south, this table is unreliable. Also note that southern latitudes must reverse the times because you look at the ecliptic from the opposite direction.

Daylight Saving Time requires advancing time by 1 hour. The use of daylight saving varies greatly both in the United States and worldwide.

E. Data on the Sun, Moon and Planets

In astrology, there are certain data regarding the Sun, Moon and planets that is useful to know. For example, the revolution of a planet around the Sun can tell much about major transits in a person's life, or how long a planet is in a sign. Below are some data that might be helpful, if not interesting.

Table 35. Data on the Sun, Moon and Planets

	PERIOD AROUND SUN (return time)	YEAR DISCOVERED	NUMBER OF MOONS	DISTANCE FROM SUN Mill. Miles	DIAMETER (Miles)	APPROXIMATE TIME IN A SIGN (Geocentric)	PERIOD OF ROTATION ON AXIS
Sun ☉	-	∞	0		865,400	1 month	24.6 days
Moon ☽	27.3 days	∞	0		2,160	2.5 days	27.3 days
Mercury ☿	87.9 days	∞	0	36	3,100	7.3 days	58.7 days
Venus ♀	224.7 days	∞	0	67	7,700	18.7 days	243.2 days
Earth ⊕	365.3 days	∞	1	93	7,927		23 hr 56 min
Mars ♂	1.88 years	∞	2	142	4,200	1.9 month	24 hr 37 min
Jupiter ♃	11.9 years	∞	16	484	88,700	0.9 year	9 hr 50 min
Saturn ♄	29.5 years	∞	21+	887	75,100	2.5 years	10hr 14 min
*Chiron ⚷	50-51 years	1977	0		about 200	5.5 to 23 years	
Uranus ♅	84 years	1781	15	1784	32,000	7 years	16.14hr
Neptune ♆	164.8 years	1846	8	2795	30,776	13.7 years	19 hr 12min
Pluto ♇	248.5 years	1930	1	3675	1430	20.7 years	6 day 9hr

* Chiron is an asteroid or trapped comet.

F. Astronomical Constants

In both astrology and astronomy there are exact constants that are useful when doing calculations and casting charts. A few of these constants are below.

Table 36. Astronomical Constants

TIME	
Mean Solar Day (24h)	24 hrs 3 min 56 sec of Sidereal Time
Mean Sidereal Day (24h)	23 hrs 56 min 4 .9 sec of Mean Solar Time
Mean Solar Second	1 ephemeris second to one part in 10x8.
1 Ephemeris Second	1/31556925975 of tropical year for 1900
LENGTH OF YEAR	
Julian	365.25 days
Tropical (equinox to equinox)	365.2422 days
Sidereal (fixed star to fixed star)	365.2564 days
Anomalistic (perihelion to perihelion)	365.2596 days
Eclipse (lunar node to lunar node)	346.6201
LENGTH OF MONTH	
Synodic (new moon to new moon)	29.5306 days
Tropical (equinox to equinox)	27.3216 days
Sidereal (fixed star to fixed star)	27.3217 days
Anomalistic (perigee to perigee)	27.5546 days
Draconic or Nodical(node to node)	27.2122 days
OTHER CONSTANTS	
Earth's Mean Velocity in Orbit	18.5 miles/second
Oblateness of the Earth	1/297
Velocity of Light	186,281.7 miles/second
Light-Year	5,880,000,000,000 miles

Refer to the Astrological Dictionary for definitions of the constants.

G. Time Zones

To cast a natal chart and obtain the house cusps, the birth time must be converted to Greenwich Mean Time (GMT) so that a standard ephemeris can be used. Some astrology programs require you to enter the birth time already adjusted to (GMT). Other programs allow you to simply enter the time zone, and the computer will automatically calculate GMT for you.

What are time zones all about? The world is divided into twenty-four time zones each separated by 15° of geographical longitude and each representing 1 hour's difference in time. The table below correlates time with longitude.

Table 37. Longitude Correlation to Time

Motion in Longitude or Arc		Clock Time
360°	=	24 hours (1 day)
30° (1 sign or house)	=	2 hours (120 minutes)
15°	=	1 hour (60 minutes)
1°	=	4 minutes
15' (minutes of motion)	=	1 minute of time
1' (minute of motion)	=	4 seconds of time

Be careful not to confuse hours, minutes and seconds of clock time with degrees, minutes and seconds of motion (arc).

Standard Time (ST) for all places in the world is calculated from Greenwich, England which is 0° longitude. In most United States astrology programs time zones east of Greenwich are negative, indicating the number of hours to be subtracted to obtain the GMT. Time zones west of Greenwich are positive, showing the number of hours to be added to obtain GMT.

To have more daylight many countries set their clocks forward one hour in the spring and back one hour in the fall. This varies greatly from country to country. Common names for this are Daylight Saving Time and Summer Time. One easy way to remember to set the clocks backward in the Fall and forward in the Spring is "*Fall Back, Spring Forward*".

The Uniform Time Act of 1966 (Public Law 89-387) put the United States on standard daylight saving time effective in 1967. DST begins from the **last Sunday in April to the Last Sunday in October**, with all time shifts at 2:00 am. A state may vote not to use daylight time, or not have the entire state in a single time zone, for example, Arizona and Hawaii.

In 1990 the United States shifted daylight saving time to begin on the **first Sunday of April**. The daylight saving regulations have helped to end some of the incredible confusion about time in the States.

The table below shows the daylight saving time dates from 1967, when the Uniform Time Act of 1966 went into effect, throughout the year 2000.

Table 38. Daylight Saving Time Dates 1967 - 2000

1966 4/24 - 10/30		
1967 4/30 - 10/29		
1968 4/28 - 10/27		
1969 4/27 - 10/26		
1970 4/26 - 10/25		
1971 4/25 - 10/31	1981 4/26 - 10/25	1991 4/7 - 10/27
1972 4/30 - 10/29	1982 4/25 - 10/31	1992 4/5 - 10/25
1973 4/29 - 10/28	1983 4/24 - 10/30	1993 4/4 - 10/31
1974 1/6 - 10/27	1984 4/29 - 10/28	1994 4/3 - 10/30
1975 2/23 - 10/26	1985 4/28 - 10/27	1995 4/2 - 10/29
1976 4/25 - 10/31	1986 4/27 - 10/26	1996 4/7 - 10/27
1977 4/24 - 10/30	1987 4/26 - 10/25	1997 4/6 - 10/26
1978 4/30 - 10/29	1988 4/24 - 10/30	1998 4/5 - 10/25
1979 4/29 - 10/28	1989 4/30 - 10/29	1999 4/4 - 10/31
1980 4/27 - 10/26	1990 4/7 - 10/27*	2000 4/2 - 10/29

**Daylight Saving Time (DST) switch from last Sunday in April to first Sunday in April*

For commerce, and the convenience of the local residents, time zones still vary in some places. Two references to identify the correct time zones are by Thomas G. Shanks: *The American Atlas* (5th edition), and *The International Atlas*. These cost $40 each but also contain place coordinates along with the time zones and changes. Less expensive, but also less comprehensive references, are by Doris Chase Doane: *Time Changes in the USA*, and *Time Changes in the World*, 1987.

Figure 60. World Map with Time Zones

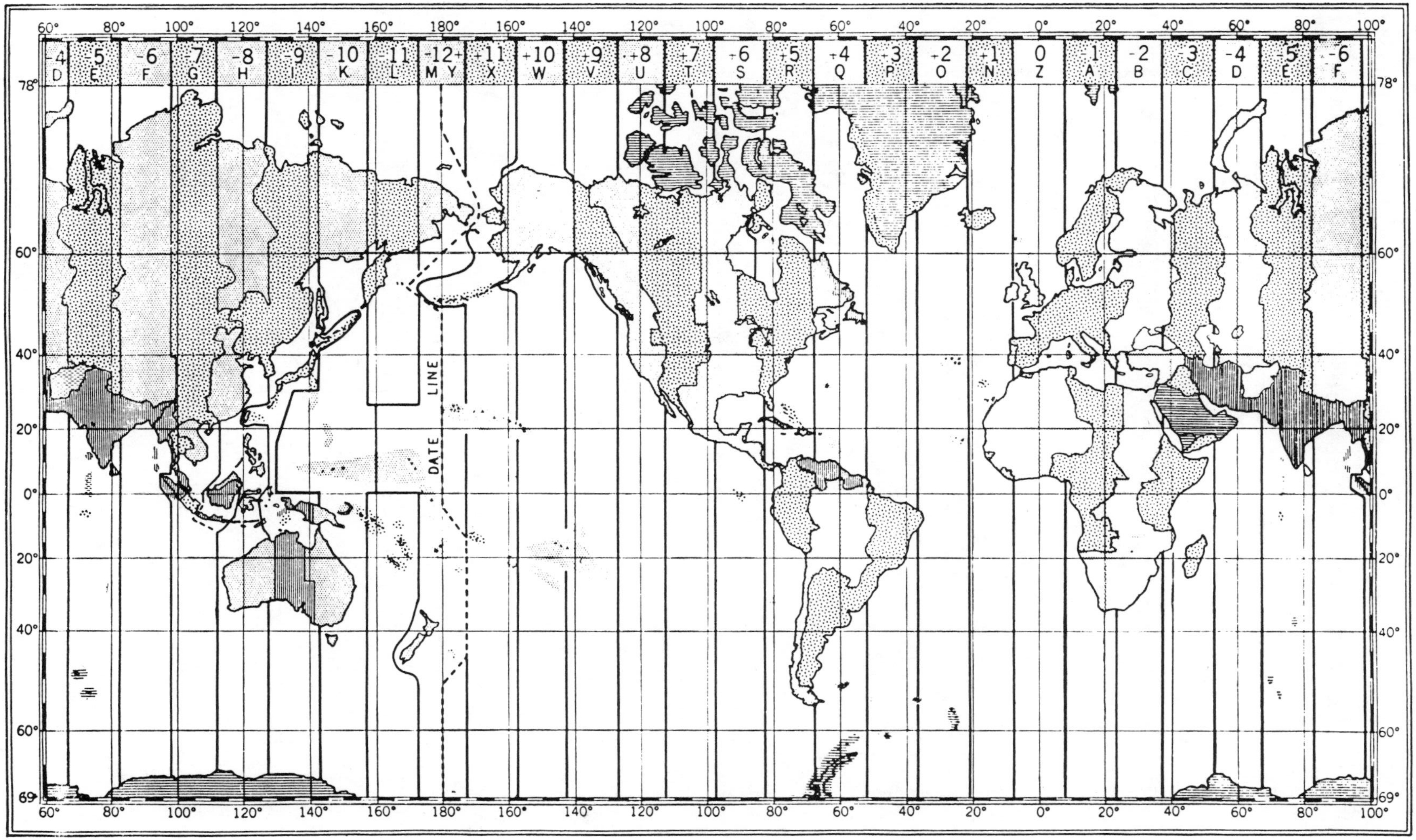

Table 39. World Time Zones

Western Hemisphere

ABBR.	FULL NAME	S.T. Meridian	HOURS TO GMT
GMT	Greenwich Mean Time	0 W 00	0
UT	Universal Time	0 W 00	0
WAT	West Africa Time	15 W 00	+1
AT	Azores Time	30 W 00	+2
BST	Brazil Standard Time	45 W 00	+3
ADT	Atlantic Daylight Time		+3
BZ2	Brazil Zone 2	45 W 00	+3
NST	Newfoundland Standard Time	52 W 30	+3:30
AST	Atlantic Standard Time	60 W 00	+4
EDT	Eastern Daylight Time		+4
EWT	Eastern War Time		+4
EST	Eastern Standard Time	75 W 00	+5
CDT	Central Daylight Time		+5
CWT	Central War Time		+5
CST	Central Standard Time	90 W 00	+6
MDT	Mountain Daylight Time		+6
MWT	Mountain War Time		+6
MST	Mountain Standard Time	105 W 00	+7
PDT	Pacific Daylight Time		+7
PWT	Pacific War Time		+7
PST	Pacific Standard Time	120 W 00	+8
YDT	Yukon Daylight Time		+8
YST	Yukon Standard Time	135 W 00	+9
AHDT	Alaska-Hawaii Daylight Time		+9
CAT	Central Alaska Standard Time	150 W 00	+10
AHST	Alaska-Hawaii Standard Time	150 W 00	+10
HST	Hawaiian Standard Time	157 W 30	+10:30
BST	Bering Standard Time	165 W 00	+11
NT	Nome Time	165 W 00	+11
IDLW	**International Date Line West**	**180 W 00**	**+12**

World Time Zones

Eastern Hemisphere

ABBR.	FULL NAME	S.T. Meridian	HOURS TO GMT
CET	Central European Time	15 E 00	-1
MET	Middle European Time	15 E 00	-1
BST	British Summer Time		-1
EET	Eastern European Time	30 E 00	-2
BDST	British Double Summer Time		-2
BT	Baghdad Time	45 E 00	-3
UZ3	USSR Zone 3	60 E 00	-4
UZ4	USSR Zone 4	50 E 00	-5
IST	Indian Standard Time	82 E 30	-5:30
UZ5	USSR Zone 5	90 E 00	-6
NST	North Sumatra Time	97 E 30	-6:30
SST	South Sumatra Time	105 E 00	-7 hr
JT	Java Time	112 E 30	-7:30
CCT	China Coast Time	120 E 00	-8
JST	Japan Standard Time	135 E 00	-9
SAST	South Australia Standard Time	142 E 30	-9:30
GST	Guam Standard Time	150 E 00	-10
		165 E 00	-11
NZT	New Zealand Time	172 E 30	-11:30
NZST	New Zealand Standard Time	180 E 00	-12
IDLE	**International Date Line East**	**180 E 00**	**-12**

H. Major World City Coordinates

Not all programs have a city atlas included for quick reference to find the coordinates (latitude and longitude) that are necessary to establish the ascendant, or rising degree. Listed below are almost 1,000 major cities worldwide, including most national capitals.

The city coordinates are listed three ways:

1. Alphabetically by City
2. Alphabetically by Country
3. Listed by Region

City	State or Provence	Country	LAT.	LONG.	Time Adjust to GMT	Abv Time	D.S. Time	1991 Daylight Savings Observed
Aberdeen	South Dakota	United States	45 N 28	98 W 29	6+	CST	5+	1st Sun April to Last Sat Oct.
Abidjan		Ivory Coast	5 N 19	4 W 01	0	GMT		No
Abilene	Texas	United States	32 N 28	99 W 43	6+	CST	5+	1st Sun April to Last Sat Oct.
Abu Dhabi		United Arab Emirat	24 N 30	54 E 28	-4			No
Accra		Ghana	5 N 33	0 W 15	0	GMT		No
Adana		Turkey	37 N 05	35 E 20	-3		-4	Last Sun March to Last Sat Sept.
Addis Ababa		Ethiopia	9 N 03	38 E 43	-3			No
Adelaide	S. Australia	Australia	34 S 56	138 E 38	-9.5			Last Sun Oct; 1st Sat March
Aden		Yeman	12 N 47	45 E 02	-3			No
Ahmadabad		India	23 N 03	72 E 41	-5.5			No
Akron	Ohio	United States	41 N 05	81 W 31	5+	EST	4+	1st Sun April to Last Sat Oct.
Al Khartum (Khartoum)		Sudan	15 N 38	32 E 33	-2	EET		No
Alamogordo	New Mexico	United States	32 N 54	105 W 57	7+	MST	6+	1st Sun April to Last Sat Oct.
Albany	New York	United States	42 N 39	73 W 45	5+	EST	4+	1st Sun April to Last Sat Oct.
Albuquerque	New Mexico	United States	35 N 05	106 W 39	7+	MST	6+	1st Sun April to Last Sat Oct.
Aleppo		Syria	36 N 14	37 E 11	-2	EET		No
Alexandria		Egypt	31 N 13	29 E 57	-2	EET		No
Alexandria	Virginia	United States	38 N 48	77 W 03	5+	EST	4+	1st Sun April to Last Sat Oct.
Algiers		Algeria	36 N 47	3 E 04	-1	CET	-2	Last Sun March to Last Sat Sept.
Allentown	Pennsylvania	United States	40 N 37	75 W 29	5+	EST	4+	1st Sun April to Last Sat Oct.
Alma-Ata	Kazakh SSR	USSR	43 N 19	76 E 56	-6		-7	Last Sun March to Last Sat Sept.
Amarillo	Texas	United States	35 N 13	101 W 50	6+	CST	5+	1st Sun April to Last Sat Oct.
Ames	Iowa	United States	42 N 02	93 W 37	6+	CST	5+	1st Sun April to Last Sat Oct.
Amman		Jordan	32 N 57	35 E 56	-2	EET	-3	1st Sun April to Last Sat Oct.
Amsterdam		Netherlands	52 N 22	4 E 54	-1	CET	-2	Last Sun March to Last Sat Sept.
Anchorage	Alaska	United States	61 N 13	149 W 34	10+	AHST	9+	1st Sun April to Last Sat Oct.
Anderson	South Carolina	United States	34 N 31	82 W 39	5+	EST	4+	1st Sun April to Last Sat Oct.
Andorra la Vella		Andorra	42 N 31	1 E 30	-1	CET	-2	Last Sun March to Last Sat Sept.
Ankara		Turkey	39 N 57	32 E 50	-3		-4	Last Sun March to Last Sat Sept.
Annapolis	Maryland	United States	38 N 59	76 W 30	5+	EST	4+	1st Sun April to Last Sat Oct.
Anshun	Guizhou	China	26 N 12	105 E 50	-8	CCT	-9	No
Antananarivo		Madagascar	185 S 51	47 E 40	-3			No
Antwerp		Belgium	51 N 13	4 E 24	-1	CET	-2	Last Sun March to Last Sat Sept.
Apia		Western Samoa	13 S 49	171 W 46	11+			No
Arequipa		Peru	16 S 27	71 W 30	5+		4+	1 Jan to 31 March
Asmera		Ethiopia	15 N 17	38 E 56	-3			No
Asunción		Paraguay	25 S 15	57 W 40	4+		3+	End Sept to End March
Athens		Greece	37 N 59	24 E 43	-2	EET	-3	Last Sun March to Last Sat Sept.
Atlanta	Georgia	United States	33 N 45	84 W 23	5+	EST	4+	1st Sun April to Last Sat Oct.
Atlantic City	New Jersey	United States	39 N 21	74 W 7	5+	EST	4+	1st Sun April to Last Sat Oct.
Auckland		New Zealand	36 S 53	174 E 45	-12		1+	Estimate Oct - Mid March
Augusta	Georgia	United States	33 N 28	81 W 58	5+	EST	4+	1st Sun April to Last Sat Oct.
Augusta	Maine	United States	44 N 19	69 W 47	5+	EST	4+	1st Sun April to Last Sat Oct.
Austin	Texas	United States	30 N 17	97 W 45	6+	CST	5+	1st Sun April to Last Sat Oct.
Baghdad		Iraq	33 N 20	44 E 24	-3	BT	-4	1st April to 30 Sept
Bakersfield	California	United States	35 N 23	119 W 01	8+	PST	7	1st Sun April to Last Sat Oct.
Baku	Azerbaijan SSR	USSR	40 N 25	49 E 50	-4		-5	Last Sun March to Last Sat Sept.
Bali	Bali	Indonesia	8 S 00	115 E 22	-7			No
Baltimore	Maryland	United States	39 N 17	76 W 37	5+	EST	4+	1st Sun April to Last Sat Oct.
Bamako		Mali	12 N 39	7 W 59	0	GMT		No
Bandar Seri Begawan		Brunei	4 N 54	114 E 57	-8	PST		No
Bandung	Java	Indonesia	7 S 00	107 E 22	-7			No
Bangalore		India	13 N 03	77 E 39	-5.5			No
Bangkok		Thailand	13 N 45	100 E 31	-7			No
Bangor	Maine	United States	44 N 48	68 W 01	5+	EST	4+	1st Sun April to Last Sat Oct.

Daylight Savings Times Deemed Reliable But Not Guaranteed

City	State or Provence	Country	LAT.	LONG.	Time Adjust to GMT	Abv Time	D.S. Time	1991 Daylight Savings Observed
Bangui		Central African Rep.	4 N 21	18 E 35	-1	CET		No
Banjul		Gambia (The)	13 N 28	16 W 39	0	GMT		No
Baranquilla		Columbia	3 N 18	74 W 40	5+			No
Barcelona		Spain	41 N 25	2 E 08	-1	CET	-2	Last Sun March to Last Sat Sept.
Basse-Terre		Guadeloupe	16 N 00	61 W 44	4+			No
Bassein	Former Burma	Union of Mayanmar	16 N 46	94 E 47	-6.5			No
Basseterre (on St. Kitts)		St. Kitts/Nevis	17 N 18	62 W 43	4+			No
Baton Rouge	Louisiana	United States	30 N 27	91 W 11	6+	CST	5+	1st Sun April to Last Sat Oct.
Battle Creek	Michigan	United States	42 N 19	85 W 11	5+	EST	4+	1st Sun April to Last Sat Oct.
Beirut		Lebanon	35 N 54	35 E 28	-3		-4	Mid May – Mid Oct
Belfast		Ireland, North	54 N 36	5 W 55	0	GMT	-1	1st Sun April to Last Sat Oct.
Belgrade		Yogoslavia	44 N 49	20 E 27	-1	CET	-2	Last Sun March to Last Sat Sept.
Belize City		Belize	17 N 31	88 W 10	6+			No
Bellingham	Washington	United States	48 N 46	122 W 29	8+	PST	7	1st Sun April to Last Sat Oct.
Belmopan		Belize	17 N 15	88 W 47	6+			No
Belo Horizonte		Brazil	19 S 54	43 W 56	3+			No
Beloit	Wisconson	United States	42 N 31	89 W 02	6+	CST	5+	1st Sun April to Last Sat Oct.
Berlin		Germany	52 N 30	13 E 25	-1	CET	-2	Last Sun March to Last Sat Sept.
Bermingham		England	52 N 30	1 W 50	0	GMT	-1	Last Sun March to Last Sat Oct.
Bern		Switzerland	46 N 57	7 E 28	-1	CET	-2	Last Sun March to Last Sat Sept.
Bilbao		Spain	43 N 12	2 W 48	-1	CET	-2	Last Sun March to Last Sat Sept.
Billings	Montana	United States	45 N 47	108 W 30	7+	MST	6+	1st Sun April to Last Sat Oct.
Binghamton	New York	United States	42 N 06	75 W 55	5+	EST	4+	1st Sun April to Last Sat Oct.
Birmingham	Alabama	United States	33 N 31	86 W 48	5+	EST	4+	1st Sun April to Last Sat Oct.
Bismarck	North Dakota	United States	46 N 48	100 W 47	6+	CST	5+	1st Sun April to Last Sat Oct.
Bissau		Guinea-Bissau	11 N 51	15 W 35	0	CET		No
Blantyre		Malawi	15 S 47	35 E 00	-2	EET		No
Bloomington	Indiana	United States	39 N 10	86 W 31	5+	EST	4+	1st Sun April to Last Sat Oct.
Bloomington	Illinois	United States	40 N 29	89 W 00	6+	CST	5+	1st Sun April to Last Sat Oct.
Bogota´		Columbia	4 N 40	74 W 05	5+			No
Boise	Idaho	United States	43 N 38	116 W 12	5+	MST	6+	1st Sun April to Last Sat Oct.
Bombay		India	18 N 58	72 E 50	-5.5			No
Bonn		Germany	50 N 44	7 E 06	-1	CET	-2	Last Sun March to Last Sat Sept.
Boston	Massachusetts	United States	42 N 22	71 W 04	5+	EST	4+	1st Sun April to Last Sat Oct.
Boulder	Colorado	United States	40 N 01	105 W 17	7+	MST	6+	1st Sun April to Last Sat Oct.
Bowling Green	Kentucky	United States	36 N 59	86 W 27	6+	CST	5+	1st Sun April to Last Sat Oct.
Brasília		Brazil	15 S 49	47 W 39	3+			No
Brasov		Romania	45 N 39	25 E 35	-2	EET	-3	Last Sun March to Last Sat Sept.
Bratislava		Czechoslovakia	48 N 09	17 E 07	-1	CET	-2	Last Sun March to Last Sat Sept.
Brattleboro	Vermont	United States	42 N 51	72 W 34	5+	EST	4+	1st Sun April to Last Sat Oct.
Brazzaville		Congo	4 S 17	15 E 14	-1	CET		No
Bremen		Germany	53 N 05	8 E 50	-1	CET	-2	Last Sun March to Last Sat Sept.
Bridgeport	Connecticut	United States	41 N 11	73 W 12	5+	EST	4+	1st Sun April to Last Sat Oct.
Bridgetown		Barbados	13 N 06	59 W 37	4+			No
Brisbane	Queensland	Australia	27 S 28	153 E 02	-10			No
Brooklyn	New York	United States	40 N 38	73 W 56	5+	EST	4+	1st Sun April to Last Sat Oct.
Brownsville	Texas	United States	25 N 54	97 W 30	6+	CST	5+	1st Sun April to Last Sat Oct.
Brussels		Belgium	50 N 51	4 E 21	-1	CET	-2	Last Sun March to Last Sat Sept.
Bucaramanga		Columbia	17 N 12	73 W 14	5+			No
Bucharest		Romania	44 N 26	26 E 06	-2	EET	-3	Last Sun March to Last Sat Sept.
Budapest		Hungary	47 N 30	19 E 05	-1	CET	-2	Last Sun March to Last Sat Sept.
Buenos Aires		Argentina	34 S 36	58 W 27	3+			No
Buffalo	New York	United States	42 N 53	78 W 53	5+	EST	4+	1st Sun April to Last Sat Oct.
Bujumbura		Burundi	3 S 24	29 E 21	-2	EET		No
Bulawayo		Zimbabwe	20 S 12	28 E 43	-2	EET		No

City	State or Provence	Country	LAT.	LONG.	Time Adjust to GMT	Abv Time	D.S. Time	1991 Daylight Savings Observed
Burlington	Vermont	United States	44 N 29	73 W 12	5+	EST	4+	1st Sun April to Last Sat Oct.
Bursa		Turkey	40 N 10	28 E 10	-3		-4	Last Sun March to Last Sat Sept.
Butte	Montana	United States	46 N 00	112 W 32	7+	MST	6+	1st Sun April to Last Sat Oct.
Cairo		Egypt	30 N 03	31 E 15	-2	EET		No
Calcutta		India	22 N 32	88 E 22	-5.5			No
Calgary	Mountain	Canada	51 N 03	114 W 03	7+	MST	6+	1st Sun April to Last Sat Oct.
Cali		Columbia	3 N 22	76 W 30	5+			No
Callao		Peru	12 S 02	77 W 07	5+		4+	1 Jan to 31 March
Camden	New Jersey	United States	39 N 56	75 W 07	5+	EST	4+	1st Sun April to Last Sat Oct.
Canberra	Canaberra	Australia	35 S 17	149 E 08	-10		-11	Last Sun Oct; 1st Sat March
Canton/Guangzhou	Guangdong	China	23 N 07	113 E 16	-8	CCT	-9	No
Cape Canaveral	Florida	United States	28 N 24	80 W 36	5+	EST	4+	1st Sun April to Last Sat Oct.
Cape Town		South Africa	33 S 55	18 E 22	-2	EET		No
Caracas		Venezuela	10 N 30	66 W 55	4+			No
Cardiff		Wales	51 N 30	3 W 18	0		-1	
Caribou	Maine	United States	46 N 52	68 W 01	5+	EST	4+	1st Sun April to Last Sat Oct.
Carlsbad	New Mexico	United States	32 N 25	104 W 14	7+	MST	6+	1st Sun April to Last Sat Oct.
Carson City	Nevada	United States	39 N 10	119 W 46	8+	PST	7+	1st Sun April to Last Sat Oct.
Cartagena		Columbia	10 N 30	75 W 40	5+			No
Cassablanca		Morocco	33 N 32	7 W 41	-1	CET	-2	Mid June to Mid Sept
Castries		St. Lucia	14 N 01	61 W 00	4+			No
Cayenne		French Guiana	4 N 57	52 W 20	3+			No
Cebu		Phillipines	10 N 22	123 E 49	-8			No
Cedar Rapids	Iowa	United States	41 N 59	91 W 40	6+	CST	5+	1st Sun April to Last Sat Oct.
Changchun	Jilin (Kirin)	China	43 N 54	125 E 20	-8	CCT		No
Charleston	South Carolina	United States	32 N 46	79 W 56	5+	EST	4+	1st Sun April to Last Sat Oct.
Charleston	West Virginia	United States	38 N 21	81 W 38	5+	EST	4+	1st Sun April to Last Sat Oct.
Charlotte	North Carolina	United States	35 N 13	80 W 51	5+	EST	4+	1st Sun April to Last Sat Oct.
Charlottesville	Virginia	United States	38 N 02	78 W 30	5+	EST	4+	1st Sun April to Last Sat Oct.
Chattanooga	Tennessee	United States	35 N 03	85 W 19	5+	EST	4+	1st Sun April to Last Sat Oct.
Chelyabinsk	Asian RSFSR	USSR	55 N 10	61 E 25	-5		-7	Last Sun March to Last Sat Sept.
Chengdu (Chengtu)	Sichuan (Szechwan)	China	30 N 30	104 E 10	-8	CCT		No
Cheyenne	Wyoming	United States	41 N 08	104 W 49	7+	MST	6+	1st Sun April to Last Sat Oct.
Chicago	Illinois	United States	41 N 52	87 W 39	6+	CST	5+	1st Sun April to Last Sat Oct.
Chiclayo		Peru	6 S 46	79 W 50	5+		4+	1 Jan to 31 March
Chilung (Keelung)		China (Taiwan)	25 N 02	121 E 48	-8	CCT		No
Chingola		Zambia	12 S 32	27 E 52	-2	EET		No
Chongquing	Sichuan (Szechwan)	China	29 N 38	107 E 30	-8	CCT		No
Cincinnati	Ohio	United States	39 N 06	84 W 31	5+	EST	4+	1st Sun April to Last Sat Oct.
Ciudad Juarez	Chihuahua	Mexico	31 N 44	106 W 28	8+		7+	1st Sun April to Last Sat Oct.
Clarksburg	West Virginia	United States	39 N 17	80 W 21	5+	EST	4+	1st Sun April to Last Sat Oct.
Cleveland	Ohio	United States	41 N 30	81 W 41	5+	EST	4+	1st Sun April to Last Sat Oct.
Cluj-Napoca		Romania	46 N 46	23 E 34	-2	EET	-3	Last Sun March to Last Sat Sept.
Cochabamaba		Boliva	17 S 24	66 W 09	4+			No
Cologne		Germany	50 N 56	6 E 57	-1	CET	-2	Last Sun March to Last Sat Sept.
Colombo		Sri Lanka	6 N 57	79 E 53	-5.5			No
Colorado Sprin	Colorado	United States	38 N 50	104 W 49	7+	MST	6+	1st Sun April to Last Sat Oct.
Columbia	South Carolina	United States	34 N 00	81 W 03	5+	EST	4+	1st Sun April to Last Sat Oct.
Columbus	Georgia	United States	32 N 28	84 W 59	5+	EST	4+	1st Sun April to Last Sat Oct.
Columbus	Ohio	United States	39 N 58	83 W 00	5+	EST	4+	1st Sun April to Last Sat Oct.
Conakry		Guinea, Republic of	9 N 30	13 W 43	0	GMT		No
Concepción		Chile	36 S 51	72 W 59	4+		3+	2nd Sun Oct; 3rd Sat March
Concord	New Hampshire	United States	43 N 12	71 W 32	5+	EST	4+	1st Sun April to Last Sat Oct.
Constanine		Algeria	36 N 28	6 E 38	-1	CET	-2	Last Sun March to Last Sat Sept.
Constanta		Romania	44 N 12	28 E 36	-2	EET	-3	Last Sun March to Last Sat Sept.

City	State or Provence	Country	LAT.	LONG.	Time Adjust to GMT	Abv Time	D.S. Time	1991 Daylight Savings Observed
Copenhagen		Denmark	55 N 41	12 E 35	-1	CET	-2	Last Sun March to Last Sat Sept.
Córdoba		Argentina	30 S 20	64 W 03	3+			No
Corpus Christi	Texas	United States	27 N 47	97 W 24	6+	CST	5+	1st Sun April to Last Sat Oct.
Cotonou		Benin	6 N 21	2 E 26	-1	GMT		No
Cumberland	Maryland	United States	39 N 39	78 W 46	5+	EST	4+	1st Sun April to Last Sat Oct.
Cupertino	California	United States	37 N 19	122 W 02	8+	PST	7	1st Sun April to Last Sat Oct.
Da Nang		Viet Nam	16 N 08	108 E 22	7+			No
Dacca		Bangladesh	23 N 43	90 E 25	-6			No
Dakar		Senegal	14 N 40	17 W 26	0	GMT		No
Dallas	Texas	United States	32 N 47	96 W 49	6+	CST	5+	1st Sun April to Last Sat Oct.
Damascus		Syria	33 N 30	36 E 18	-2	EET		No
Dar es Salaam		Tanzania	6 S 50	39 E 17	-3			No
Darwin	North Territory	Australia	12 S 28	130 E 49	-9.5			Last Sun Oct; 1st Sat March
Davenport	Iowa	United States	41 N 32	90 W 35	6+	CST	5+	1st Sun April to Last Sat Oct.
Dayton	Ohio	United States	39 N 45	84 W 12	5+	EST	4+	1st Sun April to Last Sat Oct.
Daytona Beach	Florida	United States	29 N 13	81 W 01	5+	EST	4+	1st Sun April to Last Sat Oct.
Decatur	Illinois	United States	39 N 51	88 W 57	6+	CST	5+	1st Sun April to Last Sat Oct.
Delhi		India	28 N 54	77 E 13	-5.5			No
Denver	Colorado	United States	39 N 44	104 W 59	7+	MST	6+	1st Sun April to Last Sat Oct.
Des Moines	Iowa	United States	41 N 35	93 W 37	6+	CST	5+	1st Sun April to Last Sat Oct.
Detroit	Michigan	United States	42 N 20	83 W 03	5+	EST	4+	1st Sun April to Last Sat Oct.
Djibouti		Djibouti	11 N 36	43 E 07	-3			No
Dnepropetrovsk	Ukrainian SSR	USSR	48 N 15	34 E 08	-3		-4	Last Sun March to Last Sat Sept.
Dodge City	Kansas	United States	37 N 45	100 W 01	6+	CST	5+	1st Sun April to Last Sat Oct.
Doha		Qutar	25 N 17	51 E 32	-3			No
Donetsk	Ukrainian SSR	USSR	48 N 00	37 E 35	-3		-4	Last Sun March to Last Sat Sept.
Douala		Cameroon	4 N 03	9 E 42	-1	CET		No
Douglas	England	Isle of Man	54 N 10	4 W 40	0	GMT	-1	1st Sun April to Last Sat Oct.
Dover	Delaware	United States	39 N 10	75 W 32	5+	EST	4+	1st Sun April to Last Sat Oct.
Dresden		Germany	51 N 05	13 E 45	-1	CET	-2	Last Sun March to Last Sat Sept.
Dublin		Ireland	53 N 20	6 W 15	0	GMT	-1	1st Sun April to Last Sat Oct.
Duluth	Minnesota	United States	46 N 47	92 W 07	6+	CST	5+	1st Sun April to Last Sat Oct.
Durban		South Africa	29 S 48	31 E 00	-2	EET		No
Durham	North Carolina	United States	36 N 00	78 W 54	5+	EST	4+	1st Sun April to Last Sat Oct.
Dusseldorf		Germany	51 N 14	6 E 47	-1	CET	-2	Last Sun March to Last Sat Sept.
Eau Claire	Wisconson	United States	44 N 49	91 W 30	6+	CST	5+	1st Sun April to Last Sat Oct.
Edinburgh		Scotland	55 N 57	3 W 11	0	GMT	-1	Last Sun March to Last Sat Oct.
Edmonton	Mountain	Canada	53 N 33	113 W 28	7+	MST	6+	1st Sun April to Last Sat Oct.
El Paso	Texas	United States	31 N 45	106 W 29	7+	MST	6+	1st Sun April to Last Sat Oct.
Elizabeth	New Jersey	United States	40 N 40	74 W 13	5+	EST	4+	1st Sun April to Last Sat Oct.
Elmira	New York	United States	42 N 06	76 W 48	5+	EST	4+	1st Sun April to Last Sat Oct.
Erie	Pennsylvania	United States	42 N 08	80 W 05	5+	EST	4+	1st Sun April to Last Sat Oct.
Essen		Germany	51 N 26	6 E 59	-1	CET	-2	Last Sun March to Last Sat Sept.
Eugene	Oregon	United States	44 N 05	123 W 04	8+	PST	7	1st Sun April to Last Sat Oct.
Eureka	California	United States	40 N 47	124 W 09	8+	PST	7	1st Sun April to Last Sat Oct.
Everett	Washington	United States	47 N 59	122 W 12	8+	PST	7	1st Sun April to Last Sat Oct.
Fairbanks	Alaska	United States	64 N 51	147 W 54	9+	YST	8	1st Sun April to Last Sat Oct.
Faisalabad		Pakistan	31 N 29	73 E 06	-5			No
Fargo	North Dakota	United States	46 N 53	96 W 48	6+	CST	5+	1st Sun April to Last Sat Oct.
Fayetteville	North Carolina	United States	35 N 03	78 W 53	5+	EST	4+	1st Sun April to Last Sat Oct.
Fès		Morocco	34 N 08	5 W 00	-1	CET	-2	Mid June - Mid Sept
Flagstaff	Arizona	United States	35 N 12	111 W 39	7+	MST		No
Flint	Michigan	United States	43 N 01	83 W 41	5+	EST	4+	1st Sun April to Last Sat Oct.
Florence		Italy	43 N 47	11 E 15	-1	CET	-2	Last Sun March to Last Sat Sept.
Florence	South Carolina	United States	34 N 12	79 W 46	5+	EST	4+	1st Sun April to Last Sat Oct.

City	State or Provence	Country	LAT.	LONG.	Time Adjust to GMT	Abv Time	D.S. Time	1991 Daylight Savings Observed
Ford Dodge	Iowa	United States	42 N 30	94 W 11	6+	CST	5+	1st Sun April to Last Sat Oct.
Form Myers	Florida	United States	26 N 39	81 W 52	5+	EST	4+	1st Sun April to Last Sat Oct.
Fort Collins	Colorado	United States	40 N 35	105 W 05	7+	MST	6+	1st Sun April to Last Sat Oct.
Fort Lauderdale	Florida	United States	26 N 07	80 W 08	5+	EST	4+	1st Sun April to Last Sat Oct.
Fort Wayne	Indiana	United States	41 N 04	85 W 09	5+	EST	4+	1st Sun April to Last Sat Oct.
Fort Worth	Texas	United States	32 N 45	97 W 18	7+	MST	6+	1st Sun April to Last Sat Oct.
Fort-de-France		Martinique	14 N 36	61 W 05	4+			No
Fortaleza		Brazil	3 S 35	38 W 31	3+			No
Forth Smith	Arkansas	United States	35 N 23	94 W 25	6+	CST	5+	1st Sun April to Last Sat Oct.
Frankfurt		Germany	52 N 42	13 E 37	-1	CET	-2	Last Sun March to Last Sat Sept.
Frederick	Maryland	United States	39 N 25	77 W 25	5+	EST	4+	1st Sun April to Last Sat Oct.
Freetown		Sierra Leone	8 N 29	13 W 12	0	GMT		No
Fresno	California	United States	36 N 44	119 W 47	8+	PST	7	1st Sun April to Last Sat Oct.
Fukuoka		Japan	33 N 35	130 E 23	-9			No
Funafuti		Tuvalu	8 S 31	179 E 13	-12			No
Fushun	Liaoning	China	41 N 50	124 E 00	-8	CCT		No
Gaborone		Bostwana	21 S 14	27 E 31	-2	EET		No
Gadsden	Alabama	United States	34 N 01	86 W 01	5+	EST	4+	1st Sun April to Last Sat Oct.
Gainsville	Florida	United States	29 N 40	82 W 20	5+	EST	4+	1st Sun April to Last Sat Oct.
Galati		Romania	45 N 25	28 E 05	-2	EET	-3	Last Sun March to Last Sat Sept.
Galveston	Texas	United States	29 N 18	94 W 48	7+	MST	6+	1st Sun April to Last Sat Oct.
Gary	Indiana	United States	41 N 36	87 W 20	6+	CST	5+	1st Sun April to Last Sat Oct.
Gaziantep		Turkey	37 N 10	37 E 30	-3		-4	Last Sun March to Last Sat Sept.
Gdan'sk		Poland	54 N 20	18 E 40	-1	CET	-2	Last Sun March to Last Sat Sept.
Geneva		Switzerland	46 N 14	6 E 04	-1	CET	-2	Last Sun March to Last Sat Sept.
Genoa		Italy	44 N 23	9 E 52	-1	CET	-2	Last Sun March to Last Sat Sept.
George Town (pinang)		Malaysia	5 N 21	100 E 09	-8			No
Georgetown		Cayman Islands	19 N 20	81 W 20	5+			No
Georgetown		Guyana	6 N 48	58 W 18	3+			No
Glasgow		Scotland	55 N 54	4 W 25	0	GMT	-1	Last Sun March to Last Sat Oct.
Godthaab		Greenland	64 N 11	51 W 43	4+			No
Goldsboro	North Carolina	United States	35 N 23	77 W 59	5+	EST	4+	1st Sun April to Last Sat Oct.
Gor'kij (Gorky)	European RSFSR	USSR	56 N 15	44 E 05	-4		-4	Last Sun March to Last Sat Sept.
Grand Forks	North Dakota	United States	47 N 55	97 W 03	6+	CST	5+	1st Sun April to Last Sat Oct.
Grand Island	Nebraska	United States	40 N 55	98 W 21	6+	CST	5+	1st Sun April to Last Sat Oct.
Grand Junction	Colorado	United States	39 N 04	108 W 33	7+	MST	6+	1st Sun April to Last Sat Oct.
Grand Rapids	Michigan	United States	42 N 58	85 W 40	5+	EST	4+	1st Sun April to Last Sat Oct.
Graz		Austria	47 N 05	15 E 26	-1	CET	-2	Last Sun March to Last Sat Sept.
Great Falls	Montana	United States	47 N 30	111 W 17	7+	MST	6+	1st Sun April to Last Sat Oct.
Greeley	Colorado	United States	40 N 25	104 W 42	7+	MST	6+	1st Sun April to Last Sat Oct.
Green Bay	Wisconson	United States	44 N 31	88 W 00	6+	CST	5+	1st Sun April to Last Sat Oct.
Greenboro	North Carolina	United States	36 N 04	79 W 48	5+	EST	4+	1st Sun April to Last Sat Oct.
Greenville	South Carolina	United States	34 N 51	85 W 24	5+	EST	4+	1st Sun April to Last Sat Oct.
Greenville	Mississippi	United States	33 N 24	88 W 42	6+	CST	5+	1st Sun April to Last Sat Oct.
Greenwich		England	51 N 29	00 W 00	0	GMT	-1	Last Sun March to Last Sat Oct.
Guadalajara	Jalisco	Mexico	20 N 41	103 W 21	8+		7+	1st Sun April to Last Sat Oct.
Guam		Guam	14 N 00	143 E 20	-10			No
Guatemala		Guatemala	14 N 38	90 W 31	6+			No
Guayaquil		Ecuador	2 S 16	79 W 53	5+			No
Hagerstown	Maryland	United States	39 N 39	78 W 46	5+	EST	4+	1st Sun April to Last Sat Oct.
Haiphong		Viet Nam	20 N 52	106 E 40	7+			No
Hamburg		Germany	53 N 34	10 E 02	-1	CET	-2	Last Sun March to Last Sat Sept.
Hamilton		Bermuda	23 N 18	64 W 47	4+		3+	1st Sun April to Last Sat Oct.
Hamilton	Ontario	Canada	43 N 15	79 W 52	5+		4+	1st Sun April to Last Sat Oct.
Hannover		Germany	52 N 22	9 E 45	-1	CET	-2	Last Sun March to Last Sat Sept.

City	State or Provence	Country	LAT.	LONG.	Time Adjust to GMT	Abv Time	D.S. Time	1991 Daylight Savings Observed
Hanoi		Viet Nam	21 N 01	105 E 50	7+			No
Harare		Zimbabwe	17 S 50	31 E 03	-2	EET		No
Harbin	Heilongjiang	China	45 N 47	126 E 39	-8	CCT		No
Harrisburg	Pennsylvania	United States	40 N 16	76 W 53	5+	EST	4+	1st Sun April to Last Sat Oct.
Hartford	Connecticut	United States	41 N 46	72 W 41	5+	EST	4+	1st Sun April to Last Sat Oct.
Hattiesburg	Mississippi	United States	31 N 20	89 W 17	6+	CST	5+	1st Sun April to Last Sat Oct.
Havana		Cuba	23 N 08	82 W 24	5+		4+	3rd Sat March to 3rd Sat Oct.
Helena	Montana	United States	46 N 36	112 W 02	7+	MST	6+	1st Sun April to Last Sat Oct.
Helsinki		Finland	60 N 09	24 E 58	-2	EET	-3	Last Sun March to Last Sat Sept.
Herat		Afghanistan	34 N 28	62 E 13	-4.5			No
Hilo	Hawaii	United States	19 N 44	155 W 05	10+	AHST	No	No
Hiroshima		Japan	34 N 22	132 E 25	-9			No
Hong Kong		Hong Kong	22 N 17	114 E 09	-8	CCT		No
Honiara (on Guadalcanal)		Solomon Islands	9 S 15	59 E 45	-11			No
Honolulu	Hawaii	United States	21 N 19	157 W 52	10+	AHST	No	No
Houston	Texas	United States	29 N 46	95 W 22	7+	MST	6+	1st Sun April to Last Sat Oct.
Hué		Viet Nam	16 N 28	107 E 42	7+			No
Huntsville	Alabama	United States	34 N 44	86 W 35	5+	EST	4+	1st Sun April to Last Sat Oct.
Hyderabad		India	17 N 29	78 E 28	-5.5			No
Hyderabad		Pakistan	25 N 29	68 E 28	-5			No
Ibadan		Nigeria	7 N 17	3 E 30	-1	CET		No
Independence	Missouri	United States	39 N 06	94 W 25	6+	CST	5+	1st Sun April to Last Sat Oct.
Indianapolis	Indiana	United States	39 N 46	86 W 09	5+	EST	4+	1st Sun April to Last Sat Oct.
Ipoh		Malaysia	4 N 45	101 E 05	-8			No
Irbid		Jordan	32 N 33	35 E 51	-2	EET	-3	1st Sun April to Last Sat Oct.
Irkutsk	Asian RSFSR	USSR	52 N 16	104 E 00	-8		-9	Last Sun March to Last Sat Sept.
Islamabad		Pakistan	33 N 43	75 E 17	-5			No
Istambul		Turkey	41 N 01	28 E 58	-3		-4	Last Sun March to Last Sat Sept.
Izmir		Turkey	38 N 25	27 E05	-3		-4	Last Sun March to Last Sat Sept.
Jackson	Tennessee	United States	35 N 37	88 W 49	5+	EST	4+	1st Sun April to Last Sat Oct.
Jackson	Mississippi	United States	32 N 18	90 W 12	6+	CST	5+	1st Sun April to Last Sat Oct.
Jacksonville	Florida	United States	30 N 20	81 W 39	5+	EST	4+	1st Sun April to Last Sat Oct.
Jakarta	Java	Indonesia	6 S 10	106 E 48	-7			No
Jamestown	New York	United States	42 N 06	79 W 14	5+	EST	4+	1st Sun April to Last Sat Oct.
Jeddah		Saudi Arabia	21 N 29	39 E 11	-3			No
Jefferson City	Missouri	United States	38 N 34	92 W 10	6+	CST	5+	1st Sun April to Last Sat Oct.
Jersey City	New Jersey	United States	40 N 44	74 W 04	5+	EST	4+	1st Sun April to Last Sat Oct.
Jerusalem		Israel	31 N 46	35 E 10	-2	EET	-3	Est May - Sept
Jinan	Shandong	China	36 N 40	117 E 01	-8	CCT		No
Johannesberg		South Africa	26 S 15	28 E 00	-2	EET		No
Johnson City	Tennessee	United States	36 N 19	82 W 21	5+	EST	4+	1st Sun April to Last Sat Oct.
Joplin	Missouri	United States	37 N 06	94 W 31	6+	CST	5+	1st Sun April to Last Sat Oct.
Juneau	Alaska	United States	58 N 18	134 W 25	9+	YST	8	1st Sun April to Last Sat Oct.
Kabul		Afghanistan	34 N 30	69 E 13	-4.5			No
Kalamazoo	Michigan	United States	42 N 17	85 W 35	5+	EST	4+	1st Sun April to Last Sat Oct.
Kalispell	Montana	United States	48 N 12	114 W 19	7+	MST	6+	1st Sun April to Last Sat Oct.
Kampala		Uganda	0 N 19	1 W 31	-3			No
Kananga		Zaire	6 S 14	22 E 17	-1	CET		No
Kaneohoe	Hawaii	United States	21 N 25	157 W 48	10+	AHST	No	No
Kano		Nigeria	12 N 00	8 E 30	-1	CET		No
Kanpur		India	26 N 30	80 E 10	-5.5			No
Kansas City	Kansas	United States	39 N 07	94 W 38	6+	CST	5+	1st Sun April to Last Sat Oct.
Kaohsiung		Taiwan	22 N 38	120 E 17	-8			No
Karachi		Pakistan	24 N 52	67 E 02	-5			No
Kathmandu		Nepal	27 N 43	85 E 19	5 2/3-			No

City	State or Provence	Country	LAT.	LONG.	Time Adjust to GMT	Abv Time	D.S. Time	1991 Daylight Savings Observed
Katowice		Poland	50 N 15	19 E 00	-1	CET	-2	Last Sun March to Last Sat Sept.
Kazan´	European RSFSR	USSR	55 N 50	49 E 18	-4		-5	Last Sun March to Last Sat Sept.
Keene	New Hampshire	United States	42 N 56	72 W 17	5+	EST	4+	1st Sun April to Last Sat Oct.
Key West	Florida	United States	24 N 33	81 W 47	5+	EST	4+	1st Sun April to Last Sat Oct.
Khar'kov	Ukrainian SSR	USSR	50 N 00	36 E 10	-3		-4	Last Sun March to Last Sat Sept.
Khartoum		Sudan	15 N 36	32 E 32	-2	EET		No
Kiev	Ukrainian SSR	USSR	50 N 27	30 E 32	-3		-4	Last Sun March to Last Sat Sept.
Kigali		Rwanda	1 S 59	30 E 05	-2	EET		No
Kingston		Jamaica	18 N 00	76 W 48	5+			No
Kingstown		St. Vincent	13 N 09	60 W 00	4+			No
Kinshasa		Zaire	4 S 19	15 E 18	-1	CET		No
Kitakyushu		Japan	33 N 53	130 E 50	-9			No
Kitwe		Zambia	12 S 49	28 E 13	-2	EET		No
Klamath Falls	Oregon	United States	42 N 13	121 W 46	8+	PST	7	1st Sun April to Last Sat Oct.
Knoxville	Tennessee	United States	35 N 58	83 W 55	5+	EST	4+	1st Sun April to Last Sat Oct.
Kobe		Japan	34 N 30	135 E 10	-9			No
Kowloon		Hong Kong	22 N 18	114 E 10	-8	CCT		No
Krakow		Poland	50 N 05	20 E 00	-1	CET	-2	Last Sun March to Last Sat Sept.
Kuala Lumpur		Malaysia	3 N 10	101 E 42	-8			No
Kumasi		Ghana	6 N 41	1 W 35	0	GMT		No
Kunming	Yunnan	China	25 N 04	102 E 41	-8	CCT		No
Kuwait		Kuwait	29N 23	47 E 59	-3			No
Kuybyshev	European RSFSR	USSR	53 N	50 E	-4		-5	Last Sun March to Last Sat Sept.
Kyoto		Japan	35 N 00	135 E 46	-9			No
La Paz		Bolivia	16 S 30	68 W 09	4+			No
La Plata		Argentina	34 S 54	57 W 57	3+			No
Lafayette	Indiana	United States	40 N 25	86 W 54	5+	EST	4+	1st Sun April to Last Sat Oct.
Lagos		Nigeria	6 N 27	3 E 23	-1	CET		No
Lahaina	Hawaii	United States	20 N 53	156 W 41	10+	AHST	No	No
Lahore		Pakistan	32 N 00	74 E 18	-5			No
Lake Charles	Louisiana	United States	30 N 14	93 W 13	6+	CST	5+	1st Sun April to Last Sat Oct.
Lanzhou (Lanchow)	Gansu (Kansu)	China	35 N 55	103 E 55	-8	CCT		No
Laramie	Wyoming	United States	41 N 19	105 W 35	7+	MST	6+	1st Sun April to Last Sat Oct.
Lárisa		Greece	39 N 38	22 E 25	-2	EET	-3	Last Sun March to Last Sat Sept.
Las Cruces	New Mexico	United States	32 N 19	106 W 47	7+	MST	6+	1st Sun April to Last Sat Oct.
Las Vegas	Nevada	United States	36 N 10	115 W 09	8+	PST	7	1st Sun April to Last Sat Oct.
Latakia		Syria	35 N 32	35 E 51	-2	EET		No
Lawrence	Massachusetts	United States	42 N 43	71 W 10	5+	EST	4+	1st Sun April to Last Sat Oct.
Lawton	Oklahoma	United States	34 N 37	98 W 25	6+	CST	5+	1st Sun April to Last Sat Oct.
Le Havre		France	49 N 31	0 E 07	-1	CET	-2	Last Sun March to Last Sat Sept.
Leeds		England	53 N 48	1 W 32	0	GMT	-1	Last Sun March to Last Sat Oct.
Leipzig		Germany	51 N 20	12 E 24	-1	CET	-2	Last Sun March to Last Sat Sept.
Leningrad	European RSFSR	USSR	59 N 57	30 E 20	-3		-4	Last Sun March to Last Sat Sept.
León	Jalisco	Mexico	21 N 08	101 W 41	8+		7+	1st Sun April to Last Sat Oct.
Lewiston	Maine	United States	44 N 06	70 W 13	5+	EST	4+	1st Sun April to Last Sat Oct.
Lexington	Kentucky	United States	38 N 03	84 W 30	5+	EST	4+	1st Sun April to Last Sat Oct.
Libreville		Gabon	0 N 23	9 E 26	-1	CET		No
Lihue	Hawaii	United States	21 N 59	159 W 23	10+	AHST	No	No
Lille		France	50 N 38	3 E 01	-1	CET	-2	Last Sun March to Last Sat Sept.
Lilongwe		Malawi	13 S 58	33 E 45	-2	EET		No
Lima		Peru	12 S 03	77 W 03	5+		4+	1 Jan to 31 March
Lincoln	Nebraska	United States	40 N 49	96 W 41	6+	CST	5+	1st Sun April to Last Sat Oct.
Linz		Austria	48 N 18	14 E 18	-1	CET	-2	Last Sun March to Last Sat Sept.
Lisbon		Portugal	38 N 43	9 W 10	0	GMT	-1	Last Sun March to Last Sat Sept.
Little Rock	Arkansas	United States	34 N 45	92 W 17	6+	CST	5+	1st Sun April to Last Sat Oct.

Daylight Savings Times Deemed Reliable But Not Guaranteed

City	State or Provence	Country	LAT.	LONG.	Time Adjust to GMT	Abv Time	D.S. Time	1991 Daylight Savings Observed
Liverpool		England	53 N 25	2 W 52	0	GMT	-1	Last Sun March to Last Sat Oct.
Li`ege		Belgium	50 N 38	5 E 34	-1	CET	-2	Last Sun March to Last Sat Sept.
Ljubliana		Yogoslavia	46 N 04	14 E 29	-1	CET	-2	Last Sun March to Last Sat Sept.
Lodz		Poland	51 N 46	19 E 30	-1	CET	-2	Last Sun March to Last Sat Sept.
Logan	Utah	United States	41 N 44	111 W 50	7+	MST	6+	1st Sun April to Last Sat Oct.
Lomé		Togo	6 N 08	1 E 14	0	GMT		No
London		England	51 N 30	0 W 06	0	GMT	-1	Last Sun March to Last Sat Oct.
Los Angeles	California	United States	34 N 04	118 W 15	8+	PST	7	1st Sun April to Last Sat Oct.
Louisville	Kentucky	United States	38 N 15	85 W 46	5+	EST	4+	1st Sun April to Last Sat Oct.
Luanda		Angola	8 S 48	13 E 14	-1	CET		No
Lubbock	Texas	United States	33 N 35	101 W 51	7+	MST	6+	1st Sun April to Last Sat Oct.
Lubumbashi		Zaire	11 S 40	27 E 28	-2	CET		No
Lucknow		India	26 N 54	80 E 58	-5.5			No
Luda (Dairen)	Liaoning	China	38 N 59	121 E 35	-8	CCT		No
Lusaka		Zambia	15 S 25	28 E 18	-2	EET		No
Luxembourg		Luxembourg	49 W 38	6 E 10	-1	CET	-2	Last Sun March to Last Sat Sept.
Lynchburg	Virginia	United States	37 N 25	79 W 09	5+	EST	4+	1st Sun April to Last Sat Oct.
Lyon		France	45 N 44	4 E 52	-1	CET	-2	Last Sun March to Last Sat Sept.
Macon	Georgia	United States	32 N 51	83 W 38	5+	EST	4+	1st Sun April to Last Sat Oct.
Madison	Wisconson	United States	43 N 04	89 W 24	6+	CST	5+	1st Sun April to Last Sat Oct.
Madras		India	13 N 08	80 E 15	-5.5			No
Madrid		Spain	40 N 24	3 W 41	-1	CET	-2	Last Sun March to Last Sat Sept.
Malabo		Equatorial Guinea	3 N 45	8 E 47	-1	CET		No
Malé		Maldive Islands	4 N 10	73 E 30	-5			No
Managua		Nicaragua	12 N 08	86 W 18	6+			No
Manama		Bahrain	26 N 14	50 E 35	-3			No
Manchester		England	53 N 28	2 W 14	0	GMT	-1	Last Sun March to Last Sat Oct.
Manchester	New Hampshire	United States	43 N 00	119 W 46	5+	EST	4+	1st Sun April to Last Sat Oct.
Mandalay	Former Burma	Union of Mayanmar	22 N 00	96 E 08	-6.5			No
Manhattan	New York	United States	40 N 46	73 W 59	5+	EST	4+	1st Sun April to Last Sat Oct.
Manila		Philippines	14 N 35	120 E 59	-8			No
Mankato	Minnesota	United States	44 N 10	94 W 00	6+	CST	5+	1st Sun April to Last Sat Oct.
Mannheim		Germany	49 N 30	8 E 31	-1	CET	-2	Last Sun March to Last Sat Sept.
Maputo		Mozambique	25 S 58	32 E 35	-2	EET		No
Maracaibo		Venezuela	10 N 38	71 W 45	4+			No
Marrakech		Morocco	31 N 38	8 W 00	-1	CET	-2	Mid June - Mid Sept
Marseille		France	43 N 18	5 E 25	-1	CET	-2	Last Sun March to Last Sat Sept.
Maseru		Lesotho	29 S 18	27 E 30	-2	EET		No
Mashed Soleyman		Iran	31 N 45	49 E 17	-3.5			No
Mbabane		Swaziland	26 S 19	31 E 08	-2	EET		No
Mbuji-Mayi		Zaire	6 S 09	23 E 38	-2	CET		No
Mecca		Saudi Arabia	21 N 27	39 E 50	-3			No
Medan	Sumatra	Indonesia	3 N 35	98 E 35	-7			No
Medellín		Columbia	6 N 15	75 W 35	5+			No
Medina as-Sharrb		Yeman	24 N 30	39 E 45	-3			No
Melbourne	Victoria	Australia	37 S 49	144 E 62	-10		-11	Last Sun Oct; 1st Sat March
Memphis	Tennessee	United States	35 N 08	90 W 03	6+	CST	5+	1st Sun April to Last Sat Oct.
Meridan	Mississippi	United States	32 N 22	88 W 42	6+	CST	5+	1st Sun April to Last Sat Oct.
Mexico City		Mexico	19 N 24	99 W 09	6+			No
Miami	Florida	United States	25 N 47	80 W 11	5+	EST	4+	1st Sun April to Last Sat Oct.
Milan		Italy	38 N 13	15 E 17	-1	CET	-2	Last Sun March to Last Sat Sept.
Milwaukee	Wisconson	United States	42 N47	87 W 55	6+	CST	5+	1st Sun April to Last Sat Oct.
Minneapolis	Minnesota	United States	44 N 59	93 W 16	6+	CST	5+	1st Sun April to Last Sat Oct.
Minot	North Dakota	United States	48 N 14	101 W 18	6+	CST	5+	1st Sun April to Last Sat Oct.
Minsk	Belorussin SSR	USSR	53 N 50	27 E 35	-3		-4	Last Sun March to Last Sat Sept.

City	State or Provence	Country	LAT.	LONG.	Time Adjust to GMT	Abv Time	D.S. Time	1991 Daylight Savings Observed
Missoula	Montana	United States	46 N 52	114 W 01	7+	MST	6+	1st Sun April to Last Sat Oct.
Mmabatho		Bophuthatswana	25 S 42	25 E 43	-2			No
Mobile	Alabama	United States	30 N 41	88 W 03	5+	EST	4+	1st Sun April to Last Sat Oct.
Mogadishu		Somalia	2 N 02	45 E 21	-3			No
Mombasa		Kenya	4 N 03	39 E 40	-3			No
Monaco-Ville		Monaco	43 N 44	7 E 26	-1	CET	-2	Last Sun March to Last Sat Sept.
Monroe	Louisiana	United States	32 N 30	92 W 07	6+	CST	5+	1st Sun April to Last Sat Oct.
Monrovia		Liberia	6 N 20	10 W 48	0	GMT		No
Monterrey		Mexico	25 N 43	100 W 19	6+			No
Montevideo		Uruguay	34 S 53	56 W 10	3+			No
Montpelier	Vermont	United States	44 N 16	72 W 35	5+	EST	4+	1st Sun April to Last Sat Oct.
Montre'al	Quebec	Canada	45 N 1	73 W 34	5+		4+	1st Sun April to Last Sat Oct.
Moorhead	Minnesota	United States	46 N 53	96 W 45	6+	CST	5+	1st Sun April to Last Sat Oct.
Morgantown	West Virginia	United States	39 N 38	79 W 57	5+	EST	4+	1st Sun April to Last Sat Oct.
Moroni		Comoro Islands	11 S 41	43 E 16	-3			No
Moscow	European RSFSR	USSR	55 N 45	37 E 35	-3		-4	Last Sun March to Last Sat Sept.
Moulmein	Former Burma	Union of Mayanmar	16 N 30	97 E 39	-6.5			No
Muncie	Indiana	United States	41 N 34	87 W 31	5+	EST	No	No
Munich		Germany	48 N 98	11 E 35	-1	CET	-2	Last Sun March to Last Sat Sept.
Muscat		Oman	23 N 37	58 E 37	-4			No
Muskegon	Michigan	United States	43 N 14	86 W 16	5+	EST	4+	1st Sun April to Last Sat Oct.
Muskogee	Oklahoma	United States	35 N 45	95 W 22	6+	CST	5+	1st Sun April to Last Sat Oct.
Nagoya		Japan	35 N 09	136 E 53	-9			No
Nagpur		India	21 N 12	79 E 09	-5.5			No
Nairobi		Kenya	1 S 17	36 E 48	-3			No
Nanjing (Nanking)	Jiangsu	China	32 N 04	118 E 46	-8	CCT		No
Naples		Italy	40 N 37	14 E 12	-1	CET	-2	Last Sun March to Last Sat Sept.
Naples	Florida	United States	26 N 08	81 W 48	5+	EST	4+	1st Sun April to Last Sat Oct.
Nashua	New Hampshire	United States	42 N 45	71 W 28	5+	EST	4+	1st Sun April to Last Sat Oct.
Nashville	Tennessee	United States	36 N 10	86 W 47	6+	CST	5+	1st Sun April to Last Sat Oct.
Nassau		Bahamas	25 N 05	77 W 20	5+		4+	1st Sun April to Last Sat Oct.
Ndola		Zambia	12 S 58	28 E 38	-2	EET		No
New Bedford	Massachusetts	United States	41 N 38	70 W 56	5+	EST	4+	1st Sun April to Last Sat Oct.
New Delhi		India	28 N 38	77 E 13	-5.5			No
New Haven	Connecticut	United States	41 N 18	72 W 55	5+	EST	4+	1st Sun April to Last Sat Oct.
New London	Connecticut	United States	41 N 21	72 W 06	5+	EST	4+	1st Sun April to Last Sat Oct.
New Orleans	Louisiana	United States	29 N 58	90 W 04	6+	CST	5+	1st Sun April to Last Sat Oct.
New York	New York	United States	40 N 45	73 W 57	5+	EST	4+	1st Sun April to Last Sat Oct.
Newark	New Jersey	United States	40 N 44	74 W 10	5+	EST	4+	1st Sun April to Last Sat Oct.
Newcastle (upon Tyne)		England	55 N 00	1 W 45	0	GMT	-1	Last Sun March to Last Sat Oct.
Newport	Rhode Island	United States	41 N 29	71 W 19	5+	EST	4+	1st Sun April to Last Sat Oct.
Nha Trang		Viet Nam	12 N 08	108 4 56	7+			No
Niamey		Niger	13 N 31	2 E 07	-1	CET		No
Nicosia		Cyprus	35 N 12	33 E 22	-2	EET	-3	Last Sun March to Last Sat Sept.
Nome	Alaska	United States	64 N 30	165 W 20	9+	YST	8	1st Sun April to Last Sat Oct.
North Platte	Nebraska	United States	41 N 08	100 W 46	6+	CST	5+	1st Sun April to Last Sat Oct.
Norwich	Connecticut	United States	41 N 31	72 W 05	5+	EST	4+	1st Sun April to Last Sat Oct.
Nouakchott		Mauritania	18 N 06	15 W 57	0	GMT		No
Nouméa		New Caledonia	22 S 18	166 E 48	-11			No
Novosibirsk	Asian RSFSR	USSR	55 N 09	82 E 58	-7		-8	Last Sun March to Last Sat Sept.
Nukúalofa		Tonga	21 S 08	175 W 12	11+			No
Nurnburg		Germany	49 N 28	11 E 07	-1	CET	-2	Last Sun March to Last Sat Sept.
N'djamena		Chad	12 N 07	15 E 03	-1	CET		No
Oakland	California	United States	37 N 47	124 W 09	8+	PST	7	1st Sun April to Last Sat Oct.
Oakland	California	United States	37 N 49	122 W 16	8+	PST	7	1st Sun April to Last Sat Oct.

City	State or Provence	Country	LAT.	LONG.	Time Adjust to GMT	Abv Time	D.S. Time	1991 Daylight Savings Observed
Odessa	Ukrainian SSR	USSR	46 N 28	30 E 44	-3		-4	Last Sun March to Last Sat Sept.
Ogbomosho		Nigeria	8 N 08	4 E 15	-1	CET		No
Ogden	Utah	United States	41 N 31	111 W 58	7+	MST	6+	1st Sun April to Last Sat Oct.
Oklahoma City	Oklahoma	United States	35 N 30	97 W 30	6+	CST	5+	1st Sun April to Last Sat Oct.
Olympia	Washington	United States	47 N 03	122 W 53	8+	PST	7	1st Sun April to Last Sat Oct.
Omaha	Nebraska	United States	41 N 17	96 W 01	6+	CST	5+	1st Sun April to Last Sat Oct.
Omdurman		Sudan	15 N 45	32 E 30	-2	EET		No
Omsk	Asian RSFSR	USSR	55 N 12	73 E 19	-6		-7	Last Sun March to Last Sat Sept.
Oran		Algeria	35 N 46	0 W 45	-1	CET	-2	Last Sun March to Last Sat Sept.
Oranjestad		Aruba	12 N 33	70 W 06	6.5+			No
Orlando	Florida	United States	28 N 33	81 W 23	5+	EST	4+	1st Sun April to Last Sat Oct.
Oruro		Boliva	17 S 57	66 W 59	4+			No
Osaka		Japan	34 N 40	135 E 30	-9			No
Oslo		Norway	59 N 56	10 E 45	-1	CET	-2	Last Sun March to Last Sat Sept.
Ottawa	Ontario	Canada	45 N 25	75 W 42	5+		4+	1st Sun April to Last Sat Oct.
Ouagadougou		Burkina Faso	12 N 22	1 W 31	0	GMT		No
Owensboro	Kentucky	United States	37 N 46	87 W 07	6+	CST	5+	1st Sun April to Last Sat Oct.
P'younyang		Korea, North	39 N 00	126 E 45	-9			No
Paducah	Kentucky	United States	37 N 05	88 W 37	6+	CST	5+	1st Sun April to Last Sat Oct.
Palermo		Italy	38 N 08	13 E 24	-1	CET	-2	Last Sun March to Last Sat Sept.
Panama City		Panama	8 N 57	79 W 32	5+			No
Papeete (on Tahiti)		French Polynesia	17 S 32	149 W 34	10+			No
Paramaribo		Suriname	5 N 50	55 W 13	4.5+			No
Paris		France	48 N 52	2 E 20	-1	CET	-2	Last Sun March to Last Sat Sept.
Pasadena	California	United States	34 N 09	118 W 09	8+	PST	7	1st Sun April to Last Sat Oct.
Pascagoula	Mississippi	United States	30 N 21	88 W 33	6+	CST	5+	1st Sun April to Last Sat Oct.
Paterson	New Jersey	United States	40 N 55	74 W 11	5+	EST	4+	1st Sun April to Last Sat Oct.
Pátraí		Greece	38 N 15	4 E 48	-2	EET	-3	Last Sun March to Last Sat Sept.
Peking/Beijing	Beijing Shi	China	39 N 55	116 E 25	-8	CCT		No
Peoria	Illinois	United States	40 N 42	89 W 36	6+	CST	5+	1st Sun April to Last Sat Oct.
Perm'	European RSFSR	USSR	58 N 00	56 E 15	-5		-6	Last Sun March to Last Sat Sept.
Perth	Western	Australia	31 S 57	115 E 50	-8	PST		No
Pensacola	Florida	United States	30 N 25	87 W 13	6+	CST	5+	1st Sun April to Last Sat Oct.
Peshawar	NWFP	Pakistan	34 N 01	71 E 40	-5			No
Petersburg	Virginia	United States	37 N 14	77 W 24	5+	EST	4+	1st Sun April to Last Sat Oct.
Philadelphia	Pennsylvania	United States	39 N 57	75 W 10	5+	EST	4+	1st Sun April to Last Sat Oct.
Phnum Pénh		Kampuchea	11 N 39	104 E 53	-7			No
Phoenix	Arizona	United States	60 N 07	149 W 27	7+	MST		No
Pierre	South Carolina	United States	44 N 22	100 W 21	5+	EST	4+	1st Sun April to Last Sat Oct.
Pierre	South Dakota	United States	44 N 22	100 W 20	6+	CST	5+	1st Sun April to Last Sat Oct.
Pittsburgh	Pennsylvania	United States	40 N 26	80 W 01	5+	EST	4+	1st Sun April to Last Sat Oct.
Pittsfield	Massachusetts	United States	42 N 27	73 W 15	5+	EST	4+	1st Sun April to Last Sat Oct.
Plovdiv		Bulgaria	42 N 09	24 E 43	-2	EET	-3	Last Sun March to Last Sat Sept.
Plymouth		Montserrat	16 N 42	62 W 13	4+			No
Pocatello	Idaho	United States	42 N 52	112 W 27	7+	MST	6+	1st Sun April to Last Sat Oct.
Port Louis		Mauritius	20 S 09	57 E 30	-4			No
Port Moresby		Papua New Guinea	9 S 27	147 E 08	-10			No
Port Villa	(New Hebrides)	Vanuatu	18 S 00	168 E 30	-11			No
Port-au-Prince		Haiti	18 N 33	72 W 20	5+			1st Sun April to Last Sat Oct.
Port-of-Spain		Trinidad/Tobago	10 N 39	61 W 31	4+			No
Portland	Maine	United States	43 N 39	70 W 16	5+	EST	4+	1st Sun April to Last Sat Oct.
Portland	Oregon	United States	45 N32	122 W 37	8+	PST	7	1st Sun April to Last Sat Oct.
Porto		Portugal	41 N 10	8 W 38	0	GMT	-1	Last Sun March to Last Sat Sept.
Porto Alegre		Brazil	29 S 58	51 W 11	3+			No
Portsmough	Virginia	United States	36 N 50	76 W 18	8+	PST	7	1st Sun April to Last Sat Oct.

City	State or Provence	Country	LAT.	LONG.	Time Adjust to GMT	Abv Time	D.S. Time	1991 Daylight Savings Observed
Portsmouth	New Hampshire	United States	43 N 05	70 W 45	5+	EST	4+	1st Sun April to Last Sat Oct.
Poughkeepsie	New York	United States	41 N 42	73 W 56	5+	EST	4+	1st Sun April to Last Sat Oct.
Poznan´		Poland	52 N 25	16 E 55	-1	CET	-2	Last Sun March to Last Sat Sept.
Prague		Czechoslovakia	50 N 05	14 E 26	-1	CET	-2	Last Sun March to Last Sat Sept.
Praia		Cape Verde	14 N 56	23 W 31	-2	EET		No
Pretoria		South Africa	25 S 45	28 E 11	-2	EET		No
Providence	Rhode Island	United States	41 N 49	71 W 24	5+	EST	4+	1st Sun April to Last Sat Oct.
Provo	Utah	United States	40 N 14	111 W 39	7+	MST	6+	1st Sun April to Last Sat Oct.
Pueblo	Colorado	United States	38 N 14	104 W 36	7+	MST	6+	1st Sun April to Last Sat Oct.
Pune		India	18 N 38	73 E 53	-5.5			No
Pusan		Korea, South	35 N 08	129 E 05	-9			No
Qingdao/Tsingtao	Shandong	China	36 N 05	120 E 10	-8	CCT		No
Qiqihar	Heilongjiang	China	47 N 18	124 E 00	-8	CCT		No
Québec	Québec	Canada	46 N 49	71 W 13	5+		4+	1st Sun April to Last Sat Oct.
Queens	New York	United States	40 N 43	73 W 52	5+	EST	4+	1st Sun April to Last Sat Oct.
Quezon City		Philippines	14 N 00	122 E 11	-8			No
Quito		Ecuador	0 S 13	78 W 30	5+			No
Rabat		Morocco	34 N 01	6 W 51	-1	CET	-2	Mid June - Mid Sept
Raleigh	North Carolina	United States	35 N 46	78 W 38	5+	EST	4+	1st Sun April to Last Sat Oct.
Rangoon	Former Burma	Union of Mayanmar	16 N 48	96 E 09	-6.5			No
Rapid City	South Dakota	United States	44 N 06	103 W 14	7+	MST	6+	1st Sun April to Last Sat Oct.
Rawalpindi		Pakistan	33 N 40	73 E 10	-5			No
Reading	Pennsylvania	United States	40 N 20	75 W 56	5+	EST	4+	1st Sun April to Last Sat Oct.
Recife		Brazil	8 S 09	34 W 59	3+			No
Reno	Nevada	United States	39 N 31	119 W 48	8+	PST	7	1st Sun April to Last Sat Oct.
Reykjavik		Iceland	64 N 09	21 W 57	0	CET		No
Richmond	Indiana	United States	39 N 50	84 W 54	5+	EST	No	No
Richmond	Virginia	United States	37 N 33	77 W 27	5+	EST	4+	1st Sun April to Last Sat Oct.
Rio de Janeiro		Brazil	23 S 54	43 W 14	3+			No
Riyadh		Saudi Arabia	24 N 39	46 E 42	-3			No
Road Town	Trotola	British Virgin Islands	18 N 27	64 W 37	4+			No
Roanoke	Virginia	United States	37 N 16	79 W 56	5+	EST	4+	1st Sun April to Last Sat Oct.
Rochester	New York	United States	43 N 10	77 W 37	5+	EST	4+	1st Sun April to Last Sat Oct.
Rock Springs	Wyoming	United States	41 N 35	109 W 14	7+	MST	6+	1st Sun April to Last Sat Oct.
Rockford	Illinois	United States	42 N 16	89 W 06	6+	CST	5+	1st Sun April to Last Sat Oct.
Rockville	Maryland	United States	39 N 05	77 W 09	5+	EST	4+	1st Sun April to Last Sat Oct.
Rome		Italy	41 N 54	12 E 30	-1	CET	-2	Last Sun March to Last Sat Sept.
Rosario		Argentina	32 S 58	60 W 42	3+			No
Rosseau		Dominica	15 N 18	61 W 24	4+			No
Rostov-na-Donu	European RSFSR	USSR	47 N 16	39 E 47	-3		-4	Last Sun March to Last Sat Sept.
Roswell	New Mexico	United States	33 N 24	104 W 32	7+	MST	6+	1st Sun April to Last Sat Oct.
Rotterdam		Netherlands	51 N 55	4 E 27	-1	CET	-2	Last Sun March to Last Sat Sept.
Rutland	Vermont	United States	43 N 37	72 W 58	5+	EST	4+	1st Sun April to Last Sat Oct.
Sacramento	California	United States	38 N 35	121 W 29	8+	PST	7	1st Sun April to Last Sat Oct.
Saginaw	Michigan	United States	43 N 25	83 W 57	5+	EST	4+	1st Sun April to Last Sat Oct.
Saigon (Ho Chi Minh City)		Viet Nam	10 N 45	106 E 40	7+			No
Saint Joseph	Missouri	United States	39 N46	95 W 50	6+	CST	5+	1st Sun April to Last Sat Oct.
Saint Louis	Missouri	United States	38 N 37	90 W 12	6+	CST	5+	1st Sun April to Last Sat Oct.
Saint Pierre		St. Pierre/Miquelon	46 N 46	56 W 10	3+		2+	22 April to 20 Oct
Saint-Denis		Réunion	20 S 52	55 E 27	-4			No
Salem	Oregon	United States	44 N 56	123 W 02	8+	PST	7	1st Sun April to Last Sat Oct.
Salina	Kansas	United States	38 N 50	97 W 37	6+	CST	5+	1st Sun April to Last Sat Oct.
Salt Lake City	Utah	United States	40 N 45	111 W 53	7+	MST	6+	1st Sun April to Last Sat Oct.
Saltzburg		Austria	47 N 48	13 E 04	-1	CET	-2	Last Sun March to Last Sat Sept.
Salvador		Brazil	12 S 59	38 W 27	3+			No

Daylight Savings Times Deemed Reliable But Not Guaranteed

City	State or Provence	Country	LAT.	LONG.	Time Adjust to GMT	Abv Time	D.S. Time	1991 Daylight Savings Observed
San Antonio	Texas	United States	29 N 25	98 W 30	7+	MST	6+	1st Sun April to Last Sat Oct.
San Diego	California	United States	32 N 43	117 W 09	8+	PST	7	1st Sun April to Last Sat Oct.
San Francisco	California	United States	37 N 47	112 W 25	8+	PST	7	1st Sun April to Last Sat Oct.
San José		Costa Rica	9 N 56	84 W 05	6+			No
San Jose	California	United States	37 N 20	121 W 53	8+	PST	7	1st Sun April to Last Sat Oct.
San Juan		Puerto Rico	18 N 30	66 W 10	4+			No
San Marino		San Marino	43 N 56	12 E 27	-1	CET	-2	Last Sun March to Last Sat Sept.
San Salvador		El Salvador	13 N 41	89 W 12	6+			No
Santa Barbara	California	United States	34 N 25	119 W 42	8+	PST	7	1st Sun April to Last Sat Oct.
Santa Cruz		Boliva	17 S 45	63 W 03	4+			No
Santa Fe	New Mexico	United States	35 N 41	105 W 57	7+	MST	6+	1st Sun April to Last Sat Oct.
Santiago		Chile	33 S 27	70 W 40	4+		3+	2nd Sun Oct; 3rd Sat March
Santo Domingo		Dominican Republic	18 S 29	69 W 53	4+			No
San'á		Yeman Arab Republic	15 N 23	44 E 13	-3			No
Sao Paulo		Brazil	23 S 34	46 W 38	3+			No
Sao Tome		Sao Tome	0 N 20	6 E 43	0	GMT		No
Sapporo		Japan	43 N 03	141 E 19	-9			No
Sarajevo		Yogoslavia	43 N 50	18 E 26	-1	CET	-2	Last Sun March to Last Sat Sept.
Saratov	European RSFSR	USSR	51 N 30	45 E 30	-4		-4	Last Sun March to Last Sat Sept.
Sault St. Marie	Michigan	United States	46 N 30	84 W 21	5+	EST	4+	1st Sun April to Last Sat Oct.
Savannah	Georgia	United States	32 N 05	81 W 06	5+	EST	4+	1st Sun April to Last Sat Oct.
Schenectady	New York	United States	42 N 49	75 W 57	5+	EST	4+	1st Sun April to Last Sat Oct.
Scottsbluff	Nebraska	United States	41 N 52	103 W 40	7+	MST	6+	1st Sun April to Last Sat Oct.
Scranton	Pennsylvania	United States	41 N 25	75 W 40	5+	EST	4+	1st Sun April to Last Sat Oct.
Seattle	Washington	United States	47 N 36	122 W 20	8+	PST	7	1st Sun April to Last Sat Oct.
Semarang	Java	Indonesia	7 S 03	110 E 27	-7			No
Seoul		Korea, South	37 N 33	126 E 58	-9			No
Seville		Spain	37 N 29	5 W 58	-1	CET	-2	Last Sun March to Last Sat Sept.
Seward	Alaska	United States	60 N 07	149 W 25	9+	YST	8	1st Sun April to Last Sat Oct.
Shanghai	Shanghai Shi	China	31 N 14	121 E 30	-8	CCT		No
Sheboygan	Wisconson	United States	43 N 46	87 W 45	6+	CST	5+	1st Sun April to Last Sat Oct.
Sheffield		England	53 N 23	1 W 28	0	GMT	-1	Last Sun March to Last Sat Oct.
Shenyang	Liaoning	China	41 N 45	123 E 22	-8	CCT		No
Sheridan	Wyoming	United States	44 N 48	106 W 58	7+	MST	6+	1st Sun April to Last Sat Oct.
Shreveport	Louisiana	United States	32 N 31	93 W 45	6+	CST	5+	1st Sun April to Last Sat Oct.
Shubra el Khema		Egypt	30 N 06	31 E 15	-2	EET		No
Singapore		Singapore	1 N 16	103 E 51	-8			No
Sioux Falls	South Carolina	United States	43 N 33	96 W 44	5+	EST	4+	1st Sun April to Last Sat Oct.
Sioux Falls	South Dakota	United States	43 N 33	96 W 43	6+	CST	5+	1st Sun April to Last Sat Oct.
Skopje		Yogoslavia	42 N 02	21 E 26	-1	CET	-2	Last Sun March to Last Sat Sept.
Sofia		Bulgaria	42 N 42	23 E 20	-2	EET	-3	Last Sun March to Last Sat Sept.
South Bend	Indiana	United States	41 N 41	86 W 15	5+	EST	No	No
Spartanburg	South Carolina	United States	34 N 56	81 W 57	5+	EST	4+	1st Sun April to Last Sat Oct.
Split		Yogoslavia	43 N 30	16 E 28	-1	CET	-2	Last Sun March to Last Sat Sept.
Spokane	Washington	United States	47 N 40	117 W 24	8+	PST	7	1st Sun April to Last Sat Oct.
Springfield	Massachusetts	United States	42 N 06	72 W 35	5+	EST	4+	1st Sun April to Last Sat Oct.
Springfield	Illinois	United States	39 N 48	89 W 39	6+	CST	5+	1st Sun April to Last Sat Oct.
Springfield	Missouri	United States	37 N 13	90 W 12	6+	CST	5+	1st Sun April to Last Sat Oct.
St. George's		Grenada	12 N 03	61 W 45	4+			No
St. John's		Antigua/Barbuda	17 N 06	61 W 51	5+			No
St. John's	Newfoundland	Canada	47 N 34	52 W 43	4.5+			1st Sun April to Last Sat Oct.
St. Paul	Minnesota	United States	44 N 57	93 W 06	6+	CST	5+	1st Sun April to Last Sat Oct.
St. Petersburg	Florida	United States	27 N 46	82 W 39	5+	EST	4+	1st Sun April to Last Sat Oct.
Stamford	Connecticut	United States	41 N 03	73 W 32	5+	EST	4+	1st Sun April to Last Sat Oct.
Stanley		Falkland Islands	51 S 42	57 W 50	4+			No

City	State or Provence	Country	LAT.	LONG.	Time Adjust to GMT	Abv Time	D.S. Time	1991 Daylight Savings Observed
Staten Island	New York	United States	40 N 35	74 W 09	5+	EST	4+	1st Sun April to Last Sat Oct.
Stockholm		Sweden	59 N 20	18 E 00 CK	-1	CET	-2	Last Sun March to Last Sat Sept.
Stuttgart		Germany	48 N 48	9 E 15	-1	CET	-2	Last Sun March to Last Sat Sept.
Suez Canal		Egypt	30 N 53	32 E 21	-2	EET		No
Surabaya	Java	Indonesia	7 S 23	112 E 45	-7			No
Suva (on Viti Levu)		Fiji	18 S 09	178 E 26	-12			No
Sverdlovsk	Asian RSFSR	USSR	56 N 51	60 E 36	-5		-7	Last Sun March to Last Sat Sept.
Sydney	New S. Wales	Australia	33 S 52	151 E 13	-9		-11	Last Sun Oct; 1st Sat March
Syracuse	New York	United States	43 N 03	76 W 09	5+	EST	4+	1st Sun April to Last Sat Oct.
Szczecin		Poland	53 N 25	14 E 35	-1	CET	-2	Last Sun March to Last Sat Sept.
T'aipei		Taiwan	25 N 03	121 E 30	-8			No
Tabriz		Iran	38 N 00	46 E 13	-3.5			No
Tacoma	Washington	United States	47 N 14	122 W 26	8+	PST	7	1st Sun April to Last Sat Oct.
Taegu		Korea, South	35 N 49	128 E 41	-9			No
Taichung		China (Taiwan)	24 N 10	120 E 42	-8	CCT		No
Tainan		China (Taiwan)	23 N 08	120 E 18	-8	CCT		No
Taipei		China (Taiwan)	25 N 02	121 E 38	-8	CCT		No
Taiyuan	Shanxi	China	37 N 55	112 E 30	-8	CCT		No
Tallahassee	Florida	United States	30 N 27	81 W 39	5+	EST	4+	1st Sun April to Last Sat Oct.
Tamale		Ghana	9 N 25	0 W 05	0	GMT		No
Tampere		Finland	61 N 21	23 E 39	-2	EET	-3	Last Sun March to Last Sat Sept.
Tashkent	Uzbek SSR	USSR	41 N 20	69 E 18	-6		-7	Last Sun March to Last Sat Sept.
Tbilisi	Georgian SSR	USSR	41 N 45	44 E 55	-4		-4	Last Sun March to Last Sat Sept.
Tegucigalpa		Honduras	14 N 06	87 W 13	6+			No
Tehran		Iran	35 N 40	51 E 26	-3.5			No
Tel Aviv		Israel	32 N 04	34 E 46	-2	EET	-3	Est May - Sept
Temple	Arizona	United States	33 N 25	111 W 56	7+	MST		No
Terre Haute	Indiana	United States	39 N 28	87 W 25	5+	EST	4+	1st Sun April to Last Sat Oct.
Texarkana	Arkansas	United States	33 N 26	94 W 03	6+	CST	5+	1st Sun April to Last Sat Oct.
The Hague		Netherlands	52 N 05	4 E 16	-1	CET	-2	Last Sun March to Last Sat Sept.
Thimphu		Bhutan	27 N 37	89 E 52	-6			No
Thohoyandou		Venda	23 S 00	30 E 29	2+			No
Thorshavn		Faeroe Islands	62 N 01	6 W 45	0	GMT		No
Tianjin	Tianjin Shi	China	39 N 08	117 E 14	-8	CCT		No
Timisoara		Romania	45 N 44	21 E 21	-2	EET	-3	Last Sun March to Last Sat Sept.
Tiranë		Albania	41 N 02	19 E 04	-1	CET	-2	Last Sun March to Last Sat Oct.
Tokyo		Japan	35 N 40	139 E 46	-9			No
Toledo	Ohio	United States	41 N 39	83 W 33	5+	EST	4+	1st Sun April to Last Sat Oct.
Topeka	Kansas	United States	39 N 03	95 W 40	6+	CST	5+	1st Sun April to Last Sat Oct.
Toronto	Ontario	Canada	43 N 39	79 W 22	5+		4+	1st Sun April to Last Sat Oct.
Trenton	New Jersey	United States	40 N 14	74 W 46	5+	EST	4+	1st Sun April to Last Sat Oct.
Tripoli		Libya	32 N 54	13 E 10	-2	EET		No
Trujillo		Peru	8 S 08	79 W 00	5+		4+	1 Jan to 31 March
Tucson	Arizona	United States	32 N 13	110 W 58	7+	MST		No
Tulsa	Oklahoma	United States	36 N 10	95 W 55	6+	CST	5+	1st Sun April to Last Sat Oct.
Tunis		Tunisia	36 N 48	10 E 10	-1	CET		No
Turin		Italy	45 N 05	7 E 44	-1	CET	-2	Last Sun March to Last Sat Sept.
Tuscaloosa	Alabama	United States	33 N 12	87 W 34	5+	EST	4+	1st Sun April to Last Sat Oct.
Ufa	European RSFSR	USSR	54 N 45	55 E 57	-5		-7	Last Sun March to Last Sat Sept.
Ulan Bator		Mongolia	47 N 55	106 E 45	-8		-9	1st Sun April to Last Sat Oct.
Umtala		Transkei	28 N 47	31 E 35	-2	EET		No
Utica	New York	United States	43 N 06	75 W 14	5+	EST	4+	1st Sun April to Last Sat Oct.
Vaduz		Liechtenstein	47 N 08	09 E 31	-1	CET	-2	Last Sun March to Last Sat Sept.
Valencia		Spain	39 N 26	0 W 23	-1	CET	-2	Last Sun March to Last Sat Sept.
Valencia		Venezuela	10 N 11	68 W 00	4+			No

City	State or Provence	Country	LAT.	LONG.	Time Adjust to GMT	Abv Time	D.S. Time	1991 Daylight Savings Observed
Valetta		Malta	35 N 54	14 E 31	-1	CET	-2	Last Sun March to Last Sat Sept.
Valparaíso		Chile	33 S 02	71 W 32	4+		3+	2nd Sun Oct; 3rd Sat March
Vancouver	British Columbia	Canada	49 N 16	123 W 07	8+		7+	1st Sun April to Last Sat Oct.
Varna		Bulgaria	43 N 14	27 E 58	-2	EET	-3	Last Sun March to Last Sat Sept.
Vatican City		Vatican City State	41 N 45	12 E 27	-1	CET	-2	Last Sun March to Last Sat Sept.
Venice		Italy	45 N 25	12 E 18	-1	CET	-2	Last Sun March to Last Sat Sept.
Ventura	California	United States	34 N 17	119 W 18	8+	PST	7	1st Sun April to Last Sat Oct.
Victoria		Seychelles	4 S 36	55 E 28	-4			No
Vienna		Austria	48 N 12	16 E 23	-1	CET	-2	Last Sun March to Last Sat Sept.
Vientiane		Laos	17 N 58	102 E 37	-7			No
Vladivostok	Asian RSFSR	USSR	43 N 06	131 E 47	-10		-11	Last Sun March to Last Sat Sept.
Volgograd	European RSFSR	USSR	48 N 40	42 E 20	-4		-4	Last Sun March to Last Sat Sept.
Waco	Texas	United States	31 N 33	97 W 09	7+	MST	6+	1st Sun April to Last Sat Oct.
Wallis (on Uvea)		Wallis/Futuna Islands	13 S 17	176 W 08	-12			No
Warsaw		Poland	52 N 15	21 E 00	-1	CET	-2	Last Sun March to Last Sat Sept.
Warwick	Rhode Island	United States	41 N 42	71 W 28	5+	EST	4+	1st Sun April to Last Sat Oct.
Washington	Dist. of Columbia	United States	38 N 53	77 W 00	5+	EST	4+	1st Sun April to Last Sat Oct.
Waterbury	Connecticut	United States	41 N 33	73 W 03	5+	EST	4+	1st Sun April to Last Sat Oct.
Waterloo	Iowa	United States	42 N 30	92 W 21	6+	CST	5+	1st Sun April to Last Sat Oct.
Watertown	New York	United States	43 N 59	75 W 55	5+	EST	4+	1st Sun April to Last Sat Oct.
Watertown	South Carolina	United States	44 N 54	97 W 07	5+	EST	4+	1st Sun April to Last Sat Oct.
Wausau	Wisconson	United States	44 N 58	89 W 38	6+	CST	5+	1st Sun April to Last Sat Oct.
Wellington		New Zealand	41 S 18	174 E 47	-12		1+	Last Sun March to Last Sat Oct.
Wheeling	West Virginia	United States	40 N 04	80 W 43	5+	EST	4+	1st Sun April to Last Sat Oct.
Wichita	Kansas	United States	37 N 42	97 W 20	6+	CST	5+	1st Sun April to Last Sat Oct.
Wichita Falls	Texas	United States	33 N 54	98 W 30	7+	MST	6+	1st Sun April to Last Sat Oct.
Willemstad		Netherlands Antilles	12 N 12	68 W 58	4+			No
Wilmington	Delaware	United States	39 N 45	75 W 33	5+	EST	4+	1st Sun April to Last Sat Oct.
Wilmington	North Carolina	United States	34 N 14	77 W 55	5+	EST	4+	1st Sun April to Last Sat Oct.
Windhoek		Namibia	22 S 30	17 E 00	-2	EET		No
Winnipeg	Manitoba	Canada	49 N 53	97 W 09	6+		7+	1st Sun April to Last Sat Oct.
Winston-Salem	North Carolina	United States	36 N 06	80 W 15	5+	EST	4+	1st Sun April to Last Sat Oct.
Woonsocket	Rhode Island	United States	42 N 00	71 W 31	5+	EST	4+	1st Sun April to Last Sat Oct.
Worchester	Massachusetts	United States	42 N 16	71 W 48	5+	EST	4+	1st Sun April to Last Sat Oct.
Wroclaw		Poland	51 N 07	17 E 10	-1	CET	-2	Last Sun March to Last Sat Sept.
Wuhan	Hubei (Hupei)	China	30 N 23	114 E 54	-8	CCT		No
Wuppertal		Germany	51 N 16	7 E 14	-1	CET	-2	Last Sun March to Last Sat Sept.
Xi'an	Shaanxi (Shensi)	China	34 N 20	109 E 00	-8	CCT		No
Xuzhou	Jiangsu	China	34 N 17	117 E 10	-8	CCT		No
Yakima	Washington	United States	46 N 37	120 W 30	8+	PST	7	1st Sun April to Last Sat Oct.
Yamoussoukro		Ivory Coast	6 N 49	5 W 17	0	GMT		No
Yaoundé		Cameroon	31 N 51	11 E 32	-1	CET		No
Yaren		Nauru	0 S 32	166 E 55	-12			No
Yerevan	Armenian SSR	USSR	40 N 10	44 E 30	-4		-4	Last Sun March to Last Sat Sept.
Yokohama		Japan	35 N 37	139 E 40	-9			No
Yonkers	New York	United States	40 N 56	73 W 54	5+	EST	4+	1st Sun April to Last Sat Oct.
Youngstown	Ohio	United States	41 N 06	89 W 39	5+	EST	4+	1st Sun April to Last Sat Oct.
Zagreb		Yugoslavia	45 N 50	15 E 58	-1	CET	-2	Last Sun March to Last Sat Sept.
Zarqa		Jordan	32 N 13	35 E 43	-2	EET	-3	1st Sun April to Last Sat Oct.
Zhengzhou	Henan (Honan)	China	34 N 46	113 E 42	-8	CCT		No
Zürich		Switzerland	47 N 23	8 E 32	-1	CET	-2	Last Sun March to Last Sat Sept.

MAJOR WORLD CITY COORDINATES

LISTED BY COUNTRY

Country	City	State or Provence	LAT.	LONG.	Time Adjust to GMT	Abv Time	D.S. Time	1991 Daylight Savings Observed	S.T. Meridian
Afghanistan	Herat		34 N 28	62 E 13	-4.5			No	60 E 30
Afghanistan	Kabul		34 N 30	69 E 13	-4.5			No	60 E 30
Albania	Tirane		41 N 02	19 E 04	-1	CET	-2	Last Sun March to Last Sat Oct.	15 E 00
Algeria	Algiers		36 N 47	3 E 04	-1	CET	-2	Last Sun March to Last Sat Sept.	15 E 00
Algeria	Constanine		36 N 28	6 E 38	-1	CET	-2	Last Sun March to Last Sat Sept.	15 E 00
Algeria	Oran		35 N 46	0 W 45	-1	CET	-2	Last Sun March to Last Sat Sept.	15 E 00
Andorra	Andorra la Vella		42 N 31	1 E 30	-1	CET	-2	Last Sun March to Last Sat Sept.	15 E 00
Angola	Luanda		8 S 48	13 E 14	-1	CET		No	15 E 00
Antigua/Barbuda	St. John's		17 N 06	61 W 51	5+			No	75 W 00
Argentina	Buenos Aires		34 S 36	58 W 27	3+			No	45 W 00
Argentina	Córdoba		30 S 20	64 W 03	3+			No	45 W 00
Argentina	La Plata		34 S 54	57 W 57	3+			No	45 W 00
Argentina	Rosario		32 S 58	60 W 42	3+			No	45 W 00
Aruba	Oranjestad		12 N 33	70 W 06	6.5+			No	97 W 30
Australia	Canberra	Canaberra	35 S 17	149 E 08	-10		-11	Last Sun Oct; 1st Sat March	150 E 00
Australia	Sydney	New S. Wales	33 S 52	151 E 13	-9		-11	Last Sun Oct; 1st Sat March	150 E 00
Australia	Darwin	N. Territory	12 S 28	130 E 49	-9.5			Last Sun Oct; 1st Sat March	142 E 30
Australia	Brisbane	Queensland	27 S 28	153 E 02	-10			No	150 E 00
Australia	Adelaide	S. Australia	34 S 56	138 E 38	-9.5			Last Sun Oct; 1st Sat March	142 E 30
Australia	Melbourne	Victoria	37 S 49	144 E 62	-10		-11	Last Sun Oct; 1st Sat March	150 E 00
Australia	Perth	Western	31 S 57	115 E 50	-8	PST		No	120 E 00
Austria	Graz		47 N 05	15 E 26	-1	CET	-2	Last Sun March to Last Sat Sept.	15 E 00
Austria	Linz		48 N 18	14 E 18	-1	CET	-2	Last Sun March to Last Sat Sept.	15 E 00
Austria	Saltzburg		47 N 48	13 E 04	-1	CET	-2	Last Sun March to Last Sat Sept.	15 E 00
Austria	Vienna		48 N 12	16 E 23	-1	CET	-2	Last Sun March to Last Sat Sept.	15 E 00
Bahamas	Nassau		25 N 05	77 W 20	5+		4+	1st Sun April to Last Sat Oct.	75 W 00
Bahrain	Manama		26 N 14	50 E 35	-3			No	45 E 00
Bangladesh	Dacca		23 N 43	90 E 25	-6			No	90 E 00
Barbados	Bridgetown		13 N 06	59 W 37	4+			No	60 W 00
Belgium	Antwerp		51 N 13	4 E 24	-1	CET	-2	Last Sun March to Last Sat Sept.	15 E 00
Belgium	Brussels		50 N 51	4 E 21	-1	CET	-2	Last Sun March to Last Sat Sept.	15 E 00
Belgium	Li'ege		50 N 38	5 E 34	-1	CET	-2	Last Sun March to Last Sat Sept.	15 E 00
Belize	Belize City		17 N 31	88 W 10	6+			No	90 W 00
Belize	Belmopan		17 N 15	88 W 47	6+			No	90 W 00
Benin	Cotonou		6 N 21	2 E 26	-1	GMT		No	15 E 00
Bermuda	Hamilton		23 N 18	64 W 47	4+		3+	1st Sun April to Last Sat Oct.	60 W 00
Bhutan	Thimphu		27 N 37	89 E 52	-6			No	90 E 00
Boliva	Cochabamaba		17 S 24	66 W 09	4+			No	60 W 00
Boliva	Oruro		17 S 57	66 W 59	4+			No	60 W 00
Boliva	Santa Cruz		17 S 45	63 W 03	4+			No	60 W 00
Bolivia	La Paz		16 S 30	68 W 09	4+			No	60 W 00
Bophuthatswana	Mmabatho		25 S 42	25 E 43	-2			No	30 E 00
Bostwana	Gaborone		21 S 14	27 E 31	-2	EET		No	30 E 00
Brazil	Belo Horizonte		19 S 54	43 W 56	3+			No	45 W 00
Brazil	Brasília		15 S 49	47 W 39	3+			No	45 W 00
Brazil	Fortaleza		3 S 35	38 W 31	3+			No	45 W 00
Brazil	Porto Alegre		29 S 58	51 W 11	3+			No	45 W 00
Brazil	Recife		8 S 09	34 W 59	3+			No	45 W 00
Brazil	Rio de Janeiro		23 S 54	43 W 14	3+			No	45 W 00
Brazil	Salvador		12 S 59	38 W 27	3+			No	45 W 00
Brazil	Sao Paulo		23 S 34	46 W 38	3+			No	45 W 00
British Virgin Islands	Road Town	Trotola	18 N 27	64 W 37	4+			No	60 W 00
Brunei	Bandar Seri Begawan		4 N 54	114 E 57	-8	PST		No	120 E 00
Bulgaria	Plovdiv		42 N 09	24 E 43	-2	EET	-3	Last Sun March to Last Sat Sept.	30 E 00
Bulgaria	Sofia		42 N 42	23 E 20	-2	EET	-3	Last Sun March to Last Sat Sept.	30 E 00
Bulgaria	Varna		43 N 14	27 E 58	-2	EET	-3	Last Sun March to Last Sat Sept.	30 E 00
Burkina Faso	Ouagadougou		12 N 22	1 W 31	0	GMT		No	0 W 00
Burundi	Bujumbura		3 S 24	29 E 21	-2	EET		No	30 E 00
Cameroon	Douala		4 N 03	9 E 42	-1	CET		No	15 E 00

Country	City	State or Provence	LAT.	LONG.	Time Adjust to GMT	Abv Time	D.S. Time	1991 Daylight Savings Observed	S.T. Meridian
Cameroon	Yaoundé		31 N 51	11 E 32	-1	CET		No	15 E 00
Canada	Vancouver	British Columbia	49 N 16	123 W 07	8+		7+	1st Sun April to Last Sat Oct.	120 W 00
Canada	Winnipeg	Manitoba	49 N 53	97 W 09	6+		7+	1st Sun April to Last Sat Oct.	90 W 00
Canada	Calgary	Mountain	51 N 03	114 W 03	7+	MST	6+	1st Sun April to Last Sat Oct.	105 W 00
Canada	Edmonton	Mountain	53 N 33	113 W 28	7+	MST	6+	1st Sun April to Last Sat Oct.	105 W 00
Canada	St. John's	Newfoundland	47 N 34	52 W 43	4.5+			1st Sun April to Last Sat Oct.	67 W 30
Canada	Hamilton	Ontario	43 N 15	79 W 52	5+		4+	1st Sun April to Last Sat Oct.	75 W 00
Canada	Ottawa	Ontario	45 N 25	75 W 42	5+		4+	1st Sun April to Last Sat Oct.	75 W 00
Canada	Toronto	Ontario	43 N 39	79 W 22	5+		4+	1st Sun April to Last Sat Oct.	75 W 00
Canada	Montre'al	Quebec	45 N 1	73 W 34	5+		4+	1st Sun April to Last Sat Oct.	75 W 00
Canada	Québec	Québec	46 N 49	71 W 13	5+		4+	1st Sun April to Last Sat Oct.	75 W 00
Cape Verde	Praia		14 N 56	23 W 31	-2	EET		No	30 W 00
Cayman Islands	Georgetown		19 N 20	81 W 20	5+			No	75 W 00
Central African Rep.	Bangui		4 N 21	18 E 35	-1	CET		No	15 E 00
Chad	N'djamena		12 N 07	15 E 03	-1	CET		No	15 E 00
Chile	Concepción		36 S 51	72 W 59	4+		3+	2nd Sun Oct; 3rd Sat March	60 W 00
Chile	Santiago		33 S 27	70 W 40	4+		3+	2nd Sun Oct; 3rd Sat March	60 W 00
Chile	Valparaíso		33 S 02	71 W 32	4+		3+	2nd Sun Oct; 3rd Sat March	60 W 00
China	Peking (Beijing)	Beijing Shi	39 N 55	116 E 25	-8	CCT		No	120 E 00
China	Lanzhou (Lanchow)	Gansu (Kansu)	35 N 55	103 E 55	-8	CCT		No	120 E 00
China	Canton (Guangzhou)	Guangdong	23 N 07	113 E 16	-8	CCT	-9	No	120 E 00
China	Anshun	Guizhou	26 N 12	105 E 50	-8	CCT	-9	No	120 E 00
China	Harbin	Heilongjiang	45 N 47	126 E 39	-8	CCT		No	120 E 00
China	Qiqihar	Heilongjiang	47 N 18	124 E 00	-8	CCT		No	120 E 00
China	Zhengzhou	Henan (Honan)	34 N 46	113 E 42	-8	CCT		No	120 E 00
China	Wuhan	Hubei (Hupei)	30 N 23	114 E 54	-8	CCT		No	120 E 00
China	Nanjing (Nanking)	Jiangsu	32 N 04	118 E 46	-8	CCT		No	120 E 00
China	Xuzhou	Jiangsu	34 N 17	117 E 10	-8	CCT		No	120 E 00
China	Changchun	Jilin (Kirin)	43 N 54	125 E 20	-8	CCT		No	120 E 00
China	Fushun	Liaoning	41 N 50	124 E 00	-8	CCT		No	120 E 00
China	Luda (Dairen)	Liaoning	38 N 59	121 E 35	-8	CCT		No	120 E 00
China	Shenyang	Liaoning	41 N 45	123 E 22	-8	CCT		No	120 E 00
China	Xi'an	Shaanxi (Shensi)	34 N 20	109 E 00	-8	CCT		No	120 E 00
China	Jinan	Shandong	36 N 40	117 E 01	-8	CCT		No	120 E 00
China	Qingdao (Tsingtao)	Shandong	36 N 05	120 E 10	-8	CCT		No	120 E 00
China	Shanghai	Shanghai Shi	31 N 14	121 E 30	-8	CCT		No	120 E 00
China	Taiyuan	Shanxi	37 N 55	112 E 30	-8	CCT		No	120 E 00
China	Chengdu (Chengtu)	Sichuan/Szechwan	30 N 30	104 E 10	-8	CCT		No	120 E 00
China	Chongquing	Sichuan/Szechwan	29 N 38	107 E 30	-8	CCT		No	120 E 00
China	Tianjin	Tianjin Shi	39 N 08	117 E 14	-8	CCT		No	120 E 00
China	Kunming	Yunnan	25 N 04	102 E 41	-8	CCT		No	120 E 00
China (Taiwan)	Chilung (Keelung)		25 N 02	121 E 48	-8	CCT		No	120 E 00
China (Taiwan)	Taichung		24 N 10	120 E 42	-8	CCT		No	120 E 00
China (Taiwan)	Tainan		23 N 08	120 E 18	-8	CCT		No	120 E 00
China (Taiwan)	Taipei		25 N 02	121 E 38	-8	CCT		No	120 E 00
Columbia	Baranquilla		3 N 18	74 W 40	5+			No	75 W 00
Columbia	Bogota'		4 N 40	74 W 05	5+			No	75 W 00
Columbia	Bucaramanga		17 N 12	73 W 14	5+			No	75 W 00
Columbia	Cali		3 N 22	76 W 30	5+			No	75 W 00
Columbia	Cartagena		10 N 30	75 W 40	5+			No	75 W 00
Columbia	Medellín		6 N 15	75 W 35	5+			No	75 W 00
Comoro Islands	Moroni		11 S 41	43 E 16	-3			No	45 E 00
Congo	Brazzaville		4 S 17	15 E 14	-1	CET		No	15 E 00
Costa Rica	San José		9 N 56	84 W 05	6+			No	90 W 00
Cuba	Havana		23 N 08	82 W 24	5+		4+	3rd Sat March to 3rd Sat Oct.	75 W 00
Cyprus	Nicosia		35 N 12	33 E 22	-2	EET	-3	Last Sun March to Last Sat Sept.	30 E 00
Czechoslovakia	Bratislava		48 N 09	17 E 07	-1	CET	-2	Last Sun March to Last Sat Sept.	15 E 00
Czechoslovakia	Prague		50 N 05	14 E 26	-1	CET	-2	Last Sun March to Last Sat Sept.	15 E 00
Denmark	Copenhagen		55 N 41	12 E 35	-1	CET	-2	Last Sun March to Last Sat Sept.	15 E 00

Country	City	State or Provence	LAT.	LONG.	Time Adjust to GMT	Abv Time	D.S. Time	1991 Daylight Savings Observed	S.T. Meridian
Djibouti	Djibouti		11 N 36	43 E 07	-3			No	45 E 00
Dominica	Rosseau		15 N 18	61 W 24	4+			No	60 W 00
Dominican Republic	Santo Domingo		18 S 29	69 W 53	4+			No	60 W 00
Ecuador	Guayaquil		2 S 16	79 W 53	5+			No	75 W 00
Ecuador	Quito		0 S 13	78 W 30	5+			No	75 W 00
Egypt	Alexandria		31 N 13	29 E 57	-2	EET		No	30 E 00
Egypt	Cairo		30 N 03	31 E 15	-2	EET		No	30 E 00
Egypt	Shubra el Khema		30 N 06	31 E 15	-2	EET		No	30 E 00
Egypt	Suez Canal		30 N 53	32 E 21	-2	EET		No	30 E 00
El Salvador	San Salvador		13 N 41	89 W 12	6+			No	90 W 00
England	Manchester		53 N 28	2 W 14	0	GMT	-1	Last Sun March to Last Sat Oct.	0 W 00
England	Bermingham		52 N 30	1 W 50	0	GMT	-1	Last Sun March to Last Sat Oct.	0 W 00
England	Greenwich		51 N 29	00 W 00	0	GMT	-1	Last Sun March to Last Sat Oct.	0 W 00
England	Leeds		53 N 48	1 W 32	0	GMT	-1	Last Sun March to Last Sat Oct.	0 W 00
England	Liverpool		53 N 25	2 W 52	0	GMT	-1	Last Sun March to Last Sat Oct.	0 W 00
England	London		51 N 30	0 W 06	0	GMT	-1	Last Sun March to Last Sat Oct.	0 W 00
England	Newcastle (upon Tyne)		55 N 00	1 W 45	0	GMT	-1	Last Sun March to Last Sat Oct.	0 W 00
England	Sheffield		53 N 23	1 W 28	0	GMT	-1	Last Sun March to Last Sat Oct.	0 W 00
Equatorial Guinea	Malabo		3 N 45	8 E 47	-1	CET		No	15 E 00
Ethiopia	Addis Ababa		9 N 03	38 E 43	-3			No	45 E 00
Ethiopia	Asmera		15 N 17	38 E 56	-3			No	45 E 00
Faeroe Islands	Thorshavn		62 N 01	6 W 45	0	GMT		No	0 W 00
Falkland Islands	Stanley		51 S 42	57 W 50	4+			No	60 W 00
Fiji	Suva (on Viti Levu)		18 S 09	178 E 26	-12			No	180 E 00
Finland	Helsinki		60 N 09	24 E 58	-2	EET	-3	Last Sun March to Last Sat Sept.	30 E 00
Finland	Tampere		61 N 21	23 E 39	-2	EET	-3	Last Sun March to Last Sat Sept.	30 E 00
France	Le Havre		49 N 31	0 E 07	-1	CET	-2	Last Sun March to Last Sat Sept.	15 E 00
France	Lille		50 N 38	3 E 01	-1	CET	-2	Last Sun March to Last Sat Sept.	15 E 00
France	Lyon		45 N 44	4 E 52	-1	CET	-2	Last Sun March to Last Sat Sept.	15 E 00
France	Marseille		43 N 18	5 E 25	-1	CET	-2	Last Sun March to Last Sat Sept.	15 E 00
France	Paris		48 N 52	2 E 20	-1	CET	-2	Last Sun March to Last Sat Sept.	15 E 00
French Guiana	Cayenne		4 N 57	52 W 20	3+			No	45 W 00
French Polynesia	Papeete (on Tahiti)		17 S 32	149 W 34	10+			No	150 W 00
Gabon	Libreville		0 N 23	9 E 26	-1	CET		No	15 E 00
Gambia (The)	Banjul		13 N 28	16 W 39	0	GMT		No	0 W 00
Germany	Berlin		52 N 30	13 E 25	-1	CET	-2	Last Sun March to Last Sat Sept.	15 E 00
Germany	Bonn		50 N 44	7 E 06	-1	CET	-2	Last Sun March to Last Sat Sept.	15 E 00
Germany	Bremen		53 N 05	8 E 50	-1	CET	-2	Last Sun March to Last Sat Sept.	15 E 00
Germany	Cologne		50 N 56	6 E 57	-1	CET	-2	Last Sun March to Last Sat Sept.	15 E 00
Germany	Dresden		51 N 05	13 E 45	-1	CET	-2	Last Sun March to Last Sat Sept.	15 E 00
Germany	Dusseldorf		51 N 14	6 E 47	-1	CET	-2	Last Sun March to Last Sat Sept.	15 E 00
Germany	Essen		51 N 26	6 E 59	-1	CET	-2	Last Sun March to Last Sat Sept.	15 E 00
Germany	Frankfurt		52 N 42	13 E 37	-1	CET	-2	Last Sun March to Last Sat Sept.	15 E 00
Germany	Hamburg		53 N 34	10 E 02	-1	CET	-2	Last Sun March to Last Sat Sept.	15 E 00
Germany	Hannover		52 N 22	9 E 45	-1	CET	-2	Last Sun March to Last Sat Sept.	15 E 00
Germany	Leipzig		51 N 20	12 E 24	-1	CET	-2	Last Sun March to Last Sat Sept.	15 E 00
Germany	Mannheim		49 N 30	8 E 31	-1	CET	-2	Last Sun March to Last Sat Sept.	15 E 00
Germany	Munich		48 N 98	11 E 35	-1	CET	-2	Last Sun March to Last Sat Sept.	15 E 00
Germany	Nurnburg		49 N 28	11 E 07	-1	CET	-2	Last Sun March to Last Sat Sept.	15 E 00
Germany	Stuttgart		48 N 48	9 E 15	-1	CET	-2	Last Sun March to Last Sat Sept.	15 E 00
Germany	Wuppertal		51 N 16	7 E 14	-1	CET	-2	Last Sun March to Last Sat Sept.	15 E 00
Ghana	Accra		5 N 33	0 W 15	0	GMT		No	0 W 00
Ghana	Kumasi		6 N 41	1 W 35	0	GMT		No	0 W 00
Ghana	Tamale		9 N 25	0 W 05	0	GMT		No	0 W 00
Greece	Athens		37 N 59	24 E 43	-2	EET	-3	Last Sun March to Last Sat Sept.	30 E 00
Greece	Lárisa		39 N 38	22 E 25	-2	EET	-3	Last Sun March to Last Sat Sept.	30 E 00
Greece	Pátraí		38 N 15	4 E 48	-2	EET	-3	Last Sun March to Last Sat Sept.	30 E 00
Greenland	Godthaab		64 N 11	51 W 43	4+			No	60 W 00
Grenada	St. George's		12 N 03	61 W 45	4+			No	60 W 00

Country	City	State or Provence	LAT.	LONG.	Time Adjust to GMT	Abv Time	D.S. Time	1991 Daylight Savings Observed	S.T. Meridian
Guadeloupe	Basse-Terre		16 N 00	61 W 44	4+			No	60 W 00
Guam	Guam		14 N 00	143 E 20	-10			No	150 E 00
Guatemala	Guatemala		14 N 38	90 W 31	6+			No	90 W 00
Guinea, Republic of	Conakry		9 N 30	13 W 43	0	GMT		No	0 W 00
Guinea-Bissau	Bissau		11 N 51	15 W 35	0	CET		No	0 W 00
Guyana	Georgetown		6 N 48	58 W 18	3+			No	45 W 00
Haiti	Port-au-Prince		18 N 33	72 W 20	5+			1st Sun April to Last Sat Oct.	75 W 00
Honduras	Tegucigalpa		14 N 06	87 W 13	6+			No	90 W 00
Hong Kong	Hong Kong		22 N 17	114 E 09	-8	CCT		No	120 E 00
Hong Kong	Kowloon		22 N 18	114 E 10	-8	CCT		No	120 E 00
Hungary	Budapest		47 N 30	19 E 05	-1	CET	-2	Last Sun March to Last Sat Sept.	15 E 00
Iceland	Reykjavik		64 N 09	21 W 57	0	CET		No	0 W 00
India	Ahmadabad		23 N 03	72 E 41	-5.5			No	82 E 30
India	Bangalore		13 N 03	77 E 39	-5.5			No	82 E 30
India	Bombay		18 N 58	72 E 50	-5.5			No	82 E 30
India	Calcutta		22 N 32	88 E 22	-5.5			No	82 E 30
India	Delhi		28 N 54	77 E 13	-5.5			No	82 E 30
India	Hyderabad		17 N 29	78 E 28	-5.5			No	82 E 30
India	Kanpur		26 N 30	80 E 10	-5.5			No	82 E 30
India	Lucknow		26 N 54	80 E 58	-5.5			No	82 E 30
India	Madras		13 N 08	80 E 15	-5.5			No	82 E 30
India	Nagpur		21 N 12	79 E 09	-5.5			No	82 E 30
India	New Delhi		28 N 38	77 E 13	-5.5			No	82 E 30
India	Pune		18 N 38	73 E 53	-5.5			No	82 E 30
Indonesia	Bali	Bali	8 S 00	115 E 22	-7			No	105 E 00
Indonesia	Bandung	Java	7 S 00	107 E 22	-7			No	105 E 00
Indonesia	Jakarta	Java	6 S 10	106 E 48	-7			No	105 E 00
Indonesia	Semarang	Java	7 S 03	110 E 27	-7			No	105 E 00
Indonesia	Surabaya	Java	7 S 23	112 E 45	-7			No	105 E 00
Indonesia	Medan	Sumatra	3 N 35	98 E 35	-7			No	105 E 00
Iran	Mashed Soleyman		31 N 45	49 E 17	-3.5			No	52 E 30
Iran	Tabriz		38 N 00	46 E 13	-3.5			No	52 E 30
Iran	Tehran		35 N 40	51 E 26	-3.5			No	52 E 30
Iraq	Baghdad		33 N 20	44 E 24	-3	BT	-4	1st April to 30 Sept	45 E 00
Ireland	Dublin		53 N 20	6 W 15	0	GMT	-1	1st Sun April to Last Sat Oct.	0 W 00
Ireland, North	Belfast		54 N 36	5 W 55	0	GMT	-1	1st Sun April to Last Sat Oct.	0 W 00
Isle of Man	Douglas	England	54 N 10	4 W 40	0	GMT	-1	1st Sun April to Last Sat Oct.	0 W 00
Israel	Jerusalem		31 N 46	35 E 10	-2	EET	-3	Est May - Sept	30 E 00
Israel	Tel Aviv		32 N 04	34 E 46	-2	EET	-3	Est May - Sept	30 E 00
Italy	Florence		43 N 47	11 E 15	-1	CET	-2	Last Sun March to Last Sat Sept.	15 E 00
Italy	Genoa		44 N 23	9 E 52	-1	CET	-2	Last Sun March to Last Sat Sept.	15 E 00
Italy	Milan		38 N 13	15 E 17	-1	CET	-2	Last Sun March to Last Sat Sept.	15 E 00
Italy	Naples		40 N 37	14 E 12	-1	CET	-2	Last Sun March to Last Sat Sept.	15 E 00
Italy	Palermo		38 N 08	13 E 24	-1	CET	-2	Last Sun March to Last Sat Sept.	15 E 00
Italy	Rome		41 N 54	12 E 30	-1	CET	-2	Last Sun March to Last Sat Sept.	15 E 00
Italy	Turin		45 N 05	7 E 44	-1	CET	-2	Last Sun March to Last Sat Sept.	15 E 00
Italy	Venice		45 N 25	12 E 18	-1	CET	-2	Last Sun March to Last Sat Sept.	15 E 00
Ivory Coast	Abidjan		5 N 19	4 W 01	0	GMT		No	0 W 00
Ivory Coast	Yamoussoukro		6 N 49	5 W 17	0	GMT		No	0 W 00
Jamaica	Kingston		18 N 00	76 W 48	5+			No	75 W 00
Japan	Sapporo		43 N 03	141 E 19	-9			No	135 E 00
Japan	Tokyo		35 N 40	139 E 46	-9			No	135 E 00
Japan	Fukuoka		33 N 35	130 E 23	-9			No	135 E 00
Japan	Hiroshima		34 N 22	132 E 25	-9			No	135 E 00
Japan	Kitakyushu		33 N 53	130 E 50	-9			No	135 E 00
Japan	Kobe		34 N 30	135 E 10	-9			No	135 E 00
Japan	Kyoto		35 N 00	135 E 46	-9			No	135 E 00
Japan	Nagoya		35 N 09	136 E 53	-9			No	135 E 00
Japan	Osaka		34 N 40	135 E 30	-9			No	135 E 00

Daylight Savings Times Deemed Reliable But Not Guaranteed

Country	City	State or Provence	LAT.	LONG.	Time Adjust to GMT	Abv Time	D.S. Time	1991 Daylight Savings Observed	S.T. Meridian
Japan	Yokohama		35 N 37	139 E 40	-9			No	135 E 00
Jordan	Amman		32 N 57	35 E 56	-2	EET	-3	1st Sun April to Last Sat Oct.	30 E 00
Jordan	Irbid		32 N 33	35 E 51	-2	EET	-3	1st Sun April to Last Sat Oct.	30 E 00
Jordan	Zarqa		32 N 13	35 E 43	-2	EET	-3	1st Sun April to Last Sat Oct.	30 E 00
Kampuchea	Phnum Pénh		11 N 39	104 E 53	-7			No	105 E 00
Kenya	Mombasa		4 N 03	39 E 40	-3			No	45 E 00
Kenya	Nairobi		1 S 17	36 E 48	-3			No	45 E 00
Korea, North	P'younyang		39 N 00	126 E 45	-9			No	135 E 00
Korea, South	Pusan		35 N 08	129 E 05	-9			No	135 E 00
Korea, South	Seoul		37 N 33	126 E 58	-9			No	135 E 00
Korea, South	Taegu		35 N 49	128 E 41	-9			No	135 E 00
Kuwait	Kuwait		29N 23	47 E 59	-3			No	45 E 00
Laos	Vientiane		17 N 58	102 E 37	-7			No	105 E 00
Lebanon	Beirut		35 N 54	35 E 28	-3		-4	Mid May - Mid Oct	45 E 00
Lesotho	Maseru		29 S 18	27 E 30	-2	EET		No	30 E 00
Liberia	Monrovia		6 N 20	10 W 48	0	GMT		No	0 W 00
Libya	Tripoli		32 N 54	13 E 10	-2	EET		No	30 E 00
Liechtenstein	Vaduz		47 N 08	09 E 31	-1	CET	-2	Last Sun March to Last Sat Sept.	15 E 00
Luxembourg	Luxembourg		49 W 38	6 E 10	-1	CET	-2	Last Sun March to Last Sat Sept.	15 E 00
Madagascar	Antananarivo		185 S 51	47 E 40	-3			No	45 E 00
Malawi	Blantyre		15 S 47	35 E 00	-2	EET		No	30 E 00
Malawi	Lilongwe		13 S 58	33 E 45	-2	EET		No	30 E 00
Malaysia	George Town (pinang)		5 N 21	100 E 09	-8			No	120 E 00
Malaysia	Ipoh		4 N 45	101 E 05	-8			No	120 E 00
Malaysia	Kuala Lumpur		3 N 10	101 E 42	-8			No	120 E 00
Maldive Islands	Malé		4 N 10	73 E 30	-5			No	75 E 00
Mali	Bamako		12 N 39	7 W 59	0	GMT		No	0 W 00
Malta	Valetta		35 N 54	14 E 31	-1	CET	-2	Last Sun March to Last Sat Sept.	15 E 00
Martinique	Fort-de-France		14 N 36	61 W 05	4+			No	60 W 00
Mauritania	Nouakchott		18 N 06	15 W 57	0	GMT		No	0 W 00
Mauritius	Port Louis		20 S 09	57 E 30	-4			No	60 E 00
Mexico	Ciudad Juarez	Chihuahua	31 N 44	106 W 28	8+		7+	1st Sun April to Last Sat Oct.	120 W 00
Mexico	Guadalajara	Jalisco	20 N 41	103 W 21	8+		7+	1st Sun April to Last Sat Oct.	120 W 00
Mexico	León	Jalisco	21 N 08	101 W 41	8+		7+	1st Sun April to Last Sat Oct.	120 W 00
Mexico	Mexico City		19 N 24	99 W 09	6+			No	90 W 00
Mexico	Monterrey		25 N 43	100 W 19	6+			No	90 W 00
Monaco	Monaco-Ville		43 N 44	7 E 26	-1	CET	-2	Last Sun March to Last Sat Sept.	15 E 00
Mongolia	Ulan Bator		47 N 55	106 E 45	-8		-9	1st Sun April to Last Sat Oct.	120 E 00
Montserrat	Plymouth		16 N 42	62 W 13	4+			No	60 W 00
Morocco	Cassablanca		33 N 32	7 W 41	-1	CET	-2	Mid June to Mid Sept	15 E 00
Morocco	Fès		34 N 08	5 W 00	-1	CET	-2	Mid June - Mid Sept	15 E 00
Morocco	Marrakech		31 N 38	8 W 00	-1	CET	-2	Mid June - Mid Sept	15 E 00
Morocco	Rabat		34 N 01	6 W 51	-1	CET	-2	Mid June - Mid Sept	15 E 00
Mozambique	Maputo		25 S 58	32 E 35	-2	EET		No	30 E 00
Namibia	Windhoek		22 S 30	17 E 00	-2	EET		No	30 E 00
Nauru	Yaren		0 S 32	166 E 55	-12			No	180 E 00
Nepal	Kathmandu		27 N 43	85 E 19	5 2/3-			No	82 E 30
Netherlands	Amsterdam		52 N 22	4 E 54	-1	CET	-2	Last Sun March to Last Sat Sept.	15 E 00
Netherlands	Rotterdam		51 N 55	4 E 27	-1	CET	-2	Last Sun March to Last Sat Sept.	15 E 00
Netherlands	The Hague		52 N 05	4 E 16	-1	CET	-2	Last Sun March to Last Sat Sept.	15 E 00
Netherlands Antilles	Willemstad		12 N 12	68 W 58	4+			No	60 W 00
New Caledonia	Nouméa		22 S 18	166 E 48	-11			No	175 E 00
New Zealand	Auckland		36 S 53	174 E 45	-12		1+	Estimate Oct - Mid March	180 E 00
New Zealand	Wellington		41 S 18	174 E 47	-12		1+	Last Sun March to Last Sat Oct.	180 E 00
Nicaragua	Managua		12 N 08	86 W 18	6+			No	90 W 00
Niger	Niamey		13 N 31	2 E 07	-1	CET		No	15 E 00
Nigeria	Ibadan		7 N 17	3 E 30	-1	CET		No	15 E 00
Nigeria	Kano		12 N 00	8 E 30	-1	CET		No	15 E 00
Nigeria	Lagos		6 N 27	3 E 23	-1	CET		No	15 E 00

Country	City	State or Provence	LAT.	LONG.	Time Adjust to GMT	Abv Time	D.S. Time	1991 Daylight Savings Observed	S.T. Meridian
Nigeria	Ogbomosho		8 N 08	4 E 15	-1	CET		No	15 E 00
Norway	Oslo		59 N 56	10 E 45	-1	CET	-2	Last Sun March to Last Sat Sept.	15 E 00
Oman	Muscat		23 N 37	58 E 37	-4			No	60 E 00
Pakistan	Peshawar	NWFP	34 N 01	71 E 40	-5			No	75 E 00
Pakistan	Faisalabad		31 N 29	73 E 06	-5			No	75 E 00
Pakistan	Hyderabad		25 N 29	68 E 28	-5			No	75 E 00
Pakistan	Islamabad		33 N 43	75 E 17	-5			No	75 E 00
Pakistan	Karachi		24 N 52	67 E 02	-5			No	75 E 00
Pakistan	Lahore		32 N 00	74 E 18	-5			No	75 E 00
Pakistan	Rawalpindi		33 N 40	73 E 10	-5			No	75 E 00
Panama	Panama City		8 N 57	79 W 32	5+			No	75 W 00
Papua New Guinea	Port Moresby		9 S 27	147 E 08	-10			No	150 E 00
Paraguay	Asunción		25 S 15	57 W 40	4+		3+	End Sept to End March	60 W 00
Peru	Arequipa		16 S 27	71 W 30	5+		4+	1 Jan to 31 March	75 W 00
Peru	Callao		12 S 02	77 W 07	5+		4+	1 Jan to 31 March	75 W 00
Peru	Chiclayo		6 S 46	79 W 50	5+		4+	1 Jan to 31 March	75 W 00
Peru	Lima		12 S 03	77 W 03	5+		4+	1 Jan to 31 March	75 W 00
Peru	Trujillo		8 S 08	79 W 00	5+		4+	1 Jan to 31 March	75 W 00
Philippines	Manila		14 N 35	120 E 59	-8			No	120 E 00
Philippines	Quezon City		14 N 00	122 E 11	-8			No	120 E 00
Phillipines	Cebu		10 N 22	123 E 49	-8			No	120 E 00
Poland	Gdan´sk		54 N 20	18 E 40	-1	CET	-2	Last Sun March to Last Sat Sept.	15 E 00
Poland	Katowice		50 N 15	19 E 00	-1	CET	-2	Last Sun March to Last Sat Sept.	15 E 00
Poland	Krakow		50 N 05	20 E 00	-1	CET	-2	Last Sun March to Last Sat Sept.	15 E 00
Poland	Lodz		51 N 46	19 E 30	-1	CET	-2	Last Sun March to Last Sat Sept.	15 E 00
Poland	Poznan´		52 N 25	16 E 55	-1	CET	-2	Last Sun March to Last Sat Sept.	15 E 00
Poland	Szczecin		53 N 25	14 E 35	-1	CET	-2	Last Sun March to Last Sat Sept.	15 E 00
Poland	Warsaw		52 N 15	21 E 00	-1	CET	-2	Last Sun March to Last Sat Sept.	15 E 00
Poland	Wroclaw		51 N 07	17 E 10	-1	CET	-2	Last Sun March to Last Sat Sept.	15 E 00
Portugal	Lisbon		38 N 43	9 W 10	0	GMT	-1	Last Sun March to Last Sat Sept.	0 W 00
Portugal	Porto		41 N 10	8 W 38	0	GMT	-1	Last Sun March to Last Sat Sept.	0 W 00
Puerto Rico	San Juan		18 N 30	66 W 10	4+			No	60 W 00
Qutar	Doha		25 N 17	51 E 32	-3			No	45 E 00
Réunion	Saint-Denis		20 S 52	55 E 27	-4			No	60 E 00
Romania	Brasov		45 N 39	25 E 35	-2	EET	-3	Last Sun March to Last Sat Sept.	30 E 00
Romania	Bucharest		44 N 26	26 E 06	-2	EET	-3	Last Sun March to Last Sat Sept.	30 E 00
Romania	Cluj-Napoca		46 N 46	23 E 34	-2	EET	-3	Last Sun March to Last Sat Sept.	30 E 00
Romania	Constanta		44 N 12	28 E 36	-2	EET	-3	Last Sun March to Last Sat Sept.	30 E 00
Romania	Galati		45 N 25	28 E 05	-2	EET	-3	Last Sun March to Last Sat Sept.	30 E 00
Romania	Timisoara		45 N 44	21 E 21	-2	EET	-3	Last Sun March to Last Sat Sept.	30 E 00
Rwanda	Kigali		1 S 59	30 E 05	-2	EET		No	30 E 00
San Marino	San Marino		43 N 56	12 E 27	-1	CET	-2	Last Sun March to Last Sat Sept.	15 E 00
Sao Tome	Sao Tome		0 N 20	6 E 43	0	GMT		No	0 E 00
Saudi Arabia	Jeddah		21 N 29	39 E 11	-3			No	45 E 00
Saudi Arabia	Mecca		21 N 27	39 E 50	-3			No	45 E 00
Saudi Arabia	Riyadh		24 N 39	46 E 42	-3			No	45 E 00
Scotland	Edinburgh		55 N 57	3 W 11	0	GMT	-1	Last Sun March to Last Sat Oct.	0 W 00
Scotland	Glasgow		55 N 54	4 W 25	0	GMT	-1	Last Sun March to Last Sat Oct.	0 W 00
Senegal	Dakar		14 N 40	17 W 26	0	GMT		No	0 W 00
Seychelles	Victoria		4 S 36	55 E 28	-4			No	60 E 00
Sierra Leone	Freetown		8 N 29	13 W 12	0	GMT		No	0 W 00
Singapore	Singapore		1 N 16	103 E 51	-8			No	120 E 00
Solomon Islands	Honiara (on Guadalcanal)		9 S 15	59 E 45	-11			No	175 E 00
Somalia	Mogadishu		2 N 02	45 E 21	-3			No	45 E 00
South Africa	Cape Town		33 S 55	18 E 22	-2	EET		No	30 E 00
South Africa	Durban		29 S 48	31 E 00	-2	EET		No	30 E 00
South Africa	Johannesberg		26 S 15	28 E 00	-2	EET		No	30 E 00
South Africa	Pretoria		25 S 45	28 E 11	-2	EET		No	30 E 00
Spain	Barcelona		41 N 25	2 E 08	-1	CET	-2	Last Sun March to Last Sat Sept.	15 E 00

Country	City	State or Provence	LAT.	LONG.	Time Adjust to GMT	Abv Time	D.S. Time	1991 Daylight Savings Observed	S.T. Meridian
Spain	Bilbao		43 N 12	2 W 48	-1	CET	-2	Last Sun March to Last Sat Sept.	15 E 00
Spain	Madrid		40 N 24	3 W 41	-1	CET	-2	Last Sun March to Last Sat Sept.	15 E 00
Spain	Seville		37 N 29	5 W 58	-1	CET	-2	Last Sun March to Last Sat Sept.	15 E 00
Spain	Valencia		39 N 26	0 W 23	-1	CET	-2	Last Sun March to Last Sat Sept.	15 E 00
Sri Lanka	Colombo		6 N 57	79 E 53	-5.5			No	82 E 30
St. Kitts/Nevis	Basseterre (on St. Kitts)		17 N 18	62 W 43	4+			No	60 W 00
St. Lucia	Castries		14 N 01	61 W 00	4+			No	60 W 00
St. Pierre/Miquelon	Saint Pierre		46 N 46	56 W 10	3+		2+	22 April to 20 Oct	45 W 00
St. Vincent	Kingstown		13 N 09	60 W 00	4+			No	60 W 00
Sudan	Al Khartum (Khartoum)		15 N 38	32 E 33	-2	EET		No	30 E 00
Sudan	Khartoum		15 N 36	32 E 32	-2	EET		No	30 E 00
Sudan	Omdurman		15 N 45	32 E 30	-2	EET		No	30 E 00
Suriname	Paramaribo		5 N 50	55 W 13	4.5+			No	67 W 30
Swaziland	Mbabane		26 S 19	31 E 08	-2	EET		No	30 E 00
Sweden	Stockholm		59 N 20	18 E 00 CK	-1	CET	-2	Last Sun March to Last Sat Sept.	15 E 00
Switzerland	Bern		46 N 57	7 E 28	-1	CET	-2	Last Sun March to Last Sat Sept.	15 E 00
Switzerland	Geneva		46 N 14	6 E 04	-1	CET	-2	Last Sun March to Last Sat Sept.	15 E 00
Switzerland	Zurich		47 N 23	8 E 32	-1	CET	-2	Last Sun March to Last Sat Sept.	15 E 00
Syria	Aleppo		36 N 14	37 E 11	-2	EET		No	30 E 00
Syria	Damascus		33 N 30	36 E 18	-2	EET		No	30 E 00
Syria	Latakia		35 N 32	35 E 51	-2	EET		No	30 E 00
Taiwan	Kaohsiung		22 N 38	120 E 17	-8			No	120 E 00
Taiwan	T'aipei		25 N 03	121 E 30	-8			No	120 E 00
Tanzania	Dar es Salaam		6 S 50	39 E 17	-3			No	45 E 00
Thailand	Bangkok		13 N 45	100 E 31	-7			No	105 E 00
Togo	Lomé		6 N 08	1 E 14	0	GMT		No	0 E 00
Tonga	Nukúalofa		21 S 08	175 W 12	11+			No	175 W 00
Transkei	Umtala		28 N 47	31 E 35	-2	EET		No	30 E 00
Trinidad/Tobago	Port-of-Spain		10 N 39	61 W 31	4+			No	60 W 00
Tunisia	Tunis		36 N 48	10 E 10	-1	CET		No	15 E 00
Turkey	Adana		37 N 05	35 E 20	-3		-4	Last Sun March to Last Sat Sept.	45 E 00
Turkey	Ankara		39 N 57	32 E 50	-3		-4	Last Sun March to Last Sat Sept.	45 E 00
Turkey	Bursa		40 N 10	28 E 10	-3		-4	Last Sun March to Last Sat Sept.	45 E 00
Turkey	Gaziantep		37 N 10	37 E 30	-3		-4	Last Sun March to Last Sat Sept.	45 E 00
Turkey	Istambul		41 N 01	28 E 58	-3		-4	Last Sun March to Last Sat Sept.	45 E 00
Turkey	Izmir		38 N 25	27 E05	-3		-4	Last Sun March to Last Sat Sept.	45 E 00
Tuvalu	Funafuti		8 S 31	179 E 13	-12			No	180 E 00
Uganda	Kampala		0 N 19	1 W 31	-3			No	45 E 00
Union of Mayanmar	Bassein	Former Burma	16 N 46	94 E 47	-6.5			No	97 E 30
Union of Mayanmar	Mandalay	Former Burma	22 N 00	96 E 08	-6.5			No	97 E 30
Union of Mayanmar	Moulmein	Former Burma	16 N 30	97 E 39	-6.5			No	97 E 30
Union of Mayanmar	Rangoon	Former Burma	16 N 48	96 E 09	-6.5			No	97 E 30
United Arab Emirates	Abu Dhabi		24 N 30	54 E 28	-4			No	60 E 00
United States	Birmingham	Alabama	33 N 31	86 W 48	5+	EST	4+	1st Sun April to Last Sat Oct.	75 W 00
United States	Gadsden	Alabama	34 N 01	86 W 01	5+	EST	4+	1st Sun April to Last Sat Oct.	75 W 00
United States	Huntsville	Alabama	34 N 44	86 W 35	5+	EST	4+	1st Sun April to Last Sat Oct.	75 W 00
United States	Mobile	Alabama	30 N 41	88 W 03	5+	EST	4+	1st Sun April to Last Sat Oct.	75 W 00
United States	Tuscaloosa	Alabama	33 N 12	87 W 34	5+	EST	4+	1st Sun April to Last Sat Oct.	75 W 00
United States	Anchorage	Alaska	61 N 13	149 W 34	10+	AHST	9+	1st Sun April to Last Sat Oct.	135 W 00
United States	Fairbanks	Alaska	64 N 51	147 W 54	9+	YST	8	1st Sun April to Last Sat Oct.	135 W 00
United States	Juneau	Alaska	58 N 18	134 W 25	9+	YST	8	1st Sun April to Last Sat Oct.	135 W 00
United States	Nome	Alaska	64 N 30	165 W 20	9+	YST	8	1st Sun April to Last Sat Oct.	135 W 00
United States	Seward	Alaska	60 N 07	149 W 25	9+	YST	8	1st Sun April to Last Sat Oct.	135 W 00
United States	Flagstaff	Arizona	35 N 12	111 W 39	7+	MST		No	105 W 00
United States	Phoenix	Arizona	60 N 07	149 W 27	7+	MST		No	105 W 00
United States	Temple	Arizona	33 N 25	111 W 56	7+	MST		No	105 W 00
United States	Tucson	Arizona	32 N 13	110 W 58	7+	MST		No	105 W 00
United States	Forth Smith	Arkansas	35 N 23	94 W 25	6+	CST	5+	1st Sun April to Last Sat Oct.	90 W 00
United States	Little Rock	Arkansas	34 N 45	92 W 17	6+	CST	5+	1st Sun April to Last Sat Oct.	90 W 00

Country	City	State or Provence	LAT.	LONG.	Time Adjust to GMT	Abv Time	D.S. Time	1991 Daylight Savings Observed	S.T. Meridian
United States	Texarkana	Arkansas	33 N 26	94 W 03	6+	CST	5+	1st Sun April to Last Sat Oct.	90 W 00
United States	Bakersfield	California	35 N 23	119 W 01	8+	PST	7	1st Sun April to Last Sat Oct.	120 W 00
United States	Cupertino	California	37 N 19	122 W 02	8+	PST	7	1st Sun April to Last Sat Oct.	120 W 00
United States	Eureka	California	40 N 47	124 W 09	8+	PST	7	1st Sun April to Last Sat Oct.	120 W 00
United States	Fresno	California	36 N 44	119 W 47	8+	PST	7	1st Sun April to Last Sat Oct.	120 W 00
United States	Los Angeles	California	34 N 04	118 W 15	8+	PST	7	1st Sun April to Last Sat Oct.	120 W 00
United States	Oakland	California	37 N 47	124 W 09	8+	PST	7	1st Sun April to Last Sat Oct.	120 W 00
United States	Oakland	California	37 N 49	122 W 16	8+	PST	7	1st Sun April to Last Sat Oct.	120 W 00
United States	Pasadena	California	34 N 09	118 W 09	8+	PST	7	1st Sun April to Last Sat Oct.	120 W 00
United States	Sacramento	California	38 N 35	121 W 29	8+	PST	7	1st Sun April to Last Sat Oct.	120 W 00
United States	San Diego	California	32 N 43	117 W 09	8+	PST	7	1st Sun April to Last Sat Oct.	120 W 00
United States	San Francisco	California	37 N 47	112 W 25	8+	PST	7	1st Sun April to Last Sat Oct.	120 W 00
United States	San Jose	California	37 N 20	121 W 53	8+	PST	7	1st Sun April to Last Sat Oct.	120 W 00
United States	Santa Barbara	California	34 N 25	119 W 42	8+	PST	7	1st Sun April to Last Sat Oct.	120 W 00
United States	Ventura	California	34 N 17	119 W 18	8+	PST	7	1st Sun April to Last Sat Oct.	120 W 00
United States	Boulder	Colorado	40 N 01	105 W 17	7+	MST	6+	1st Sun April to Last Sat Oct.	105 W 00
United States	Colorado Springs	Colorado	38 N 50	104 W 49	7+	MST	6+	1st Sun April to Last Sat Oct.	105 W 00
United States	Denver	Colorado	39 N 44	104 W 59	7+	MST	6+	1st Sun April to Last Sat Oct.	105 W 00
United States	Fort Collins	Colorado	40 N 35	105 W 05	7+	MST	6+	1st Sun April to Last Sat Oct.	105 W 00
United States	Grand Junction	Colorado	39 N 04	108 W 33	7+	MST	6+	1st Sun April to Last Sat Oct.	105 W 00
United States	Greeley	Colorado	40 N 25	104 W 42	7+	MST	6+	1st Sun April to Last Sat Oct.	105 W 00
United States	Pueblo	Colorado	38 N 14	104 W 36	7+	MST	6+	1st Sun April to Last Sat Oct.	105 W 00
United States	Bridgeport	Connecticut	41 N 11	73 W 12	5+	EST	4+	1st Sun April to Last Sat Oct.	75 W 00
United States	Hartford	Connecticut	41 N 46	72 W 41	5+	EST	4+	1st Sun April to Last Sat Oct.	75 W 00
United States	New Haven	Connecticut	41 N 18	72 W 55	5+	EST	4+	1st Sun April to Last Sat Oct.	75 W 00
United States	New London	Connecticut	41 N 21	72 W 06	5+	EST	4+	1st Sun April to Last Sat Oct.	75 W 00
United States	Norwich	Connecticut	41 N 31	72 W 05	5+	EST	4+	1st Sun April to Last Sat Oct.	75 W 00
United States	Stamford	Connecticut	41 N 03	73 W 32	5+	EST	4+	1st Sun April to Last Sat Oct.	75 W 00
United States	Waterbury	Connecticut	41 N 33	73 W 03	5+	EST	4+	1st Sun April to Last Sat Oct.	75 W 00
United States	Dover	Delaware	39 N 10	75 W 32	5+	EST	4+	1st Sun April to Last Sat Oct.	75 W 00
United States	Wilmington	Delaware	39 N 45	75 W 33	5+	EST	4+	1st Sun April to Last Sat Oct.	75 W 00
United States	Washington	Dist. of Columbia	38 N 53	77 W 00	5+	EST	4+	1st Sun April to Last Sat Oct.	75 W 00
United States	Cape Canaveral	Florida	28 N 24	80 W 36	5+	EST	4+	1st Sun April to Last Sat Oct.	75 W 00
United States	Daytona Beach	Florida	29 N 13	81 W 01	5+	EST	4+	1st Sun April to Last Sat Oct.	75 W 00
United States	Form Myers	Florida	26 N 39	81 W 52	5+	EST	4+	1st Sun April to Last Sat Oct.	75 W 00
United States	Fort Lauderdale	Florida	26 N 07	80 W 08	5+	EST	4+	1st Sun April to Last Sat Oct.	75 W 00
United States	Gainsville	Florida	29 N 40	82 W 20	5+	EST	4+	1st Sun April to Last Sat Oct.	75 W 00
United States	Jacksonville	Florida	30 N 20	81 W 39	5+	EST	4+	1st Sun April to Last Sat Oct.	75 W 00
United States	Key West	Florida	24 N 33	81 W 47	5+	EST	4+	1st Sun April to Last Sat Oct.	75 W 00
United States	Miami	Florida	25 N 47	80 W 11	5+	EST	4+	1st Sun April to Last Sat Oct.	75 W 00
United States	Naples	Florida	26 N 08	81 W 48	5+	EST	4+	1st Sun April to Last Sat Oct.	75 W 00
United States	Orlando	Florida	28 N 33	81 W 23	5+	EST	4+	1st Sun April to Last Sat Oct.	75 W 00
United States	Pensacola	Florida	30 N 25	87 W 13	6+	CST	5+	1st Sun April to Last Sat Oct.	90 W 00
United States	St. Petersburg	Florida	27 N 46	82 W 39	5+	EST	4+	1st Sun April to Last Sat Oct.	75 W 00
United States	Tallahassee	Florida	30 N 27	81 W 39	5+	EST	4+	1st Sun April to Last Sat Oct.	75 W 00
United States	Atlanta	Georgia	33 N 45	84 W 23	5+	EST	4+	1st Sun April to Last Sat Oct.	75 W 00
United States	Augusta	Georgia	33 N 28	81 W 58	5+	EST	4+	1st Sun April to Last Sat Oct.	75 W 00
United States	Columbus	Georgia	32 N 28	84 W 59	5+	EST	4+	1st Sun April to Last Sat Oct.	75 W 00
United States	Macon	Georgia	32 N 51	83 W 38	5+	EST	4+	1st Sun April to Last Sat Oct.	75 W 00
United States	Savannah	Georgia	32 N 05	81 W 06	5+	EST	4+	1st Sun April to Last Sat Oct.	75 W 00
United States	Hilo	Hawaii	19 N 44	155 W 05	10+	AHST	No	No	150 W 00
United States	Honolulu	Hawaii	21 N 19	157 W 52	10+	AHST	No	No	150 W 00
United States	Kaneohoe	Hawaii	21 N 25	157 W 48	10+	AHST	No	No	150 W 00
United States	Lahaina	Hawaii	20 N 53	156 W 41	10+	AHST	No	No	150 W 00
United States	Lihue	Hawaii	21 N 59	159 W 23	10+	AHST	No	No	150 W 00
United States	Boise	Idaho	43 N 38	116 W 12	5+	MST	6+	1st Sun April to Last Sat Oct.	105 W 00
United States	Pocatello	Idaho	42 N 52	112 W 27	7+	MST	6+	1st Sun April to Last Sat Oct.	105 W 00
United States	Bloomington	Illinois	40 N 29	89 W 00	6+	CST	5+	1st Sun April to Last Sat Oct.	90 W 00
United States	Chicago	Illinois	41 N 52	87 W 39	6+	CST	5+	1st Sun April to Last Sat Oct.	90 W 00

Country	City	State or Provence	LAT.	LONG.	Time Adjust to GMT	Abv Time	D.S. Time	1991 Daylight Savings Observed	S.T. Meridian
United States	Decatur	Illinois	39 N 51	88 W 57	6+	CST	5+	1st Sun April to Last Sat Oct.	90 W 00
United States	Peoria	Illinois	40 N 42	89 W 36	6+	CST	5+	1st Sun April to Last Sat Oct.	90 W 00
United States	Rockford	Illinois	42 N 16	89 W 06	6+	CST	5+	1st Sun April to Last Sat Oct.	90 W 00
United States	Springfield	Illinois	39 N 48	89 W 39	6+	CST	5+	1st Sun April to Last Sat Oct.	90 W 00
United States	Bloomington	Indiana	39 N 10	86 W 31	5+	EST	4+	1st Sun April to Last Sat Oct.	75 W 00
United States	Fort Wayne	Indiana	41 N 04	85 W 09	5+	EST	4+	1st Sun April to Last Sat Oct.	75 W 00
United States	Gary	Indiana	41 N 36	87 W 20	6+	CST	5+	1st Sun April to Last Sat Oct.	90 W 00
United States	Indianapolis	Indiana	39 N 46	86 W 09	5+	EST	4+	1st Sun April to Last Sat Oct.	75 W 00
United States	Lafayette	Indiana	40 N 25	86 W 54	5+	EST	4+	1st Sun April to Last Sat Oct.	75 W 00
United States	Muncie	Indiana	41 N 34	87 W 31	5+	EST	No	No	75 W 00
United States	Richmond	Indiana	39 N 50	84 W 54	5+	EST	No	No	75 W 00
United States	South Bend	Indiana	41 N 41	86 W 15	5+	EST	No	No	75 W 00
United States	Terre Haute	Indiana	39 N 28	87 W 25	5+	EST	4+	1st Sun April to Last Sat Oct.	75 W 00
United States	Ames	Iowa	42 N 02	93 W 37	6+	CST	5+	1st Sun April to Last Sat Oct.	90 W 00
United States	Cedar Rapids	Iowa	41 N 59	91 W 40	6+	CST	5+	1st Sun April to Last Sat Oct.	90 W 00
United States	Davenport	Iowa	41 N 32	90 W 35	6+	CST	5+	1st Sun April to Last Sat Oct.	90 W 00
United States	Des Moines	Iowa	41 N 35	93 W 37	6+	CST	5+	1st Sun April to Last Sat Oct.	90 W 00
United States	Ford Dodge	Iowa	42 N 30	94 W 11	6+	CST	5+	1st Sun April to Last Sat Oct.	90 W 00
United States	Waterloo	Iowa	42 N 30	92 W 21	6+	CST	5+	1st Sun April to Last Sat Oct.	90 W 00
United States	Dodge City	Kansas	37 N 45	100 W 01	6+	CST	5+	1st Sun April to Last Sat Oct.	90 W 00
United States	Kansas City	Kansas	39 N 07	94 W 38	6+	CST	5+	1st Sun April to Last Sat Oct.	90 W 00
United States	Salina	Kansas	38 N 50	97 W 37	6+	CST	5+	1st Sun April to Last Sat Oct.	90 W 00
United States	Topeka	Kansas	39 N 03	95 W 40	6+	CST	5+	1st Sun April to Last Sat Oct.	90 W 00
United States	Wichita	Kansas	37 N 42	97 W 20	6+	CST	5+	1st Sun April to Last Sat Oct.	90 W 00
United States	Bowling Green	Kentucky	36 N 59	86 W 27	6+	CST	5+	1st Sun April to Last Sat Oct.	90 W 00
United States	Lexington	Kentucky	38 N 03	84 W 30	5+	EST	4+	1st Sun April to Last Sat Oct.	75 W 00
United States	Louisville	Kentucky	38 N 15	85 W 46	5+	EST	4+	1st Sun April to Last Sat Oct.	75 W 00
United States	Owensboro	Kentucky	37 N 46	87 W 07	6+	CST	5+	1st Sun April to Last Sat Oct.	90 W 00
United States	Paducah	Kentucky	37 N 05	88 W 37	6+	CST	5+	1st Sun April to Last Sat Oct.	90 W 00
United States	Baton Rouge	Louisiana	30 N 27	91 W 11	6+	CST	5+	1st Sun April to Last Sat Oct.	90 W 00
United States	Lake Charles	Louisiana	30 N 14	93 W 13	6+	CST	5+	1st Sun April to Last Sat Oct.	90 W 00
United States	Monroe	Louisiana	32 N 30	92 W 07	6+	CST	5+	1st Sun April to Last Sat Oct.	90 W 00
United States	New Orleans	Louisiana	29 N 58	90 W 04	6+	CST	5+	1st Sun April to Last Sat Oct.	90 W 00
United States	Shreveport	Louisiana	32 N 31	93 W 45	6+	CST	5+	1st Sun April to Last Sat Oct.	90 W 00
United States	Augusta	Maine	44 N 19	69 W 47	5+	EST	4+	1st Sun April to Last Sat Oct.	75 W 00
United States	Bangor	Maine	44 N 48	68 W 01	5+	EST	4+	1st Sun April to Last Sat Oct.	75 W 00
United States	Caribou	Maine	46 N 52	68 W 01	5+	EST	4+	1st Sun April to Last Sat Oct.	75 W 00
United States	Lewiston	Maine	44 N 06	70 W 13	5+	EST	4+	1st Sun April to Last Sat Oct.	75 W 00
United States	Portland	Maine	43 N 39	70 W 16	5+	EST	4+	1st Sun April to Last Sat Oct.	75 W 00
United States	Annapolis	Maryland	38 N 59	76 W 30	5+	EST	4+	1st Sun April to Last Sat Oct.	75 W 00
United States	Baltimore	Maryland	39 N 17	76 W 37	5+	EST	4+	1st Sun April to Last Sat Oct.	75 W 00
United States	Cumberland	Maryland	39 N 39	78 W 46	5+	EST	4+	1st Sun April to Last Sat Oct.	75 W 00
United States	Frederick	Maryland	39 N 25	77 W 25	5+	EST	4+	1st Sun April to Last Sat Oct.	75 W 00
United States	Hagerstown	Maryland	39 N 39	78 W 46	5+	EST	4+	1st Sun April to Last Sat Oct.	75 W 00
United States	Rockville	Maryland	39 N 05	77 W 09	5+	EST	4+	1st Sun April to Last Sat Oct.	75 W 00
United States	Boston	Massachusetts	42 N 22	71 W 04	5+	EST	4+	1st Sun April to Last Sat Oct.	75 W 00
United States	Lawrence	Massachusetts	42 N 43	71 W 10	5+	EST	4+	1st Sun April to Last Sat Oct.	75 W 00
United States	New Bedford	Massachusetts	41 N 38	70 W 56	5+	EST	4+	1st Sun April to Last Sat Oct.	75 W 00
United States	Pittsfield	Massachusetts	42 N 27	73 W 15	5+	EST	4+	1st Sun April to Last Sat Oct.	75 W 00
United States	Springfield	Massachusetts	42 N 06	72 W 35	5+	EST	4+	1st Sun April to Last Sat Oct.	75 W 00
United States	Worchester	Massachusetts	42 N 16	71 W 48	5+	EST	4+	1st Sun April to Last Sat Oct.	75 W 00
United States	Battle Creek	Michigan	42 N 19	85 W 11	5+	EST	4+	1st Sun April to Last Sat Oct.	75 W 00
United States	Detroit	Michigan	42 N 20	83 W 03	5+	EST	4+	1st Sun April to Last Sat Oct.	75 W 00
United States	Flint	Michigan	43 N 01	83 W 41	5+	EST	4+	1st Sun April to Last Sat Oct.	75 W 00
United States	Grand Rapids	Michigan	42 N 58	85 W 40	5+	EST	4+	1st Sun April to Last Sat Oct.	75 W 00
United States	Kalamazoo	Michigan	42 N 17	85 W 35	5+	EST	4+	1st Sun April to Last Sat Oct.	75 W 00
United States	Muskegon	Michigan	43 N 14	86 W 16	5+	EST	4+	1st Sun April to Last Sat Oct.	75 W 00
United States	Saginaw	Michigan	43 N 25	83 W 57	5+	EST	4+	1st Sun April to Last Sat Oct.	75 W 00
United States	Sault St. Marie	Michigan	46 N 30	84 W 21	5+	EST	4+	1st Sun April to Last Sat Oct.	75 W 00

Daylight Savings Times Deemed Reliable But Not Guaranteed

Country	City	State or Provence	LAT.	LONG.	Time Adjust to GMT	Abv Time	D.S. Time	1991 Daylight Savings Observed	S.T. Meridian
United States	Duluth	Minnesota	46 N 47	92 W 07	6+	CST	5+	1st Sun April to Last Sat Oct.	90 W 00
United States	Mankato	Minnesota	44 N 10	94 W 00	6+	CST	5+	1st Sun April to Last Sat Oct.	90 W 00
United States	Minneapolis	Minnesota	44 N 59	93 W 16	6+	CST	5+	1st Sun April to Last Sat Oct.	90 W 00
United States	Moorhead	Minnesota	46 N 53	96 W 45	6+	CST	5+	1st Sun April to Last Sat Oct.	90 W 00
United States	St. Paul	Minnesota	44 N 57	93 W 06	6+	CST	5+	1st Sun April to Last Sat Oct.	90 W 00
United States	Greenville	Mississippi	33 N 24	88 W 42	6+	CST	5+	1st Sun April to Last Sat Oct.	90 W 00
United States	Hattiesburg	Mississippi	31 N 20	89 W 17	6+	CST	5+	1st Sun April to Last Sat Oct.	90 W 00
United States	Jackson	Mississippi	32 N 18	90 W 12	6+	CST	5+	1st Sun April to Last Sat Oct.	90 W 00
United States	Meridan	Mississippi	32 N 22	88 W 42	6+	CST	5+	1st Sun April to Last Sat Oct.	90 W 00
United States	Pascagoula	Mississippi	30 N 21	88 W 33	6+	CST	5+	1st Sun April to Last Sat Oct.	90 W 00
United States	Independence	Missouri	39 N 06	94 W 25	6+	CST	5+	1st Sun April to Last Sat Oct.	90 W 00
United States	Jefferson City	Missouri	38 N 34	92 W 10	6+	CST	5+	1st Sun April to Last Sat Oct.	90 W 00
United States	Joplin	Missouri	37 N 06	94 W 31	6+	CST	5+	1st Sun April to Last Sat Oct.	90 W 00
United States	Saint Joseph	Missouri	39 N46	95 W 50	6+	CST	5+	1st Sun April to Last Sat Oct.	90 W 00
United States	Saint Louis	Missouri	38 N 37	90 W 12	6+	CST	5+	1st Sun April to Last Sat Oct.	90 W 00
United States	Springfield	Missouri	37 N 13	90 W 12	6+	CST	5+	1st Sun April to Last Sat Oct.	90 W 00
United States	Billings	Montana	45 N 47	108 W 30	7+	MST	6+	1st Sun April to Last Sat Oct.	105 W 00
United States	Butte	Montana	46 N 00	112 W 32	7+	MST	6+	1st Sun April to Last Sat Oct.	105 W 00
United States	Great Falls	Montana	47 N 30	111 W 17	7+	MST	6+	1st Sun April to Last Sat Oct.	105 W 00
United States	Helena	Montana	46 N 36	112 W 02	7+	MST	6+	1st Sun April to Last Sat Oct.	105 W 00
United States	Kalispell	Montana	48 N 12	114 W 19	7+	MST	6+	1st Sun April to Last Sat Oct.	105 W 00
United States	Missoula	Montana	46 N 52	114 W 01	7+	MST	6+	1st Sun April to Last Sat Oct.	105 W 00
United States	Grand Island	Nebraska	40 N 55	98 W 21	6+	CST	5+	1st Sun April to Last Sat Oct.	90 W 00
United States	Lincoln	Nebraska	40 N 49	96 W 41	6+	CST	5+	1st Sun April to Last Sat Oct.	90 W 00
United States	North Platte	Nebraska	41 N 08	100 W 46	6+	CST	5+	1st Sun April to Last Sat Oct.	90 W 00
United States	Omaha	Nebraska	41 N 17	96 W 01	6+	CST	5+	1st Sun April to Last Sat Oct.	90 W 00
United States	Scottsbluff	Nebraska	41 N 52	103 W 40	7+	MST	6+	1st Sun April to Last Sat Oct.	105 W 00
United States	Carson City	Nevada	39 N 10	119 W 46	8+	PST	7+	1st Sun April to Last Sat Oct.	120 W 00
United States	Las Vegas	Nevada	36 N 10	115 W 09	8+	PST	7	1st Sun April to Last Sat Oct.	120 W 00
United States	Reno	Nevada	39 N 31	119 W 48	8+	PST	7	1st Sun April to Last Sat Oct.	120 W 00
United States	Concord	New Hampshire	43 N 12	71 W 32	5+	EST	4+	1st Sun April to Last Sat Oct.	75 W 00
United States	Keene	New Hampshire	42 N 56	72 W 17	5+	EST	4+	1st Sun April to Last Sat Oct.	75 W 00
United States	Manchester	New Hampshire	43 N 00	119 W 46	5+	EST	4+	1st Sun April to Last Sat Oct.	75 W 00
United States	Nashua	New Hampshire	42 N 45	71 W 28	5+	EST	4+	1st Sun April to Last Sat Oct.	75 W 00
United States	Portsmouth	New Hampshire	43 N 05	70 W 45	5+	EST	4+	1st Sun April to Last Sat Oct.	75 W 00
United States	Atlantic City	New Jersey	39 N 21	74 W 7	5+	EST	4+	1st Sun April to Last Sat Oct.	75 W 00
United States	Camden	New Jersey	39 N 56	75 W 07	5+	EST	4+	1st Sun April to Last Sat Oct.	75 W 00
United States	Elizabeth	New Jersey	40 N 40	74 W 13	5+	EST	4+	1st Sun April to Last Sat Oct.	75 W 00
United States	Jersey City	New Jersey	40 N 44	74 W 04	5+	EST	4+	1st Sun April to Last Sat Oct.	75 W 00
United States	Newark	New Jersey	40 N 44	74 W 10	5+	EST	4+	1st Sun April to Last Sat Oct.	75 W 00
United States	Paterson	New Jersey	40 N 55	74 W 11	5+	EST	4+	1st Sun April to Last Sat Oct.	75 W 00
United States	Trenton	New Jersey	40 N 14	74 W 46	5+	EST	4+	1st Sun April to Last Sat Oct.	75 W 00
United States	Alamogordo	New Mexico	32 N 54	105 W 57	7+	MST	6+	1st Sun April to Last Sat Oct.	105 W 00
United States	Albuquerque	New Mexico	35 N 05	106 W 39	7+	MST	6+	1st Sun April to Last Sat Oct.	105 W 00
United States	Carlsbad	New Mexico	32 N 25	104 W 14	7+	MST	6+	1st Sun April to Last Sat Oct.	105 W 00
United States	Las Cruces	New Mexico	32 N 19	106 W 47	7+	MST	6+	1st Sun April to Last Sat Oct.	105 W 00
United States	Roswell	New Mexico	33 N 24	104 W 32	7+	MST	6+	1st Sun April to Last Sat Oct.	105 W 00
United States	Santa Fe	New Mexico	35 N 41	105 W 57	7+	MST	6+	1st Sun April to Last Sat Oct.	105 W 00
United States	Albany	New York	42 N 39	73 W 45	5+	EST	4+	1st Sun April to Last Sat Oct.	75 W 00
United States	Binghamton	New York	42 N 06	75 W 55	5+	EST	4+	1st Sun April to Last Sat Oct.	75 W 00
United States	Brooklyn	New York	40 N 38	73 W 56	5+	EST	4+	1st Sun April to Last Sat Oct.	75 W 00
United States	Buffalo	New York	42 N 53	78 W 53	5+	EST	4+	1st Sun April to Last Sat Oct.	75 W 00
United States	Elmira	New York	42 N 06	76 W 48	5+	EST	4+	1st Sun April to Last Sat Oct.	75 W 00
United States	Jamestown	New York	42 N 06	79 W 14	5+	EST	4+	1st Sun April to Last Sat Oct.	75 W 00
United States	Manhattan	New York	40 N 46	73 W 59	5+	EST	4+	1st Sun April to Last Sat Oct.	75 W 00
United States	New York	New York	40 N 45	73 W 57	5+	EST	4+	1st Sun April to Last Sat Oct.	75 W 00
United States	Poughkeepsie	New York	41 N 42	73 W 56	5+	EST	4+	1st Sun April to Last Sat Oct.	75 W 00
United States	Queens	New York	40 N 43	73 W 52	5+	EST	4+	1st Sun April to Last Sat Oct.	75 W 00
United States	Rochester	New York	43 N 10	77 W 37	5+	EST	4+	1st Sun April to Last Sat Oct.	75 W 00

Country	City	State or Provence	LAT.	LONG.	Time Adjust to GMT	Abv Time	D.S. Time	1991 Daylight Savings Observed	S.T. Meridian
United States	Schenectady	New York	42 N 49	75 W 57	5+	EST	4+	1st Sun April to Last Sat Oct.	75 W 00
United States	Staten Island	New York	40 N 35	74 W 09	5+	EST	4+	1st Sun April to Last Sat Oct.	75 W 00
United States	Syracuse	New York	43 N 03	76 W 09	5+	EST	4+	1st Sun April to Last Sat Oct.	75 W 00
United States	Utica	New York	43 N 06	75 W 14	5+	EST	4+	1st Sun April to Last Sat Oct.	75 W 00
United States	Watertown	New York	43 N 59	75 W 55	5+	EST	4+	1st Sun April to Last Sat Oct.	75 W 00
United States	Yonkers	New York	40 N 56	73 W 54	5+	EST	4+	1st Sun April to Last Sat Oct.	75 W 00
United States	Charlotte	North Carolina	35 N 13	80 W 51	5+	EST	4+	1st Sun April to Last Sat Oct.	75 W 00
United States	Durham	North Carolina	36 N 00	78 W 54	5+	EST	4+	1st Sun April to Last Sat Oct.	75 W 00
United States	Fayetteville	North Carolina	35 N 03	78 W 53	5+	EST	4+	1st Sun April to Last Sat Oct.	75 W 00
United States	Goldsboro	North Carolina	35 N 23	77 W 59	5+	EST	4+	1st Sun April to Last Sat Oct.	75 W 00
United States	Greenboro	North Carolina	36 N 04	79 W 48	5+	EST	4+	1st Sun April to Last Sat Oct.	75 W 00
United States	Raleigh	North Carolina	35 N 46	78 W 38	5+	EST	4+	1st Sun April to Last Sat Oct.	75 W 00
United States	Wilmington	North Carolina	34 N 14	77 W 55	5+	EST	4+	1st Sun April to Last Sat Oct.	75 W 00
United States	Winston-Salem	North Carolina	36 N 06	80 W 15	5+	EST	4+	1st Sun April to Last Sat Oct.	75 W 00
United States	Bismarck	North Dakota	46 N 48	100 W 47	6+	CST	5+	1st Sun April to Last Sat Oct.	90 W 00
United States	Fargo	North Dakota	46 N 53	96 W 48	6+	CST	5+	1st Sun April to Last Sat Oct.	90 W 00
United States	Grand Forks	North Dakota	47 N 55	97 W 03	6+	CST	5+	1st Sun April to Last Sat Oct.	90 W 00
United States	Minot	North Dakota	48 N 14	101 W 18	6+	CST	5+	1st Sun April to Last Sat Oct.	90 W 00
United States	Akron	Ohio	41 N 05	81 W 31	5+	EST	4+	1st Sun April to Last Sat Oct.	75 W 00
United States	Cincinnati	Ohio	39 N 06	84 W 31	5+	EST	4+	1st Sun April to Last Sat Oct.	75 W 00
United States	Cleveland	Ohio	41 N 30	81 W 41	5+	EST	4+	1st Sun April to Last Sat Oct.	75 W 00
United States	Columbus	Ohio	39 N 58	83 W 00	5+	EST	4+	1st Sun April to Last Sat Oct.	75 W 00
United States	Dayton	Ohio	39 N 45	84 W 12	5+	EST	4+	1st Sun April to Last Sat Oct.	75 W 00
United States	Toledo	Ohio	41 N 39	83 W 33	5+	EST	4+	1st Sun April to Last Sat Oct.	75 W 00
United States	Youngstown	Ohio	41 N 06	89 W 39	5+	EST	4+	1st Sun April to Last Sat Oct.	75 W 00
United States	Lawton	Oklahoma	34 N 37	98 W 25	6+	CST	5+	1st Sun April to Last Sat Oct.	90 W 00
United States	Muskogee	Oklahoma	35 N 45	95 W 22	6+	CST	5+	1st Sun April to Last Sat Oct.	90 W 00
United States	Oklahoma City	Oklahoma	35 N 30	97 W 30	6+	CST	5+	1st Sun April to Last Sat Oct.	90 W 00
United States	Tulsa	Oklahoma	36 N 10	95 W 55	6+	CST	5+	1st Sun April to Last Sat Oct.	90 W 00
United States	Eugene	Oregon	44 N 05	123 W 04	8+	PST	7	1st Sun April to Last Sat Oct.	120 W 00
United States	Klamath Falls	Oregon	42 N 13	121 W 46	8+	PST	7	1st Sun April to Last Sat Oct.	120 W 00
United States	Portland	Oregon	45 N32	122 W 37	8+	PST	7	1st Sun April to Last Sat Oct.	120 W 00
United States	Salem	Oregon	44 N 56	123 W 02	8+	PST	7	1st Sun April to Last Sat Oct.	120 W 00
United States	Allentown	Pennsylvania	40 N 37	75 W 29	5+	EST	4+	1st Sun April to Last Sat Oct.	75 W 00
United States	Erie	Pennsylvania	42 N 08	80 W 05	5+	EST	4+	1st Sun April to Last Sat Oct.	75 W 00
United States	Harrisburg	Pennsylvania	40 N 16	76 W 53	5+	EST	4+	1st Sun April to Last Sat Oct.	75 W 00
United States	Philadelphia	Pennsylvania	39 N 57	75 W 10	5+	EST	4+	1st Sun April to Last Sat Oct.	75 W 00
United States	Pittsburgh	Pennsylvania	40 N 26	80 W 01	5+	EST	4+	1st Sun April to Last Sat Oct.	75 W 00
United States	Reading	Pennsylvania	40 N 20	75 W 56	5+	EST	4+	1st Sun April to Last Sat Oct.	75 W 00
United States	Scranton	Pennsylvania	41 N 25	75 W 40	5+	EST	4+	1st Sun April to Last Sat Oct.	75 W 00
United States	Newport	Rhode Island	41 N 29	71 W 19	5+	EST	4+	1st Sun April to Last Sat Oct.	75 W 00
United States	Providence	Rhode Island	41 N 49	71 W 24	5+	EST	4+	1st Sun April to Last Sat Oct.	75 W 00
United States	Warwick	Rhode Island	41 N 42	71 W 28	5+	EST	4+	1st Sun April to Last Sat Oct.	75 W 00
United States	Woonsocket	Rhode Island	42 N 00	71 W 31	5+	EST	4+	1st Sun April to Last Sat Oct.	75 W 00
United States	Anderson	South Carolina	34 N 31	82 W 39	5+	EST	4+	1st Sun April to Last Sat Oct.	75 W 00
United States	Charleston	South Carolina	32 N 46	79 W 56	5+	EST	4+	1st Sun April to Last Sat Oct.	75 W 00
United States	Columbia	South Carolina	34 N 00	81 W 03	5+	EST	4+	1st Sun April to Last Sat Oct.	75 W 00
United States	Florence	South Carolina	34 N 12	79 W 46	5+	EST	4+	1st Sun April to Last Sat Oct.	75 W 00
United States	Greenville	South Carolina	34 N 51	85 W 24	5+	EST	4+	1st Sun April to Last Sat Oct.	75 W 00
United States	Pierre	South Carolina	44 N 22	100 W 21	5+	EST	4+	1st Sun April to Last Sat Oct.	75 W 00
United States	Sioux Falls	South Carolina	43 N 33	96 W 44	5+	EST	4+	1st Sun April to Last Sat Oct.	75 W 00
United States	Spartanburg	South Carolina	34 N 56	81 W 57	5+	EST	4+	1st Sun April to Last Sat Oct.	75 W 00
United States	Watertown	South Carolina	44 N 54	97 W 07	5+	EST	4+	1st Sun April to Last Sat Oct.	75 W 00
United States	Aberdeen	South Dakota	45 N 28	98 W 29	6+	CST	5+	1st Sun April to Last Sat Oct.	90 W 00
United States	Pierre	South Dakota	44 N 22	100 W 20	6+	CST	5+	1st Sun April to Last Sat Oct.	90 W 00
United States	Rapid City	South Dakota	44 N 06	103 W 14	7+	MST	6+	1st Sun April to Last Sat Oct.	105 W 00
United States	Sioux Falls	South Dakota	43 N 33	96 W 43	6+	CST	5+	1st Sun April to Last Sat Oct.	90 W 00
United States	Chattanooga	Tennessee	35 N 03	85 W 19	5+	EST	4+	1st Sun April to Last Sat Oct.	75 W 00
United States	Jackson	Tennessee	35 N 37	88 W 49	5+	EST	4+	1st Sun April to Last Sat Oct.	75 W 00

Daylight Savings Times Deemed Reliable But Not Guaranteed

Country	City	State or Provence	LAT.	LONG.	Time Adjust to GMT	Abv Time	D.S. Time	1991 Daylight Savings Observed	S.T. Meridian
United States	Johnson City	Tennessee	36 N 19	82 W 21	5+	EST	4+	1st Sun April to Last Sat Oct.	75 W 00
United States	Knoxville	Tennessee	35 N 58	83 W 55	5+	EST	4+	1st Sun April to Last Sat Oct.	75 W 00
United States	Memphis	Tennessee	35 N 08	90 W 03	6+	CST	5+	1st Sun April to Last Sat Oct.	90 W 00
United States	Nashville	Tennessee	36 N 10	86 W 47	6+	CST	5+	1st Sun April to Last Sat Oct.	90 W 00
United States	Abilene	Texas	32 N 28	99 W 43	6+	CST	5+	1st Sun April to Last Sat Oct.	90 W 00
United States	Amarillo	Texas	35 N 13	101 W 50	6+	CST	5+	1st Sun April to Last Sat Oct.	90 W 00
United States	Austin	Texas	30 N 17	97 W 45	6+	CST	5+	1st Sun April to Last Sat Oct.	90 W 00
United States	Brownsville	Texas	25 N 54	97 W 30	6+	CST	5+	1st Sun April to Last Sat Oct.	90 W 00
United States	Corpus Christi	Texas	27 N 47	97 W 24	6+	CST	5+	1st Sun April to Last Sat Oct.	90 W 00
United States	Dallas	Texas	32 N 47	96 W 49	6+	CST	5+	1st Sun April to Last Sat Oct.	90 W 00
United States	El Paso	Texas	31 N 45	106 W 29	7+	MST	6+	1st Sun April to Last Sat Oct.	105 W 00
United States	Fort Worth	Texas	32 N 45	97 W 18	7+	MST	6+	1st Sun April to Last Sat Oct.	105 W 00
United States	Galveston	Texas	29 N 18	94 W 48	7+	MST	6+	1st Sun April to Last Sat Oct.	105 W 00
United States	Houston	Texas	29 N 46	95 W 22	7+	MST	6+	1st Sun April to Last Sat Oct.	105 W 00
United States	Lubbock	Texas	33 N 35	101 W 51	7+	MST	6+	1st Sun April to Last Sat Oct.	105 W 00
United States	San Antonio	Texas	29 N 25	98 W 30	7+	MST	6+	1st Sun April to Last Sat Oct.	105 W 00
United States	Waco	Texas	31 N 33	97 W 09	7+	MST	6+	1st Sun April to Last Sat Oct.	105 W 00
United States	Wichita Falls	Texas	33 N 54	98 W 30	7+	MST	6+	1st Sun April to Last Sat Oct.	105 W 00
United States	Logan	Utah	41 N 44	111 W 50	7+	MST	6+	1st Sun April to Last Sat Oct.	105 W 00
United States	Ogden	Utah	41 N 31	111 W 58	7+	MST	6+	1st Sun April to Last Sat Oct.	105 W 00
United States	Provo	Utah	40 N 14	111 W 39	7+	MST	6+	1st Sun April to Last Sat Oct.	105 W 00
United States	Salt Lake City	Utah	40 N 45	111 W 53	7+	MST	6+	1st Sun April to Last Sat Oct.	105 W 00
United States	Brattleboro	Vermont	42 N 51	72 W 34	5+	EST	4+	1st Sun April to Last Sat Oct.	75 W 00
United States	Burlington	Vermont	44 N 29	73 W 12	5+	EST	4+	1st Sun April to Last Sat Oct.	75 W 00
United States	Montpelier	Vermont	44 N 16	72 W 35	5+	EST	4+	1st Sun April to Last Sat Oct.	75 W 00
United States	Rutland	Vermont	43 N 37	72 W 58	5+	EST	4+	1st Sun April to Last Sat Oct.	75 W 00
United States	Alexandria	Virginia	38 N 48	77 W 03	5+	EST	4+	1st Sun April to Last Sat Oct.	75 W 00
United States	Charlottesville	Virginia	38 N 02	78 W 30	5+	EST	4+	1st Sun April to Last Sat Oct.	75 W 00
United States	Lynchburg	Virginia	37 N 25	79 W 09	5+	EST	4+	1st Sun April to Last Sat Oct.	75 W 00
United States	Petersburg	Virginia	37 N 14	77 W 24	5+	EST	4+	1st Sun April to Last Sat Oct.	75 W 00
United States	Portsmough	Virginia	36 N 50	76 W 18	8+	PST	7	1st Sun April to Last Sat Oct.	120 W 00
United States	Richmond	Virginia	37 N 33	77 W 27	5+	EST	4+	1st Sun April to Last Sat Oct.	75 W 00
United States	Roanoke	Virginia	37 N 16	79 W 56	5+	EST	4+	1st Sun April to Last Sat Oct.	75 W 00
United States	Bellingham	Washington	48 N 46	122 W 29	8+	PST	7	1st Sun April to Last Sat Oct.	120 W 00
United States	Everett	Washington	47 N 59	122 W 12	8+	PST	7	1st Sun April to Last Sat Oct.	120 W 00
United States	Olympia	Washington	47 N 03	122 W 53	8+	PST	7	1st Sun April to Last Sat Oct.	120 W 00
United States	Seattle	Washington	47 N 36	122 W 20	8+	PST	7	1st Sun April to Last Sat Oct.	120 W 00
United States	Spokane	Washington	47 N 40	117 W 24	8+	PST	7	1st Sun April to Last Sat Oct.	120 W 00
United States	Tacoma	Washington	47 N 14	122 W 26	8+	PST	7	1st Sun April to Last Sat Oct.	120 W 00
United States	Yakima	Washington	46 N 37	120 W 30	8+	PST	7	1st Sun April to Last Sat Oct.	120 W 00
United States	Charleston	West Virginia	38 N 21	81 W 38	5+	EST	4+	1st Sun April to Last Sat Oct.	75 W 00
United States	Clarksburg	West Virginia	39 N 17	80 W 21	5+	EST	4+	1st Sun April to Last Sat Oct.	75 W 00
United States	Morgantown	West Virginia	39 N 38	79 W 57	5+	EST	4+	1st Sun April to Last Sat Oct.	75 W 00
United States	Wheeling	West Virginia	40 N 04	80 W 43	5+	EST	4+	1st Sun April to Last Sat Oct.	75 W 00
United States	Beloit	Wisconson	42 N 31	89 W 02	6+	CST	5+	1st Sun April to Last Sat Oct.	90 W 00
United States	Eau Claire	Wisconson	44 N 49	91 W 30	6+	CST	5+	1st Sun April to Last Sat Oct.	90 W 00
United States	Green Bay	Wisconson	44 N 31	88 W 00	6+	CST	5+	1st Sun April to Last Sat Oct.	90 W 00
United States	Madison	Wisconson	43 N 04	89 W 24	6+	CST	5+	1st Sun April to Last Sat Oct.	90 W 00
United States	Milwaukee	Wisconson	42 N47	87 W 55	6+	CST	5+	1st Sun April to Last Sat Oct.	90 W 00
United States	Sheboygan	Wisconson	43 N 46	87 W 45	6+	CST	5+	1st Sun April to Last Sat Oct.	90 W 00
United States	Wausau	Wisconson	44 N 58	89 W 38	6+	CST	5+	1st Sun April to Last Sat Oct.	90 W 00
United States	Cheyenne	Wyoming	41 N 08	104 W 49	7+	MST	6+	1st Sun April to Last Sat Oct.	105 W 00
United States	Laramie	Wyoming	41 N 19	105 W 35	7+	MST	6+	1st Sun April to Last Sat Oct.	105 W 00
United States	Rock Springs	Wyoming	41 N 35	109 W 14	7+	MST	6+	1st Sun April to Last Sat Oct.	105 W 00
United States	Sheridan	Wyoming	44 N 48	106 W 58	7+	MST	6+	1st Sun April to Last Sat Oct.	105 W 00
Uruguay	Montevideo		34 S 53	56 W 10	3+			No	45 W 00
USSR	Yerevan	Armenian SSR	40 N 10	44 E 30	-4		-4	Last Sun March to Last Sat Sept.	45 E 00
USSR	Chelyabinsk	Asian RSFSR	55 N 10	61 E 25	-5		-7	Last Sun March to Last Sat Sept.	75 E 00
USSR	Irkutsk	Asian RSFSR	52 N 16	104 E 00	-8		-9	Last Sun March to Last Sat Sept.	120 E 00

Daylight Savings Times Deemed Reliable But Not Guaranteed

Country	City	State or Provence	LAT.	LONG.	Time Adjust to GMT	Abv Time	D.S. Time	1991 Daylight Savings Observed	S.T. Meridian
USSR	Novosibirsk	Asian RSFSR	55 N 09	82 E 58	-7		-8	Last Sun March to Last Sat Sept.	105 E 00
USSR	Omsk	Asian RSFSR	55 N 12	73 E 19	-6		-7	Last Sun March to Last Sat Sept.	90 E 00
USSR	Sverdlovsk	Asian RSFSR	56 N 51	60 E 36	-5		-7	Last Sun March to Last Sat Sept.	75 E 00
USSR	Vladivostok	Asian RSFSR	43 N 06	131 E 47	-10		-11	Last Sun March to Last Sat Sept.	150 E 00
USSR	Baku	Azerbaijan SSR	40 N 25	49 E 50	-4		-5	Last Sun March to Last Sat Sept.	60 E 00
USSR	Minsk	Belorussin SSR	53 N 50	27 E 35	-3		-4	Last Sun March to Last Sat Sept.	45 E 00
USSR	Gor'kij (Gorky)	European RSFSR	56 N 15	44 E 05	-4		-4	Last Sun March to Last Sat Sept.	45 E 00
USSR	Kazan'	European RSFSR	55 N 50	49 E 18	-4		-5	Last Sun March to Last Sat Sept.	60 E 00
USSR	Kuybyshev	European RSFSR	53 N	50 E	-4		-5	Last Sun March to Last Sat Sept.	60 E 00
USSR	Leningrad	European RSFSR	59 N 57	30 E 20	-3		-4	Last Sun March to Last Sat Sept.	45 E 00
USSR	Moscow	European RSFSR	55 N 45	37 E 35	-3		-4	Last Sun March to Last Sat Sept.	45 E 00
USSR	Perm'	European RSFSR	58 N 00	56 E 15	-5		-6	Last Sun March to Last Sat Sept.	75 E 00
USSR	Rostov-na-Donu	European RSFSR	47 N 16	39 E 47	-3		-4	Last Sun March to Last Sat Sept.	45 E 00
USSR	Saratov	European RSFSR	51 N 30	45 E 30	-4		-4	Last Sun March to Last Sat Sept.	45 E 00
USSR	Ufa	European RSFSR	54 N 45	55 E 57	-5		-7	Last Sun March to Last Sat Sept.	75 E 00
USSR	Volgograd	European RSFSR	48 N 40	42 E 20	-4		-4	Last Sun March to Last Sat Sept.	45 E 00
USSR	Tbilisi	Georgian SSR	41 N 45	44 E 55	-4		-4	Last Sun March to Last Sat Sept.	45 E 00
USSR	Alma-Ata	Kazakh SSR	43 N 19	76 E 56	-6		-7	Last Sun March to Last Sat Sept.	90 E 00
USSR	Dnepropetrovsk	Ukrainian SSR	48 N 15	34 E 08	-3		-4	Last Sun March to Last Sat Sept.	45 E 00
USSR	Donetsk	Ukrainian SSR	48 N 00	37 E 35	-3		-4	Last Sun March to Last Sat Sept.	45 E 00
USSR	Khar'kov	Ukrainian SSR	50 N 00	36 E 10	-3		-4	Last Sun March to Last Sat Sept.	45 E 00
USSR	Kiev	Ukrainian SSR	50 N 27	30 E 32	-3		-4	Last Sun March to Last Sat Sept.	45 E 00
USSR	Odessa	Ukrainian SSR	46 N 28	30 E 44	-3		-4	Last Sun March to Last Sat Sept.	45 E 00
USSR	Tashkent	Uzbek SSR	41 N 20	69 E 18	-6		-7	Last Sun March to Last Sat Sept.	90 E 00
Vanuatu	Port Villa	New Hebrides	18 S 00	168 E 30	-11			No	165 E 00
Vatican City State	Vatican City		41 N 45	12 E 27	-1	CET	-2	Last Sun March to Last Sat Sept.	15 E 00
Venda	Thohoyandou		23 S 00	30 E 29	2+			No	30 E 00
Venezuela	Caracas		10 N 30	66 W 55	4+			No	60 W 00
Venezuela	Maracaibo		10 N 38	71 W 45	4+			No	60 W 00
Venezuela	Valencia		10 N 11	68 W 00	4+			No	60 W 00
Viet Nam	Da Nang		16 N 08	108 E 22	7+			No	105 E 00
Viet Nam	Haiphong		20 N 52	106 E 40	7+			No	105 E 00
Viet Nam	Hanoi		21 N 01	105 E 50	7+			No	105 E 00
Viet Nam	Hué		16 N 28	107 E 42	7+			No	105 E 00
Viet Nam	Nha Trang		12 N 08	108 4 56	7+			No	105 E 00
Viet Nam	Saigon (Ho Chi Minh City)		10 N 45	106 E 40	7+			No	105 E 00
Wales	Cardiff		51 N 30	3 W 18	0		-1		0 W 00
Wallis/Futuna Islands	Wallis (on Uvea)		13 S 17	176 W 08	-12			No	180 W 00
Western Samoa	Apia		13 S 49	171 W 46	11+			No	172 W 30
Yeman	Aden		12 N 47	45 E 02	-3			No	45 E 00
Yeman	Medina as-Sharrb		24 N 30	39 E 45	-3			No	45 E 00
Yeman Arab Republic	San'á		15 N 23	44 E 13	-3			No	45 E 00
Yogoslavia	Belgrade		44 N 49	20 E 27	-1	CET	-2	Last Sun March to Last Sat Sept.	15 E 00
Yogoslavia	Ljubliana		46 N 04	14 E 29	-1	CET	-2	Last Sun March to Last Sat Sept.	15 E 00
Yogoslavia	Sarajevo		43 N 50	18 E 26	-1	CET	-2	Last Sun March to Last Sat Sept.	15 E 00
Yogoslavia	Skopje		42 N 02	21 E 26	-1	CET	-2	Last Sun March to Last Sat Sept.	15 E 00
Yogoslavia	Split		43 N 30	16 E 28	-1	CET	-2	Last Sun March to Last Sat Sept.	15 E 00
Yugoslavia	Zagreb		45 N 50	15 E 58	-1	CET	-2	Last Sun March to Last Sat Sept.	15 E 00
Zaire	Kananga		6 S 14	22 E 17	-1	CET		No	15 E 00
Zaire	Kinshasa		4 S 19	15 E 18	-1	CET		No	15 E 00
Zaire	Lubumbashi		11 S 40	27 E 28	-2	CET		No	30 E 00
Zaire	Mbuji-Mayi		6 S 09	23 E 38	-2	CET		No	30 E 00
Zambia	Chingola		12 S 32	27 E 52	-2	EET		No	30 E 00
Zambia	Kitwe		12 S 49	28 E 13	-2	EET		No	30 E 00
Zambia	Lusaka		15 S 25	28 E 18	-2	EET		No	30 E 00
Zambia	Ndola		12 S 58	28 E 38	-2	EET		No	30 E 00
Zimbabwe	Bulawayo		20 S 12	28 E 43	-2	EET		No	30 E 00
Zimbabwe	Harare		17 S 50	31 E 03	-2	EET		No	30 E 00

MAJOR WORLD CITY COORDINATES

LISTED BY REGION

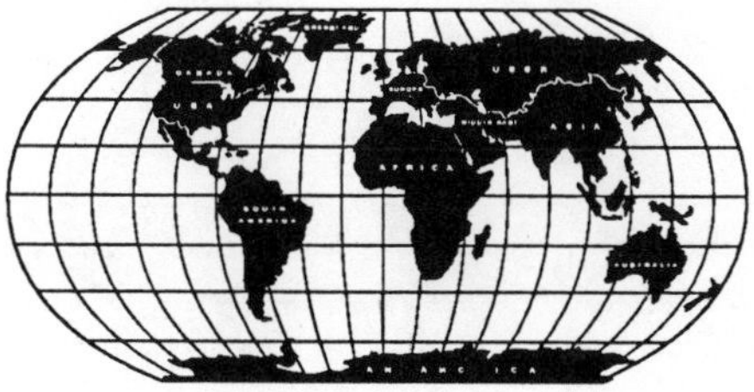

REGION	Country	City	State or Provence	LAT.	LONG.	Time Adjust to GMT	Abv Time	D.S. Time
Africa	Algeria	Constanine		36 N 28	6 E 38	-1	CET	-2
Africa	Algeria	Oran		35 N 46	0 W 45	-1	CET	-2
Africa	Angola	Luanda		8 S 48	13 E 14	-1	CET	
Africa	Benin	Cotonou		6 N 21	2 E 26	-1	GMT	
Africa	Bophuthatswana	Mmabatho		25 S 42	25 E 43	-2		
Africa	Bostwana	Gaborone		21 S 14	27 E 31	-2	EET	
Africa	Burkina Faso	Ouagadougou		12 N 22	1 W 31	0	GMT	
Africa	Burundi	Bujumbura		3 S 24	29 E 21	-2	EET	
Africa	Cameroon	Douala		4 N 03	9 E 42	-1	CET	
Africa	Cameroon	Yaoundé		31 N 51	11 E 32	-1	CET	
Africa	Cape Verde	Praia		14 N 56	23 W 31	-2	EET	
Africa	Central African Rep.	Bangui		4 N 21	18 E 35	-1	CET	
Africa	Chad	N'djamena		12 N 07	15 E 03	-1	CET	
Africa	Comoro Islands	Moroni		11 S 41	43 E 16	-3		
Africa	Congo	Brazzaville		4 S 17	15 E 14	-1	CET	
Africa	Djibouti	Djibouti		11 N 36	43 E 07	-3		
Africa	Egypt	Alexandria		31 N 13	29 E 57	-2	EET	
Africa	Egypt	Cairo		30 N 03	31 E 15	-2	EET	
Africa	Egypt	Shubra el Khema		30 N 06	31 E 15	-2	EET	
Africa	Egypt	Suez Canal		30 N 53	32 E 21	-2	EET	
Africa	Equatorial Guinea	Malabo		3 N 45	8 E 47	-1	CET	
Africa	Ethiopia	Addis Ababa		9 N 03	38 E 43	-3		
Africa	Ethiopia	Asmera		15 N 17	38 E 56	-3		
Africa	Gabon	Libreville		0 N 23	9 E 26	-1	CET	
Africa	Gambia (The)	Banjul		13 N 28	16 W 39	0	GMT	
Africa	Ghana	Accra		5 N 33	0 W 15	0	GMT	
Africa	Ghana	Kumasi		6 N 41	1 W 35	0	GMT	
Africa	Ghana	Tamale		9 N 25	0 W 05	0	GMT	
Africa	Guinea, Republic of	Conakry		9 N 30	13 W 43	0	GMT	
Africa	Guinea-Bissau	Bissau		11 N 51	15 W 35	0	CET	
Africa	Ivory Coast	Abidjan		5 N 19	4 W 01	0	GMT	
Africa	Ivory Coast	Yamoussoukro		6 N 49	5 W 17	0	GMT	
Africa	Kenya	Mombasa		4 N 03	39 E 40	-3		
Africa	Kenya	Nairobi		1 S 17	36 E 48	-3		
Africa	Kuwait	Kuwait		29N 23	47 E 59	-3		
Africa	Lebanon	Beirut		35 N 54	35 E 28	-3		-4
Africa	Lesotho	Maseru		29 S 18	27 E 30	-2	EET	
Africa	Liberia	Monrovia		6 N 20	10 W 48	0	GMT	
Africa	Libya	Tripoli		32 N 54	13 E 10	-2	EET	
Africa	Madagascar	Antananarivo		185 S 51	47 E 40	-3		
Africa	Malawi	Blantyre		15 S 47	35 E 00	-2	EET	
Africa	Malawi	Lilongwe		13 S 58	33 E 45	-2	EET	
Africa	Mali	Bamako		12 N 39	7 W 59	0	GMT	
Africa	Mauritania	Nouakchott		18 N 06	15 W 57	0	GMT	
Africa	Morocco	Cassablanca		33 N 32	7 W 41	-1	CET	-2
Africa	Morocco	Fès		34 N 08	5 W 00	-1	CET	-2
Africa	Morocco	Marrakech		31 N 38	8 W 00	-1	CET	-2
Africa	Morocco	Rabat		34 N 01	6 W 51	-1	CET	-2
Africa	Mozambique	Maputo		25 S 58	32 E 35	-2	EET	
Africa	Namibia	Windhoek		22 S 30	17 E 00	-2	EET	
Africa	Niger	Niamey		13 N 31	2 E 07	-1	CET	

REGION	Country	City	State or Provence	LAT.	LONG.	Time Adjust to GMT	Abv Time	D.S. Time
Africa	Nigeria	Ibadan		7 N 17	3 E 30	-1	CET	
Africa	Nigeria	Kano		12 N 00	8 E 30	-1	CET	
Africa	Nigeria	Lagos		6 N 27	3 E 23	-1	CET	
Africa	Nigeria	Ogbomosho		8 N 08	4 E 15	-1	CET	
Africa	Rwanda	Kigali		1 S 59	30 E 05	-2	EET	
Africa	Senegal	Dakar		14 N 40	17 W 26	0	GMT	
Africa	Sierra Leone	Freetown		8 N 29	13 W 12	0	GMT	
Africa	Solomon Islands	Honiara (on Guadalcanal)		9 S 15	59 E 45	-11		
Africa	Somalia	Mogadishu		2 N 02	45 E 21	-3		
Africa	South Africa	Cape Town		33 S 55	18 E 22	-2	EET	
Africa	South Africa	Durban		29 S 48	31 E 00	-2	EET	
Africa	South Africa	Johannesberg		26 S 15	28 E 00	-2	EET	
Africa	South Africa	Pretoria		25 S 45	28 E 11	-2	EET	
Africa	Sudan	Al Khartum (Khartoum)		15 N 38	32 E 33	-2	EET	
Africa	Sudan	Khartoum		15 N 36	32 E 32	-2	EET	
Africa	Sudan	Omdurman		15 N 45	32 E 30	-2	EET	
Africa	Swaziland	Mbabane		26 S 19	31 E 08	-2	EET	
Africa	Tanzania	Dar es Salaam		6 S 50	39 E 17	-3		
Africa	Togo	Lomé		6 N 08	1 E 14	0	GMT	
Africa	Transkei	Umtala		28 N 47	31 E 35	-2	EET	
Africa	Tunisia	Tunis		36 N 48	10 E 10	-1	CET	
Africa	Uganda	Kampala		0 N 19	1 W 31	-3		
Africa	Venda	Thohoyandou		23 S 00	30 E 29	2+		
Africa	Zaire	Kananga		6 S 14	22 E 17	-1	CET	
Africa	Zaire	Kinshasa		4 S 19	15 E 18	-1	CET	
Africa	Zaire	Lubumbashi		11 S 40	27 E 28	-2	CET	
Africa	Zaire	Mbuji-Mayi		6 S 09	23 E 38	-2	CET	
Africa	Zambia	Chingola		12 S 32	27 E 52	-2	EET	
Africa	Zambia	Kitwe		12 S 49	28 E 13	-2	EET	
Africa	Zambia	Lusaka		15 S 25	28 E 18	-2	EET	
Africa	Zambia	Ndola		12 S 58	28 E 38	-2	EET	
Africa	Zimbabwe	Bulawayo		20 S 12	28 E 43	-2	EET	
Africa	Zimbabwe	Harare		17 S 50	31 E 03	-2	EET	
Africa	Algeria	Algiers		36 N 47	3 E 04	-1	CET	-2
Asia	Afghanistan	Herat		34 N 28	62 E 13	-4.5		
Asia	Afghanistan	Kabul		34 N 30	69 E 13	-4.5		
Asia	Bangladesh	Dacca		23 N 43	90 E 25	-6		
Asia	Bhutan	Thimphu		27 N 37	89 E 52	-6		
Asia	Brunei	Bandar Seri Begawan		4 N 54	114 E 57	-8	PST	
Asia	China	Peking (Beijing)	Beijing Shi	39 N 55	116 E 25	-8	CCT	
Asia	China	Lanzhou (Lanchow)	Gansu (Kansu)	35 N 55	103 E 55	-8	CCT	
Asia	China	Canton (Guangzhou)	Guangdong	23 N 07	113 E 16	-8	CCT	-9
Asia	China	Anshun	Guizhou	26 N 12	105 E 50	-8	CCT	-9
Asia	China	Harbin	Heilongjiang	45 N 47	126 E 39	-8	CCT	
Asia	China	Qiqihar	Heilongjiang	47 N 18	124 E 00	-8	CCT	
Asia	China	Zhengzhou	Henan (Honan)	34 N 46	113 E 42	-8	CCT	
Asia	China	Wuhan	Hubei (Hupei)	30 N 23	114 E 54	-8	CCT	
Asia	China	Nanjing (Nanking)	Jiangsu	32 N 04	118 E 46	-8	CCT	
Asia	China	Xuzhou	Jiangsu	34 N 17	117 E 10	-8	CCT	
Asia	China	Changchun	Jilin (Kirin)	43 N 54	125 E 20	-8	CCT	
Asia	China	Fushun	Liaoning	41 N 50	124 E 00	-8	CCT	

REGION	Country	City	State or Provence	LAT.	LONG.	Time Adjust to GMT	Abv Time	D.S. Time
Asia	China	Luda (Dairen)	Liaoning	38 N 59	121 E 35	-8	CCT	
Asia	China	Shenyang	Liaoning	41 N 45	123 E 22	-8	CCT	
Asia	China	Xi'an	Shaanxi (Shensi)	34 N 20	109 E 00	-8	CCT	
Asia	China	Jinan	Shandong	36 N 40	117 E 01	-8	CCT	
Asia	China	Qingdao (Tsingtao)	Shandong	36 N 05	120 E 10	-8	CCT	
Asia	China	Shanghai	Shanghai Shi	31 N 14	121 E 30	-8	CCT	
Asia	China	Taiyuan	Shanxi	37 N 55	112 E 30	-8	CCT	
Asia	China	Chengdu (Chengtu)	Sichuan (Szechwan)	30 N 30	104 E 10	-8	CCT	
Asia	China	Chongquing	Sichuan (Szechwan)	29 N 38	107 E 30	-8	CCT	
Asia	China	Tianjin	Tianjin Shi	39 N 08	117 E 14	-8	CCT	
Asia	China	Kunming	Yunnan	25 N 04	102 E 41	-8	CCT	
Asia	China (Taiwan)	Chilung (Keelung)		25 N 02	121 E 48	-8	CCT	
Asia	China (Taiwan)	Taichung		24 N 10	120 E 42	-8	CCT	
Asia	China (Taiwan)	Tainan		23 N 08	120 E 18	-8	CCT	
Asia	China (Taiwan)	Taipei		25 N 02	121 E 38	-8	CCT	
Asia	Hong Kong	Hong Kong		22 N 17	114 E 09	-8	CCT	
Asia	Hong Kong	Kowloon		22 N 18	114 E 10	-8	CCT	
Asia	India	Ahmadabad		23 N 03	72 E 41	-5.5		
Asia	India	Bangalore		13 N 03	77 E 39	-5.5		
Asia	India	Bombay		18 N 58	72 E 50	-5.5		
Asia	India	Calcutta		22 N 32	88 E 22	-5.5		
Asia	India	Delhi		28 N 54	77 E 13	-5.5		
Asia	India	Hyderabad		17 N 29	78 E 28	-5.5		
Asia	India	Kanpur		26 N 30	80 E 10	-5.5		
Asia	India	Lucknow		26 N 54	80 E 58	-5.5		
Asia	India	Madras		13 N 08	80 E 15	-5.5		
Asia	India	Nagpur		21 N 12	79 E 09	-5.5		
Asia	India	New Delhi		28 N 38	77 E 13	-5.5		
Asia	India	Pune		18 N 38	73 E 53	-5.5		
Asia	Indonesia	Bandung	Java	7 S 00	107 E 22	-7		
Asia	Indonesia	Jakarta	Java	6 S 10	106 E 48	-7		
Asia	Indonesia	Semarang	Java	7 S 03	110 E 27	-7		
Asia	Indonesia	Surabaya	Java	7 S 23	112 E 45	-7		
Asia	Indonesia	Medan	Sumatra	3 N 35	98 E 35	-7		
Asia	Japan	Sapporo		43 N 03	141 E 19	-9		
Asia	Japan	Tokyo		35 N 40	139 E 46	-9		
Asia	Japan	Fukuoka		33 N 35	130 E 23	-9		
Asia	Japan	Hiroshima		34 N 22	132 E 25	-9		
Asia	Japan	Kitakyushu		33 N 53	130 E 50	-9		
Asia	Japan	Kobe		34 N 30	135 E 10	-9		
Asia	Japan	Kyoto		35 N 00	135 E 46	-9		
Asia	Japan	Nagoya		35 N 09	136 E 53	-9		
Asia	Japan	Osaka		34 N 40	135 E 30	-9		
Asia	Japan	Yokohama		35 N 37	139 E 40	-9		
Asia	Kampuchea	Phnum Pénh		11 N 39	104 E 53	-7		
Asia	Korea, North	P'younyang		39 N 00	126 E 45	-9		
Asia	Korea, South	Pusan		35 N 08	129 E 05	-9		
Asia	Korea, South	Seoul		37 N 33	126 E 58	-9		
Asia	Korea, South	Taegu		35 N 49	128 E 41	-9		
Asia	Laos	Vientiane		17 N 58	102 E 37	-7		
Asia	Malaysia	George Town (pinang)		5 N 21	100 E 09	-8		

REGION	Country	City	State or Provence	LAT.	LONG.	Time Adjust to GMT	Abv Time	D.S. Time
Asia	Malaysia	Ipoh		4 N 45	101 E 05	-8		
Asia	Malaysia	Kuala Lumpur		3 N 10	101 E 42	-8		
Asia	Mongolia	Ulan Bator		47 N 55	106 E 45	-8		-9
Asia	Nepal	Kathmandu		27 N 43	85 E 19	5 2/3-		
Asia	Pakistan	Peshawar	NWFP	34 N 01	71 E 40	-5		
Asia	Pakistan	Faisalabad		31 N 29	73 E 06	-5		
Asia	Pakistan	Hyderabad		25 N 29	68 E 28	-5		
Asia	Pakistan	Islamabad		33 N 43	75 E 17	-5		
Asia	Pakistan	Karachi		24 N 52	67 E 02	-5		
Asia	Pakistan	Lahore		32 N 00	74 E 18	-5		
Asia	Pakistan	Rawalpindi		33 N 40	73 E 10	-5		
Asia	Philippines	Manila		14 N 35	120 E 59	-8		
Asia	Philippines	Quezon City		14 N 00	122 E 11	-8		
Asia	Phillipines	Cebu		10 N 22	123 E 49	-8		
Asia	Singapore	Singapore		1 N 16	103 E 51	-8		
Asia	Taiwan	Kaohsiung		22 N 38	120 E 17	-8		
Asia	Taiwan	T'aipei		25 N 03	121 E 30	-8		
Asia	Thailand	Bangkok		13 N 45	100 E 31	-7		
Asia	Union of Mayanmar	Bassein	Former Burma	16 N 46	94 E 47	-6.5		
Asia	Union of Mayanmar	Mandalay	Former Burma	22 N 00	96 E 08	-6.5		
Asia	Union of Mayanmar	Moulmein	Former Burma	16 N 30	97 E 39	-6.5		
Asia	Union of Mayanmar	Rangoon	Former Burma	16 N 48	96 E 09	-6.5		
Asia	USSR	Chelyabinsk	Asian RSFSR	55 N 10	61 E 25	-5		-7
Asia	USSR	Irkutsk	Asian RSFSR	52 N 16	104 E 00	-8		-9
Asia	USSR	Novosibirsk	Asian RSFSR	55 N 09	82 E 58	-7		-8
Asia	USSR	Omsk	Asian RSFSR	55 N 12	73 E 19	-6		-7
Asia	USSR	Sverdlovsk	Asian RSFSR	56 N 51	60 E 36	-5		-7
Asia	USSR	Vladivostok	Asian RSFSR	43 N 06	131 E 47	-10		-11
Asia	Viet Nam	Da Nang		16 N 08	108 E 22	7+		
Asia	Viet Nam	Haiphong		20 N 52	106 E 40	7+		
Asia	Viet Nam	Hanoi		21 N 01	105 E 50	7+		
Asia	Viet Nam	Hué		16 N 28	107 E 42	7+		
Asia	Viet Nam	Nha Trang		12 N 08	108 4 56	7+		
Asia	Viet Nam	Saigon (Ho Chi Minh City)		10 N 45	106 E 40	7+		
Atlantic Ocean	Falkland Islands	Stanley		51 S 42	57 W 50	4+		
Australia	Australia	Canberra	Canaberra	35 S 17	149 E 08	-10		-11
Australia	Australia	Sydney	New S. Wales	33 S 52	151 E 13	-9		-11
Australia	Australia	Darwin	Northern Territory	12 S 28	130 E 49	-9.5		
Australia	Australia	Brisbane	Queensland	27 S 28	153 E 02	-10		
Australia	Australia	Adelaide	S. Australia	34 S 56	138 E 38	-9.5		
Australia	Australia	Melbourne	Victoria	37 S 49	144 E 62	-10		-11
Australia	Australia	Perth	Western	31 S 57	115 E 50	-8	PST	
Caribbean	Antigua/Barbuda	St. John's		17 N 06	61 W 51	5+		
Caribbean	Aruba	Oranjestad		12 N 33	70 W 06	6.5+		
Caribbean	Bahamas	Nassau		25 N 05	77 W 20	5+		4+
Caribbean	Barbados	Bridgetown		13 N 06	59 W 37	4+		
Caribbean	Bermuda	Hamilton		23 N 18	64 W 47	4+		3+
Caribbean	British Virgin Islands	Road Town	Trotola	18 N 27	64 W 37	4+		
Caribbean	Cayman Islands	Georgetown		19 N 20	81 W 20	5+		
Caribbean	Cuba	Havana		23 N 08	82 W 24	5+		4+
Caribbean	Dominica	Rosseau		15 N 18	61 W 24	4+		

REGION	Country	City	State or Provence	LAT.	LONG.	Time Adjust to GMT	Abv Time	D.S. Time
Caribbean	Dominican Republic	Santo Domingo		18 S 29	69 W 53	4+		
Caribbean	Grenada	St. George's		12 N 03	61 W 45	4+		
Caribbean	Guadeloupe	Basse-Terre		16 N 00	61 W 44	4+		
Caribbean	Haiti	Port-au-Prince		18 N 33	72 W 20	5+		
Caribbean	Indonesia	Bali	Bali	8 S 00	115 E 22	-7		
Caribbean	Jamaica	Kingston		18 N 00	76 W 48	5+		
Caribbean	Montserrat	Plymouth		16 N 42	62 W 13	4+		
Caribbean	Netherlands Antilles	Willemstad		12 N 12	68 W 58	4+		
Caribbean	St. Kitts/Nevis	Basseterre (on St. Kitts)		17 N 18	62 W 43	4+		
Caribbean	St. Lucia	Castries		14 N 01	61 W 00	4+		
Caribbean	St. Vincent	Kingstown		13 N 09	60 W 00	4+		
Caribbean	Trinidad/Tobago	Port-of-Spain		10 N 39	61 W 31	4+		
Europe	Albania	Tiranë		41 N 02	19 E 04	-1	CET	-2
Europe	Andorra	Andorra la Vella		42 N 31	1 E 30	-1	CET	-2
Europe	Austria	Graz		47 N 05	15 E 26	-1	CET	-2
Europe	Austria	Linz		48 N 18	14 E 18	-1	CET	-2
Europe	Austria	Saltzburg		47 N 48	13 E 04	-1	CET	-2
Europe	Austria	Vienna		48 N 12	16 E 23	-1	CET	-2
Europe	Belgium	Antwerp		51 N 13	4 E 24	-1	CET	-2
Europe	Belgium	Brussels		50 N 51	4 E 21	-1	CET	-2
Europe	Belgium	Li`ege		50 N 38	5 E 34	-1	CET	-2
Europe	Bulgaria	Plovdiv		42 N 09	24 E 43	-2	EET	-3
Europe	Bulgaria	Sofia		42 N 42	23 E 20	-2	EET	-3
Europe	Bulgaria	Varna		43 N 14	27 E 58	-2	EET	-3
Europe	Czechoslovakia	Bratislava		48 N 09	17 E 07	-1	CET	-2
Europe	Czechoslovakia	Prague		50 N 05	14 E 26	-1	CET	-2
Europe	Denmark	Copenhagen		55 N 41	12 E 35	-1	CET	-2
Europe	England	Manchester		53 N 28	2 W 14	0	GMT	-1
Europe	England	Bermingham		52 N 30	1 W 50	0	GMT	-1
Europe	England	Greenwich		51 N 29	00 W 00	0	GMT	-1
Europe	England	Leeds		53 N 48	1 W 32	0	GMT	-1
Europe	England	Liverpool		53 N 25	2 W 52	0	GMT	-1
Europe	England	London		51 N 30	0 W 06	0	GMT	-1
Europe	England	Newcastle (upon Tyne)		55 N 00	1 W 45	0	GMT	-1
Europe	England	Sheffield		53 N 23	1 W 28	0	GMT	-1
Europe	Faeroe Islands	Thorshavn		62 N 01	6 W 45	0	GMT	
Europe	Finland	Helsinki		60 N 09	24 E 58	-2	EET	-3
Europe	Finland	Tampere		61 N 21	23 E 39	-2	EET	-3
Europe	France	Le Havre		49 N 31	0 E 07	-1	CET	-2
Europe	France	Lille		50 N 38	3 E 01	-1	CET	-2
Europe	France	Lyon		45 N 44	4 E 52	-1	CET	-2
Europe	France	Marseille		43 N 18	5 E 25	-1	CET	-2
Europe	France	Paris		48 N 52	2 E 20	-1	CET	-2
Europe	Germany	Berlin		52 N 30	13 E 25	-1	CET	-2
Europe	Germany	Bonn		50 N 44	7 E 06	-1	CET	-2
Europe	Germany	Bremen		53 N 05	8 E 50	-1	CET	-2
Europe	Germany	Cologne		50 N 56	6 E 57	-1	CET	-2
Europe	Germany	Dresden		51 N 05	13 E 45	-1	CET	-2
Europe	Germany	Dusseldorf		51 N 14	6 E 47	-1	CET	-2
Europe	Germany	Essen		51 N 26	6 E 59	-1	CET	-2
Europe	Germany	Frankfurt		52 N 42	13 E 37	-1	CET	-2

REGION	Country	City	State or Provence	LAT.	LONG.	Time Adjust to GMT	Abv Time	D.S. Time
Europe	Germany	Hamburg		53 N 34	10 E 02	-1	CET	-2
Europe	Germany	Hannover		52 N 22	9 E 45	-1	CET	-2
Europe	Germany	Leipzig		51 N 20	12 E 24	-1	CET	-2
Europe	Germany	Mannheim		49 N 30	8 E 31	-1	CET	-2
Europe	Germany	Munich		48 N 98	11 E 35	-1	CET	-2
Europe	Germany	Nurnburg		49 N 28	11 E 07	-1	CET	-2
Europe	Germany	Stuttgart		48 N 48	9 E 15	-1	CET	-2
Europe	Germany	Wuppertal		51 N 16	7 E 14	-1	CET	-2
Europe	Greece	Athens		37 N 59	24 E 43	-2	EET	-3
Europe	Greece	Lárisa		39 N 38	22 E 25	-2	EET	-3
Europe	Greece	Pátraí		38 N 15	4 E 48	-2	EET	-3
Europe	Hungary	Budapest		47 N 30	19 E 05	-1	CET	-2
Europe	Iceland	Reykjavik		64 N 09	21 W 57	0	CET	
Europe	Ireland	Dublin		53 N 20	6 W 15	0	GMT	-1
Europe	Ireland, North	Belfast		54 N 36	5 W 55	0	GMT	-1
Europe	Isle of Man	Douglas	England	54 N 10	4 W 40	0	GMT	-1
Europe	Italy	Florence		43 N 47	11 E 15	-1	CET	-2
Europe	Italy	Genoa		44 N 23	9 E 52	-1	CET	-2
Europe	Italy	Milan		38 N 13	15 E 17	-1	CET	-2
Europe	Italy	Naples		40 N 37	14 E 12	-1	CET	-2
Europe	Italy	Palermo		38 N 08	13 E 24	-1	CET	-2
Europe	Italy	Rome		41 N 54	12 E 30	-1	CET	-2
Europe	Italy	Turin		45 N 05	7 E 44	-1	CET	-2
Europe	Italy	Venice		45 N 25	12 E 18	-1	CET	-2
Europe	Liechtenstein	Vaduz		47 N 08	09 E 31	-1	CET	-2
Europe	Luxembourg	Luxembourg		49 W 38	6 E 10	-1	CET	-2
Europe	Netherlands	Amsterdam		52 N 22	4 E 54	-1	CET	-2
Europe	Netherlands	Rotterdam		51 N 55	4 E 27	-1	CET	-2
Europe	Netherlands	The Hague		52 N 05	4 E 16	-1	CET	-2
Europe	Norway	Oslo		59 N 56	10 E 45	-1	CET	-2
Europe	Poland	Gdan´sk		54 N 20	18 E 40	-1	CET	-2
Europe	Poland	Katowice		50 N 15	19 E 00	-1	CET	-2
Europe	Poland	Krakow		50 N 05	20 E 00	-1	CET	-2
Europe	Poland	Lodz		51 N 46	19 E 30	-1	CET	-2
Europe	Poland	Poznan´		52 N 25	16 E 55	-1	CET	-2
Europe	Poland	Szczecin		53 N 25	14 E 35	-1	CET	-2
Europe	Poland	Warsaw		52 N 15	21 E 00	-1	CET	-2
Europe	Poland	Wroclaw		51 N 07	17 E 10	-1	CET	-2
Europe	Portugal	Lisbon		38 N 43	9 W 10	0	GMT	-1
Europe	Portugal	Porto		41 N 10	8 W 38	0	GMT	-1
Europe	Romania	Brasov		45 N 39	25 E 35	-2	EET	-3
Europe	Romania	Bucharest		44 N 26	26 E 06	-2	EET	-3
Europe	Romania	Cluj-Napoca		46 N 46	23 E 34	-2	EET	-3
Europe	Romania	Constanta		44 N 12	28 E 36	-2	EET	-3
Europe	Romania	Galati		45 N 25	28 E 05	-2	EET	-3
Europe	Romania	Timisoara		45 N 44	21 E 21	-2	EET	-3
Europe	San Marino	San Marino		43 N 56	12 E 27	-1	CET	-2
Europe	Scotland	Edinburgh		55 N 57	3 W 11	0	GMT	-1
Europe	Scotland	Glasgow		55 N 54	4 W 25	0	GMT	-1
Europe	Spain	Barcelona		41 N 25	2 E 08	-1	CET	-2
Europe	Spain	Bilbao		43 N 12	2 W 48	-1	CET	-2

REGION	Country	City	State or Provence	LAT.	LONG.	Time Adjust to GMT	Abv Time	D.S. Time
Europe	Spain	Madrid		40 N 24	3 W 41	-1	CET	-2
Europe	Spain	Seville		37 N 29	5 W 58	-1	CET	-2
Europe	Spain	Valencia		39 N 26	0 W 23	-1	CET	-2
Europe	Sweden	Stockholm		59 N 20	18 E 00 CK	-1	CET	-2
Europe	Switzerland	Bern		46 N 57	7 E 28	-1	CET	-2
Europe	Switzerland	Geneva		46 N 14	6 E 04	-1	CET	-2
Europe	Switzerland	Zürich		47 N 23	8 E 32	-1	CET	-2
Europe	USSR	Yerevan	Armenian SSR	40 N 10	44 E 30	-4		-4
Europe	USSR	Baku	Azerbaijan SSR	40 N 25	49 E 50	-4		-5
Europe	USSR	Minsk	Belorussin SSR	53 N 50	27 E 35	-3		-4
Europe	USSR	Gor'kij (Gorky)	European RSFSR	56 N 15	44 E 05	-4		-4
Europe	USSR	Kazan'	European RSFSR	55 N 50	49 E 18	-4		-5
Europe	USSR	Kuybyshev	European RSFSR	53 N	50 E	-4		-5
Europe	USSR	Leningrad	European RSFSR	59 N 57	30 E 20	-3		-4
Europe	USSR	Moscow	European RSFSR	55 N 45	37 E 35	-3		-4
Europe	USSR	Perm'	European RSFSR	58 N 00	56 E 15	-5		-6
Europe	USSR	Rostov-na-Donu	European RSFSR	47 N 16	39 E 47	-3		-4
Europe	USSR	Saratov	European RSFSR	51 N 30	45 E 30	-4		-4
Europe	USSR	Ufa	European RSFSR	54 N 45	55 E 57	-5		-7
Europe	USSR	Volgograd	European RSFSR	48 N 40	42 E 20	-4		-4
Europe	USSR	Tbilisi	Georgian SSR	41 N 45	44 E 55	-4		-4
Europe	USSR	Alma-Ata	Kazakh SSR	43 N 19	76 E 56	-6		-7
Europe	USSR	Dnepropetrovsk	Ukrainian SSR	48 N 15	34 E 08	-3		-4
Europe	USSR	Donetsk	Ukrainian SSR	48 N 00	37 E 35	-3		-4
Europe	USSR	Khar'kov	Ukrainian SSR	50 N 00	36 E 10	-3		-4
Europe	USSR	Kiev	Ukrainian SSR	50 N 27	30 E 32	-3		-4
Europe	USSR	Odessa	Ukrainian SSR	46 N 28	30 E 44	-3		-4
Europe	USSR	Tashkent	Uzbek SSR	41 N 20	69 E 18	-6		-7
Europe	Vatican City State	Vatican City		41 N 45	12 E 27	-1	CET	-2
Europe	Wales	Cardiff		51 N 30	3 W 18	0		-1
Europe	Yogoslavia	Belgrade		44 N 49	20 E 27	-1	CET	-2
Europe	Yogoslavia	Ljubliana		46 N 04	14 E 29	-1	CET	-2
Europe	Yogoslavia	Sarajevo		43 N 50	18 E 26	-1	CET	-2
Europe	Yogoslavia	Skopje		42 N 02	21 E 26	-1	CET	-2
Europe	Yogoslavia	Split		43 N 30	16 E 28	-1	CET	-2
Europe	Yugoslavia	Zagreb		45 N 50	15 E 58	-1	CET	-2
Indian Ocean	Maldive Islands	Malé		4 N 10	73 E 30	-5		
Indian Ocean	Mauritius	Port Louis		20 S 09	57 E 30	-4		
Indian Ocean	Réunion	Saint-Denis		20 S 52	55 E 27	-4		
Indian Ocean	Seychelles	Victoria		4 S 36	55 E 28	-4		
Indian Ocean	Sri Lanka	Colombo		6 N 57	79 E 53	-5.5		
Mediterranean	Cyprus	Nicosia		35 N 12	33 E 22	-2	EET	-3
Mediterranean	Malta	Valetta		35 N 54	14 E 31	-1	CET	-2
Mediterranean	Monaco	Monaco-Ville		43 N 44	7 E 26	-1	CET	-2
Middle East	Bahrain	Manama		26 N 14	50 E 35	-3		
Middle East	Iran	Mashed Soleyman		31 N 45	49 E 17	-3.5		
Middle East	Iran	Tabriz		38 N 00	46 E 13	-3.5		
Middle East	Iran	Tehran		35 N 40	51 E 26	-3.5		
Middle East	Iraq	Baghdad		33 N 20	44 E 24	-3	BT	-4
Middle East	Israel	Jerusalem		31 N 46	35 E 10	-2	EET	-3
Middle East	Israel	Tel Aviv		32 N 04	34 E 46	-2	EET	-3

REGION	Country	City	State or Provence	LAT.	LONG.	Time Adjust to GMT	Abv Time	D.S. Time
Middle East	Jordan	Amman		32 N 57	35 E 56	-2	EET	-3
Middle East	Jordan	Irbid		32 N 33	35 E 51	-2	EET	-3
Middle East	Jordan	Zarqa		32 N 13	35 E 43	-2	EET	-3
Middle East	Oman	Muscat		23 N 37	58 E 37	-4		
Middle East	Qutar	Doha		25 N 17	51 E 32	-3		
Middle East	Saudi Arabia	Jeddah		21 N 29	39 E 11	-3		
Middle East	Saudi Arabia	Mecca		21 N 27	39 E 50	-3		
Middle East	Saudi Arabia	Riyadh		24 N 39	46 E 42	-3		
Middle East	Syria	Aleppo		36 N 14	37 E 11	-2	EET	
Middle East	Syria	Damascus		33 N 30	36 E 18	-2	EET	
Middle East	Syria	Latakia		35 N 32	35 E 51	-2	EET	
Middle East	Turkey	Adana		37 N 05	35 E 20	-3		-4
Middle East	Turkey	Ankara		39 N 57	32 E 50	-3		-4
Middle East	Turkey	Bursa		40 N 10	28 E 10	-3		-4
Middle East	Turkey	Gaziantep		37 N 10	37 E 30	-3		-4
Middle East	Turkey	Istambul		41 N 01	28 E 58	-3		-4
Middle East	Turkey	Izmir		38 N 25	27 E05	-3		-4
Middle East	United Arab Emir	Abu Dhabi		24 N 30	54 E 28	-4		
Middle East	Yeman	Aden		12 N 47	45 E 02	-3		
Middle East	Yeman	Medina as-Sharrb		24 N 30	39 E 45	-3		
Middle East	Yeman Arab Republic	San'á		15 N 23	44 E 13	-3		
North America	Canada	Vancouver	British Columbia	49 N 16	123 W 07	8+		7+
North America	Canada	Winnipeg	Manitoba	49 N 53	97 W 09	6+		7+
North America	Canada	Calgary	Mountain	51 N 03	114 W 03	7+	MST	6+
North America	Canada	Edmonton	Mountain	53 N 33	113 W 28	7+	MST	6+
North America	Canada	St. John's	Newfoundland	47 N 34	52 W 43	4.5+		
North America	Canada	Hamilton	Ontario	43 N 15	79 W 52	5+		4+
North America	Canada	Ottawa	Ontario	45 N 25	75 W 42	5+		4+
North America	Canada	Toronto	Ontario	43 N 39	79 W 22	5+		4+
North America	Canada	Montre'al	Quebec	45 N 1	73 W 34	5+		4+
North America	Canada	Québec	Québec	46 N 49	71 W 13	5+		4+
North America	Greenland	Godthaab		64 N 11	51 W 43	4+		
North America	Mexico	Ciudad Juarez	Chihuahua	31 N 44	106 W 28	8+		7+
North America	Mexico	Guadalajara	Jalisco	20 N 41	103 W 21	8+		7+
North America	Mexico	León	Jalisco	21 N 08	101 W 41	8+		7+
North America	Mexico	Mexico City		19 N 24	99 W 09	6+		
North America	Mexico	Monterrey		25 N 43	100 W 19	6+		
North America	St. Pierre/Miquelon	Saint Pierre		46 N 46	56 W 10	3+		2+
North America	United States	Birmingham	Alabama	33 N 31	86 W 48	5+	EST	4+
North America	United States	Gadsden	Alabama	34 N 01	86 W 01	5+	EST	4+
North America	United States	Huntsville	Alabama	34 N 44	86 W 35	5+	EST	4+
North America	United States	Mobile	Alabama	30 N 41	88 W 03	5+	EST	4+
North America	United States	Tuscaloosa	Alabama	33 N 12	87 W 34	5+	EST	4+
North America	United States	Anchorage	Alaska	61 N 13	149 W 34	10+	AHST	9+
North America	United States	Fairbanks	Alaska	64 N 51	147 W 54	9+	YST	8
North America	United States	Juneau	Alaska	58 N 18	134 W 25	9+	YST	8
North America	United States	Nome	Alaska	64 N 30	165 W 20	9+	YST	8
North America	United States	Seward	Alaska	60 N 07	149 W 25	9+	YST	8
North America	United States	Flagstaff	Arizona	35 N 12	111 W 39	7+	MST	
North America	United States	Phoenix	Arizona	60 N 07	149 W 27	7+	MST	
North America	United States	Temple	Arizona	33 N 25	111 W 56	7+	MST	

REGION	Country	City	State or Provence	LAT.	LONG.	Time Adjust to GMT	Abv Time	D.S. Time
North America	United States	Tucson	Arizona	32 N 13	110 W 58	7+	MST	
North America	United States	Forth Smith	Arkansas	35 N 23	94 W 25	6+	CST	5+
North America	United States	Little Rock	Arkansas	34 N 45	92 W 17	6+	CST	5+
North America	United States	Texarkana	Arkansas	33 N 26	94 W 03	6+	CST	5+
North America	United States	Bakersfield	California	35 N 23	119 W 01	8+	PST	7
North America	United States	Cupertino	California	37 N 19	122 W 02	8+	PST	7
North America	United States	Eureka	California	40 N 47	124 W 09	8+	PST	7
North America	United States	Fresno	California	36 N 44	119 W 47	8+	PST	7
North America	United States	Los Angeles	California	34 N 04	118 W 15	8+	PST	7
North America	United States	Oakland	California	37 N 47	124 W 09	8+	PST	7
North America	United States	Oakland	California	37 N 49	122 W 16	8+	PST	7
North America	United States	Pasadena	California	34 N 09	118 W 09	8+	PST	7
North America	United States	Sacramento	California	38 N 35	121 W 29	8+	PST	7
North America	United States	San Diego	California	32 N 43	117 W 09	8+	PST	7
North America	United States	San Francisco	California	37 N 47	112 W 25	8+	PST	7
North America	United States	San Jose	California	37 N 20	121 W 53	8+	PST	7
North America	United States	Santa Barbara	California	34 N 25	119 W 42	8+	PST	7
North America	United States	Ventura	California	34 N 17	119 W 18	8+	PST	7
North America	United States	Boulder	Colorado	40 N 01	105 W 17	7+	MST	6+
North America	United States	Colorado Springs	Colorado	38 N 50	104 W 49	7+	MST	6+
North America	United States	Denver	Colorado	39 N 44	104 W 59	7+	MST	6+
North America	United States	Fort Collins	Colorado	40 N 35	105 W 05	7+	MST	6+
North America	United States	Grand Junction	Colorado	39 N 04	108 W 33	7+	MST	6+
North America	United States	Greeley	Colorado	40 N 25	104 W 42	7+	MST	6+
North America	United States	Pueblo	Colorado	38 N 14	104 W 36	7+	MST	6+
North America	United States	Bridgeport	Connecticut	41 N 11	73 W 12	5+	EST	4+
North America	United States	Hartford	Connecticut	41 N 46	72 W 41	5+	EST	4+
North America	United States	New Haven	Connecticut	41 N 18	72 W 55	5+	EST	4+
North America	United States	New London	Connecticut	41 N 21	72 W 06	5+	EST	4+
North America	United States	Norwich	Connecticut	41 N 31	72 W 05	5+	EST	4+
North America	United States	Stamford	Connecticut	41 N 03	73 W 32	5+	EST	4+
North America	United States	Waterbury	Connecticut	41 N 33	73 W 03	5+	EST	4+
North America	United States	Dover	Delaware	39 N 10	75 W 32	5+	EST	4+
North America	United States	Wilmington	Delaware	39 N 45	75 W 33	5+	EST	4+
North America	United States	Washington	Dist. of Columbia	38 N 53	77 W 00	5+	EST	4+
North America	United States	Cape Canaveral	Florida	28 N 24	80 W 36	5+	EST	4+
North America	United States	Daytona Beach	Florida	29 N 13	81 W 01	5+	EST	4+
North America	United States	Form Myers	Florida	26 N 39	81 W 52	5+	EST	4+
North America	United States	Fort Lauderdale	Florida	26 N 07	80 W 08	5+	EST	4+
North America	United States	Gainsville	Florida	29 N 40	82 W 20	5+	EST	4+
North America	United States	Jacksonville	Florida	30 N 20	81 W 39	5+	EST	4+
North America	United States	Key West	Florida	24 N 33	81 W 47	5+	EST	4+
North America	United States	Miami	Florida	25 N 47	80 W 11	5+	EST	4+
North America	United States	Naples	Florida	26 N 08	81 W 48	5+	EST	4+
North America	United States	Orlando	Florida	28 N 33	81 W 23	5+	EST	4+
North America	United States	Pensacola	Florida	30 N 25	87 W 13	6+	CST	5+
North America	United States	St. Petersburg	Florida	27 N 46	82 W 39	5+	EST	4+
North America	United States	Tallahassee	Florida	30 N 27	81 W 39	5+	EST	4+
North America	United States	Atlanta	Georgia	33 N 45	84 W 23	5+	EST	4+
North America	United States	Augusta	Georgia	33 N 28	81 W 58	5+	EST	4+
North America	United States	Columbus	Georgia	32 N 28	84 W 59	5+	EST	4+

REGION	Country	City	State or Provence	LAT.	LONG.	Time Adjust to GMT	Abv Time	D.S. Time
North America	United States	Macon	Georgia	32 N 51	83 W 38	5+	EST	4+
North America	United States	Savannah	Georgia	32 N 05	81 W 06	5+	EST	4+
North America	United States	Hilo	Hawaii	19 N 44	155 W 05	10+	AHST	No
North America	United States	Honolulu	Hawaii	21 N 19	157 W 52	10+	AHST	No
North America	United States	Kaneohoe	Hawaii	21 N 25	157 W 48	10+	AHST	No
North America	United States	Lahaina	Hawaii	20 N 53	156 W 41	10+	AHST	No
North America	United States	Lihue	Hawaii	21 N 59	159 W 23	10+	AHST	No
North America	United States	Boise	Idaho	43 N 38	116 W 12	5+	MST	6+
North America	United States	Pocatello	Idaho	42 N 52	112 W 27	7+	MST	6+
North America	United States	Bloomington	Illinois	40 N 29	89 W 00	6+	CST	5+
North America	United States	Chicago	Illinois	41 N 52	87 W 39	6+	CST	5+
North America	United States	Decatur	Illinois	39 N 51	88 W 57	6+	CST	5+
North America	United States	Peoria	Illinois	40 N 42	89 W 36	6+	CST	5+
North America	United States	Rockford	Illinois	42 N 16	89 W 06	6+	CST	5+
North America	United States	Springfield	Illinois	39 N 48	89 W 39	6+	CST	5+
North America	United States	Bloomington	Indiana	39 N 10	86 W 31	5+	EST	4+
North America	United States	Fort Wayne	Indiana	41 N 04	85 W 09	5+	EST	4+
North America	United States	Gary	Indiana	41 N 36	87 W 20	6+	CST	5+
North America	United States	Indianapolis	Indiana	39 N 46	86 W 09	5+	EST	4+
North America	United States	Lafayette	Indiana	40 N 25	86 W 54	5+	EST	4+
North America	United States	Muncie	Indiana	41 N 34	87 W 31	5+	EST	No
North America	United States	Richmond	Indiana	39 N 50	84 W 54	5+	EST	No
North America	United States	South Bend	Indiana	41 N 41	86 W 15	5+	EST	No
North America	United States	Terre Haute	Indiana	39 N 28	87 W 25	5+	EST	4+
North America	United States	Ames	Iowa	42 N 02	93 W 37	6+	CST	5+
North America	United States	Cedar Rapids	Iowa	41 N 59	91 W 40	6+	CST	5+
North America	United States	Davenport	Iowa	41 N 32	90 W 35	6+	CST	5+
North America	United States	Des Moines	Iowa	41 N 35	93 W 37	6+	CST	5+
North America	United States	Ford Dodge	Iowa	42 N 30	94 W 11	6+	CST	5+
North America	United States	Waterloo	Iowa	42 N 30	92 W 21	6+	CST	5+
North America	United States	Dodge City	Kansas	37 N 45	100 W 01	6+	CST	5+
North America	United States	Kansas City	Kansas	39 N 07	94 W 38	6+	CST	5+
North America	United States	Salina	Kansas	38 N 50	97 W 37	6+	CST	5+
North America	United States	Topeka	Kansas	39 N 03	95 W 40	6+	CST	5+
North America	United States	Wichita	Kansas	37 N 42	97 W 20	6+	CST	5+
North America	United States	Bowling Green	Kentucky	36 N 59	86 W 27	6+	CST	5+
North America	United States	Lexington	Kentucky	38 N 03	84 W 30	5+	EST	4+
North America	United States	Louisville	Kentucky	38 N 15	85 W 46	5+	EST	4+
North America	United States	Owensboro	Kentucky	37 N 46	87 W 07	6+	CST	5+
North America	United States	Paducah	Kentucky	37 N 05	88 W 37	6+	CST	5+
North America	United States	Baton Rouge	Louisiana	30 N 27	91 W 11	6+	CST	5+
North America	United States	Lake Charles	Louisiana	30 N 14	93 W 13	6+	CST	5+
North America	United States	Monroe	Louisiana	32 N 30	92 W 07	6+	CST	5+
North America	United States	New Orleans	Louisiana	29 N 58	90 W 04	6+	CST	5+
North America	United States	Shreveport	Louisiana	32 N 31	93 W 45	6+	CST	5+
North America	United States	Augusta	Maine	44 N 19	69 W 47	5+	EST	4+
North America	United States	Bangor	Maine	44 N 48	68 W 01	5+	EST	4+
North America	United States	Caribou	Maine	46 N 52	68 W 01	5+	EST	4+
North America	United States	Lewiston	Maine	44 N 06	70 W 13	5+	EST	4+
North America	United States	Portland	Maine	43 N 39	70 W 16	5+	EST	4+
North America	United States	Annapolis	Maryland	38 N 59	76 W 30	5+	EST	4+

REGION	Country	City	State or Provence	LAT.	LONG.	Time Adjust to GMT	Abv Time	D.S. Time
North America	United States	Baltimore	Maryland	39 N 17	76 W 37	5+	EST	4+
North America	United States	Cumberland	Maryland	39 N 39	78 W 46	5+	EST	4+
North America	United States	Frederick	Maryland	39 N 25	77 W 25	5+	EST	4+
North America	United States	Hagerstown	Maryland	39 N 39	78 W 46	5+	EST	4+
North America	United States	Rockville	Maryland	39 N 05	77 W 09	5+	EST	4+
North America	United States	Boston	Massachusetts	42 N 22	71 W 04	5+	EST	4+
North America	United States	Lawrence	Massachusetts	42 N 43	71 W 10	5+	EST	4+
North America	United States	New Bedford	Massachusetts	41 N 38	70 W 56	5+	EST	4+
North America	United States	Pittsfield	Massachusetts	42 N 27	73 W 15	5+	EST	4+
North America	United States	Springfield	Massachusetts	42 N 06	72 W 35	5+	EST	4+
North America	United States	Worchester	Massachusetts	42 N 16	71 W 48	5+	EST	4+
North America	United States	Battle Creek	Michigan	42 N 19	85 W 11	5+	EST	4+
North America	United States	Detroit	Michigan	42 N 20	83 W 03	5+	EST	4+
North America	United States	Flint	Michigan	43 N 01	83 W 41	5+	EST	4+
North America	United States	Grand Rapids	Michigan	42 N 58	85 W 40	5+	EST	4+
North America	United States	Kalamazoo	Michigan	42 N 17	85 W 35	5+	EST	4+
North America	United States	Muskegon	Michigan	43 N 14	86 W 16	5+	EST	4+
North America	United States	Saginaw	Michigan	43 N 25	83 W 57	5+	EST	4+
North America	United States	Sault St. Marie	Michigan	46 N 30	84 W 21	5+	EST	4+
North America	United States	Duluth	Minnesota	46 N 47	92 W 07	6+	CST	5+
North America	United States	Mankato	Minnesota	44 N 10	94 W 00	6+	CST	5+
North America	United States	Minneapolis	Minnesota	44 N 59	93 W 16	6+	CST	5+
North America	United States	Moorhead	Minnesota	46 N 53	96 W 45	6+	CST	5+
North America	United States	St. Paul	Minnesota	44 N 57	93 W 06	6+	CST	5+
North America	United States	Greenville	Mississippi	33 N 24	88 W 42	6+	CST	5+
North America	United States	Hattiesburg	Mississippi	31 N 20	89 W 17	6+	CST	5+
North America	United States	Jackson	Mississippi	32 N 18	90 W 12	6+	CST	5+
North America	United States	Meridan	Mississippi	32 N 22	88 W 42	6+	CST	5+
North America	United States	Pascagoula	Mississippi	30 N 21	88 W 33	6+	CST	5+
North America	United States	Independence	Missouri	39 N 06	94 W 25	6+	CST	5+
North America	United States	Jefferson City	Missouri	38 N 34	92 W 10	6+	CST	5+
North America	United States	Joplin	Missouri	37 N 06	94 W 31	6+	CST	5+
North America	United States	Saint Joseph	Missouri	39 N46	95 W 50	6+	CST	5+
North America	United States	Saint Louis	Missouri	38 N 37	90 W 12	6+	CST	5+
North America	United States	Springfield	Missouri	37 N 13	90 W 12	6+	CST	5+
North America	United States	Billings	Montana	45 N 47	108 W 30	7+	MST	6+
North America	United States	Butte	Montana	46 N 00	112 W 32	7+	MST	6+
North America	United States	Great Falls	Montana	47 N 30	111 W 17	7+	MST	6+
North America	United States	Helena	Montana	46 N 36	112 W 02	7+	MST	6+
North America	United States	Kalispell	Montana	48 N 12	114 W 19	7+	MST	6+
North America	United States	Missoula	Montana	46 N 52	114 W 01	7+	MST	6+
North America	United States	Grand Island	Nebraska	40 N 55	98 W 21	6+	CST	5+
North America	United States	Lincoln	Nebraska	40 N 49	96 W 41	6+	CST	5+
North America	United States	North Platte	Nebraska	41 N 08	100 W 46	6+	CST	5+
North America	United States	Omaha	Nebraska	41 N 17	96 W 01	6+	CST	5+
North America	United States	Scottsbluff	Nebraska	41 N 52	103 W 40	7+	MST	6+
North America	United States	Carson City	Nevada	39 N 10	119 W 46	8+	PST	7+
North America	United States	Las Vegas	Nevada	36 N 10	115 W 09	8+	PST	7
North America	United States	Reno	Nevada	39 N 31	119 W 48	8+	PST	7
North America	United States	Concord	New Hampshire	43 N 12	71 W 32	5+	EST	4+
North America	United States	Keene	New Hampshire	42 N 56	72 W 17	5+	EST	4+

REGION	Country	City	State or Provence	LAT.	LONG.	Time Adjust to GMT	Abv Time	D.S. Time
North America	United States	Manchester	New Hampshire	43 N 00	119 W 46	5+	EST	4+
North America	United States	Nashua	New Hampshire	42 N 45	71 W 28	5+	EST	4+
North America	United States	Portsmouth	New Hampshire	43 N 05	70 W 45	5+	EST	4+
North America	United States	Atlantic City	New Jersey	39 N 21	74 W 7	5+	EST	4+
North America	United States	Camden	New Jersey	39 N 56	75 W 07	5+	EST	4+
North America	United States	Elizabeth	New Jersey	40 N 40	74 W 13	5+	EST	4+
North America	United States	Jersey City	New Jersey	40 N 44	74 W 04	5+	EST	4+
North America	United States	Newark	New Jersey	40 N 44	74 W 10	5+	EST	4+
North America	United States	Paterson	New Jersey	40 N 55	74 W 11	5+	EST	4+
North America	United States	Trenton	New Jersey	40 N 14	74 W 46	5+	EST	4+
North America	United States	Alamogordo	New Mexico	32 N 54	105 W 57	7+	MST	6+
North America	United States	Albuquerque	New Mexico	35 N 05	106 W 39	7+	MST	6+
North America	United States	Carlsbad	New Mexico	32 N 25	104 W 14	7+	MST	6+
North America	United States	Las Cruces	New Mexico	32 N 19	106 W 47	7+	MST	6+
North America	United States	Roswell	New Mexico	33 N 24	104 W 32	7+	MST	6+
North America	United States	Santa Fe	New Mexico	35 N 41	105 W 57	7+	MST	6+
North America	United States	Albany	New York	42 N 39	73 W 45	5+	EST	4+
North America	United States	Binghamton	New York	42 N 06	75 W 55	5+	EST	4+
North America	United States	Brooklyn	New York	40 N 38	73 W 56	5+	EST	4+
North America	United States	Buffalo	New York	42 N 53	78 W 53	5+	EST	4+
North America	United States	Elmira	New York	42 N 06	76 W 48	5+	EST	4+
North America	United States	Jamestown	New York	42 N 06	79 W 14	5+	EST	4+
North America	United States	Manhattan	New York	40 N 46	73 W 59	5+	EST	4+
North America	United States	New York	New York	40 N 45	73 W 57	5+	EST	4+
North America	United States	Poughkeepsie	New York	41 N 42	73 W 56	5+	EST	4+
North America	United States	Queens	New York	40 N 43	73 W 52	5+	EST	4+
North America	United States	Rochester	New York	43 N 10	77 W 37	5+	EST	4+
North America	United States	Schenectady	New York	42 N 49	75 W 57	5+	EST	4+
North America	United States	Staten Island	New York	40 N 35	74 W 09	5+	EST	4+
North America	United States	Syracuse	New York	43 N 03	76 W 09	5+	EST	4+
North America	United States	Utica	New York	43 N 06	75 W 14	5+	EST	4+
North America	United States	Watertown	New York	43 N 59	75 W 55	5+	EST	4+
North America	United States	Yonkers	New York	40 N 56	73 W 54	5+	EST	4+
North America	United States	Charlotte	North Carolina	35 N 13	80 W 51	5+	EST	4+
North America	United States	Durham	North Carolina	36 N 00	78 W 54	5+	EST	4+
North America	United States	Fayetteville	North Carolina	35 N 03	78 W 53	5+	EST	4+
North America	United States	Goldsboro	North Carolina	35 N 23	77 W 59	5+	EST	4+
North America	United States	Greenboro	North Carolina	36 N 04	79 W 48	5+	EST	4+
North America	United States	Raleigh	North Carolina	35 N 46	78 W 38	5+	EST	4+
North America	United States	Wilmington	North Carolina	34 N 14	77 W 55	5+	EST	4+
North America	United States	Winston-Salem	North Carolina	36 N 06	80 W 15	5+	EST	4+
North America	United States	Bismarck	North Dakota	46 N 48	100 W 47	6+	CST	5+
North America	United States	Fargo	North Dakota	46 N 53	96 W 48	6+	CST	5+
North America	United States	Grand Forks	North Dakota	47 N 55	97 W 03	6+	CST	5+
North America	United States	Minot	North Dakota	48 N 14	101 W 18	6+	CST	5+
North America	United States	Akron	Ohio	41 N 05	81 W 31	5+	EST	4+
North America	United States	Cincinnati	Ohio	39 N 06	84 W 31	5+	EST	4+
North America	United States	Cleveland	Ohio	41 N 30	81 W 41	5+	EST	4+
North America	United States	Columbus	Ohio	39 N 58	83 W 00	5+	EST	4+
North America	United States	Dayton	Ohio	39 N 45	84 W 12	5+	EST	4+
North America	United States	Toledo	Ohio	41 N 39	83 W 33	5+	EST	4+

REGION	Country	City	State or Provence	LAT.	LONG.	Time Adjust to GMT	Abv Time	D.S. Time
North America	United States	Youngstown	Ohio	41 N 06	89 W 39	5+	EST	4+
North America	United States	Lawton	Oklahoma	34 N 37	98 W 25	6+	CST	5+
North America	United States	Muskogee	Oklahoma	35 N 45	95 W 22	6+	CST	5+
North America	United States	Oklahoma City	Oklahoma	35 N 30	97 W 30	6+	CST	5+
North America	United States	Tulsa	Oklahoma	36 N 10	95 W 55	6+	CST	5+
North America	United States	Eugene	Oregon	44 N 05	123 W 04	8+	PST	7
North America	United States	Klamath Falls	Oregon	42 N 13	121 W 46	8+	PST	7
North America	United States	Portland	Oregon	45 N32	122 W 37	8+	PST	7
North America	United States	Salem	Oregon	44 N 56	123 W 02	8+	PST	7
North America	United States	Allentown	Pennsylvania	40 N 37	75 W 29	5+	EST	4+
North America	United States	Erie	Pennsylvania	42 N 08	80 W 05	5+	EST	4+
North America	United States	Harrisburg	Pennsylvania	40 N 16	76 W 53	5+	EST	4+
North America	United States	Philadelphia	Pennsylvania	39 N 57	75 W 10	5+	EST	4+
North America	United States	Pittsburgh	Pennsylvania	40 N 26	80 W 01	5+	EST	4+
North America	United States	Reading	Pennsylvania	40 N 20	75 W 56	5+	EST	4+
North America	United States	Scranton	Pennsylvania	41 N 25	75 W 40	5+	EST	4+
North America	United States	Newport	Rhode Island	41 N 29	71 W 19	5+	EST	4+
North America	United States	Providence	Rhode Island	41 N 49	71 W 24	5+	EST	4+
North America	United States	Warwick	Rhode Island	41 N 42	71 W 28	5+	EST	4+
North America	United States	Woonsocket	Rhode Island	42 N 00	71 W 31	5+	EST	4+
North America	United States	Anderson	South Carolina	34 N 31	82 W 39	5+	EST	4+
North America	United States	Charleston	South Carolina	32 N 46	79 W 56	5+	EST	4+
North America	United States	Columbia	South Carolina	34 N 00	81 W 03	5+	EST	4+
North America	United States	Florence	South Carolina	34 N 12	79 W 46	5+	EST	4+
North America	United States	Greenville	South Carolina	34 N 51	85 W 24	5+	EST	4+
North America	United States	Pierre	South Carolina	44 N 22	100 W 21	5+	EST	4+
North America	United States	Sioux Falls	South Carolina	43 N 33	96 W 44	5+	EST	4+
North America	United States	Spartanburg	South Carolina	34 N 56	81 W 57	5+	EST	4+
North America	United States	Watertown	South Carolina	44 N 54	97 W 07	5+	EST	4+
North America	United States	Aberdeen	South Dakota	45 N 28	98 W 29	6+	CST	5+
North America	United States	Pierre	South Dakota	44 N 22	100 W 20	6+	CST	5+
North America	United States	Rapid City	South Dakota	44 N 06	103 W 14	7+	MST	6+
North America	United States	Sioux Falls	South Dakota	43 N 33	96 W 43	6+	CST	5+
North America	United States	Chattanooga	Tennessee	35 N 03	85 W 19	5+	EST	4+
North America	United States	Jackson	Tennessee	35 N 37	88 W 49	5+	EST	4+
North America	United States	Johnson City	Tennessee	36 N 19	82 W 21	5+	EST	4+
North America	United States	Knoxville	Tennessee	35 N 58	83 W 55	5+	EST	4+
North America	United States	Memphis	Tennessee	35 N 08	90 W 03	6+	CST	5+
North America	United States	Nashville	Tennessee	36 N 10	86 W 47	6+	CST	5+
North America	United States	Abilene	Texas	32 N 28	99 W 43	6+	CST	5+
North America	United States	Amarillo	Texas	35 N 13	101 W 50	6+	CST	5+
North America	United States	Austin	Texas	30 N 17	97 W 45	6+	CST	5+
North America	United States	Brownsville	Texas	25 N 54	97 W 30	6+	CST	5+
North America	United States	Corpus Christi	Texas	27 N 47	97 W 24	6+	CST	5+
North America	United States	Dallas	Texas	32 N 47	96 W 49	6+	CST	5+
North America	United States	El Paso	Texas	31 N 45	106 W 29	7+	MST	6+
North America	United States	Fort Worth	Texas	32 N 45	97 W 18	7+	MST	6+
North America	United States	Galveston	Texas	29 N 18	94 W 48	7+	MST	6+
North America	United States	Houston	Texas	29 N 46	95 W 22	7+	MST	6+
North America	United States	Lubbock	Texas	33 N 35	101 W 51	7+	MST	6+
North America	United States	San Antonio	Texas	29 N 25	98 W 30	7+	MST	6+

REGION	Country	City	State or Provence	LAT.	LONG.	Time Adjust to GMT	Abv Time	D.S. Time
North America	United States	Waco	Texas	31 N 33	97 W 09	7+	MST	6+
North America	United States	Wichita Falls	Texas	33 N 54	98 W 30	7+	MST	6+
North America	United States	Logan	Utah	41 N 44	111 W 50	7+	MST	6+
North America	United States	Ogden	Utah	41 N 31	111 W 58	7+	MST	6+
North America	United States	Provo	Utah	40 N 14	111 W 39	7+	MST	6+
North America	United States	Salt Lake City	Utah	40 N 45	111 W 53	7+	MST	6+
North America	United States	Brattleboro	Vermont	42 N 51	72 W 34	5+	EST	4+
North America	United States	Burlington	Vermont	44 N 29	73 W 12	5+	EST	4+
North America	United States	Montpelier	Vermont	44 N 16	72 W 35	5+	EST	4+
North America	United States	Rutland	Vermont	43 N 37	72 W 58	5+	EST	4+
North America	United States	Alexandria	Virginia	38 N 48	77 W 03	5+	EST	4+
North America	United States	Charlottesville	Virginia	38 N 02	78 W 30	5+	EST	4+
North America	United States	Lynchburg	Virginia	37 N 25	79 W 09	5+	EST	4+
North America	United States	Petersburg	Virginia	37 N 14	77 W 24	5+	EST	4+
North America	United States	Portsmough	Virginia	36 N 50	76 W 18	8+	PST	7
North America	United States	Richmond	Virginia	37 N 33	77 W 27	5+	EST	4+
North America	United States	Roanoke	Virginia	37 N 16	79 W 56	5+	EST	4+
North America	United States	Bellingham	Washington	48 N 46	122 W 29	8+	PST	7
North America	United States	Everett	Washington	47 N 59	122 W 12	8+	PST	7
North America	United States	Olympia	Washington	47 N 03	122 W 53	8+	PST	7
North America	United States	Seattle	Washington	47 N 36	122 W 20	8+	PST	7
North America	United States	Spokane	Washington	47 N 40	117 W 24	8+	PST	7
North America	United States	Tacoma	Washington	47 N 14	122 W 26	8+	PST	7
North America	United States	Yakima	Washington	46 N 37	120 W 30	8+	PST	7
North America	United States	Charleston	West Virginia	38 N 21	81 W 38	5+	EST	4+
North America	United States	Clarksburg	West Virginia	39 N 17	80 W 21	5+	EST	4+
North America	United States	Morgantown	West Virginia	39 N 38	79 W 57	5+	EST	4+
North America	United States	Wheeling	West Virginia	40 N 04	80 W 43	5+	EST	4+
North America	United States	Beloit	Wisconson	42 N 31	89 W 02	6+	CST	5+
North America	United States	Eau Claire	Wisconson	44 N 49	91 W 30	6+	CST	5+
North America	United States	Green Bay	Wisconson	44 N 31	88 W 00	6+	CST	5+
North America	United States	Madison	Wisconson	43 N 04	89 W 24	6+	CST	5+
North America	United States	Milwaukee	Wisconson	42 N47	87 W 55	6+	CST	5+
North America	United States	Sheboygan	Wisconson	43 N 46	87 W 45	6+	CST	5+
North America	United States	Wausau	Wisconson	44 N 58	89 W 38	6+	CST	5+
North America	United States	Cheyenne	Wyoming	41 N 08	104 W 49	7+	MST	6+
North America	United States	Laramie	Wyoming	41 N 19	105 W 35	7+	MST	6+
North America	United States	Rock Springs	Wyoming	41 N 35	109 W 14	7+	MST	6+
North America	United States	Sheridan	Wyoming	44 N 48	106 W 58	7+	MST	6+
Pacific Ocean	Fiji	Suva (on Viti Levu)		18 S 09	178 E 26	-12		
Pacific Ocean	French Polynesia	Papeete (on Tahiti)		17 S 32	149 W 34	10+		
Pacific Ocean	Guam	Guam		14 N 00	143 E 20	-10		
Pacific Ocean	Nauru	Yaren		0 S 32	166 E 55	-12		
Pacific Ocean	New Caledonia	Nouméa		22 S 18	166 E 48	-11		
Pacific Ocean	New Zealand	Auckland		36 S 53	174 E 45	-12		1+
Pacific Ocean	New Zealand	Wellington		41 S 18	174 E 47	-12		1+
Pacific Ocean	Papua New Guinea	Port Moresby		9 S 27	147 E 08	-10		
Pacific Ocean	Tuvalu	Funafuti		8 S 31	179 E 13	-12		
South America	Argentina	Buenos Aires		34 S 36	58 W 27	3+		
South America	Argentina	Córdoba		30 S 20	64 W 03	3+		
South America	Argentina	La Plata		34 S 54	57 W 57	3+		

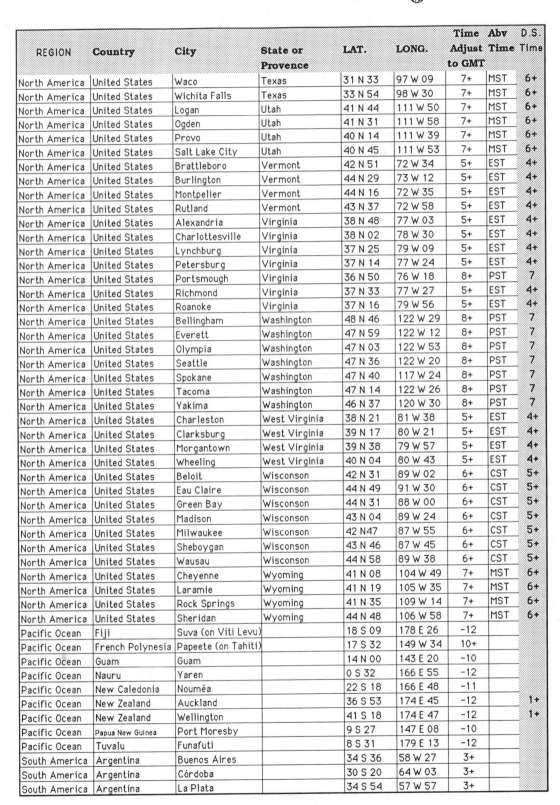

REGION	Country	City	State or Provence	LAT.	LONG.	Time Adjust to GMT	Abv Time	D.S. Time
South America	Argentina	Rosario		32 S 58	60 W 42	3+		
South America	Belize	Belize City		17 N 31	88 W 10	6+		
South America	Belize	Belmopan		17 N 15	88 W 47	6+		
South America	Boliva	Cochabamaba		17 S 24	66 W 09	4+		
South America	Boliva	Oruro		17 S 57	66 W 59	4+		
South America	Boliva	Santa Cruz		17 S 45	63 W 03	4+		
South America	Bolivia	La Paz		16 S 30	68 W 09	4+		
South America	Brazil	Belo Horizonte		19 S 54	43 W 56	3+		
South America	Brazil	Brasília		15 S 49	47 W 39	3+		
South America	Brazil	Fortaleza		3 S 35	38 W 31	3+		
South America	Brazil	Porto Alegre		29 S 58	51 W 11	3+		
South America	Brazil	Recife		8 S 09	34 W 59	3+		
South America	Brazil	Rio de Janeiro		23 S 54	43 W 14	3+		
South America	Brazil	Salvador		12 S 59	38 W 27	3+		
South America	Brazil	Sao Paulo		23 S 34	46 W 38	3+		
South America	Chile	Concepción		36 S 51	72 W 59	4+		3+
South America	Chile	Santiago		33 S 27	70 W 40	4+		3+
South America	Chile	Valparaíso		33 S 02	71 W 32	4+		3+
South America	Columbia	Baranquilla		3 N 18	74 W 40	5+		
South America	Columbia	Bogota´		4 N 40	74 W 05	5+		
South America	Columbia	Bucaramanga		17 N 12	73 W 14	5+		
South America	Columbia	Cali		3 N 22	76 W 30	5+		
South America	Columbia	Cartagena		10 N 30	75 W 40	5+		
South America	Columbia	Medellín		6 N 15	75 W 35	5+		
South America	Costa Rica	San José		9 N 56	84 W 05	6+		
South America	Ecuador	Guayaquil		2 S 16	79 W 53	5+		
South America	Ecuador	Quito		0 S 13	78 W 30	5+		
South America	El Salvador	San Salvador		13 N 41	89 W 12	6+		
South America	French Guiana	Cayenne		4 N 57	52 W 20	3+		
South America	Guatemala	Guatemala		14 N 38	90 W 31	6+		
South America	Guyana	Georgetown		6 N 48	58 W 18	3+		
South America	Honduras	Tegucigalpa		14 N 06	87 W 13	6+		
South America	Nicaragua	Managua		12 N 08	86 W 18	6+		
South America	Panama	Panama City		8 N 57	79 W 32	5+		
South America	Paraguay	Asunción		25 S 15	57 W 40	4+		3+
South America	Peru	Arequipa		16 S 27	71 W 30	5+		4+
South America	Peru	Callao		12 S 02	77 W 07	5+		4+
South America	Peru	Chiclayo		6 S 46	79 W 50	5+		4+
South America	Peru	Lima		12 S 03	77 W 03	5+		4+
South America	Peru	Trujillo		8 S 08	79 W 00	5+		4+
South America	Puerto Rico	San Juan		18 N 30	66 W 10	4+		
South America	Suriname	Paramaribo		5 N 50	55 W 13	4.5+		
South America	Uruguay	Montevideo		34 S 53	56 W 10	3+		
South America	Venezuela	Caracas		10 N 30	66 W 55	4+		
South America	Venezuela	Maracaibo		10 N 38	71 W 45	4+		
South America	Venezuela	Valencia		10 N 11	68 W 00	4+		
South Pacific	Tonga	Nukúalofa		21 S 08	175 W 12	11+		
South Pacific	Vanuatu	Port Villa	(New Hebrides)	18 S 00	168 E 30	-11		
South Pacific	Wallis/Futuna Islands	Wallis (on Uvea)		13 S 17	176 W 08	-12		
South Pacific	Western Samoa	Apia		13 S 49	171 W 46	11+		
West Indies	Martinique	Fort-de-France		14 N 36	61 W 05	4+		

Daylight Savings Times Deemed Reliable But Not Guaranteed

REFERENCES AND BIBLIOGRAPHY

Abell, George O., *Realm of the Universe*, Saunders College, West Washington Square, Philadelphia, PA., 19105, USA, 1980.

Alexander, Roy, *The Astrology of Choice: A Counseling Approach*, Samuel Weiser, Inc., P.O. Box 612, York Beach, Maine, 03910, USA, 1985.

Arroyo, Stephen, *Astrology, Karma & Transformation: The Inner Dimensions of the Birth Chart*, CRCS Publications, P.O. Box 20850, Reno, Nevada, 89515, USA.

Arroyo, Stephen, *Relationships and Life Cycles: Modern Dimensions of Astrology*, CRCS Publications, P.O. Box 20850, Reno, Nevada, 89515, USA, 1979.

Bailey, Alice A., *Esoteric Astrology: A Treatise on the Seven Rays*, Vol III., Lucis Publishing Company, New York, USA, 1979.

Ballard, Juliet Brooke, *The Hidden Laws of Earth: Based on the Edgar Cayce Readings*, A.R.E. Press, Virginia Beach, Virginia, USA, 1987.

Binder, Jamie, *Planets in Work: a Complete Guide to Vocational Astrology*, ACS Publications, Box 34487, San Diego, California, 92103-0802, USA, 1988.

Blue Star Level III User's Guide, Matrix Software, 315 Marion Avenue, Big Rapids, Michigan, 49307, USA.

Bulfinch, Thomas, *The Age of Fable or Beauties of Mythology*, David McKay, Philadelphia, USA, 1898.

Burt, Kathleen, *Archetypes of the Zodiac*, Llewellyn Publications, Saint Paul, Minnesota 55164-0383, USA, 1988.

Capt, Raymond E., *The Glory of the Stars: A Study of the Zodiac*, Artisan Sales, P.O. Box 1497, Thousand Oaks, California 91360 USA, 1983.

Cole, John, N., *Sun Reflections: Images for the New Solar Age*, Rodale Press, Emmaus, Pennsylvania, USA, 1981.

Cozzi, Steve, *Planets in Locality: Exploring Local Space Astrology*, Llewellyn Publications, St. Paul, Minnesota, 55164-0383, USA, 1988.

Davison, Ronald, *Synastry: Understanding Human Relations through Astrology*, Aurora Press, 205 Third Avenue, New York, NY, 10003, USA, 1986.

deVore, Nicholas, *Encyclopedia of Astrology*, Bonanza Books, Philosophical Library, New York, NY. USA, 1974.

Doane, Doris Chase, *Time Changes in the USA*, 1985 and *Time Changes in the World*, 1987, both published by the American Federation of Astrologers, 6535 South Rural Road, Tempe, Arizona 85283, USA.

Dobyns, Zipporah, *Working With Local Space*, All About Astrology Series (No. 9), Astro Computing Services, P.O. Box 16430, San Diego, California 92116-0430, USA.

Ebertin, Reinhold, *The Combination of Stellar Influences*, American Federation of Astrologers, Inc., 6535 S. Rural Road, Tempe, Arizona 85283, USA, 1972.

Espenshade, Edward Jr, Editor, *Rand McNally Goodes World Atlas*, 18th edition, 1990.

Freeman, Martin, *Forecasting by Astrology: A Comprehensive Manual of Interpretation and Technique*, The Aquarian Press, Wellingborough, Northamptionshire, U.K., 1982.

Frontiers in Astronomy, Readings from *Scientific American*, Edited by W. H. Freeman, 660 Market Street, San Francisco, California 94104, USA, 1970.

Gauquelin, Michel, *Birth-Times: A Scientific Investigation of the Secrets of Astrology*, Hill and Wang, New York, New York, USA, 1983.

Gauquelin, Michel, *Cosmic Influences on Human Behavior: Planetary Factors in Personality*, Aurora Press, 205 Third Avenue, 2A, New York, NY, 10003, USA, 1985.

George, Demetra, *Asteroid Goddesses*, ACS Publications, Inc., P.O. Box 16430, San Diego, California, 92116-0430, USA, 1987.

Gettings, Fred, *The Dictionary of Astrology*, Routledge & Kegan Paul, 9 Part Street, Boston, Mass. 02108, USA, 1985.

Gettings, Fred, *Dictionary of Occult, Hermetic and Alchemical Sigils*, Routledge & Kegan Paul, 9 Park Street, Boston, Mass. 02108, USA, 1981.

Gleadow,Rupert, *The Origin of the Zodiac*, Castle Books, New York, USA, 1968.

Goodavage, Joseph F., *Astrology: The Space Age Science*, New American Library, Inc. New York, New York, USA, Castle Books, New, York, USA, 1968.

Gribbin, J.R. and Plagemann, S.H., *The Jupiter Effect: Planets as Triggers of Devastating Earthquakes*, Vintage Books, New York, New York, USA, 1974.

Hall, Manly P., *Astrological Keywords*, Littlefield Adams Quality Paperbacks, Savage, Maryland, USA, 1958.

Hand, Robert, *Horoscope Symbols*, Whitford Press, 1981, West Chester, Pennsylvania, 19380. USA, 1981.

Hand, Robert, *Planets in Composite: Analyzing Human Relationships*, Whitford Press, West Chester, Pennsylvania. 19380, USA, 1975.

Hand, Robert, *Planets in Transit: Life Cycles for Living*, Whitford Press, West Chester, Pennsylvania, USA, 1987.

Hand, Robert, *Planets in Youth: Patterns of Early Development*, Whitford Press, West Chester, Pennsylvania, USA, 1977.

Hand, Robert and Sweeney, William, *Documentation for Astrolabe's NOVA Series Version 2.10*, Astrolabe Astro-Graphics Services, Inc., Box 1750, 350 Underpass Road, Brewster, Mass. 02631, USA, 1988.

Haskell, Dennis, *Graphic Astrology: The Gamma Edition*, User's Documentation, Time Cycles Research, Waterford, Connecticut, USA, 1987.

Hastings, Nancy Anne, *Secondary Progressions: Time to Remember*, Samuel Weiser, Inc, York Beach, Maine, USA, 1984.

Hastings, Nancy Anne, *The Practice of Prediction: The Astrologer's Handbook of Techniques Used to Accurately Forecast the Future*, Samuel Weiser, Inc, York Beach, Maine, USA, 1989.

Henry, William, *How to Use Dials*, All About Astrology Series (No 8), Astro Computing Services, P.O. Box 16430, San Diego, California 92116-0430, USA.

Jacobson, Roger A., *The Language of Uranian Astrology*, Uranian Publications, Inc., P.O. Box 114, Franksville, Wisconsin, 53126-0114, USA, 1975.

Jenkins, Palden, *Living in Time: Learning to Experience Astrology in Your Life*, Gateway Books, 19 Circus Place, Bath, BA1 2PW, England, UK, 1987.

Kirby, Babs and Stubbs, Janey, *Interpreting Solar and Lunar Returns: a Psychological Approach*, Element Books, Longmead, Shaftesbury, Dorset, England, 1990.

The Kimberton Hills Agricultural Calendar: a Guide for Understanding the Influence of Cosmic Rhythm in Farming and Gardening, Kimberton Hills Publications, P.O. Box 155, Kimberton, PA, 19442, annual publication.

Lewis, Jim and Guttman, Ariel, *The Astro*Carto*Graphy Book of Maps: The Astrology of Relocation*, Llewellen Publications, St. Paul, Minnesota, USA, 1989.

Lehman, J. Lee, *The Ultimate Asteroid Book*, Whitford Press, 1469 Morstein Road, West Chester, Pennsylvania 19380, USA, 1988.

Leinbach, Esther V., *Degrees of the Zodiac*, Macoy Publishing, Richmond, Virginia, USA, 1981.

Ling, Kim, *The Moon Book*, Johnson Publishing Co., 1880 South 57th Court, Boulder, Colorado, 80301, USA.

Llewellyn's Moon Sign Book & Lunar Planting Guide, Llewellyn Publications, P.O. Box 64383, Saint Paul, MN, 55164. Annual publication.

Lundsted, Betty, *Transits: The Time of Your Life*, Samuel Weiser, Inc, York Beach, Maine, USA, 1981.

Lynch, John, Editor, *The Coffee Table Book of Astrology*, The Viking Press, Inc., 625 Madison Avenue, New York 22, New York, USA, 1962.

Lofthus, Myran, *A Spiritual Approach to Astrology*, CRCS Publications, P.O. Box 20850, Reno, Nevada, 89515, USA, 1983.

Makransky, Jerry, "Primary Directions", article in the *National Council for Geocosmic Research Journal*, 78 Hubbard Avenue, Stamford, Ct. 06905, USA.

Marks, Tracy, *The Astrology of Self-Discovery*, CRCS Publications, P.O. Box 20850, Reno, Nevada, 89515, USA, 1985.

Martin, Vivian B., *Astrocycles: How to Make the Major Planetary Cycles Work for You*, Ballantine Books, New York, New York, USA, 1991.

Mayo, Jeff, *The Astrologer's Astronomical Handbook*, L.N. Fowler & Co., 1201/3 High Road, Chadwell Heath, Romford, Esses RM6 4DH, England, 1979.

McEvers, Joan (ed), *The Astrology of the Macrocosm: New Directions in Mundane Astrology*, Llewellyn's New World Astrology Series, Llewellyn Publications, St. Paul, Minnesota, USA, 1990.

Mercury Hour: The Astrologer's Astrological Magazine, Edith Custer, C-7, 3509 Waterlick Road, Lynchburg, Virginia 24502, USA.

Meyer, Michael, *A Handbook for the Humanistic Astrologer*, Anchor Press/Doubleday, Garden City, New York, USA, 1974.

Morford, Mark and Lenardon, Robert J., *Classical Mythology*, David McKay Company, Inc. and Longman, Inc., New York, USA, 1977.

Murchie, Guy, *Music of the Spheres*, The Riverside Press, Cambridge, Massachusetts, 1961.

Muzzio, John, *Astrological Life Scripts: Mythological Archetypes in the Natal Horoscope*, Seek-it Publications, P.O. Box 1074, Birmingham, Michigan, 48-12, USA, 1986.

National Council for Geocosmic Research Journal, 78 Hubbard Avenue, Stamfort, CT, 06905, USA.

Oken, Alan, *Alan Oken's Complete Astrology*, Bantan Books, 666 Fifth Avenue, New York, New York, USA, 1980.

Oken, Alan, *Soul-Centered Astrology: A Key to Your Expanding Self*, Bantam Books, 666 Fifth Avenue, New York, New York, 10103, USA, 1990.

Pelletier, Robert, *Planets in Houses: Experiencing Your Environment*, Para Research, Inc, 85 Eastern Avenue, Glouchester, Massachusetts, 01930, USA, 1978.

Parker, Derek and Julia, *The New Compleat Astrologer: The New Twenty-First Century Edition*, Crown Publishers, Inc, 225 Park Avenue South, New York, N.Y., 10003, USA.

Pottenger, Maritha, *The East Point and the Antivertex*, All About Astrology Series (No 4), Astro Computing Services, P.O. Box 16430, San Diego, California 92116-0430, USA.

Pottenger, Maritha, *What are Astrolocality Maps?*, All About Astrology Series (No 1), Astro Computing Services, P.O. Box 16430, San Diego, California 92116-0430, USA, 1983.

Pottenger, Mark, *CCRS Horoscope Program Documentation*, 1990, 838 5th Avenue, Los Angeles, California 90005. USA.

Powell, Robert, *Hermetic Astrology Volumes I and II*, Powell & Hermetika Verlag, 8921 Kinsau, West Germany, 1989.

Powell, Robert, *The Zodiac: A Historical Survey*, All About Astrology Series (No 3), Astro Computing Services, P.O. Box 16430, San Diego, California 92116-0430, USA.

Riotte, Louise, *Astrological Gardening: the Ancient Wisdom of Successful Planting and Harvesting by the Stars*, Storey Communications, Inc., Schoolhouse Road, Pownal, Vermont, 05261, USA.

Rudhyar, Dane, *An Astrological Mandala: the Cycle of Transformations and its 360 Symbolic Phases*, Vantage Books, New York, USA, 1974.

Rudhyar, Dane, *An Astrological Triptych: Gifts of the Spirit, The Way Through the Illumined Road*, ASI Publishers, 127 Madison Avenue, New York, N.Y. 10016, USA.

Rudhyar, Dane, *The Galactic Dimension of Astrology: The Sun is Also a Star*, Aurora Press, 205 Third Avenue, 2A, New York, N.Y. 10003, USA, 1975.

Rudhyar, Dane, *The Lunation Cycle: A Key to the Understanding of Personality*, Aurora Press, 205 Third Avenue 2A, New York, New York, 10003, USA, 1986.

Rudhyar, Dane, *The Planetarization of Consciousness*, ASI Publishers, 127 Madison Avenue, New York, New York, USA, 1977.

Ruperti, Alexander, *Cycles of Becoming: The Planetary Pattern of Growth*, CCRS Publications P.O. 4307, Vancover, Washington, 98662, USA, 1978.

Sandbach, John, *Degree Analysis: Dwadashamsas and Deeper Meanings*, (1978) and *Degree Analysis Part II: Chandra Symbols in the*

Horoscope, (1984) Seek-it Publications, Box 1074 Brimingham, Michigan 48012, USA.

Sepharial, *Sepharial's New Dictionary of Astrology*, ACRO Publishing, 219 Part Avenue South, New York, NY, 10003, USA, 1972.

Shanks, Thomas G., *The American Atlas: U.S. Longitudes and Latitudes Time Changes and Time Zones*, 5th edition, March, 1990, and *The International Atlas*, Second Edition, 1988, ACS Publications, P.O. Box 16430, San Diego, California, 92116-0430, USA.

Simms, Maria Kay, *Dial Detective: Investigations with the 90° Dial, An Illustrated Introduction to Uranian Astrology*, ACS Publications, Inc., P.O. Box 34487, San Diego, California, 92103-0802, USA, 1989.

Smith, C. Michael, "Astrology in the 90s: Modern Tools of the Trade" Article in *The Mountain Astrologer*, July-July 1991, P.O. Box 11292, Berkley, California, 94701, USA.

Smoluchowski, Roman, *The Solar System*, Scientific American Books, W. H. Freeman and Company, 41 Madison Avenue, New York, N.Y. 10010, USA, 1983.

Townley, John, *Astrological Life Cycles, A Planetary Guide to Personal and Career Opportunities*, Destiny Books, 1 Park Street, Rochester, Vermont, 05767, USA, 1987.

Thomas, Robert B., *The Old Farmer's Almanac*, 1991, Yankee Publishing, Inc., Dublin, New Hampshire 03444, USA, 1991.

Wedeck, H.E., *Dictionary of Astrology*, The Citadel Press, Secaucus, New Jersey, USA, 1973.

World Holiday and Time Guide, 1990, J.P. Morgan & Co., 60 Wall Street, New York, NY, 10260, USA.

Yott, Donald H., *Astrology and Reincarnation*, Samuel Weiser, Inc. Box 612, York Beach, Maine, 03910, USA, 1989.

INDEX

A

D

E

F

G

H

N

O

P

Q

R

S

T

U

About the Author

Patricia Foreman has a varied background that has been primarily focused in the sciences and public service. She attended Purdue University and graduated from both the Colleges of Pharmacy and Agriculture. Her graduate studies at Indiana University gave her a Master's in Public Administration with majors in Health Systems Administration and International Affairs. Her many awards include a Fullbright Fellowship and an appointment as a Presidential Executive Management Intern in Washington, D.C. She has worked for the United Nations and has provided technical health related consulting services to the World Bank, World Health Organization, United States Agency for International Development, and other international donor agencies.

Pat is currently working for a nonprofit organization that provides health care assistance to third world countries. She also is a practicing pharmacist. Her work is greatly supplemented by computers and she has formally taught the use of computers in international courses worldwide. She has also written user's documentation to accompany specialty computer programs created for managing pharmaceutical supply systems.

Her interest in astrology was fueled by her use of computers to cast charts and a life long fascination with the metaphysical sciences. She teaches astrology at the University of Vermont's Church Street Center for Continuing Education. She entered this world on the New Moon of Scorpio.

In compiling this book, Pat drew upon her scientific background and, with a systematic approach, focused on all aspects of combining computers with astrology. Enjoying writing, research and astrology, the result was this comprehensive reference book that was over four years in preparation.

Textue de Sphaera. Sarobosco, 1538

Did you borrow this copy? Want to give a gift?
If so, order your own personal copy so that you, or a friend, will have this reference to use day after day.

Yes, Please send the book(s) indicated below:

Type or print clearly

Name ____________________
Address ____________________
City __________ State _____
Zip _____ Country ________
Phone (___) ______________

Please send a gift to:

Name ____________________
Address ____________________
City __________ State _____
Zip _____ Country ________
Phone (___) ______________

Book Title	How Many	Price Each	Total
Computers and Astrology: A Universal User's Guide and Reference by Patricia L. Foreman		$19.95	
Backyard Market Gardener: A Masters Guide to Selling What You Grow (Forthcoming in December 1991) by Andrew W. Lee		$19.95	
Subtotal			
Vermont Residents add 5% sales tax			
Postage & Handling: $3.00 for 1 - 3 books, 50¢ for each additional book, extra to ship outside U.S.*			
Total Enclosed (U.S. dollars only)			

Payment: Please check payment method.
[ ] Check or Money Order (Payable to Good Earth Publications) [ ] VISA [ ] MasterCard

Card Number _ _ _ _ - _ _ _ _ - _ _ _ _ - _ _ _ _ Expires: __ __

Cardholder's Signiture ____________________ Daytime Phone (___) ________

Mail to *Good Earth Publications*
Box 4352 - CA
Burlington, Vermont 05406-4352
Phone and Fax: 802-985-8184

Bulk purchase inquiries invited.

*We ship ground UPS within the 48 contiguous states. Please give full street address and allow 2 weeks for delivery time. UPS will not deliver to P.O. Box addresses. FPO, APO, Alaska and Hawaii orders are sent by 4th class mail, allow 6 weeks for delivery. Orders shipped outside the US are sent by surface mail - allow 8 to 12 weeks delivery. Overseas mail charges are approximately double domestic postage and handling charges depending upon the weight. Satisfaction Fully Guaranteed !

THANK YOU FOR YOUR ORDER!

Did you borrow this copy? Want to give a gift?
If so, order your own personal copy so that you, or a friend, will have this reference to use day after day.

Yes, Please send the book(s) indicated below:

Type or print clearly

Name ______________________
Address ____________________
City ___________ State _____
Zip ______ Country ________
Phone (   ) ______________

Please send a gift to:

Name ______________________
Address ____________________
City ___________ State _____
Zip ______ Country ________
Phone (   ) ______________

Book Title	How Many	Price Each	Total
Computers and Astrology: A Universal User's Guide and Reference by Patricia L. Foreman		$19.95	
Backyard Market Gardener: A Masters Guide to Selling What You Grow (Forthcoming in December 1991) by Andrew W. Lee		$19.95	
Subtotal			
Vermont Residents add 5% sales tax			
Postage & Handling: $3.00 for 1 - 3 books, 50¢ for each additional book, extra to ship outside U.S.*			
Total Enclosed (U.S. dollars only)			

Payment: Please check payment method.
[ ] Check or Money Order (Payable to Good Earth Publications) [ ] VISA [ ] MasterCard

Card Number ____-____-____-____ Expires: __ __

Cardholder's Signiture ________________ Daytime Phone (   ) __________

Mail to *Good Earth Publications*
Box 4352 - CA
Burlington, Vermont 05406-4352
Phone and Fax: 802-985-8184

Bulk purchase inquiries invited.

*We ship ground UPS within the 48 contiguous states. Please give full street address and allow 2 weeks for delivery time. UPS will not deliver to P.O. Box addresses. FPO, APO, Alaska and Hawaii orders are sent by 4th class mail, allow 6 weeks for delivery. Orders shipped outside the US are sent by surface mail - allow 8 to 12 weeks delivery. Overseas mail charges are approximately double domestic postage and handling charges depending upon the weight. Satisfaction Fully Guaranteed !

THANK YOU FOR YOUR ORDER!

MY NOTES

MY NOTES

MY NOTES

MY NOTES

MY NOTES

MY NOTES

MY NOTES

MY NOTES